A HISTORICAL INTRODUCTION TO ENGLISH LAW

There are some stories that need to be told anew to every generation. This book tells one such story. It explores the historical origins of the common law and explains why that story needs to be understood by all who study or come into contact with English law. The book functions as the prequel to what students learn during their law degrees or for the SQE. It can be read in preparation for, or as part of, modules introducing the study of English law or as a starting point for specialist modules on legal history or aspects of legal history. This book will not only help students understand and contextualise their study of the current law but it will also show them that the options they have to change the law are greater than they might assume from just studying the current law.

Russell Sandberg is a Professor of Law at Cardiff University. He is the author of *Law and Religion* (Cambridge, 2011), *Religion, Law and Society* (Cambridge, 2014) and *Subversive Legal History: A Manifesto for the Future of Legal Education* (Routledge, 2021).

A HISTORICAL INTRODUCTION TO ENGLISH LAW

Genesis of the Common Law

RUSSELL SANDBERG
Cardiff University

Shaftesbury Road, Cambridge CB2 8EA, United Kingdom

One Liberty Plaza, 20th Floor, New York, NY 10006, USA

477 Williamstown Road, Port Melbourne, VIC 3207, Australia

314–321, 3rd Floor, Plot 3, Splendor Forum, Jasola District Centre, New Delhi – 110025, India

103 Penang Road, #05-06/07, Visioncrest Commercial, Singapore 238467

Cambridge University Press is part of Cambridge University Press & Assessment, a department of the University of Cambridge.

We share the University's mission to contribute to society through the pursuit of education, learning and research at the highest international levels of excellence.

www.cambridge.org
Information on this title: www.cambridge.org/highereducation/isbn/9781108423335

DOI: 10.1017/9781316106990

© Russell Sandberg 2023

This publication is in copyright. Subject to statutory exception and to the provisions of relevant collective licensing agreements, no reproduction of any part may take place without the written permission of Cambridge University Press & Assessment.

First published 2023

A catalogue record for this publication is available from the British Library.

A Cataloging-in-Publication data record for this book is available from the Library of Congress

ISBN 978-1-107-09058-3 Hardback
ISBN 978-1-107-46273-1 Paperback

Cambridge University Press & Assessment has no responsibility for the persistence or accuracy of URLs for external or third-party internet websites referred to in this publication and does not guarantee that any content on such websites is, or will remain, accurate or appropriate.

To Emma, with love.

Contents

Prologue: The Man of Law's Tale		*page* xi
1	**The Need for Legal History**	1
	I Introduction	1
	II Maitland and the Common Law	4
	III Why History?	7
	1 History Contextualises Law	8
	2 History as Comparative Law	9
	3 History Shows That Law Is Not Fixed	9
	4 History Highlights the Necessity of Legal Change	9
	5 History Highlights the Nature of Legal Change	10
	6 History Questions the Relationship between Law and Society	10
	7 History Serves as Critique	11
	IV Stories of the Common Law	12
	V Conclusions	16
2	**The Architects of Legal History**	19
	I Introduction	19
	II The Intellectual History Tradition	20
	III The Social History Tradition	22
	IV Radical Approaches	26
	1 Critical Legal History	26
	2 Feminist Legal History	30
	3 Critical Race Theory	35
	4 Subversive Legal History	38
	V Conclusions	41
3	**The Anglo-Saxon Legacy**	45
	I Introduction	45
	II The Seamless Web	46
	III From Feud to Compensation	49

1 The Blood Feud	50
2 Compensating Wrongs	52
3 Fault	53
IV The Late Anglo-Saxon Legal System	55
1 Laws	56
2 Courts	57
3 Proof	61
V Conclusions	62

4	The Norman Conquest (c.1066–1154)	65
	I Introduction	65
	II What Have the Normans Ever Done for Us?	66
	III Feudalism	70
	1 Feudal Tenures	72
	2 Feudal Incidents	74
	3 Feudal Courts	75
	4 The Sarum Oath	76
	IV The Position of Slaves and Women	77
	V Conclusions	79

5	The Father of the Common Law (c.1154–1215)	85
	I Introduction	85
	II The Becket Controversy	86
	III The Angevin Advance	88
	IV The Writ System	92
	1 Maitland and *The Forms of Action*	94
	2 The Writ of Right	95
	3 The Possessory Assizes	97
	4 The Writs of Entry	100
	5 The Maitland–Milsom Debate	102
	V Conclusions	109

6	The Myth of Magna Carta (c.1215–1272)	113
	I Introduction	113
	II The Great Charter?	115
	1 Feudalism	116
	2 Courts	117
	3 Governance	119
	4 Immigration	120
	III The Origins of Parliament	123
	1 Magna Carta and the Charter of the Forest	125
	2 The Statute of Merton 1235	126

3 The Provisions of Oxford 1258 and the Provisions of Westminster 1259	127
4 The Statute of Marlborough 1267	128
IV Women under Medieval Law	131
V Conclusions	134

7 The English Justinian (c.1272–1307) 137

I Introduction	137
II The Statutes of Edward I	139
1 The Statute of Westminster 1275	141
2 The Statute of Wales 1284	142
3 The Statute of Westminster II 1285	143
III The Decline of Feudalism	145
IV The Origins of the Law of Obligations	148
1 Covenant	149
2 Trespass	150
V Conclusions	153

8 The Black Death (c.1307–1485) 157

I Introduction	157
II The Origins of Labour Law	159
1 The Ordinance of Labourers 1349	163
2 The Statute of Labourers 1351	164
III Effect upon the Legal System	166
IV Effect upon Substantive Law	169
1 The Action on the Case	169
2 Assumpsit	173
3 Treason	177
4 Murder	179
V Conclusions	182

9 The Tudor Transformation (c.1485–1603) 189

I Introduction	189
II The Legal Renaissance	191
1 The Common Law Courts	196
2 The New Conciliar Courts	199
3 The Court of Chancery	201
III The Reformation of Statute Law	205
1 Regulating the Relationship with Rome	209
2 Cromwell's Constitutional Clash	210
3 A Religious Revolution	211

IV The Tudor Common Law	215
1 Consideration	215
2 Ejectment	218
3 Trusts	219
4 Murder and Manslaughter	223
V Conclusions	229
10 The Stuart Suicide (c.1603–1649)	233
I Introduction	233
II Coke the Lawyer	236
1 Disputes with the Ecclesiastical Courts	238
2 Tensions between the King and the Common Law	239
3 The Conflict with Chancery	241
4 The End of Coke's Judicial Career	242
5 Coke the Parliamentarian	243
III Coke the Husband	247
IV Coke the Jurist	251
V Conclusions	256
Epilogue: Destiny of the Common Law	261
Afterword	269
Index	272

Prologue

The Man of Law's Tale

It was five thousand years since all of life on Earth had been destroyed. Just before the solar flares hit the planet, representatives from the human race had boarded a giant space ship. Aboard that ship, named 'Freedonia', those representatives entered cryogenic chambers and underwent suspended animation. For five thousand years, they were asleep out amongst the stars. They were only to be revived once it was safe to return to the Earth.

Five thousand years previously, the Council of the World Executive had decided that in order to preserve and eventually replicate humanity's achievements, the ship would be peopled with representatives from each country. Furthermore, reflecting the highly compartmentalised society that existed at the time and the need to build a new earth society, there would be one representative from each occupation within the delegation from each country.

Now, as the survivors of the human race were revived from their suspended animation, the commanders of the mission met not only with the lead representatives from each of the countries but also with the representatives from each occupation so that lessons could be learnt from their previous experiences on their return to the purified Earth.

Today, the commanders were meeting with the lawyers and the time had come for them to meet with the volunteer who had boarded the ship to represent the English legal profession. The Man of Law shook hands with the commanders. It was his first meeting for five thousand years; it was their sixth meeting that morning.

One of the commanders began the meeting with a frown. 'We do not seem to have a copy of your country's constitution in the electronic depository', he shrugged, already tired of administrative errors.

'Ah', the Man of Law exclaimed, 'that is because we don't have one. Well, there's no one written constitution or constitutional document. Instead, our constitutional rules are scattered in a variety of legal forms.'

The commander frowned further. 'And what about your code of civil law and your code of criminal law'?, he enquired, scrolling on the electronic screen in front of him trying unsuccessfully to find them.

'We don't have any codes of law as such', replied the Man of Law, pushing up his glasses. 'The law of England is to be found in many different sources but the two most important types are Acts of Parliament – often called statutes – which are made and passed by Parliament to which the monarch then gives Royal Assent; and the decisions made by judges.'

'Do you not even distinguish between civil and criminal law?' responded the commander, treating himself to a short laugh.

'Yes, of course, we distinguish the two', replied the Man of Law, grabbing his lapels. 'Criminal law largely applies to rules that are enforced by the State. So, criminal cases usually the form of "*R* v. *Bloggs*", R being short for the Crown, personifying that they are being brought by the State. Technically R stands for "Rex" if the monarch is male or "Regina" if the monarch is female.'

The commander nodded, which the Man of Law took as encouragement to continue his lecture.

'In contrast, civil cases are usually between two individuals. So, the case is referenced as "*Bloggs* v. *Jones*". Oh, and by the way, the word "v" is written as "v" but pronounced as "and". The two parties are known as the claimant (the person bringing the claim, who used to be known as the plaintiff) and the defendant (the person defending the claim). There's a variety of different forms of civil law and they can be distinguished in different ways. There's property law and there's the law of agreements, known as contract law. There's also the law of private wrongs, known as tort law – that's from the French word meaning "wrong". That covers the situation where, say, I commit a wrong against you: if it's a criminal wrong, then the State could prosecute me; but if you suffer damage, then you could sue me in tort.'

The Man of Law paused for breath and the commander took advantage of this to interrupt. 'So, English law was made by the judges then?' he enquired.

'Well', replied the Man of Law, 'that's an interesting question. Parliament is supreme and creates the law through Acts of Parliament. And technically, the judges are there to declare or apply the law rather than to create it. However, as they apply the law to new circumstances, they are inevitably creating law. We call that – well, we called that – the common law.'

The commander's frown increased further.

'It's not a free for all', exclaimed the Man of Law, 'because of the system of precedent. Basically, the decisions of higher courts are binding on lower courts. The principle that the case establishes becomes binding precedent. We call that part of the judgment the *ratio decidendi*, to give you the Latin. Other things that the judge says that are not the point that determines the judgment are known as *obiter dicta*. Working out what is *ratio* and what is *obiter* in a legal judgment is a key lawyerly skill. It's often not clear cut.'

The commander interjected, 'So you are telling me that English law has no singular constitutional document, no criminal or civil codes and that your role is to find and interpret laws in thousands of Acts of Parliament and how they have been interpreted by the common law judges?'

The Man of Law nodded.

'But how can we get a sense of your achievements and accomplishments then?' the commander continued. 'How can we see how your law has developed? How can we understand English law if there is no one constitution or code, no singular book of law?'

'Ah', interrupted the Man of Law. 'There is no book. But there was a man.'

The Man of Law proceeded to tell the commander that many books had been written that sought to describe the common law at any one moment and that as time went on many books had been written devoted to exploring in detail particular areas of English law such as criminal law or contract law. However, he noted, one author stood out: 'the legal historian Frederic William Maitland (1850–1906).'

'The common law developed in a pragmatic and piecemeal way', the Man of Law continued. 'It had no singular author but developed over time with each generation adapting it to fit their circumstances and needs. It was characterised by change but also by continuity. And that means that the English common law can only be truly understood historically.'

The commander nodded and the Man of Law warmed to his theme.

'You cannot really understand the common law as a whole', the Man of Law continued. 'You can only ever see parts of it. One approach, favoured by the law schools, was to explore the common law bit by bit, examining each area and what the law was at that time, looking at statutes and the decisions of senior courts. But that only gives you part of the picture. English law needs to be understood historically.'

'And this Maitland fellow was the pioneer of the historical study of the common law?' asked the commander.

The Man of Law grinned and proceeded to explain that, although there had been important legal historians before and after Maitland, it was Maitland who is seen as the founder of the study of English legal history. It was his work that established the framework for understanding the history of the common law, and it was Maitland who stressed the need to understand the past in its own terms rather than reading back later expectations and values.

'I see', replied the commander. 'But if we look at English law through a man's work rather than looking at a constitution or a code, are we not just seeing his interpretation?'

'That is true', considered the Man of Law. 'You could say that the common law is really a collection of memories that became stories and those stories then mutate into being histories. But you are right: they are always interpretations. It is important that we retell the stories of the common law but also that we question and are critical about those stories. We need to cast critical light upon the stories that the common law tells and the stories that we forget. We need to listen to Maitland but also need to dialogue with him.'

The commander paused and considered this before asking, 'What are the main stories of the common law? What do we need to know in order to understand the development of English law and to shape its future?'

'There are so many stories', the Man of Law replied. 'One group of stories surrounds the origins of the common law – its genesis. These are the stories about how the legal system developed in England before and after the Norman Conquest of 1066 during the medieval period up to and including the Civil War. It is not a continuous tale of progress, far from it. It's a tale – no it's a number of tales – of how legal ideas and institutions adapted, developed and then fell out of use; how they grew and regressed; and how law is always moulded by human hands and shaped by human experience. The common law is created by people and also effects people, advantaging some and disadvantaging others.'

The commander nodded. The Man of Law then proceeded to tell the stories that you will find in this book.

1

The Need for Legal History

'The only direct utility of legal history ... lies in the lesson that each generation has an enormous power of shaping its own law. I don't think that the study of legal history would make men fatalists; I doubt that it would make them conservatives. I am sure that it would free them from superstitions and teach them that they have free hands'.

Frederic W Maitland, 'Letter from Maitland to AV Dicey, c. July 1896', Quoted in C H S Fifoot, *Frederic William Maitland* (Harvard University Press, 1971) 143.

I   Introduction

This book is addressed to you as law students and prospective law students, and seeks to tell you what you are unlikely to be told as part of your law degree, course or examination. It provides the 'back stories' of some of the main topics that you are likely to study during your degree. It will explain where the common law comes from and will explore the early origins of some of the main subjects that you will study on your degree such as constitutional law, land law, contract law, tort law, criminal law and the law of equity and trusts. It is a prequel to the conventional law degree. This book is designed to give you a head start and should mean that your study of the current law makes more sense.

The chapters that follow tell some of the main stories of the history of English law. They focus on stories told about the origins of the common law, tracing elements of the development of English law from around the time of the Norman Conquest to the outbreak of the Civil War in the Stuart period. Before we time travel through the centuries, this chapter and the following chapter pause to explore why a historical approach to law is needed and what it entails. You might want to skip these chapters for now and begin with Chapter 3, which starts our collection of stories about the origins of the common law. However, the discussions in these chapters are necessary because most introductions to and accounts of English law do not take a historical perspective.

On the face of it, it is perfectly reasonable that law schools ignore history. It is unclear why law students should bother looking at history. Every generation thinks that the challenges they face are unique. We are constantly being told that the legal, political, social, economic and moral problems that we face are unprecedented. Law students are encouraged to look towards the future, not back at the past. History is simply the study of out-of-date law.

The role of the law student is to understand, critically evaluate and apply the law as it stands today, not the law from the medieval or Stuart periods, and to suggest changes for the future. The central method of the law degree is what is known as doctrinal or 'black letter' legal study – that is, the study of primary legal materials (mainly legislation and case law) in their own terms. The role of the law student is to develop a thorough knowledge of the law as it applies today. Law schools train you to become jurists. Lord Goff summed this up well in an article:

The prime task of the jurist is to take the cases and statutes which provide the raw material of the law on any particular topic; and by a critical re-appraisal of that raw material, to build up a systematic statement of the law on the relevant topic in a coherent form, often combined with proposals of how the law can be beneficially developed in the future.[1]

However, by not taking a historical approach, many accounts present the common law as being autonomous, natural and universal. This is shown by how often we talk about 'the law'. It is assumed that the law has always been similar to how it is today and will continue to evolve in a similar manner. This means that it is often accepted that legal change must be slow, piecemeal and conservative, working within clearly laid out parameters. These ideas about the law are perpetuated in law schools and in legal practice.

History is usually neglected by lawyers. When lawyers do refer to history, they misuse it. They tend to do so simply as a means of understanding what the law is today. Law textbooks will frequently cite statutes and cases from centuries ago and law lectures will often review how a case law has developed over time. However, law teachers and students are typically not interested in understanding these developments in the legal, social and political context of their times. They are seldom interested in the historical trajectory of areas of law or key legal ideas. Rather, old laws are typically cited either because they are still the source of law on a particular topic or because they help explain the current law, which is usually presented as a significant improvement. This common way in which lawyers use history is not history at all. Frederic W Maitland (1850–1906) gave the following example:

A lawyer finds on his table a case about rights of common which sends him to the Statute of Merton. But is it really the law of 1236 that he wants to know? No, it is the ultimate result of the interpretations set on the statute by the judges of twenty generations. The more modern the decision the more valuable for his purpose. That process by which old principles and old phrases are charged with new content, is from the lawyer's point of view an evolution of the true intent and meaning of the old law; from the historian's point of view it is almost a necessity a process of perversion and misunderstanding.[2]

---

[1] Lord Goff of Chieveley, 'Judge, Jurist and Legislature' (1987) 2(1) *Denning Law Journal* 79, 92.
[2] Frederic W Maitland, 'Why the History of English Law Has Not Been Written' in HAL Fisher (ed.), *Collected Papers of Frederic William Maitland, Downing Professor of the Laws of England* (Cambridge University Press, 1911) vol. 1, 480, 490–1.

Introduction 3

As Robert W Gordon has put it, history is misused in law schools because they give 'present effect' to materials from the past.[3] The picture usually drawn is a linear line of progress. The law has evolved and cleansed itself, fixing or at least lessening the problem. These progress narratives are ubiquitous in law textbooks, lectures and seminars. As Carolyn Steedman has noted, '[T]he lawyer's "history" was about harmony, not difference, about making the past of the law conform to the present and to the future.'[4] History in this sense is used to stabilise the present.

This book argues that history can be used in a different sense, because looking at its history sheds a different light upon law. History can be used to subvert the present. It can challenge rather than stabilise what we think we know about 'the law'. Reference to history shows that there were once other ways of doing things. Taking a historical perspective reveals that the legal landscape is not pre-determined and that significant amounts of legal change can occur. The study of the current law in isolation tends to suggest that only modest legal change can occur within the confines of the system. By contrast, a historical approach shows that the system itself is not universal and modest incremental development of the status quo is not inevitable. Comparison with the past underscores how the law and legal institutions are not fixed but are constructed, and that every line drawn in the law and everything the law holds as sacred is arbitrary. Every rule, every institution, everything we take for granted about the law once did not exist or at least did not exist in its present form. As Jim Phillips pointed out, it shows us that 'we think of as the law today, and then assume to have always been the case, has in fact not always predominated', and this underlines that 'ways of thinking other than conventional wisdom are possible'.[5] This means that other possibilities are possible because they once were possible. Legal change can be achieved on a greater scale than what is often imagined.

This means that a greater range of possibilities is available to us now. A historical approach to law shows that every sacred principle, distinction and dividing line drawn in the law has not always been there and so does not need to be there in its current form in the future. By showing that laws once operated differently in the past, we can appreciate how laws can be used more creatively in the future. This means that legal change is possible on a greater scale than is often imagined. This radical purpose of legal history was stressed by Maitland in the passage from his letter quoted earlier in this chapter. Exploring law from a historical perspective underlines 'the lesson that each generation has an enormous power of shaping its own law'.[6] The message of this book is that law students have 'free hands' as citizens and potentially as the legal professionals of tomorrow.

This book demonstrates how the historical study of English law is necessary in terms of showing that you have 'free hands', but also informing you of the true extent to the choices available to you. This introductory chapter provides a run-through of some of the main arguments. It will fall into three sections. Section II will explain what the common law is

---

[3] Robert W Gordon, *Taming the Past: Essays on Law in History and History in Law* (Cambridge University Press, 2017) 223.

[4] Carolyn Steedman, *History and the Law: A Love Story* (Cambridge University Press, 2020) 9.

[5] Jim Phillips, 'Why Legal History Matters' (2010) 41 *Victoria University of Wellington Law Review* 293, 310.

[6] Frederic W Maitland, 'Letter from Maitland to AV Dicey, c. July 1896', quoted in CHS Fifoot, *Frederic William Maitland* (Harvard University Press, 1971) 143.

4 *The Need for Legal History*

and provide an introduction to Maitland, our chosen tour guide. Section III will identify seven reasons why a historical approach to law is needed.[7] Section IV of the chapter provides a brief guide to further reading and an outline of the chapters that follow, which will explore some of the stories of the common law.

II   Maitland and the Common Law

There are numerous stories that can be told about the history of the common law, from various different perspectives. This book provides a historical introduction to the common law by exploring stories told about its origins and early development. It uses the work of Frederic W Maitland as our tour guide. Maitland's work in the nineteenth century has now become the orthodox account of the history of the common law. This is so ingrained today that it is taken for granted and now rarely told. This book revisits Maitland's stories; it retells them but also questions them. This subverts our understanding not only of the historical genesis of the common law but of law and legal change generally.

This section will begin by introducing our tour guide, Frederic W Maitland, and his emphasis upon the historical study of law. However, before going any further, it is necessary to explain the definition of 'common law'. The term is used in a vague and a specific sense. In a vague sense, common law is sometimes used as a label to describe the entire system of law in England and Wales, and to contrast it to 'civil law' jurisdictions based on Roman law and the tradition of codifying law into books or codes. The label is sometimes used synonymously with the phrase 'English law'.

This book, however, uses common law in its specific sense. Common law specifically refers to the 'unwritten' general law of the land as administered by the royal courts. As Maitland noted, the word 'common' is used to mean 'general'.[8] The term common law refers to the generally applicable law that governs the whole kingdom and the people in it. In other words, it is the law that is common to the whole land. Common law is used in particular to describe the law as administered by royal courts. It is the law that is declared and applied in the courts of the land, the law as adjudicated by judges in what are referred to as the common law courts.

It is perhaps easiest to define the common law negatively; to say what the common law is not. Maitland observed that the common law can be contrasted with three main other types of law. The first contrast is with statute law, also known as legislation. This is the law enacted by Parliament and other similar bodies. This is why the common law is often referred to as 'unwritten law', because it is not found or based on any legislative text. The second contrast is between the common law and local or personal customary law. Such local or personal laws or customs are not 'general' law, in that they are not common to the whole land. The third contrast distinguishes the common law from forms of law administered by other courts. These other forms of law include the law of the Church administered

---

[7] This draws upon chapter 1 of Russell Sandberg, *Subversive Legal History: A Manifesto for the Future of Legal Education* (Routledge, 2021).

[8] Frederic W Maitland, *The Constitutional History of England* (Cambridge University Press, 1941 [1908]) 22. Dates in square brackets denote date of initial publication.

by the Church courts, and this has historically included other types of law such as the law of equity, as this book will discuss.

This book examines the origins of English law and will use the label common law in the more specific sense referred to by Maitland. This book tells some of the stories of how the common law began, how it largely replaced local law and customs, and how it was affected by the growth of statute law and the rise of other forms of law. However, it is important not to overplay these developments. The growth of the common law never eclipsed other forms of law. Our focus will be on the early development of the common law, but it is possible and important to note that other stories can be told about the other laws that existed and still exist. Our focus on the common law reflects that of Maitland. He will be our guide in recounting these tales; though we will see how later legal historians have challenged and developed his accounts.

Every work on the history of the common law that has been written since the end of the nineteenth century has been influenced by Maitland. As SFC Milsom commented, his work remains 'a still living authority', providing 'the foundation of all we know about the history of common law'.[9] Historians of the common law still begin their study through the eyes of Maitland: 'Their questions still take the form: was Maitland right?'[10] Although a number of seminal works have been published before and since, Maitland is seen as the founder of the study of English legal history. This reputation rests upon both the legacy of Maitland's work and his development of a distinct legal history method.

Maitland produced a diverse body of writing that set the content and tone for what the historical study of the common law entailed. As Milsom noted, Maitland's 'lifetime's worth of seemingly miraculous writing' has resulted in a 'superhuman myth engulfing him'.[11] Perhaps his best-known work was his *The History of English Law*, co-authored with Frederick Pollock, which is popularly known as 'Pollock and Maitland'.[12] The nickname of that book is ironic, however, given that Pollock (then the most well-known of the two authors) contributed very little to the book.[13] One of Pollock's limited contributions to the book was his chapter devoted to the Anglo-Saxon period, which was so disliked by Maitland that he then attempted to write the remainder of the book before Pollock could.[14] The two volumes of 'Pollock and Maitland' cover the period up to 1272, providing a sketch of early English legal history and a discussion of the doctrines of English law in the early Middle Ages.

Maitland's other most influential publications consist of a number of books published after his death and based on the lectures he delivered to his students at Cambridge. These books were based upon their notes. This includes a series of lectures on *The Constitutional*

---

[9] SFC Milsom, 'Introduction' in Frederick Pollock and Frederic W Maitland (eds.), *The History of English Law* (2nd ed., Cambridge University Press, 1968 [1898]) vol. 1, xxiii, ixxi, xxiv.

[10] This is underlined by Milsom's introduction to the reissued second edition of the legendary 'Pollock and Maitland', which concluded: 'Maitland himself would probably wish his work to be superseded. There is little sign that this will happen soon' (ibid. ixxiii).

[11] SFC Milsom, 'Maitland' (2001) 60(2) *Cambridge Law Journal* 265.

[12] Pollock and Maitland, *The History of English Law*. The first edition was published in 1895, with a second edition in 1898.

[13] As Pollock noted, 'the greater share of the execution belongs to Mr Maitland, both as to the actual writing and as to the detailed research which was constantly required' (ibid. vi).

[14] Frederic W Maitland, 'Maitland to Vinogradoff' (1982), quoted in Fifoot, *Frederic William Maitland* 137.

History of England, which provided a sketch of the position in 1307, 1509, 1625, 1702 and 1887–8 (which was, for Maitland and his students, the present day).[15] It therefore provided a sequel in terms of chronology to 'Pollock and Maitland' but had a narrower focus. At first glance, it would seem that the other books based on his university lectures had a narrower focus still. His lectures on *The Forms of Action* and *Equity* have been published together and separately.[16] Despite first appearances, they are actually the broadest of all of Maitland's legal works. *The Forms of Action* provides a history of the main developments of the common law up to the time in which Maitland was speaking. His published lectures on *Equity* explored the development of the equitable jurisdiction that was to supplement the common law throughout its history. In addition to these publications for which Maitland is most renowned today, he also authored a number of lesser-known books,[17] collections of essays[18] and numerous articles.[19]

Maitland's reputation also rests upon his method: he pioneered the use of primary legal materials. He was acclaimed for his introductions to numerous editions of primary materials prepared for the Selden Society and other organisations. The Selden Society has been referred to as 'the living memorial which perpetuates not only the work but also the spirit of Maitland'.[20] Formed in 1886 with Maitland serving as its literary director until the end of his life, the Selden Society reflected the second aspect of Maitland's legacy: it entrenched the method of examining the history of English law by excavating the original primary sources, looking at the actual records of decisions made at the time. The volumes published by the Selden Society, several of which were edited by Maitland, provided modern English-language translations of key legal documents and records from throughout history, with lengthy introductory essays that placed the texts into their contexts. The method of painstakingly examining primary legal sources is often dated back to Maitland, not only because he used the method in his works but also given his role in the foundation of the Selden Society, which continues this work. Maitland has enjoyed the reputation of being 'the legal historian's historian'.[21] His work has been celebrated not only by lawyers but also historians. For Michael Lobban, Maitland 'was one of the central figures who helped to turn the study of history into a professional pursuit, in which the scholar was

---

[15] Maitland, *The Constitutional History of England*.

[16] Frederic W Maitland, *Equity, Also the Form of Action at Common Law* (Cambridge University Press, 1909); Frederic W Maitland, *The Forms of Action at Common Law* (Cambridge University Press, 1965 [1936]); Frederic W Maitland, *Equity: A Course of Lectures* (Cambridge University Press, 1969 [1936]).

[17] On legal history, see: Frederic W Maitland, *Justice and Police* (Macmillan, 1885); Frederic W Maitland and Francis C Montague, *A Sketch of English Legal History* (GP Putman's Sons, 1998 [1915]). This body of work stands apart from work on political philosophy completed at the start and the end of his career: his 1875 dissertation (reprinted as Frederic W Maitland, *A Historical Sketch of Liberty and Equality* (Liberty Fund, 2000)); his translation of the work of Otto von Gierke (*Political Theories of the Middle Age* (Cambridge University Press, 1900)); and a range of late essays (Frederic W Maitland, *State, Trust and Corporation* (Cambridge University Press, 2003 [1911])). His last publication was a work of biography: Frederic W Maitland, *The Life and Letters of Leslie Stephen* (Duckworth, 1906).

[18] Frederic W Maitland, *Domesday Book and Beyond* (Cambridge University Press, 1897); Frederic W Maitland, *Roman Canon Law in the Church of England* (Methuen & Co., 1898).

[19] Collected in Fisher, *Collected Papers of Frederic William Maitland, Downing Professor of the Laws of England*. For Maitland's letters, see: CHS Fifoot (ed.), *The Letters of Frederic Maitland* (Harvard University Press, 1965) and P Zutshi, *The Letters of Frederic William Maitland* (Selden Society, 1995) vol. 2.

[20] Theodore FT Plucknett, 'Frederic William Maitland' (1951) 26 *New York University Law Review* 10.

[21] KJM Smith and JPS McLaren, 'History's Living Legacy: An Outline of "Modern" Historiography of the Common Law' (2001) 21 *Legal Studies* 251, 261.

encouraged to spend long hours in the archives reading primary sources'.[22] Maitland's work also emphasised to historians the importance of looking at law. He regarded legal documents as being 'the best, often the only evidence that we have for social and economic history, for the history of morality, for the history of practical religion'.[23]

Despite ill health, Maitland produced a body of work of which the quality and quantity was impressive, almost superhuman, drawing upon mostly original sources to produce authoritative accounts that were both accessible but also demonstrated an eye to detail. His work continues to set not only the scene but the standard for legal historians. His influence upon how we understand the history of the common law is so ingrained that it is often taken for granted. In this book, Maitland will be used explicitly as our tour guide. As we will see, his work shapes our knowledge, the key debates and methods that legal historians continue to use. This is not to say that it should not be questioned. Indeed, this book will seek to dialogue with him, looking at subsequent research rather than treating Maitland as the last word on the topic. This is probably what Maitland would have wanted. When 'Pollock and Maitland' was reissued in 1968, the text was left unchanged on the basis that the work so reflected the touch of a master that it could only be weakened by editing it.[24] The only addition was a new introduction by SFC Milsom, who is widely celebrated as the greatest legal historian who worked in the late twentieth century. Interestingly, Milsom's introduction begun by observing that:

Maitland, I think, would have been saddened by this re-issue of his book, and not only by the inadequacy of an introductory essay that is the sole addition of what last left his hands just seventy years ago. He felt sorry for those whose work became classical: it meant that vitality had been lost from the enterprise they had loved.[25]

This book will show that Maitland's work remains vital and alive today. As we go through the centuries, we will constantly return to the publications mentioned earlier. Maitland's work remains an important, foundational and sometimes controversial part of the stories that make up the history of the English common law. It may be questioned first, however, why it is worth telling these stories at all.

III   Why History?

There are numerous reasons why people study law. At degree level, perhaps the main reasons for selecting law are the subject itself and the career possibilities that it enables. Law is seen as a rigorous academic subject that scrutinises real world issues. It covers all aspects of human life and is visible not only in the public debates of the time but also in our everyday lives. Most news stories have a legal dimension, as do most of our activities: not just the 'big events' in our lives such as renting a flat or getting married, but also every purchase that we make and what we are permitted and prohibited to do throughout our lives. To study law then is to study life, and law students develop the skill of being able to

---

[22] Michael Lobban, 'The Varieties of Legal History' (2012) 5 *Clio@Themis* 1, 4.
[23] Maitland, 'Why the History of English Law Has Not Been Written' 480, 486.
[24] Pollock and Maitland, *The History of English Law.*   [25] Milsom, 'Introduction' xxiii.

simultaneously master the details while also keeping an eye on the larger picture. This is why a law degree opens so many doors in terms of a career. The skills developed though studying law are those that are essential in a range of jobs, and, of course, prepare you if you wish to have a career in law, whether as a barrister or a solicitor.

The claim made in this book is that studying law historically will further improve the knowledge and skills that you develop as part of your legal studies. Studying law historically will make you a better law student, and will make sense of the subjects that you will study in your law degree. It will place the modules that you will study within a broader picture, and you will understand how law has developed in the ways that it has. Studying legal history will also improve your career prospects and improve your ability to problem solve, to question and to suggest new and innovative solutions.

The need for and potential of a truly historical approach can be illustrated by using a novel analogy.[26] Your experience as a law student is like that of a reader who has only read a chapter somewhere towards the end of a novel. By focusing on that one chapter, the reader has little if no grasp of the story so far, the extent to which the current chapter moves that story on or what is likely to come next. The same experience is true of students studying most law modules. You become experts on a very small part of the story and have little insight as to how the story has previously developed and its likely future trajectory. Indeed, you are unlikely to appreciate that it is a story, that the current system came from somewhere and, crucially, that there was a time when things were done differently. Reading those previous chapters would not necessarily show a linear movement towards progress. When read in detail, chapters in the historical development of areas of law (like chapters in a novel) often do not advance the plot directly but rather complicate or reverse plot points. Indeed, this is why starting with the later chapter and then looking back often leads to confusion. The benefit of hindsight colours the interpretation and makes a journey that was complicated and unintended look straightforward and deliberate. But focusing solely upon a later chapter without even glancing backwards is worse still: it gives the reader no understanding of the chapters yet to come and of earlier plot points that may become significant. It limits the frame of analysis.

Studying law from a historical angle will enrich your study of law. As Maitland's letter suggested, it unlocks the potential of law, broadening out the picture and showing that radical options have been possible and so can be possible.[27] The remainder of this section will unpack this further by exploring seven (overlapping) reasons why law students should study history.[28]

1   *History Contextualises Law*

History is one way of thinking about law in a larger context.[29] It enables an understanding of law within the context of political, social and economic forces.[30] A historical perspective allows us to understand where we are going by showing us where we have come from. This should not be about instilling a linear narrative of progress but showing the

---

[26] Sandberg, *Subversive Legal History* 9.   [27] Maitland, 'Maitland to AV Dicey, c. July 1896' 143.

[28] This draws upon Sandberg, *Subversive Legal History* 11–16.

[29] Robin L West, *Teaching Law: Justice, Politics and the Demands of Professionalism* (Cambridge University Press, 2014) 191.

[30] John McLaren 'The Legal Historian, Masochist or Missionary? A Canadian's Reflection' (1994) 5 *Legal Education Review* 67.

complicated forward and backward trajectories that have resulted in the current position and the effect of political, social and economic pressures. A historical approach to law is an interdisciplinary endeavour that introduces students to the ideas and methods from elsewhere in the university. This means, in the words of Jim Phillips, that a historical approach to law teaches 'law students not only analytical skills and substantive knowledge, but also a deeper understanding of the nature of law'.[31]

2 *History as Comparative Law*

Comparative law enables law students to understand law more deeply by comparing the legal system that they are studying with another jurisdiction. While comparative law traditionally does this by exploring different legal systems across space, using history as a form of comparative law approach does this across time.[32] This approach uses the past to highlight the nature and form of the current law and to critique it by showing that other ways of doing things has been possible. This not only means seeing the past from which something can be learnt but also seeing the past as being different.[33] This requires us to consider the past in its own terms and to become immersed in the past to such an extent that this 'forces us to probe our beliefs, compare them to the features we encounter elsewhere, and expose our assumptions to scrutiny and evaluation'.[34] By seeing how things operated differently in the past, our impression and understanding of the present changes.

3 *History Shows That Law Is Not Fixed*

As Phillips notes, a historical perspective shows that law 'is not a set of abstract ahistorical and universal principles'.[35] A historical approach shows how law has changed and how the actual changes that occur have not been inevitable. This suggests that further change is possible and that this change is similarly likely to be unpredictable. History shows how law is contingent. It underscores how law is in flux and is shaped by a range of internal and external factors. Understanding law as a historical construction underscores that law is the product of human interaction and is the response to the specific challenges of a particular time. This suggests that the reconstruction of the law is possible and necessary in light of new challenges.

4 *History Highlights the Necessity of Legal Change*

A historical approach to law teaches us that the current law is not perfect and is not necessarily the finished product. The way in which legal actors have grappled with problems

---

[31] Phillips, 'Why Legal History Matters' 294.

[32] For an application and discussion of this, see John H Baker, *English Law under Two Elizabeths: The Late Tudor Legal World and the Present* (Cambridge University Press, 2021). It is possible to combine the two: comparative legal history is the historical comparison of more than one jurisdiction. See David Ibbetson, 'The Challenges of Comparative Legal History' (2013) 1(1) *Comparative Legal History* 1 and subsequent articles in that journal.

[33] Jonathan Rose, 'Studying the Past: The Nature and Development of Legal History as an Academic Discipline' (2010) 31(2) *The Journal of Legal History* 101, 101–2.

[34] Jeremy Webber 'The Past and Foreign Countries' (2006) 10 *Legal History* 1.   [35] Phillips, 'Why Legal History Matters' 295.

10   *The Need for Legal History*

over time in different social conditions shows the pragmatic and therefore ultimately unpolished nature of law. As John McLaren put it, legal history 'provides a valuable antidote to the arrogant belief that we are likely to produce a legal regime of innate comprehensibility, completeness, intellectual perfection and practical attractiveness'.[36] More optimistically, it also shows that since the legal landscape is not pre-determined, significant amounts of legal change can occur. A historical perspective requires us to disregard progress narratives that limit legal change to modest incremental developments.

5   *History Highlights the Nature of Legal Change*

A historical perspective does not only show that change is possible and necessary, reference to a longer time scale also enables a more sophisticated understanding of legal change. As Alan Watson has argued, historical approaches can provide a 'way to measure the speed – or absence thereof – of a response to changed circumstances'.[37] They can also show the factors that tend to lead to change, how change comes about and the effectiveness of different forms of change. Historical analysis focuses on the complex relationship between change and continuity. This includes exploring how continuity can often accompany change. It also involves examining the relationship between legal and social change including the two may be out of sync. Watson noted that in addition to studying change and innovation, we should also study situations when 'a legal change did not occur when society changed'.[38] A historical perspective can highlight and critique common generalisations. It can question linear simplifications that reduce legal and social change to straightforward sequences of cause and effect, and that overplay the intentional evolution of legal and social change, ignoring how every cause arose in instances where a range of choices were possible. History presented in all its complexity can question the progress narratives where, as Rosemary Auchmuty put it, 'there is always a sense in that law is essentially benevolent and will get there in the end'.[39] A historical approach showing the ebbs and flows of legal change can be used to question simplistic and misleading narratives of progress and can broaden the question of cause and effect to take into account overlooked developments.

6   *History Questions the Relationship between Law and Society*

A historical approach raises the question of the extent to which legal change is the product of internal developments within the legal system or of external social and political influences. As John McLaren observed, a historical approach allows legal change to be understood 'in a way which is sensitive not only to doctrinal and institutional development' as well as recognising 'the political, social and economic forces which have shaped or

---

[36] McLaren 'The Legal Historian, Masochist or Missionary?' 83.
[37] Alan Watson, *Legal Origins and Legal Change* (Hambledon Press, 1991) 72.
[38] Alan Watson, 'Legal Change: Sources of Law and Legal Culture' (1983) 131(5) *University of Pennsylvania Law Review* 1121, 1123; reprinted as Watson, *Legal Origins and Legal Change*, chapter 7.
[39] Rosemary Auchmuty, 'Land Law and Equity and Trusts' in Caroline Hunter (ed.) *Integrating Socio-legal Studies into the Law Curriculum* (Palgrave, 2012) 69, 76.

Why History?

affected the law, and what that may suggest about the relationship between legal develop-ment and those influences in our own era'.[40] Reference to history reveals how legal change is not simply the product of the legal system by highlighting the roles played by individuals and pressure groups. As Auchmuty has pointed out, a historical approach can highlight 'the power struggles, the opposition to reform and the agency of those campaigners who ultimately succeeded, or not'.[41] It can therefore correct the way that 'students are led to believe that the law has evolved through internal reform rather than as a result of radical movements'.[42] A historical approach can be used to critique the claim that law is entirely autonomous whilst recognising that legal institutions and actors are distinct and that law has its own discourse. A historical approach can show how the legal and the social interact, and indeed how a distinct line between the two cannot be drawn. History has much to contribute to questions concerning how law should be defined and distinguished from other forms of social control. As Lobban has observed, '[A]n historical perspective, which focuses on the distinct nature of legal thought, and its different operations in different eras and contexts, can open the way for a better understanding of the distinct nature of law and ... its relation to society.'[43] He noted that:

Rather than asking how "law" impacts on "society" in general, we may learn more by looking at particular aspects of law impacting on particular aspects of society. For such an enterprise, the historian's method – with its keen focus on the particular context and its scepticism for grand theory – seems in many ways the most useful one.[44]

7   *History Serves as Critique*

These reasons for the importance of a historical approach to law cumulatively suggest that a historical approach serves as a critique: a way of challenging and questioning law. As Rowan Williams has commented, '[G]ood history makes us think again about the defin-ition of things we thought we understood pretty well, because it engages not just with what is familiar but with what is strange.'[45] It makes us question what we know by showing that law is contingent, malleable and capable of change; it questions the dividing lines that have been drawn around the law, what is included and excluded in textbooks and lectures and the idea that law is autonomous and objective. As Morton Horwitz noted, a historical approach reveals that 'principles of mainstream scholars are historically contingent', and this unsettles the orthodox approach that 'regards history as subversive because it exposes the rationalising enterprise'.[46] A historical approach subverts the common understandings of law and the ways in which legal actors stabilise the law by making the messy realities fit within existing systems and categories. David Sugarman went as far as to argue that legal

---

[40] McLaren, 'The Legal Historian, Masochist or Missionary?' 87.   [41] Auchmuty, 'Land Law and Equity and Trusts' 76.
[42] Ibid. 77.
[43] Michael Lobban, 'Sociology, History and the "Internal" Study of Law' in Richard Nobles and David Schiff (eds.) *Law, Society and Community: Socio-legal Essays in Honour of Roger Cotterrell* (Ashgate, 2014) 48.
[44] Ibid. 56–7.   [45] Rowan Williams, *Why Study the Past?* (Longman and Todd, 2005) 1.
[46] Morton J Horwitz, 'The Historical Contingency of the Role of History' (1981) 90 *Yale Law Journal* 1057.

12   *The Need for Legal History*

history should 'take on the mantle of an all-purpose subversive, illuminating the connections between legal, socio-economic and political change, thereby enlarging and supplementing the study of law'.[47]

The seven reasons also highlight the importance of the historical study of law as an interdisciplinary means of contextualising and critiquing law. A historical approach therefore transforms how we see law. It shows us that law is constructed and shaped to fit the needs of different times. It is not a fully autonomous system and is not as stable, rational or inevitable as it may first appear. A historical approach can and should be radical, showing that we can achieve legal change on a larger scale than often assumed possible. These seven reasons for adopting this approach to law therefore require us to go further than using materials from the past to explain the current law. They oblige us to challenge and supersede the progress narratives that regard the past as being backwards and that view change in a straightforward linear way whereby legal change is the inevitable result of the legal system constantly improving over time.

IV   Stories of the Common Law

The need for and value of a historical approach to law will be demonstrated throughout this book. The chapters that follow tell some of the main stories of the historical origins of the common law. They provide a succinct account of some of the ways in which the common law developed from just before the Norman Conquest to around the outbreak of the Civil War. The focus will be on the development of some of the main principles, structures and institutions. The purpose is not to provide an exhaustive account of the historical development of English law but rather to tell some of the main stories of the common law that will be of most relevance in terms of providing the context for your study of the law today. The book also seeks to introduce you to the existing rich literature on legal history and does this by drawing upon this secondary material in the text itself through copious footnoting. This is designed to be the first book you read on the history of English law, but not the last.

You are encouraged to follow up the references in order to read more widely on the topic and to assess my interpretations. These references, however, are just the tip of the iceberg. Given the size of the literature, perhaps a few additional words are necessary in terms of further reading generally.[48] The works of Sir John Baker and SFC Milsom should be at the top of your reading list.[49] Their textbooks complement this book since while our introductory survey is chronological, their detailed accounts are largely arranged by areas of law.[50] Thomas Watkin's book provides an authoritative account in respect of Wales, which also

---

[47] David Sugarman, 'Writing "Law and Society"' Histories (1992) 55(5) *Modern Law Review* 292, 292.

[48] For a detailed but now slightly dated guide to the terrain, see the essays in WD Hines (ed.) *English Legal History: A Bibliography and Guide to the Literature* (Garland, 1990).

[49] John H Baker, *An Introduction to English Legal History* (5th ed., Oxford University Press, 2019); SFC Milsom, *Historical Foundations of the Common Law* (2nd ed., Butterworths, 1981). See also their collected papers: John H Baker, *Collected Papers on English Legal History* (Cambridge University Press, 2013); SFC Milsom, *Studies in the History of the Common Law* (Hambledon Press, 1985).

[50] Their co-authored casebook will also be invaluable in terms of private law: John H Baker and SFC Milsom, *Sources of English Legal History* (2nd ed., Oxford University Press, 2010). The publications of the Selden Society will also be invaluable, especially the introductions to the primary materials in each volume.

Stories of the Common Law

casts a different light upon the English common law.[51] It also complements this book in that our focus will be on the English common law. In terms of areas of law, the recent leading book-length general accounts of the history of constitutional law, land law and the law of contract and tort can be found in the works of Ann Lyon, Brian Simpson and David Ibbetson, respectively.[52] For a chronological and comprehensive account of English law, the various entries published to date in *The Oxford History of the Laws of England* are now authoritative.[53] Those interested in modern English legal history have been well-served by the publication of a number of general works in recent years.[54] There are, of course, countless books on particular periods, handbooks, collected volumes of papers by particular scholars, edited collections, specialist book series, and articles in specialist and general law journals, not to mention the significant literature produced in other jurisdictions and cognate disciplines. And, if you wish to read more on the need for and importance of a historical approach to law, then *Subversive Legal History* develops many of the points in this book.[55]

Of course, in addition to these works, there is a rich earlier literature that can be consulted (albeit with some caution given subsequent research), chiefly the work of Maitland, which will serve as the guide throughout this book.[56] Our choice of tour guide reflects the exalted position that Maitland has within English legal history, but we will dialogue with rather than critically accept Maitland's work and the assumptions and values upon which it was based.

This is reflected in Chapter 2 of this book, 'The Architects of Legal History'. Although we will be taking Maitland as our main tour guide, it is important to note how various forms of legal history have developed since his day. The chapter will introduce the various

---

[51] Thomas G Watkin, *The Legal History of Wales* (2nd ed., University of Wales Press, 2012). See also Richard Ireland, *Land of White Gloves? A History of Crime and Punishment in Wales* (Routledge, 2015) and the publications of the Welsh Legal History Society.

[52] Ann Lyon, *Constitutional History of the United Kingdom* (2nd ed., Routledge, 2016); AW Brian Simpson, *An Introduction to the History of Land Law* (2nd ed., Oxford University Press, 1986); AW Brian Simpson, History *of the Common Law of Contract* (Clarendon Press, 1987); David J Ibbetson, *A Historical Introduction to the Law of Obligations* (Oxford University Press, 1999). Though now dated, I would also recommend the work of Fifoot on particular writs within the law of obligations: CHS Fifoot, *History and Sources of the Common Law* (Stevens & Sons, 1949). In terms of criminal law, the focus tends to be more on criminal justice, but the nearest comparisons in terms of a general account of his history include: John Briggs, Christopher Harrison, Angus McInnes and David Vincent, *Crime and Punishment in England: An Introductory History* (University College London Press, 1996); KJM Smith, *Lawyers, Legislators and Theorists: Developments in English Criminal Jurisprudence 1800–1957* (Clarendon Press, 1998); Philip Rawlings, *Crime and Power: A History of Criminal Justice 1688–1998* (Longman, 1999); John Hostettler, *A History of Criminal Justice in England and Wales* (Waterside Press, 2009). The books in the 'Landmark Cases in' series published by Hart are also invaluable and now cover a number of areas of law.

[53] Richard H Helmholz, *The Oxford History of the Laws of England Volume I: The Canon Law and Ecclesiastical Jurisdiction from 597 to 1640s* (Oxford University Press, 2004); John Hudson, *The Oxford History of the Laws of England Volume II: 871–1216* (Oxford University Press, 2012); John H Baker, *The Oxford History of the Laws of England Volume VI: 1483–1558* (Oxford University Press, 2003); William Cornish, J Stuart Anderson, Ray Cocks et al., *The Oxford History of the Laws of England Volumes XI, XXII and XIII: 1820–1914* (Oxford University Press, 2010).

[54] AH Manchester, *Modern Legal History* (Butterworths, 1980); G R Rubin and David Sugarman (eds.) *Law, Economy & Society: Essays in the History of English Law 1750–1914* (Professional Books, 1984); William R Cornish, Stephen Banks, Charles Mitchell, Paul Mitchell and Rebecca Probert, *Law and Society in England 1750–1950* (2nd ed., Hart 2019); Ian Ward, *English Legal Histories* (Hart, 2020).

[55] Sandberg, *Subversive Legal History*. There is also an increasing literature on legal history and legal theory. See Chloë Kennedy, 'Immanence and Transcendence: History's Roles in Normative Legal Theory' (2017) 8(3) *Jurisprudence* 557, and the essays in Maksymilian del Mar and Michael Lobban (eds.), *Legal Theory and Legal History* (Ashgate, 2014) and Maksymilian del Mar and Michael Lobban (eds.) *Law in Theory and History: New Essays on a Neglected Dialogue* (Hart, 2016). For discussion on the interplay between legal history and the sociology of law, see Chloë Kennedy, 'Sociology of Law and Legal History' in Jiři Přibaň (ed.) *Research Handbook on the Sociology of Law* (Edward Elgar, 2020) 31.

[56] For a survey, see Smith and McLaren, 'History's Living Legacy' 251.

perspectives. It will begin by distinguishing between what may be referred to as the intellectual history tradition in legal history, which explores the development of legal ideas within legal sources, and the social history tradition, which explores legal changes within their social context.[57] It will demonstrate that both approaches complement one another, and that, although Maitland is often regarded as a significant figure in the intellectual history tradition, some of his work can also be situated in the social history tradition. Further, it will be shown that Maitland's work often demonstrated what may be styled a radical approach to legal history. The chapter will conclude by examining a number of radical perspectives that have been taken to the interaction between law and history, namely critical legal history, feminist legal history, critical race theory, and my own call for a subversive legal history. These approaches are presented so that you can critique and apply insights from these perspectives as we re-tell and question the conventional stories of the genesis of the common law.

The remaining chapters explore the origins of the common law by taking a chronological approach. Although each chapter explores a particular time period, some creative license has been taken so that the discussion of certain topics can be concentrated in a particular chapter. Where chapters begin and end, what they include and exclude, is arbitrary and a matter of choice. This also applies to the question of where the book begins and where it ends. Several conventional accounts of the origins of English law begin with the Norman Conquest of 1066. However, many other accounts – including that of Maitland – begin just before the Conquest, exploring how centralised authority developed in the late Anglo-Saxon period. This is the focus of Chapter 3, 'The Anglo-Saxon Legacy', which explores the debate of the importance of this period by examining the characteristics of the late Anglo-Saxon legal system. This account then continues in Chapter 4, 'The Norman Conquest (c.1066–1154)', which examines the significance and after effects of the Conquest upon the development of the common law. This chapter introduces the concept of feudalism, which would be of great significance in terms of developing English land law, but which actually undermined the development of a common law by feudal lords presiding over their own feudal courts for their tenants. The king's law and protection were only afforded to his own personal tenants. Although there were some developments that allowed royal justice to extend more widely, such innovations stopped during the time appropriately known as the Anarchy at the end of this period. It was during the reign of Henry II (1154–89) that, to quote Maitland, that the exceptional became normal, and royal justice was available to anyone who could bring their case within a certain formula, known as a writ.[58] This is discussed in Chapter 5, 'The Father of the Common Law (c.1154–1215)', the title of which refers to the title often bestowed upon Henry II, the first monarch from the House of Plantagenet. The chapter focuses on the development of the writ system during and in the aftermath of Henry's reign in relation to what we now call land law, and whether this marked a move to centralisation, which replaced the feudal system.

---

[57] Sandberg, *Subversive Legal History* chapter 3.
[58] Frederic W Maitland, *The Forms of Action at Common Law* (Cambridge University Press, 1965 [1909]) 21.

Chapter 6, 'The Myth of Magna Carta (c.1215–1272)' explores the most well-known English constitutional text and the period that followed its enactment. It explores how Magna Carta was a much more mundane and feudal document than its reputation suggests. It also examines how it was by no means the sole kingly concession during this period and discusses the origins of Parliament and how this affected the common law. This story is continued in Chapter 7, 'The English Justinian (c.1272–1307)', the title of which refers to the nickname given to Edward I (1272–1307), who was likened to the Roman Emperor Justinian I, who codified Roman law, on the basis that Edward's reign saw a significant increase in the number and importance of statutes. The chapter explores the main statutes but also explores common law developments at this time, examining the early development of what is sometimes called the law of obligations or the laws of contract and tort (examining the writs of covenant and trespass). Chapter 8, 'The Black Death (c.1307–1485)', completes our examination of the long Plantagenet period, which culminated in the bloody War of the Roses. However, as the chapter title makes plain, the focus is on the impact that the deadly plague of this period had upon law and order. The chapter explores the different interpretations made of the importance of the Black Death, and surveys developments of this period such as the origins of what we would today call employment law, significant increases in the effectiveness of the administration of justice chiefly through increased powers for Justices of the Peace, and important developments in both law of obligations (exploring how actions on the case developed from the writ of trespass and how it further developed into the action on the case for assumpsit) and the criminal law (focusing on treason and murder).

This brings us to another significant turning point in English history and so too the history of the common law, the reign of the Tudor monarchs. Our penultimate chapter, 'The Tudor Transformation (c.1485–1603)', explores the extent to which this period saw a legal renaissance. It examines developments in the common law courts but also explores the development of new conciliar courts outside the common law, most notably Star Chamber and the Court of Equity, which were to prove influential. It also examines the further rise in the use and importance of statute law in this period, demonstrating that the Reformation statutes that split England from the Roman Catholic Church underscored the power of Parliamentary statute. Attention is also given to some developments in the common law courts during this period concerning the law of obligations (the development of the principle of consideration in contract law), property law (the development of the writ of ejectment that replaced the older land law writs and the origins of the law of trusts) and criminal law (the development of the distinction between murder and manslaughter).

Our final chapter, 'The Stuart Suicide (c.1603–1649)', examines the early Stuart period in the years leading to the Civil War. This ending point, though necessarily arbitrary, has been chosen because of the entwinement between centralised royal power and the origins of the common law described in previous chapters means that it can be said that the common law had reached a level of maturity when it was able to survive for an extended period of time without a monarch. The Civil War further provides an appropriate conclusion to our survey given that it was the culmination of the conflicts between the king and his advisers that date back centuries to Magna Carta and before. The chapter explores this final time period by exploring the work, behaviour and legacy of Sir Edward Coke, who has been likened to the Shakespeare of the law, and who is often seen as the bridge between the medieval and the modern laws.[59] Yet, in noting that Coke was active in both the Tudor and early Stuart period and by recognising that his work was to be influential for centuries to come, this final chapter also illustrates how chopping the history of the common law up into chapters emphasises change at the cost of continuity and runs the risk of presenting an evolutionary narrative of progress. It is clear, however, that this chapter provides a semi-colon rather than a full stop to the account of the development of the common law.

V   Conclusions

Anthony Bradney once wrote, somewhat provocatively, that in order to 'become a law student the student must forget who he or she is'.[60] What he meant by this was that the law degree and its focus on doctrinal legal study (the attempt to study law solely through the internal evidence of legal sources) makes law students think in a particular way. 'Thinking like a lawyer' means that you ask certain questions and do not ask other questions. This is necessary in terms of understanding the letter of the law, but it is insufficient. You need to think like a lawyer but also question like a citizen. Mastery of the details of the law degree need to be combined with a curious spirit, an ability to identify and challenge power imbalances, and the determination to question whether there is a need for an alternative approach. This chapter and this book argue that studying legal history can help you with this. A historical approach is necessary in terms of allowing you to spot and to question what you as law students are socialised into being. History can question the assumptions, biases, principles, categorisations and expectations that result from the study of the current law. Rather than being used to stabilise the present, a historical approach can subvert it.

A historical approach challenges what we think we know about the law. It reveals other possibilities. It shows how legal ideas, principles, distinctions and institutions that we think of as fixed have been different in the past and therefore can be different in the future. It flies in the face of expectations that regard the legal system as being autonomous and timeless. The study of legal history corrects the impressions that are often formed through the study of the current law. It underscores that law is not universal but is rather the construction of people at particular times responding to particular circumstances. It challenges the progress narratives that underpin common understandings of the law. A historical approach questions everything, including the careful lines constructed around each law school module. As Maitland put it, law is a 'living body' and so cannot be compartmentalised, because all parts of the body depend upon each other.[61]

A historical approach to law can revolutionise how students see law. It opens the door to a range of additional questions and possibilities. It has the potential to liberate law students. It unsettles what we know and are taught about the law. It can help ensure that you do not

---

[59] William S Holdsworth, 'Sir Edward Coke' (1935) 5(3) *Cambridge Law Journal* 332, 344.
[60] Anthony Bradney, 'Law as a Parasitic Discipline' (1998) 25(1) *Journal of Law and Society* 71, 77.
[61] Maitland, *The Constitutional History of England* 539.

forget who you are, as Bradney warned. Legal history can, in the words of Maitland, free us from 'superstitions'.[62] The chapters that follow will help equip you in order to analyse, critique and subvert law historically. A historical approach will, in the words of our tour guide, demonstrate that you and your generation have the enormous power of shaping your own laws and 'teach us that we have free hands'.

---

[62] Maitland, 'Maitland to AV Dicey, c. July 1896' 143.

'And, if it be true, as said by others, that there are many reasons why history should be taught, let it not be forgotten that, whether we like it or no, history will be written. The number of men in England who at the present time are writing history of some sort or another must be very large ... The study of interactions and interdependences is but just beginning, and no one can foresee the end. There is much to be done by schools of history; there will be more to be done every year'.

Frederic W Maitland, 'Introduction' in Frederic W Maitland *et al*, *Essays on the Teaching of History* (Cambridge University Press, 2013 [1901]) ix, xviii, Xx.

2

The Architects of Legal History

I Introduction

This chapter introduces the various types of historical research on law. There are different ways in which the numerous approaches of legal history can be conceptualised. The following will draw upon a remark by John Baker that: 'Law flits uncomfortably between intellectual and social history.'[1] This chapter will maintain that a similar comment can be made about legal history work. Within the numerous forms of historical writings about law, it is possible to highlight two major traditions: one that examines law from an intellectual history dimension (exploring the development of legal ideas) and the other that looks at law from a social history dimension (exploring the development of interface between law and society).[2]

This chapter will develop this understanding by exploring in turn the intellectual history and social history traditions within legal history. It will also explain that these two traditions overlap and why both can be dated back to the work of Frederic Maitland. It will also examine why this conceptualisation is to be preferred over other distinctions drawn between types of legal history work. Section IV will then introduce particular radical movements within the historical study of law that transcend the two traditions. This will begin by looking at critical legal history, an approach that has had more influence in the United States than on this side of 'the Pond'. However, as we will see, this approach has been developed into growing literatures on gender and race, and we will introduce in turn the literature that critiques law from those perspectives. The critical turn has also been the catalyst for the development of what has been referred to elsewhere as subversive legal history. These radical approaches can all be contrasted with the more conservative approach whereby history is used to stabilise the present.[3]

---

[1] John H Baker, 'Criminal Courts and Procedure, 1550–1800' in JS Cockbourn (ed.) *Crime in England 1500–1800* (Methuen, 1977) 15, 15.

[2] This distinction was formulated in Russell Sandberg, *Subversive Legal History: A Manifesto for the Future of Legal Education* (Routledge, 2021) chapter 3. This distinction is used in preference to distinctions between old and new or internal and external legal histories, as discussed in ibid. chapter 2.

[3] Robert W Gordon, 'The Past as Authority and as Social Critic: Stabilizing and Destabilizing Functions of History in Legal Argument' in Terrence J McDonald (ed.) *The Historic Turn in the Human Sciences* (University of Michigan Press, 1996) 339, 350.

As we will see, a subversive approach argues that most accounts of the common law have adopted the wrong scientific framework to understand the historical development of law. Most accounts and most lawyers implicitly accept and perpetuate that the common law is characterised by evolution: the idea of progressive improvement over time. Such a perspective means that legal history is simply the story of improvement over time and we have little to learn from the past. It will be argued that, rather than the dominant assumptions of evolution (the idea of progressive improvement over time), the development of law is actually characterised by entropy (the idea of increasing complexity and chaos). This perspective discards the assumption of a linear march towards progress. It reveals that there was nothing inevitable about the development of English law and that legal change is often pragmatic. This means that legal history is necessary in that it shows us how legal ideas and institutions are the product of their times and that the development of English law is often far from planned. A historical approach shows us the roads not taken, and how legal ideas and institutions have not always been as they are today and so do not have to be as they are now in the future. A subversive approach can therefore subvert assumptions that we have of the law and of law reform. This chapter sets the scene for the rest of the book, which will explore what this chaotic understanding of the development of the English common law entails.

II   The Intellectual History Tradition

Intellectual history is often known as the 'history of ideas'. It can be defined as the 'systematic study of the content of those ideas and of their transmission, translation, diffusion and reception'.[4] An intellectual history approach seeks 'to produce causal explanations for the appearance (and disappearance) of those ideas, to trace the influence of a given idea over time, and to de-familiarise current ideas and concepts about law as a first step in the process of reforming them'.[5]

Legal history in the intellectual history tradition, therefore, examines the development of legal ideas. Baker introduced his book in *The Oxford History of the Laws of England* by stating that the focus of the book and of the series was 'the intellectual and institutional framework within which the lawyers' opinions were formed and their arguments devised, the processes of litigation managed and recorded, and the legislative changes achieved'.[6] The intellectual history of law includes what Michael Lobban described as the study of law as 'a specialist intellectual technique':[7] the study of law as interpretation and reinterpretation, of legal argumentation and of the development of legal discourse. This includes the consideration of how law has been understood and presented over time and so is the analysis of works on law as well as of the law itself, scrutinising the question of authorship and possible unreliable narration in relation to both.

---

[4] Richard Whatmore, *What Is Intellectual History?* (Polity Press, 2016) 13–14.
[5] Assaf Likhovski, 'The Intellectual History of Law' in Markus D Dubber and Christopher Tomlins (eds.), *The Oxford Handbook of Legal History* (Oxford University Press, 2018) 151, 151.
[6] John H Baker, *The Oxford History of the Laws of England Volume VI: 1483–1558* (Oxford University Press, 2003) vi.
[7] Michael Lobban, 'Sociology, History and the "Internal" Study of Law' in Richard Nobles and David Schiff (eds.) *Law, Society and Community: Socio-legal Essays in Honour of Roger Cotterrell* (Ashgate, 2014) 39, 51.

The Intellectual History Tradition

As Robert W Gordon pointed out, the word 'intellectual' here does not mean that the study is limited to what he called 'the high falutin' theorizers' such as 'the producers of legal thought, or the producers of legal doctrine or writers'.[8] It also includes those involved with legal ideas and institutions, the 'people who are arguing, justifying, categorizing and often simply describing history'. The intellectual history of law, therefore, includes popular understandings of law: what Assaf Likhovski referred to as 'the history of legal consciousness – that is, the study of the ideas that laypersons have about law and its institutions'.[9] It requires the study of particular communities at particular times and how they understand, distinguish and perpetuate legal ideas.[10]

As we have seen, the method of painstakingly examining primary legal sources is often dated back to Maitland, not only because of his works but also given his role in the foundation of the Selden Society. Maitland recognised his role in founding the intellectual history tradition. He wrote that: 'The History of law must be a history of ideas. It must represent, not merely what men have done and said, but what men have thought in bygone ages.'[11] Maitland's work lay the foundation not only for the legal history works that followed in the first half of the twentieth century, the works of Paul Vinogradoff (1854–1925), William Holdsworth (1897–1944), Theodore Plucknett (1897–1965) and CHS Fifoot (1899–1975), amongst others, but also inspired the next generation of historians 'who were interested not in the doctrines of law as such, but who were interested in law as one of the means of governance in medieval society'.[12] This included the likes of Thomas F Tout (1855–1929), Frank M Stenton (1880–1967), Doris M Stenton (1894–1971) and GO Sayles (1901–94). The same thing happened in the late twentieth century, with Maitland's influence extending not only to the legal historians working in law schools, most notably SFC Milsom (1923–2016), Brian Simpson (1931–2011), David Ibbetson and John Baker, but also a number of 'non-lawyer legal historians' such as James Holt (1922–2014), Patrick Wormald (1947–2004), Paul Hyams, Paul Brand and John Hudson.[13]

However, it is the work of Milsom that epitomised the intellectual history tradition within legal history.[14] Milsom recognised that legal history can be understood as part of intellectual history. For Milsom, the history of law is 'not just part of social and economic history. To use uncomfortably large words, it is the intellectual history of society.'[15] For Lobban, it was Milsom's work that brought about 'the real revolution'.[16] Milsom was interested in how legal ideas change over time through the way in which cases were argued and decided. His work reinvigorated legal history by regarding it as an intellectual puzzle, the purpose of which was not to shed light on the current law but rather to reconstruct a

---

[8] Robert W Gordon, 'Some Final Observations on Legal Intellectual History' (2016) 64 *Buffalo Law Review* 215, 215.
[9] Likhovski, 'The Intellectual History of Law' 151.
[10] Richard Nobles and David Schiff, 'Introduction' in Nobles and Schiff, Law, Society and Community 1, 4.
[11] Frederic W Maitland, *Domesday Book and Beyond* (Fontana, 1960) 415.
[12] Michael Lobban, 'The Varieties of Legal History' (2012) 5 *Clio@Themis* 17, 17.
[13] Jonathan Rose, 'Studying the Past: The Nature and Development of Legal History as an Academic Discipline' (2010) 31(2) *The Journal of Legal History* 101, 118–19. Dates have not been given for those historians who are still alive.
[14] Most notably in SFC Milsom, *Historical Foundations of the Common Law* (2nd ed., Butterworths, 1981), but see also the collection of his essays published as SFC Milsom, *Studies in the History of the Common Law* (Hambledon Press, 1985). An important reflection on his historical method can be found in SFC Milsom, *A Natural History of the Common Law* (Columbia University Press, 2003).
[15] SFC Milsom, 'Maitland' (2001) 60(2) *Cambridge Law Journal* 265, 270.   [16] Lobban, 'The Varieties of Legal History' 11.

22   *The Architects of Legal History*

different earlier legal world. He was concerned with how in each age practitioners sought to get their client out of the legal difficulties of the day. Milsom's work considered the past in its own terms. Milsom's great lesson was that legal historians 'had to attempt to think like a lawyer of the age they were studying'.[17] Legal historians 'had to grasp the fact that terms and concepts which hold one meaning for us held a different meaning in different times'. Milsom's work has proved to be influential. As Lobban has noted, 'legal scholars following Milsom have largely concentrated on those areas which have generated the most legal doctrine, and the knottiest problems for lawyers to wrestle with'.[18] This has meant that such work, however, has tended to focus on the medieval and early modern periods, and upon the history of civil rather than criminal law.[19]

A further innovation in the intellectual history tradition has been the development of 'legal archaeology', which was developed in Simpson's later work. Simpson pioneered an approach often referred to as 'legal archaeology', this entailed focusing upon a leading case and then reconstructing 'the exact factual matrices, the personalities and the clashes which led to the famous decisions'.[20] As Simpson put it, although there are differences (including that legal historians do not tend to regularly destroy their evidence), this approach can be likened to archaeology in that it seeks to 'reconstruct and make sense of the past':

> Cases need to be treated as what they are, fragments of antiquity, and we need, like, archaeologists, gently to free these fragments from the overburden of legal dogmatic, and try, by relating them to other evidence, which has been sought outside the law library, to make sense of them as events in history and incidents in the evolution of the law.[21]

Although a number of studies of legal archaeology have followed,[22] these have largely not been incorporated into the legal history canon. As Ian Ward noted, 'Simpson and his anecdotes were cast to the margins. Which to some might seem diminishing; but to others, conversely a mark of esteem.'[23] It is Milsom's approach that has defined how legal history is seen. Legal historians following Maitland and Milsom have focused on legal doctrine and have not examined, 'except in a most general sense, any connection between such changes and underlying social or economic forces.'[24] Yet, in the late twentieth century, an important change occurred and a new tradition of historical scholarship on law developed.

III   The Social History Tradition

Social history examines the interaction of social groups and social structures over time. It can be defined as being 'the study of economic, political, and social structures, the analysis

---

[17] Ibid. 11.   [18] Ibid. 12.

[19] Philip Handler, 'Legal History' in Dawn Watkins and Mandy Burton (eds.), *Research Methods in Law* (2nd ed., Routledge, 2018) 103, 104.

[20] Sarah E Hamill, 'Review of Legal History' (2019) 28(4) *Social & Legal Studies* 538, 542.

[21] AW Brian Simpson, *Leading Cases in the Common Law* (Oxford University Press, 1995) 12.

[22] See, notably, Cynthia S Gorman, 'Feminist Legal Archaeology, Domestic violence and the Raced-Gendered juridical Boundaries of U.S. Asylum Law' (2019) 51(5) *EPA: Economy and Space* 1050 and Emma Nottingham, 'Digging into Legal Archaeology: A Methodology for Case Study Research' (2022) 49(S1) *Journal of Law and Society* S16.

[23] Ian Ward, *English Legal Histories* (Hart, 2019) 13.

[24] Stuart Anderson, 'The Lawyer as Historian' (1981) 44 *Modern Law Review* 227, 227.

of collectivities – groups defined by class, occupation, sex, family position, geographic location, ethnicity, religion, etc. – in the past'.[25] Social history brings to the fore the lived lives of individuals and groups in the past. In the words of GM Trevelyan, social history entails the study of 'the daily life of the inhabitants of the land in past ages'.[26] It 'adds new stories or new voices and characters to old stories' and 'deepens and broadens the contexts of our stories'.[27]

Legal history in the social history tradition examines the history of law as one social institution amongst other social institutions (e.g., the economy, family, education, media, religion and so on) and within the setting of society as a whole. It is the study of how law interacts with its social environment and how its social environment interacts with law. It is the historical study of the non-legal origins, causes, motivations, assumptions, consequences that are of relevance to the history of law, and of non-legal sources and their relationship with legal sources, using a blend of methodologies. Social history places law into its sociological context. However, this process is two-way. As Laura F Edwards pointed out, reference to law is also integral and transformational for social history: '[L]egal history then changes our view of social history, by exposing the law's presence in places and relationships that most historians imagine to be far distant from anything remotely legal.'[28] As Christopher Brooks noted, '[T]he intriguing thing about "the law" is that it appears to offer a tantalising opportunity to transcend the divide between political and social history.'[29]

The social history approach was pioneered by the work of EP Thompson (1924–93) and his protégés at the history department at Warwick University, which 'opened up interest in the legal history of the eighteenth and nineteenth centuries, encouraged scholars to consider how law was experienced within society and especially by the poor and unenfranchised, raising a host of awkward questions about the claimed objectivity and rationality of law in history'.[30] As well as prospering in history departments, this began to have an effect upon law schools from around the 1970s.[31] This was part of the broader contextual and interdisciplinary approach that started to develop in law schools that was known as socio-legal studies. Many of the scholars who conducted this work did not see themselves as legal historians. They tended to be either employed by history departments rather than law schools or worked within law schools but saw themselves as socio-legal scholars. Their work explored 'the interface between the legal and the social' and has brought about a 'veritable renaissance to the writing of legal history'. As Sarah E Hamill has put it:

---

[25] Louise A Tilly, 'Social History and Its Critics' (1980) 9(5) *Theory and Society* 668, 668.

[26] GM Trevelyan, *English Social History* (Longmans, 1944) vii.

[27] Francis G Couvares, 'Telling a Story in Context; or, What's Wrong with Social History?' (1980) 9(5) *Theory and Society* 674, 675.

[28] Laura F Edwards, 'Law as Social History' in Dubber and Tomlins, *The Oxford Handbook of Legal History* 119, 120.

[29] Christopher W Brooks, *Law, Politics and Society in Early Modern England* (Cambridge University Press, 2008) 10.

[30] KJM Smith and JPS McLaren 'History's Living Legacy: An Outline of "Modern" Historiography of the Common Law' (2001) 21 *Legal Studies* 251, 308.

[31] Smith and McLaren note that before that 'arguably the only out and out attempt at an "external" narrative account of the full span of English legal history was Alan Harding's *A Social History of English Law* (Penguin, 1966)' (ibid. 272).

'Good' legal history is no longer an endless 'and then' of judicial decisions but a 'why this at this time' approach. Legal historians are expected to read around the law and capture the contexts which shaped it.[32]

Writers in the social history tradition have engaged with periods and areas of law that were previously neglected. Although David Sugarman has noted that the 'the boundaries of the subject have spread in almost every conceivable direction,'[33] certain areas and topics have achieved particular attention. The focus has been on modern history,[34] exploring the political, social, economic and cultural causes and effects of changes, including a number of works that focus on gender,[35] as well as the importance of non-legal developments.[36] There has also been a particular focus upon the history of criminal justice,[37] which underscores the difference in approach between writers in this tradition and those in the intellectual history tradition who have largely focuses on the medieval period and paid little attention to criminal law. Indeed, Milsom famously wrote that 'the miserable history of crime in England can be shortly told. Nothing worth-while was created.'[38] Another difference is that the notable expansion in the range of sources used has arisen in part due to the different focus of this work. The nature of the work means that a range of non-legal sources are also used, ranging from statistical date, newspapers, biographies and beyond. As Steve Hedley has observed, accounts of modern legal history have 'retreated from the black-letter tradition'.[39] Although they continue to make reference to what the law was, they use legal materials in a different way. As Carolyn Steedman has put it, practitioners of social history are interested in 'legal proceedings as stories or narrative sources'.[40]

Yet, despite these apparent differences, it is clear that the intellectual history and social history traditions overlap. There is no clear dividing line between the two dimensions. Indeed, the two dimensions are recognised precisely in order to underscore that they are both valid and complementary to each other. It is commonly accepted that the fields of intellectual and social history complement one another rather than battle one another. Richard Whatmore underlined that 'intellectual historians accept that ... ideas are social forces'.[41] And Gordon has noted that 'the history of legal ideas is an important branch of the history of

---

[32] Hamill, 'Review of Legal History' 540.
[33] David Sugarman, 'Writing "Law and Society"' Histories' (1992) 55(5) *Modern Law Review* 292, 299.
[34] See, e.g., AH Manchester, *Modern Legal History* (Butterworths, 1980); William R Cornish and Geoffrey de N Clark, *Law and Society in England 1750–1950* (Sweet and Maxwell, 1989) (a new edition of this was published as William R Cornish, Stephen Banks, Charles Mitchell, Paul Mitchell and Rebecca Probert, *Law and Society in England 1750–1950* (2nd ed., Hart, 2019)); and the work cited by David Sugarman and GR Rubin, 'Towards a New History of Law and Material Society in England 1750–1914' in GR Rubin and David Sugarman (eds.), *Law, Economy & Society* (Professional Books, 1984) 1.
[35] See, e.g., Laura Gowing, *Domestic Dangers: Women, Words and Sex in Early Modern London* (Oxford University Press, 1996) and Garthine Walker, *Crime, Gender and Social Order in Early Modern British History* (Cambridge University Press, 2009).
[36] Leading works include EP Thompson, *Whigs and Hunters* (Allen Lane, 1975) and Douglas Hay, Peter Linebaugh, John G Rule, EP Thompson and Cal Winslow, *Albion's Fatal Tree* (Allen Lane, 1975).
[37] Christopher W Brooks's work provides an exception to this, focusing on civil law: David Sugarman, 'Promoting Dialogue between History and Socio-legal Studies: The Contribution of Christopher W Brooks and the "Legal Turn in Early Modern English History' (2017) 44(S1) *Journal of Law and Society* S37.
[38] Milsom, *Historical Foundations of the Common Law* 403.
[39] Steve Hedley, '"Superior Knowledge or Revelation": An Approach to Modern Legal History' (1987) 18 *Anglo-American Law Review* 177, 177.
[40] Carolyn Steedman, *History and the Law: A Love Story* (Cambridge University Press, 2020) 221.
[41] Whatmore, *What Is Intellectual History?* 9.

The Social History Tradition 25

political and economic thought, of the way in which people try to explain, justify and rationalize the social arrangements under which they live'.[42]

The overlap between the intellectual history and social history traditions is underscored by the way in which the work of Maitland is seen as the founder of both types.[43] As we have seen, his work clearly explored institutional and doctrinal developments, mapping the history of legal ideas. Yet, as Jonathan Rose has pointed out, even Maitland's most doctrinal work was 'not purely legal, as he understands the relationship of law to a broader social and political context'.[44] Maitland's work as a whole freely danced across disciplinary divisions, with Maitland authoring works that drew upon and became renowned in other forms of history and political science. For Rose, this means that 'Maitland is both the discipline's most important pioneer and one whose work connects with legal history's more recent manifestations.' As GR Elton observed, for Maitland, 'historical enquiry demanded the subversion of what had been said before'.[45]

The conception of the intellectual history and social history traditions adopted here is in preference to other distinctions that are usually drawn between internal and external legal history,[46] old and new legal history,[47] textual and contextual legal history,[48] and various other similar formulations.[49] As argued in *Subversive Legal History*, these labels are all insufficient because they tend to suggest a rivalry between the two different forms, with the second form often being presented as a corrective or improvement of the first.[50] By contrast, understanding the types of legal history by reference to the intellectual history and social history traditions shows that such work is complementary. It is not a question of one being newer than the other, or more sophisticated than the other. Moreover, while other divisions are concerned mainly with the way that historical research is conducted, focusing on the intellectual history social history traditions within legal history highlights the focus of the analysis. There are, however, many other different dimensions within legal history scholarship.[51] Many of these do not fit within either the intellectual history or social history traditions. This is especially true of a number of radical approaches that have emerged.

---

[42] Robert J Gordon, 'Book Review: *Tort in America: An Intellectual History*' (1980–91) 94 *Harvard Law Review* 903, 906.

[43] Lobban, 'The Varieties of Legal History' 4.   [44] Rose, 'Studying the Past' 114, 115.

[45] GR Elton, *F W Maitland* (George Weidenfeld and Nicolson, 1985) 21.

[46] E.g., David Ibbetson, 'What Is Legal History a History Of' in Andrew Lewis and Michael Lobban (eds.), *Law and History* (Oxford University Press, 2004) 33.

[47] Alan Hunt, 'The New Legal History: Prospects and Perspectives' (1986) 10 *Contemporary Crises* 201.

[48] Russell Sandberg and Norman Doe, 'Textual and Contextual Legal History' in Norman Doe and Russell Sandberg (eds.), *Law and History: Critical Concepts* (Routledge, 2017) 1.

[49] Rosemary Hunter distinguishes *legal* history, which 'focuses on primarily on statutes, cases and judges (and legal practice), and legal *history*, which 'explores the legal dimension of historical problems' (Rosemary Hunter, 'Australian Legal History in Context' (2003) 21 *Law and History Review* 607, 613). The first form has also been called the 'orthodox' or 'classical' legal history (Hunt, 'The New Legal History' 202; Rose, 'Studying the Past' 117), while the second form has been called 'socio-legal history' (Christopher W Brooks, *Lawyers, Litigation and English Society since 1450* (Hambledon Press, 1998) 179) or has been understood as not being history at all and as just coming under a 'socio-legal' or 'law in context' banner.

[50] See Sandberg, *Subversive Legal History* chapter 2 for a fuller discussion.

[51] *The Oxford Handbook of Legal History* takes a slightly different approach to what has been proposed here. It has a section dedicated to approaches to legal history that includes chapters on legal history as legal scholarship, social history, political history, intellectual history, doctrinal history, cultural history and economic history as well as a number of related chapters.

IV   Radical Approaches

The development of social history in history departments and of socio-legal studies in law schools was part of a critical and interdisciplinary turn in humanities scholarship in the late twentieth century. This led to the development of a number of movements, which this section will now discuss. This section will focus on critical legal history and how this has developed and been superseded by feminist legal history and critical race theory, as well as how it has been developed by my own work on subversive legal history. These radical approaches transcend the intellectual history and social history traditions. The critical legal history movement is often seen as part of the social history tradition. However, as we will see, it also has an often overlooked intellectual history dimension.

1   *Critical Legal History*

The critical legal history movement grew in the late twentieth century as part of the wider critical turn within the humanities as a whole and as a development of the critical legal studies movement in law schools in particular. Critical legal studies provided a radical critique of the orthodox legal position.[52] It provided a critique of the idea of law as an autonomous, objective and legitimate normative mechanism.[53] It questioned the dominant assumption that law provided an objective means to resolve the conflict between individual and social interests. As Alan Hunt noted, critical legal studies stressed that law was actually a mere pragmatic response 'which reflects the unequal distribution of power and resources whilst claiming to act in the name of a set of universal social values'.[54] Critical legal studies stressed how every judge was 'a political actor effecting a particular political agenda'.[55] Gordon wrote that the critical approach was based on two main ideas: 'false legitimation', that is, 'the complacent idea that the legal system in force is about as efficient, just and rational a system that it could be'; and 'false necessity', the idea that the legal system 'could not be reformed except in minor ways without risking economic and political catastrophe'.[56]

The lines between critical legal studies and critical legal history are blurred, in that much work within critical legal studies has been historical. Gordon observed that critical legal writers had 'probably devoted more pages to historical description – particularly the intellectual history of legal doctrine – than to anything else'.[57] Both movements were larger in the United States than in the United Kingdom. The main authors of critical legal history in the United States are Morton Horwitz and Robert W Gordon, while in the United Kingdom, the main author is David Sugarman.[58]

---

[52] See, e.g., Roberto Mangaberia Unger, *The Critical Legal Studies Movement: Another Time, A Greater Task* (Verso, 2015).
[53] Alan Hunt, 'The Theory of Critical Legal Studies' (1986) 6 *Oxford Journal of Legal Studies* 1, 4.   [54] Ibid. 5.
[55] Ian Ward, *Introduction to Critical Legal Theory* (2nd ed., Cavendish, 2004) 144.
[56] Robert W Gordon, *Taming the Past: Essays on Law in History and History in Law* (Cambridge University Press, 2017) 220.
[57] Ibid. 221.
[58] See Morton J Horwitz, *The Transformation of American Law 1780–1860* (Harvard University Press, 1977); Morton J Horwitz, *The Transformation of American Law 1870–1960: The Crisis of Legal Orthodoxy* (Oxford University Press, 1992); Robert W Gordon, 'Critical Legal Histories' (1984) 36 *Stanford Law Review* 57; Sugarman and Rubin, 'Towards a New History of Law and Material Society in England, 1750–1914'.

Radical Approaches 27

Like critical legal studies, there are 'considerable variations in the style focus and method of work produced' under the label of critical legal history.[59] Indeed, the very notion that there is a 'correct' theory or method is anathematic to critical scholars. That said, critical legal history can be understood as a 'strongly revisionist' approach that views law 'as inherently historical and with an ideological role'.[60] Critical legal history is political, not in the sense that it takes a particular political stance, but that it is directly concerned with questions of power. It articulates, emphasises and directs critical fire at power imbalances. It realises that conventional historical narratives are constructs.

Hunt has argued that critical legal history's 'primary target is a Whig interpretation of legal history which perceives the past as the forebear of the contemporary legal system through a unilinear trajectory'.[61] The label 'Whig history', originated by Herbert Butterfield,[62] describes a mode of 'big history' writing that long outlasted the Whig Party.[63] This approach presents history within a narrative of progress, depicting the 'the past as a journey to democracy or the past as a story of class struggle'.[64] As Ward noted, Whig histories stressed how 'a series of "great" things accounted for the past of English constitutional history, and the same past assured the future'.[65] This approach, which critical legal history set itself in opposition to, emphasised a narrative of evolutionary progress.

This has been underlined in the work of Gordon in 'Critical Legal Histories',[66] which argued that the background assumptions found in the work of legal scholars can be described as 'evolutionary functionalism'.[67] For Gordon, evolutionary functionalism is so entrenched that it is almost unnoticeable. Gordon's term describes a number of ideas and assumptions that assemble around two ideas. The first idea is that of evolution: this refers to a basic Darwinian understanding that regards history as a constant, linear process of progress and improvement. The second is functionalism: this refers to a school of thought in social theory dating back to Emile Durkheim[68] and Talcott Parsons[69] that understands society as being comprised like the human body of various parts that perform different functions in order for society as a whole to operate as the result of order and consensus.[70]

For Gordon, evolutionary functionalism is comprised of five threads:[71] first, law and society are separate categories and law is autonomous; second, societies have needs that drive them and limit the possibilities of social experimentation; third, societies follow an objective, determined, progressive social evolutionary path and law assumes this; fourth, legal systems are described and explained in terms of their functional responsiveness to social needs (whether they have satisfied, or failed to satisfy, the functional requirements of

---

[59] Cf. Peter Fitzpatrick and Alan Hunt, 'Critical Legal Studies: Introduction' (1987) 14(1) *Journal of Law and Society* 1, 1.
[60] Rose, 'Studying the Past' 121.   [61] Hunt, 'The New Legal History' 202–3.
[62] Herbert Butterfield, *The Whig Interpretation of History* (G Bell & Sons, 1931)   [63] Ward, *English Legal Histories* 4.
[64] Sugarman, 'Writing "Law and Society"' Histories' 299.
[65] Ian Ward, *Writing the Victorian Constitution* (Palgrave, 2018) 19.
[66] Gordon, 'Critical Legal Histories' 57, reprinted as chapter 11 of Gordon, *Taming the Past*.
[67] The concept was referred to as 'adaptation theory' in Gordon's earlier work. Robert W Gordon, 'Historicism in Legal Scholarship' (1981) 90 *Yale Law Review* 1017, reprinted as chapter 10 of Gordon, *Taming the Past*.
[68] On which, see Roger Cotterrell, *Emile Durkheim: Law in a Moral Domain* (Stanford University Press, 1999).
[69] On which, see A Javier Trevino, *Talcott Parsons on Law and the Legal System* (Cambridge Scholars Publishing, 2008).
[70] This organic analogy is similar to Maitland's description of law as a 'living body', discussed in the last chapter of this book: Frederic W Maitland, *The Constitutional History of England* (Cambridge University Press, 1941 [1908]) 539.
[71] Gordon, *Taming the Past* 223–9.

each stage of social development); and fifth, the legal system adapts to changing social needs in that, although legal changes can be dysfunctional for short periods, adaption is the normal course. This is reflected in the idea that the 'common law over time tends to work itself pure', that legal doctrine has become 'ever more certain and predictable as well as more adaptable to social needs; and that the law has 'become more and more efficient'.[72]

Gordon observed that the critical approach counters evolutionary functionalism. A critical approach argues that this representation obscures the way in which these processes are actually manufactured by people.[73] Legal forms and practices are political products that arise from the struggles of conflict. A critical approach shows that the course of historical development is not determined by any uniform evolutionary path. There is no necessary link between social and legal change ('Comparable social conditions (both within the same and across societies) have generated contrary legal responses, and comparable legal forks have produced contrary social effects'[74]); law is neither an objective response to objective historical processes nor a neutral technology adapted to the needs of that particular society. Gordon insisted that law and society are 'inextricably mixed'.[75] As he put it, '[I]t is just about impossible to describe any set of "basic" social practices without describing the legal relations among the people involved.'[76] Indeed, 'legal categories affect social perceptions' to such an extent that law persuades that 'the world described in its images and categories is the only attainable world in which a sane person would want to live'. This hides the extent to which law is 'founded upon contradictions' and the chief job of law is 'to keep those oppositions from becoming too starkly obvious'.[77] Legal history written in the evolutionary functionalist mode seeks to hide and/or normalise this. By contrast, legal history written in the critical mode seeks to highlight and question this. As Gordon put it, critical legal historiography becomes 'the intellectual history of the rise and fall of paradigm structures of thought designed to mediate contradictions'.[78]

The reference here to 'intellectual history' is important. Critical legal history is often understood as being an example of social history, in that it focuses on the effect of external factors on law. It is concerned with the relationship between law and society. However, Gordon's account makes it clear that critical legal history also uses intellectual history, in that it is concerned with the internal development of legal ideas. Gordon did not argue that the study of doctrinal legal sources be abandoned, but argued 'for studying law embedded in everyday practice as well'.[79] He wrote that '[T]his special kind of doctrinal history is surely the most distinctive Critical contribution.'[80] Yet, it is striking how few of Gordon's followers have pursued this line of inquiry.[81] Gordon himself has backtracked a little, claiming that he was writing for a specific audience and 'was not trying to privilege the history of legal doctrine over other kinds of legal history' and 'not identifying "critical"

---

[72] Ibid. 229.   [73] For fuller discussion of the seven 'partial critiques' that inform critical approaches, see ibid. 261.
[74] Ibid. 261.   [75] Ibid. 266.   [76] Ibid. 262.   [77] Ibid. 273.   [78] Ibid. 274.
[79] Robert W Gordon, '"Critical Legal Histories Revisited": A Response' (2012) 37 *Law & Social Inquiry* 200, 208.
[80] Gordon, *Taming the Past* 274.
[81] Susanna L Blumenthal, 'Of Mandarins, Legal Consciousness, and the Cultural Turn in US Legal History' (2012) 37 *Law & Social Inquiry* 167, 177–8.

Radical Approaches   29

history with the history of doctrine'.[82] His later work has described the critical approach more generally. In his short essay 'The Arrival of Critical Historicism', he described 'critical history' as:

any approach to the past that produces disturbances in the field – that inverts or scrambles familiar narratives of stasis, recovery or progress; anything that advances rival perspectives (such of those as the losers rather than the winners) for surveying developments, or that posits alternative trajectories that might have produced a very different present – in short any approach that unsettles the familiar strategies that we use to tame the past in order to normalize the present.[83]

Christopher Tomlins has called this approach 'utterly subversive'.[84] Read in conjunction with Gordon's earlier work, it can be said that critical legal history is a disturbance that seeks to unsettle and critique the notion that law is autonomous, objective and predictable, and complicates accounts of legal and social change that are based upon these liberal expectations. It challenges progress myths of legal evolution and the associated conservative belief that legal change can occur within the system. Critical legal history 'shows the way in which our most basic legal categories and distinctions (e.g. that between "public" and "private" realms) are both the product of, and themselves give rise to, political and ideological struggles among different people'.[85] It is inherently revisionist, necessarily challenging and invariably contentious, controversial and divisive.

Mariana Valverde has written that critical legal studies is now 'a mature, if not frankly elderly, literature'.[86] Most accounts agree that the critical legal studies movement burnt out in the 1990s, though 'the echoes of its intervention are still audible in legal scholarship'.[87] The same is true of critical legal history. As Tomlins has noted, 'The "subversive" conjunction between history and critical legal studies . . . has ended' and this is 'a marker of intellectual exhaustion'.[88] However, others have commented that critical legal studies has evolved rather than simply declined, and that one way in which it has evolved is in the particular areas of feminist and race theories.[89]

The heirs to the critical movement have focused their critique in various different ways. Many have fore-grounded types of inequality such as class, race, religion, sexuality and gender. The following sections will look at radical movements that have focuses on gender and race. It will begin by looking at feminist legal history. Like critical legal history, this has developed the most in the United States. However, as the next section will discuss, in

---

[82] Gordon, 'Critical Legal Histories Revisited' 205.

[83] Robert Gordon, 'The Arrival of Critical Historicism' (1997) 49 *Stanford Law Review* 1023, 1024. It is a curious irony that this description is itself a functional definition.

[84] Christopher Tomlins, 'After Critical Legal History: Scope, Scale, Structure' (2012) 8 *Annual Review of Law and Social Science* 31, 37.

[85] Charles Barzun, 'Causation, Legal History, and Legal Doctrine' (2016) 64 *Buffalo Law Review* 81, 86.

[86] Mariana Valverde, *Chronotopes of Law: Jurisdiction, Scale and Governance* (Routledge, 2015) 47, 31.

[87] Christopher Tomlins, 'What Is Left of the Law and Society Paradigm after Critique? Revisiting Gordon's "Critical Legal Histories' (2012) 37 *Law & Social Inquiry* 155, 156.

[88] Christopher Tomlins, 'Law and History' in Keith E Whittington, R Daniel Kelemen and Gregory A Calderia (eds.) *The Oxford Handbook of Law and Politics* (Oxford University Press, 2008) 723, 730.

[89] Ward, *Introduction to Critical Legal Theory* 145.

30   *The Architects of Legal History*

recent years, feminist legal history has developed as a movement in the United Kingdom, and now arguably has become the main heir to the critical movement of the late twentieth century.[90]

2   *Feminist Legal History*

The field of feminist legal studies arose in the 1980s 'virtually simultaneously in Canada, the US, Britain, Australia and Scandinavia' and can be understood as being both 'an off-shoot of critical legal studies' and 'a development from the women's movement more generally'.[91] Its influence upon British law schools was slowly felt but formed part of what Emily Jackson and Nicola Lacey have referred to as the 'gradual intellectualisation of law schools'.[92] This meant that by the dawn of the new millennium, feminist legal studies constituted 'a significant body of scholarship, competing with other jurisprudential theories for distinguished journals and texts'.[93] Feminism became one of, if not the, main critical approaches used in British law schools.

Yet, the influence of feminist approaches upon legal scholarship has been uneven and varied. It has remained true that most legal history 'scholarship in the UK and Ireland largely ignores women', in that 'at best it plays down women's perspectives and agency and at worst reduces mentions of women to the occasional paragraph'.[94] Yet, in recent years, a growing literature has developed in the United Kingdom that emphasises gender and that focuses on these missing stories.[95] This is epitomised by the project and book on Women's Legal Landmarks,[96] as well as the emerging literature that includes work by Rosemary Auchmuty, Erika Rackley, Joanne Conaghan and Sharon Thompson.

These works can be labelled as feminist legal history rather than as women's history. As June Purvis has noted, women's history is 'a history that takes women as its subject matter but is not necessarily informed by the ideas and theories that would constitute a feminist analysis'.[97] Feminist legal history, by contrast, draws upon the 'well established and vigorously theorized sub-discipline of feminist history' and goes beyond the collecting and assembling the facts, in that it 'seeks to produce a new, accurate, inclusive account'.[98] As Rackley and Auchmuty have put it, feminist legal history draws upon women's legal

---

[90] For a comparison between the United States and the United Kingdom, see Maria Drakopoilou, 'Feminist Historiography of Law: An Exposition and Proposition' in Dubber and Tomlins, *The Oxford Handbook of Legal History* 603, 603.

[91] Joanne Conaghan, 'Labour Law and Feminist Method' (2017) 33(1) *International Journal of Comparative Labour Law* 93; MDA Freeman, *Lloyds Introduction to Jurisprudence* (9th ed., Sweet & Maxwell, 2014) 1079.

[92] Emily Jackson and Nicola Lacey, 'Introducing Feminist Legal Theory' in James Penner, David Schiff and Richard Nobles (eds.) *Introduction to Jurisprudence and Legal Theory* (Butterworths, 2002) 779, 780.

[93] Joanne Conaghan, 'Reassessing the Feminist Theoretical Project in Law' (2000) 27(3) *Journal of Law and Society* 351, 352.

[94] Erika Rackley and Rosemary Auchmuty, 'Women's Legal Landmarks: An Introduction' in Erika Rackley and Rosemary Auchmuty (eds.), *Women's Legal Landmarks: Celebrating the History of Women and Law in the UK and Ireland* (Hart, 2018) 1, 4.

[95] The following draws upon chapter 4 of Sandberg, *Subversive Legal History*.

[96] Rackley and Auchmuty, *Women's Legal Landmarks*.

[97] June Purvis, 'Doing Feminist Women's History: Researching the Lives of Women in the Suffragette Movement in Edwardian England' in Mary Maynard and June Purvis (eds.), *Researching Women's Lives from a Feminist Perspective* (Taylor & Francis, 1994) 166, 167.

[98] Rackley and Auchmuty, 'Women's Legal Landmarks' 4–5.

Radical Approaches 31

history: 'in practice, the stories and narratives of women 'in', 'and' and 'of' law – what we might call "women's legal history" – are the building blocks of feminist legal history. It is through these histories that feminist legal history is able to expose and contest'.[99]

This approach is sometimes referred to as 'engendering' legal history: re-adding the stories of women.[100] This entails asking what Auchmuty called the 'woman question' – '[W]here are the women in this account?'[101] It then requires 'including women's stories, experiences, and voices (often hidden, ignored and silenced in dominant narratives)'. However, engendering legal history requires more than just writing women into the history of law. As Felice Batlan has argued, 'it produces a new history, creating possibilities of re-narrations and the potential for fresh interpretations'.[102] Moreover, this requires more than just re-writing legal stories where women already appear. As Batlan argued, engendering legal history is not only valuable in relation to areas such as domestic relations and family law where 'issues of women and gender readily appear'. It is also useful – possibly even more useful – when applied to 'those areas of law that on the surface appear to be ungendered'.[103]

Engendering legal history can be said to have three main effects. First, it questions assumptions. As Batlan has written, focusing on gender 'makes us question some of our basic assumptions about legal history'.[104] Second, engendering legal history questions the explanations that have previously been given for legal and social change. As Batlan put it, 'How does gender account for changes in law that historians have traditionally interpreted as the result of economic change? How does out understanding of the individuals' relationship to the state change when domestic relations law stands not at the periphery of law, but at its core?'[105] Third, and crucially, engendering legal history brings to the fore the issue of power dynamics. The questioning of assumptions and explanations enable legal historians to 'uncover the many mechanisms by which men have retained power for themselves in law'.[106] Focusing on gender also shows how 'power becomes effectuated – that is, made real and material'.[107] This is what makes it an explicitly feminist project. As Thompson has put it, a feminist approach 'seeks to transform our understanding of the past by writing' stories 'back into legal history, while confronting the question of why [they have] been excluded from accounts'.[108]

However, defining what feminism means is difficult. There are a wide range of perspectives and traditions within feminist thought. A taxonomy of schools of feminist thought such as the liberal, radical, cultural and postmodern are often identified.[109] However, as Vanessa Munro has convincingly argued, talk of such classifications runs the risk that we 'lose sight of the basic and fundamental convictions that continue to

---

[99] Erika Rackley and Rosemary Auchmuty, 'The Case for Feminist Legal History' (2020) 40(4) *Oxford Journal of Legal Studies* 878, 889.

[100] Tracy A Thomas and Tracey J Boisseua, 'Introduction: Law, History, and Feminism' in Tracy A Thomas and Tracey J Boisseua (eds.), *Feminist Legal History: Essays on Women and Law* (New York University Press, 2011) 1.

[101] Rackley and Auchmuty, 'Women's Legal Landmarks' 5.

[102] Felice Batlan, 'Engendering Legal History' (2005) 30(4) *Law & Society Inquiry* 823, 823. [103] Ibid. 837. [104] Ibid. 832.

[105] Ibid. 824.

[106] Rosemary Auchmuty, 'Recovering Lost Lives: Researching Women in Legal History' (2015) 42 *Journal of Law and Society* 34, 34.

[107] Sandra Harding, *Whose Science, Whose Knowledge* (Cornell University Press, 2013) 150.

[108] Sharon Thompson, *Quiet Revolutionaries: The Married Women's Association and Family Law* (Hart, 2022) 13.

[109] Patrica A Cain, 'Feminism and the Limits of Equality' (1990) 24 *Georgia Law Review* 803.

32   *The Architects of Legal History*

animate and unite theorists across these divides'.[110] Although feminists are wary of attempts to identify essential or fundamental principles, this does not mean that identifying trends and general features of feminism is impossible.[111] Feminism in this context can be understood as a dynamic '*process* of engagement or interaction – a dynamic *movement* of ideas', which 'places distinctive substantive issues on the agenda of legal scholarship and legal theory'.[112] In particular, a feminist approach focuses on gender as a structural and ideological means of subordination and exclusion. For Conaghan, 'the application of a gender lens works to: (1) expose the operation of gender bias and neglect; (2) destabilise the normative and conceptual infrastructure; and (3) historicise and contextualise the field'.[113]

Five features of a feminist approach to law may be identified.[114] First, feminism is a grounded approach. A feminist lens dispenses the usual 'top-down' analysis to instead focus on actual lived experiences, operating from the ground up.[115] This involves examining the everyday experiences of how women interact with the law. This is summed up by the conviction that 'the personal is the political'. It also requires a wider range of sources than conventionally used in doctrinal legal scholarship, including the use of non-legal sources.[116]

Second, feminist scholarship exposes binary understandings about gender roles and social life. As Munro noted, '[W]omen are identified with domestic and family life, with reproduction and with passive but accessible (hetro) sexuality.'[117] A feminist legal approach shows how these gendered understandings are articulated in law – 'the myriad ways in which law constructs gender by invoking images of 'woman'' – and how this leads to and perpetuates structural disadvantage.[118] As Thompson observed, '[F]eminist analyses can usefully break down the boundaries between public and private.'[119]

Third, feminist approaches highlight how ideas are gendered. It is not just legal structures and institutions (and subjective understandings of such structures and institutions) that are gendered. A feminist approach can uncover the gendered nature of legal concepts and ideas themselves (and their application). This can include taking 'a sceptical approach towards claims of law's rationality and neutrality'.[120] A feminist approach emphasises how law is not a 'neutral arbiter'.[121] This questions the very foundations of the legal system since, as Thompson observed, '[T]he notion of law's neutrality is a

---

[110] Vanessa Munro, *Law and Politics at the Perimeter: Re-evaluating Key Debates in Feminist Theory* (Hart, 2007) 11. Carole Pateman has suggested that such 'classification of feminists … suggests that feminism is always secondary, a supplement to other doctrines' (Carole Pateman, *The Sexual Contract* (Polity Press, 1988) x).
[111] Joanne Conaghan, 'The Making of a Field of the Building of a Wall? Feminist Legal Studies and Law, Gender and Sexuality' (2009) 17 *Feminist Legal Studies* 303, 304.
[112] Conaghan, 'Reassessing the Feminist Theoretical Project in Law' 356; Jackson and Lacey, 'Introducing Feminist Legal Theory' 789.
[113] Conaghan, 'Labour Law and Feminist Method' 100.
[114] Sandberg, *Subversive Legal History* 91 *et seq*. See also the 'six substantive and methodological characteristics of feminist legal history' identified by Rackley and Auchmuty, 'The Case for Feminist Legal History' 889– 902.
[115] There is 'a rejection of abstraction and commitment to the importance of context' (Vanessa Munro, 'The Master's Tools? A Feminist Approach to Legal and Lay Decision-Making' in Watkins and Burton, *Research Methods in Law* 194, 196).
[116] Thompson, *Quiet Revolutionaries* 9.   [117] Munro, *Law and Politics at the Perimeter* 12.
[118] Conaghan, 'Reassessing the Feminist Theoretical Project in Law' 361.   [119] Thompson, *Quiet Revolutionaries* 14.
[120] Munro, 'The Master's Tools' 196.   [121] Thompson, *Quiet Revolutionaries* 15.

Radical Approaches 33

powerful force which helps maintain public confidence in the legal system and reinforces the assumption that the law will be applied equally to everyone.'[122] A feminist approach is critical in that it 'invites the application of a gender lens to a seemingly genderless space or operation and 'helps to flush out any hidden norms lurking unacknowledged behind a gender-neutral façade'.[123] It shows how gender is actually 'analytically central' to and 'deeply constitutive' of law.

Fourth, feminist approaches can emphasise the agency of those experiencing disadvantage, subordination and exclusion. A feminist perspective brings to the fore the experiences and achievements of women.[124] This is overlooked in traditional legal histories where women are 'portrayed as the passive recipients of legal and social change, as subjects rather than initiators of legal reform'.[125] This requires attention to be paid only to voices that are heard less often. For instance, as Thompson has commented: 'While the arrests, hunger strikes and civil disobedience of the suffragettes is part of mainstream feminist history, the quieter work of feminist groups established in the aftermath of these campaigns has largely been consigned to oblivion.'[126] A feminist approach also reveals the nature of legal change recognising the agency of women. This is in contrast to conventional accounts that present 'hard-fought-for legal change, for example, as a simple response to shifts in "social attitudes"'.[127] As Thompson has noted, dominant accounts of 'legal developments are often blinkered as those producing these accounts have focused mostly (or even solely) on the work of institutions' that have historically been led by men, meaning that 'women – and the grass roots pressure groups led by women – are obliterated from the story of reform'.[128] A grounded feminist approach, by contrast, can reveal the importance of the role of activism not only where such activism was successful but also where it was seemingly unsuccessful. As Thompson asserted: 'For legal historians, however, investigating why change did *not* happen can be as important as exploring why it did.'[129] A feminist approach can understand why change is slowly achieved, how it is often the result of compromise and can point to the importance of piecemeal achievements.[130] Crucially, a feminist approach focuses on the power dynamics at play in particular situations. In Thompson's words, it 'directs critical fire at how social and legal structures create and reinforce power imbalances'.[131] A feminist approach does not assume that men

---

[122] Ibid. 16.   [123] Conaghan, 'Labour Law and Feminist Method' 101.

[124] Recent years have seen increased attention paid to legal biography generally. See, William Cornish, *Life Stories and Legal Histories* (Selden Society, 2015); David Sugarman, 'From Legal Biography to Legal Life Writing: Broadening Conceptions of Legal History and Socio-legal Scholarship' (2015) 42(1) *Journal of Law and Society* 7 and the other essays published in that special issue; Victoria Barnes, Catharine MacMillan and Stefan Vogenauer, 'On Legal Biography' (2020) 41(2) *Journal of Legal History* 115 and the other essays published in that special issue; and the discussion in Thompson, *Quiet Revolutionaries* 49 *et seq.*

[125] Rackley and Auchmuty, 'The Case for Feminist Legal History' 884, 881.   [126] Thompson, *Quiet Revolutionaries* 3.

[127] Rackley and Auchmuty, 'The Case for Feminist Legal History' 884, 881.   [128] Thompson, *Quiet Revolutionaries* 14.

[129] Ibid. 155. See also ibid. 145–9. Thompson's account of the Married Women's Association highlights the importance of their supposed failures. She noted that not only can failures be precursors to successes but that the association saw its results differently than orthodox accounts have assumed. She cited one Executive Committee report that 'described their work as being more notable for its "ricochets" than its "bulls-eyes"': 'The "bulls-eyes" are marked clearly by a new statute or precedent. The ricochets are the ostensible failures, that did in fact leave their mark.' The report concluded that: 'Experience has taught us not to expect the bulls-eyes, but to view with satisfaction such ricochets as have furthered our cause': ibid. 227.

[130] See ibid. 178 *et seq.*   [131] Ibid. 14.

necessarily have an oppressive role, but 'it recognises that there is a power dimension between men and women'.[132] This involves paying attention 'to the tacit understandings affecting intimate relationships'.[133]

Fifth, a feminist approach seeks to bring about social change. As Conaghan put it, feminism is concerned 'not just with describing or interpreting social arrangements but also with changing them, that is, with prescribing and effecting transformation, informed by a range of normative ideals including sexual equality, social justice, and individual self-development'.[134] This means that feminist scholarship can, and often does have, a political dimension.[135] As Rackley and Auchmuty have put it: 'Feminist legal history is a call to arms to anyone who cares about the position of women in law, and society generally.'[136] Feminist legal history, as with feminist legal studies generally, both expresses and interrogates feminism as a political movement.[137]

However, there are other focuses upon race, religion, class or sexuality that could perform similar and equally necessary correctives. This is recognised in the feminist literature on intersectionality, which has stressed that people have a range of overlapping identities and are not solely defined by their gender. In this literature, the focus has 'shifted away from the concept of gender as an isolated category of analysis towards a concern with the way in which gender intersects with other categories of identity for purposes of understanding and combating inequality'.[138] This literature emerged in the 1990s as part of a growing recognition of the need to broaden the representational base of feminism to take better account, substantively and strategically, of differences between women buoyed by a 'a keen suspicion of categories of categories in general and of the category "woman" in particular'.[139] This is known as anti-essentialism. The literature on intersectionality has led to increased analysis of other forms of inequality, such as sexuality.[140] There is also a significant literature on race and the law, which has a strong historical component.[141] In recent years, particular attention has been afforded to a particular approach known as critical race theory.

---

[132] Sharon Thompson, *Prenuptial Agreements and the Presumption of Free Choice: Issues of Power in Theory and Practice* (Hart, 2015) 9.

[133] Sharon Thompson, 'Feminist Relational Contract Theory: A New Model for Family Property Agreements' (2018) 45(4) *Journal of Law and Society* 617, 629.

[134] Conaghan, 'Reassessing the Feminist Theoretical Project in Law' 375.

[135] For Erika Rackley and Rosemary Auchmuty, 'feminist legal history is, then, at root a political project': Erika Rackley and Rosemary Auchmuty, 'Women's Legal Landmarks: An Introduction' in Rackley and Auchmuty, *Women's Legal Landmarks* 1, 5.

[136] Rackley and Auchmuty, 'The Case for Feminist Legal History' 902.

[137] Conaghan, 'Reassessing the Feminist Theoretical Project in Law' 355, 356.

[138] Joanne Conaghan, 'Intersectionality and the Feminist Project in Law' in Emily Grabham, Davina Cooper, Jane Krishnadas and Didi Herman (eds.), *Intersectionality and Beyond: Law, Power and the Politics of Location* (Routledge, 2009) 21, 21.

[139] Munro, *Law and Politics at the Perimeter* 23

[140] On which see, e.g., Caroline Derry, *Lesbianism and the Criminal Law: Three Centuries of Legal Regulation in England and Wales* (Palgrave, 2020); David Minto, 'Queering Law's Empire: Domination and Domain in the Sexing up of Legal History' in Dubber and Tomlins, *The Oxford Handbook of Legal History* 641; Luisa Stella de Oliveira Coutinho Silva, 'Sexy Legal History: Mapping Sexualities in a Handbook' (2019) 27 *Rechtsgeschichte – Legal History* 260.

[141] For an excellent example, see Bharat Malkani, *Slavery and the Death Penalty: A Study in Abolition* (Routledge, 2018).

3 Critical Race Theory

Critical race theory can be dated back to a particular workshop held on 8 July 1989 in Madison, Wisconsin.[142] Although this workshop was entitled 'New Developments in Critical Race Theory', which suggested that the movement already existed, the name 'critical race theory' was created for this event.[143] Critical race theory became a movement of activists and scholars who were 'engaged in studying and transforming the relationship among race, racism and power'.[144] It was at first a movement in American law schools, focusing on how racism was institutionalised in and by law.[145] It sprang from a realisation that the advances of the civil rights era of the 1960s in America had stalled and were being rolled back.[146] A generation of scholars, including Derrick Bell (1930–2011), Richard Delgado, Alan Freeman, Charles Lawrence, Mari Matsuda, Patricia Williams and Kimberlé Williams Crenshaw, realised that 'new theories and strategies were needed to combat the subtler forms of racism that were gaining ground'.

The critical race theory movement considered many of the same issues that were being explored in work on civil rights and ethnic studies but placed these issues in a broader setting, including history.[147] Moreover, as Delgado and Jean Stefancic pointed out, critical race theory rejected the focus on incremental step-by-step progress as advocated by traditional civil rights discourse. Rather, critical race theory questioned the very foundations of society: It explored the biases within and the effect of supposedly neutral provisions, including the law. It was designed 'not only to name, but to be a tool for rooting out inequality and injustice'.[148] Critical race theory drew upon both the radical approaches of both critical legal studies and feminism. This included taking a sceptical approach to triumphal accounts of history and their evolutionary progress narratives, as well as scrutinising the relationship between power and the construction of social roles and the 'unseen, largely invisible collection of patterns and habits' that allow domination to occur.[149]

Like other radical approaches, there are many different strands of critical race theory and significant tension about whether it has any central propositions and, if so, how these can be articulated. However, Delgado and Stefancic suggested that many critical race scholars would agree on the following six propositions.[150]

The first proposition is that 'racism is ordinary, not aberrational', in that racism is perpetuated in 'the usual way society does business, the common, everyday experience of most people'.[151] This means that racism is difficult to address and cannot be addressed by

---

[142] There were also pre-workshop formations that often gathered in hotel rooms and in other spaces often before, during and after professional conferences. Kimberlé Williams Crenshaw, 'Twenty Years of Critical Race Theory: Looking Back to Move Forward' (2011) 43(5) *Connecticut Law Review* 1253, 1298.

[143] Ibid. 1263.

[144] Richard Delgado and Jean Stefancic, *Critical Race Theory: An Introduction* (3rd ed., New York University Press, 2017) 3.

[145] Derrick A Bell, 'Who's Afraid of Critical Race Theory?' (1995) *University of Illinois Law Review* 893, 898.

[146] Delgado and Stefancic, Critical Race Theory 4.   [147] Ibid. 3.

[148] A Javier Treviño, Michelle A Harris and Derron Wallace, 'What's So Critical about Critical Race Theory?' (2008) 11(1) *Contemporary Justice Review* 7, 8.

[149] Delgado and Stefancic, Critical Race Theory 5.   [150] Ibid. 8–11.

[151] Ibid. 8. This proposition is expressed in Charles R Lawrence, 'The Id, the Ego, and Equal Protection: Reckoning with Unconscious Racism' (1987) 39 *Stanford Law Review* 317 and Derrick Bell, *Faces at the Bottom of the Well: The Permanence of Racism* (Basic Books, 2018 [1992]).

liberal approaches that seek a 'colour blind' approach and formal equality in the sense of treating everyone the same because such policies can 'remedy only the most blatant forms of discrimination'.

The second proposition is known as 'interest convergence' or 'material determination'. This is the idea that racism serves important purposes for the dominant group, who therefore have little reason to eradicate it.[152] This means that the changes that do occur that seem to be a triumph of civil rights are often nothing of the sort and actually result from the self-interests of the white elites.[153] Racism is not only the result of 'matters of thinking, mental categorization, attitude and discourse' but is also the means by 'which society allocates privilege and status'.[154] This has been cemented into law.[155]

The 'social construction' thesis is the third proposition. This holds that, rather than being biological and objective, inherent or fixed, race is actually the product of social thoughts and relations: '[R]aces are categories that society invents, manipulates, or retires when convenient.'[156] The articulation of race as a social construction has become 'a mantra' in critical race theory.[157] This does not deny the fact of biology and genetics but stresses the importance of nurture over nature. As Delgado and Stefancic put it:

People with common origins share certain physical traits, of course, such as skin color, physique, and hair texture. But these constitute only an extremely small portion of their genetic endowment, are dwarfed by what we have in common, and have little or nothing to do with distinctively human, higher-order traits, such as personality, intelligence, and moral behavior.[158]

The fourth proposition is 'differential racialisation'. This is 'the idea that each race has its own origins and ever-revolving history'.[159] This means that race was never simply 'out there' to be discovered but was invented 'in a quite literal sense'.[160] Differential racialisation highlights 'the ways the dominant society racializes different minority groups at different times, in response to shifting needs'.[161] This means that popular images and stereotypes of various minority groups also shift over time.

Adherence to 'intersectionality and anti-essentialism' represents the fifth proposition. This means that no one is defined by one 'single, easily stated, unitary identity', such as their race. Rather, everyone has 'potentially conflicting, overlapping identities, loyalties and allegiances'.[162] As with feminist approaches, critical race scholars increasingly stress

---

[152] Delgado and Stefancic, Critical Race Theory 9.
[153] See Derrick Bell, *Silent Covenants: Brown v Board of Education and the Unfulfilled Hopes for Racial Reform* (Oxford University Press, 2005).
[154] Delgado and Stefancic, Critical Race Theory 21.
[155] See Cheryl I Harris, 'Whiteness as Property' (1993) 106 *Harvard Law Review* 1709.
[156] Delgado and Stefancic, Critical Race Theory 9.
[157] Robert S Chang, 'Critiquing "Race" and Its Uses: Critical Race Theory's Uncompleted Argument' in Francisco Valdes, Jerome McCristal Culp and Angela P Harris (eds.), *Crossroads, Directions, and a New Critical Race Theory* (Temple University Press, 2002) 87.
[158] Delgado and Stefancic, *Critical Race Theory* 9.   [159] Ibid. 10.
[160] Robert L. Hayman, Jr and Nancy Levit, 'Un-natural Things: Constructions of Race, Gender, and Disability' in Valdes, McCristal Culp and Harris, Crossroads, Directions, and a New Critical Race Theory 159, 159.
[161] Delgado and Stefancic, *Critical Race Theory* 10.
[162] Ibid. 11. For a classic statement, see Kimberlé Williams Crenshaw, 'Demarginalizing the Intersection of Race and Sex: A Black Feminist Critique of Antidiscrimination Doctrine, Feminist Theory and Antiracist Politics' (1989) 1(8) *University of Chicago Legal Forum* 139.

Radical Approaches 37

how forms of identities interact and clash. A number of off-shoots of critical race theory have developed to explore this.

The sixth proposition is the 'voice of colour' thesis. This sits uncomfortably with the fifth proposition in that it holds that 'because of their different histories and experiences with oppression' minority races are able to communicate to majority matters that the majority are unlikely to know.[163] As Delgado and Stefancic put it, minority status 'brings with it a presumed competence, to speak out about race and racism'. This is articulated in the 'legal storytelling' movement, which urges minority racial groups 'to recount their experiences with racism and the legal system and to apply their own unique perspectives to assess law's master narratives'.[164] This use of allegorical stories, as found in the work of Bell and Williams, draws 'on a long history with roots doing back to the slave narratives, tales written by black captives to describe their condition and unmask the gentility that white plantation society pretended to'.[165] As with feminism, this is a grounded approach that reveals the everyday experiences and culture of the group. It opens a window onto ignored or alternative realities because 'members of this country's dominant racial group cannot easily grasp what it is like to be nonwhite'.[166] It therefore provides a cure for silence: 'Stories can give them a voice and reveal that other people have similar experiences.'[167] It can often have a 'destructive function' whereby counter-stories are used 'to challenge, displace, or mock these pernicious narratives and beliefs'.[168] It serves 'as a way of countering the metanarratives – the images, preconceptions, and myths – that have been propagated by the dominant culture of hegemonic Whiteness as a way of maintaining racial inequality'.[169] This informs the methodological approach taken by critical race theory: 'writing and lecturing is characterized by frequent use of the first person, storytelling, narrative, allegory, interdisciplinary treatment of law, and the unapologetic use of creativity'.[170]

This is not to say that all critical race theory work is characterised by the use of 'literary models as a more helpful vehicle than legal precedent'.[171] Bell, who pioneered such work,[172] also wrote an influential textbook on the topic.[173] Moreover, many critical race theorists were legal historians and so the critical race theory literature often included work that explored law historically. For Delgado and Stefancic, revisionist history was one of hallmarks of the movement: such work 're-examines America's historical record, replacing comforting majoritarian interpretations of events with ones that square more accurately with minorities' experience'.[174] Such accounts achieve this by providing the evidence that has sometimes been suppressed to support those new interpretations. This requires exploring a wider range of sources. The work of Kendall Thomas, for instance, sought to explore a legal history of a US Supreme Court decision 'from the bottom up' by allowing the people involved to speak for themselves.[175] Such work also questions the autonomy of the

---

[163] Delgado and Stefancic, *Critical Race Theory* 11.   [164] Ibid.   [165] Ibid. 45.   [166] Ibid. 46.   [167] Ibid. 51.
[168] Ibid. 49, 50.   [169] Treviño, Harris and Wallace, 'What's So Critical about Critical Race Theory?' 8.
[170] Bell, 'Who's Afraid of Critical Race Theory?' 899.   [171] Bell, Faces at the Bottom of the Well xxi.
[172] See ibid. and Derrick Bell, *And We Are Not Saved: The Elusive Quest for Racial Justice* (Basic Books, 1989).
[173] Derrick Bell, *Race, Racism and American Law* (6th ed., Aspen, 2008 [1980]).
[174] Delgado and Stefancic, *Critical Race Theory* 25.
[175] Kendall Thomas, '*Rouge et Noir* Reread: A Popular Constitutional History of the Angelo Herndon Case' (1992) 65 *Southern Californian Law Review* 2599.

law and linear ideas of progress. Delgado and Stefancic noted that revisionism holds 'that to understand the zigs and zags of black, Latino and Asian fortunes, one must look to matters like profit, labor supply, international relations and the interest of elite whites.'[176]

The relationship between critical race theory and legal history is therefore complicated. H Timothy Lovelace, Jr commented that in the United States, 'critical race theory had become embedded in legal history', at least in relation to the history of civil rights.[177] Critical race theory has, however, been much less influential in Europe.[178] It has been in the field of education that critical race theory has had most influence in England since the early 2000s.[179] There has been growing literatures on race and the law, on law and cultural diversity, and on legal pluralism, but these typically do not explicitly endorse critical race theory. History has a limited place in such work and with the exception of work on topics such as slavery and civil rights, work on English legal history tend to pay little attention to race.

4   *Subversive Legal History*

Subversive legal history draws upon and develops critical legal studies and critical legal history.[180] It recognises that these movements were of their time. Critical legal studies was 'a disruptive engagement in a particular circumstance'.[181] This means that rather than refighting old battles, there is a need to take inspiration from these movements while developing them. This involves a change in name because the 'critical' label is itself controversial and divisive. The word is loaded given its association with the critical legal studies movement. The term is also vague, in that the word 'critical' is used to refer to any sort of judgment. As Panu Minkkinen has noted, '"[C]ritical judgment" is a generic intellectual skill that all researchers are supposed to be able to apply.'[182] Moreover, a critical approach is also by definition always a response to something else: 'to be critical is always to be critical *of* something'.[183] And this means that it is shaped by the assumptions, values and content of whatever is being criticised. A critique runs the risk of being merely an act of de-construction. It does not necessarily enable the necessary next step of re-construction.

This is a key point of subversive legal history: the act of subversion requires not only the questioning, critiquing and de-construction of law. It also requires subversive acts of re-construction. This distinguishes it from the critical movements of the past. Writing over twenty years after the publication of 'Critical Legal Histories', Gordon conceded that '[T]he potential contributions of historical learning to rebuilding society – as contrasted

---

[176] Delgado and Stefancic, *Critical Race Theory* 25.

[177] H Timothy Lovelace Jr, 'Critical Race Theory and the Political Uses of Legal History' in Dubber and Tomlins, *The Oxford Handbook of Legal History* 621, 625.

[178] Mathias Moschel, *Law, Lawyers and Race: Critical Race theory from the US to Europe* (Routledge, 2016).

[179] Paul Warmington, 'Critical Race Theory in England: Impact and Opposition' (2020) 27(1) *Global Studies in Culture and Power* 20. See also Namita Chakrabarty, Lorna Roberts and John Preston, 'Critical Race Theory in England' (2012)15(1) *Race, Ethnicity and Education* 1.

[180] Sandberg, *Subversive Legal History.*   [181] Unger, *The Critical Legal Studies Movement* 4.

[182] Panu Minkkinen, 'Critical Legal "Method" as Attitude' in Watkins and Burton, *Research Methods in Law* 146, 146.

[183] Ibid. 150.

Radical Approaches 39

simply to combating the fatalistic sense that no change is possible – are still not so clear.'[184] Re-construction is at the heart of subversive legal history. It describes a radical approach that is not limited to one form of inequality but that sees historical analysis as a method to de-construct and re-construct our understandings of law.

A subversive approach causes three important disturbances to occur.[185] First, the narrative of law is disturbed by focusing on the question of power, complicating linear accounts of progression and rewriting conventional accounts to emphasise the agency of individuals and movements both in terms of campaigning for reform and also in using law strategically. This is an act of re-construction, in that an alternative story is provided that not only identifies, challenges and disrupts the dominant narrative but also supersedes it. Second, the sources of law are disturbed by requiring a much wider range of primary and secondary materials than those normally used in legal studies. This is in itself subversive because, as Auchmuty and Rackley have noted, using 'secondary sources written by historians as well as non-legal records, runs counter to the training of many legal scholars, who are not only not familiar with this material, but have been trained to disregard it – to rely only on strictly legal sources'.[186] This requires seeking out 'voices in autobiographical accounts, oral histories, the press, fiction even; to look beyond self-referential legal historical accounts and to immerse ourselves in secondary sources'.[187] Third, the discipline of law is disturbed, including its assumptions and explanations concerning disciplines of knowledge. A subversive approach questions how conventional accounts are perpetuated in law schools. As Conaghan noted, a critical approach 'troubles categories, blurs boundaries, subverts meanings and contests normative priorities'.[188] A hallmark of subversive legal history is the critical disturbance (de- and re-construction) of the conventional stories that law schools perpetuate. This reveals that the stories law schools tell are authored stories and are therefore constructed, biased and partial. Moreover, subversive legal history reveals that the stories that are told are all imbued with similar values: They are founded upon what Gordon called evolutionary functionalism.[189]

A subversive approach becomes an exercise in re-construction, in that it explores whether an alternative exists to the underpinning narrative of evolutionary functionalism. It suggests that the wrong scientific framework to understand the historical development of law has been adopted: Rather than the dominant assumptions of evolution, the development of law is actually characterised by entropic complexity (the idea of increasing complexity and chaos).[190] The concept of entropy denotes the gradual decline into disorder. Such an approach would see such chaos – uncertainty, nuance and flexibility – as normal. This reverses the usual approach to the common law, which 'assumes that although the law may appear to be irrational, chaotic and particularistic, if one digs deep enough and knows that one is looking for, then it will soon become evident that the law is

---

[184] Gordon, 'The Past as Authority and as Social Critic' 364–5.   [185] Sandberg, *Subversive Legal History* 97 *et seq.*

[186] Rosemary Auchmuty and Erika Rackley, 'Feminist Legal Biography: A Model for All Legal Life Stories' (2020) 41(2) *The Journal of Legal History* 186, 192.

[187] Rackley and Auchmuty, 'The Case for Feminist Legal History' 892.

[188] Conaghan, 'Labour Law and Feminist Method' 114.   [189] Gordon, *Taming the Past* 221.

[190] See Sandberg, *Subversive Legal History* chapter 5.

an internally coherent and unified system of rules'.[191] This new approach draws upon three different but complementary literatures: social entropy theory, chaos theory and complexity theory.[192]

Regarding entropic complexity as the norm insists that the first impressions of the chaos of law were not mistaken. In *Subversive Legal History*, it was suggested that entropic complexity can be said to have the following seven characteristics.[193] First, entropic complexity rejects the evolutionary aspect of evolutionary functionalism. Law is 'untimely';[194] it neither operates in linear nor progressive ways. This means that rather than focusing on origins or end points, there is a need to explore the intellectual history of the ebb and flow of legal ideas.

Second, entropic complexity rejects the functionalist aspect of evolutionary functionalism. Traditionally, social scientists and humanities scholars have relied upon the concept of equilibrium rather than entropy. An approach based on entropic complexity shows that equilibrium is not the default. Law is a complex system, and the natural result of a complex system is entropy. This means that lack of order and unpredictability are the norm; uncertainty, nuance and flexibility are the default.

Third, consequentially, entropic complexity liberates the way in which we understand and analyse law. This all opens up significantly the prospects of legal change on a much wider level. It also underscores the limits of law and that law is not about providing a solution in the same way as solving a mathematical equation.

Fourth, this complicates but makes more important the role of the legal historian. The task of tracing developments becomes more complex and multi-causal, reflecting the lack of a clear distinction between the social and the legal. Prediction is difficult but not impossible since entropic complexity does not result in complete anarchy. It simply requires the acceptance that complexity renders it virtually impossible for us to make accurate predictions.[195]

Fifth, entropic complexity stresses the need to examine individuals and systems. This approach underlines the importance of agency of individuals and their social groups. Attention also needs to be paid to how complex systems grow from the actions of individuals and social groups. These complex systems – such as law – develop their own artificial intelligence; they emerge and develop a life of their own that equates to more than the sum of their parts. Law is a complex system and communications within that system need to be an object of study.

Sixth, entropic complexity emphasises the dynamic interconnectedness of systems, and therefore shows that individual systems cannot be studied in isolation. Complex systems –

---

[191] David Sugarman, 'Legal Theory, the Common Law Mind and the Making of the Textbook Tradition' in William Twinning (ed.), *Legal Theory and the Common Law* (Blackwell, 1986) 26, 26.

[192] It explicitly draws upon three works that have applied these theories in the context of law: David Collins, 'The Chaos Machine: The WTO in a Social Entropy Model of the World Trading System' (2014) 34(2) *Oxford Journal of Legal Studies* 353; Robert E Scott, 'Chaos Theory and the Justice Paradox' (1993) 35 *William & Mary Law Review* 329; and Jamie Murray, Thomas E Webb and Steven Wheatley (eds.), *Complexity Theory and Law: Mapping an Emergent Jurisprudence* (Routledge, 2019).

[193] Sandberg, *Subversive Legal History* 133–4.

[194] Kathryn McNeilly, 'Are Rights Out of Time? International Human Rights Law, Temporality, and Radical Social Change' (2019) 28(6) *Social and Legal Studies* 817.

[195] Niall Ferguson 'Introduction – Virtual History: Towards a "Chaotic" Theory of the Past' in Niall Ferguson (ed.), *Virtual History: Alternatives and Counterfactuals* (Papermac, 1998) 1, 77.

Conclusions 41

such as law – are self-organising but not fully autonomous. They have an open and contested interaction with other systems. The legal and the non-legal cannot be adequately distinguished from one another but are interpenetrative.[196]

Seventh, entropic complexity requires a subversive approach to the analysis of law that recognises that the artificial intelligence of law is constructed and shaped by particular people with their own biases, assumptions and values. A subversive approach disturbs the way in which we see the system by focusing on agency, especially the agency of those who have been previously marginalised. It also requires the questioning, de-construction and re-construction of concepts, ideas and boundaries, including those around areas of study.

Subversive legal history, therefore, shifts the lens by questioning and superseding the dominant evolutionary functionalist approach. This requires new approaches. One alternative method discussed in *Subversive Legal History* is to adopt a counterfactual analysis.[197] Counterfactual legal history asks the 'what if' question; it traces what would have been the outcome if a different path had been taken. Comparison of this alternative timeline with what actually happened can shed light upon the effect of the variable in question. Indeed, this underscores how a subversive approach regards legal history as an important method rather than a specialist subject that can be kept separate from the rest of the law curriculum. This book is an application of this approach. In *Subversive Legal History*, it was argued that:

Law schools need to teach the history of the common law … The focus needs to be on ensuring that all law students are introduced to the conventional histories of the common law … Law students need to be aware of these stories in order to question them, in order to be subversive … And there is a need for texts that introduce the conventional stories and authors of those stories, enabling students to understand these before they question them.[198]

This is what this book aims to achieve. It provides a way by which all law students can be introduced to the conventional histories of the common law. However, as we go through the centuries, we will question the conventional stories told by the Man of Law as we recount them. We will show how they are authored, revealing and debating with the ghost of Maitland and paying attention to how he and other legal historians have shaped the common understandings. Our journey will show how the history of the common law is inherently chaotic: It is not a story of progress but rather one of accidents; a collection of tales of panic rather than order, showing how law is used pragmatically at a time of crisis. This book will provide you with the conventional account of the historical development of the common law for you to question, subvert and challenge using the radical approaches that have been described in this chapter.

V   Conclusions

This chapter has explored different approaches to legal history. It began by exploring the two traditions inspired by intellectual history and social history respectively. It then

---

[196] Roger Cotterrell, 'Why Must Legal Ideas Be Interpreted Sociologically?' (1998) 25 *Journal of Law and Society* 171, reprinted as Roger Cotterrell, *Law, Culture and Society* (Ashgate, 2006) chapter 3.
[197] See Sandberg, *Subversive Legal History* chapter 6.   [198] Ibid. 222–3.

explored a series of what we have called radical approaches. These radical approaches – critical legal history, feminist legal history, critical race theory and subversive legal history – are all heirs to the critical legal studies movement and they all not only stress the importance of studying law in context but also to analysing the internal development of law. This underscores the importance of both the intellectual history and social history traditions. A historical approach to law can highlight both the internal development of law and its external relations to other social institutions, groups and to society itself. This provides a further reason why a historical approach can be useful.

Indeed, this chapter has further shown that a historical approach is necessary in terms of questioning the default narratives that are entrenched and into which law students are commonly socialised. History can question the assumptions, biases, principles, categorisations and expectations that result from the study of the current law. A historical approach can ensure that doctrinal study does not result in indoctrination. It opens the door to a range of additional questions and possibilities. These first two chapters of this book have provided a background to the trip through the centuries that will occur in the rest of this book and has shown why a historical approach to law is required. The chapters that follow will equip you to analyse, critique and subvert law historically. They will enable you to begin to develop a historical understanding of the law by providing a historical introduction to the genesis of the English common law.

'Such is the unity of all history that anyone who endeavours to tell a piece of it must feel that his first sentence tears a seamless web'.

Frederick Pollock and Frederic W Maitland,
The History of English Law (2nd ed, vol 1,
Cambridge University Press, 1968 [1898]) 1.

3

The Anglo-Saxon Legacy

I   Introduction

This chapter begins our examination of the origins of the common law. There are three candidates for the period in which the common law can be said to have truly begun. Most commentators, including Frederic W Maitland, regard the Norman Conquest of 1066 as being a decisive moment. The victory of William of Normandy in the Battle of Hastings was undoubtedly a major turning point in English history: It saw the death of a king, the replacement of a ruling class and the demise of Anglo-Saxon England. However, Hastings was not the birth place of the English common law and William I (1066–87) was not its midwife. A strong argument can be made that it was during the earlier Anglo-Saxon period that the origins of common law ideas, institutions and values can be found. Moreover, a compelling argument can also be made that a recognisable common law only emerged a century after the Conquest during the reign of Henry II (1154–89), the first Plantagenet king. The importance of this period is stressed in Maitland's account of the development of English law.

The next three chapters will explore each of these three periods in turn, arguing that all three periods were important to the development of the English common law and that the common law did not begin in an orderly deliberate way. It was rather a pragmatic response to the need to maintain order built upon a number of quirks that existed at the time. This nuances but does not generally contradict the story told by Maitland. It reveals, however, that it was Maitland and his successors that have created the story of the systematic evolution of the English common law, emphasising the later parts of its early development because these are the most orderly and because they resemble the modern legal system. This is not to deny that the common law and its components were created. The argument is rather that the cultivation of the common law was simply a means by which the end of social control was achieved. No one set out to create the common law.

This chapter will examine the legacy of the Anglo-Saxon period (before 1066).[1] The next chapter will analyse the actual effect of 1066 upon English law and the legal

---

[1] It is usually understood that the Anglo-Saxon period lasted around 500 years. However, there is disagreement as to the dating. Compare, for example, Stenton's account, which begins c.550, with that of Blair, which begins c.440: Frank M Stenton, *The Oxford History of England – Anglo-Saxon England* (3rd ed., Oxford University Press, 1971); John Blair, 'The Anglo-Saxon Period' in Kenneth O Morgan (ed.), *The Oxford History of Britain* (Oxford University Press, 2010) 66.

significance of the reigns of the Norman kings.[2] Chapter 5 will then examine how the common law developed during the early Plantagenet period (also known as the Angevin period),[3] focusing in particular upon the reign of Henry II (1154–89), who is often referred to as the 'father of the common law'. In the next two chapters, we will see how Maitland emphasises and possibly over-states the importance of the Norman and Plantagenet kings as the founders and architects of the common law. By contrast, in this chapter, we will see how Maitland underplayed and perhaps understated the importance of the Anglo-Saxon period on the formation of the common law. This lack of emphasis upon the Anglo-Saxon inheritance has been influential. SFC Milsom's book begins as follows: 'The common law is the by product of an administrative triumph, the way in which the government of England came to be centralised and specialised during the centuries after the Conquest.'[4]

This chapter will show that the centuries *before* the Conquest were also important to the development of the common law. As Milsom conceded, William the Conqueror 'took over a going concern one to which he claimed lawful title; and he expressly confirmed the laws of his predecessors'.[5] This chapter will explore what the Anglo-Saxon inheritance was. Section II will look at the historical debate as to where the history of English law begins and the importance that should be placed on the Anglo-Saxon period. It will contrast the still influential approach of Maitland with more recent scholars, most notably Patrick Wormald. Section III will then outline what is considered to be the major achievement of the long Anglo-Saxon period as a whole: the move from feud to compensation. Section IV will then explore how what we would call the legal system had developed by the end of the Anglo-Saxon period. It will ask what William the Conqueror inherited and to what extent this provided some foundation for the English common law.

II   The Seamless Web

The starting point for any historical study is invariably arbitrary. As Maitland pointed out, '[S]uch is the unity of all history that anyone who endeavours to tell a piece of it must feel that his first sentence tears a seamless web.'[6] However, even though it is possible to begin much earlier, for instance, by reference to Roman law,[7] most modern-day English legal historians follow Maitland back to 1066.[8] Maitland's approach, at least in 'Pollock and

---

[2] Namely, William I (1066–87), William II (1087–100), Henry I (1100–35) and Stephen (1135–54).

[3] Henry II (1154–89) was the first of a line of fourteen Plantagenet kings that lasted until the death of Richard II on Bosworth Field in 1485. For convenience, the Plantagenet kings are usually divided into three: the Angevins, the Lancastrians and the Yorkists. See, e.g., ED Delderfield, *Kings and Queens of England and Great Britain* (2nd ed., David and Charles, 1970) 35.

[4] SFC Milsom, *Historical Foundations of the Common Law* (2nd ed., Butterworths, 1981) 11.   [5] Ibid.

[6] Frederick Pollock and Frederic W Maitland, *The History of English Law*, vol. 1 (2nd ed., Cambridge University Press, 1968 [1898]) 1.

[7] Thomas G Watkin, *The Legal History of Wales* (2nd ed., University of Wales Press, 2012) begins with pre-Roman Britain. See also the prologue on the Roman law pre-history provided by David J Ibbetson, *A Historical Introduction to the Law of Obligations* (Oxford University Press, 1999).

[8] Milsom, *Historical Foundations of the Common Law*; AW Brian Simpson, *An Introduction to the History of Land Law* (2nd ed., Oxford University Press, 1986); Raoul C van Caenegem, *The Birth of the English Common Law* (Cambridge University Press, 1988); John Hostettler, *A History of Criminal Justice in England and Wales* (Waterside Press, 2009); Ann Lyon, *Constitutional History of the United Kingdom* (2nd ed., Routledge, 2016); John Hudson, *The Formation of the English Common Law* (2nd ed., Routledge 2018); John H Baker, *An Introduction to English Legal History* (5th ed., Butterworths, 2019). *The Oxford History of the Laws of England* begin with reign of King Alfred (871–99), though a free-standing first volume on ecclesiastical jurisdiction begins in 597; John Hudson, *The Oxford History of the Laws of England Volume II: 871–1216* (Oxford University Press, 2012);

The Seamless Web 47

Maitland', was to focus on 'Anglo-Saxon legal antiquities, but only in so far as they are connected with, and tend to throw light upon, the subsequent history of the laws of England'.[9] The chapter on 'Anglo-Saxon Law' in 'Pollock and Maitland' was one of the few contributions to the text that was by Pollock rather than by Maitland and, although the discussion of legal doctrines in the second part of the book does sometimes begin with discussion of the Anglo-Saxon position, even here the focus is very much upon the Anglo-Saxon inheritance and the position in 1066 immediately before the Conquest. The focus was not on the Anglo-Saxon period as such, though Maitland later returned to the topic with a collection of essays and a new chapter in the second edition of 'Pollock and Maitland', which provided a pan-European opening to the book, explored 'The Dark Age of Legal History'.[10] However, it is the general approach of 'Pollock and Maitland' that has proved to be most influential; the starting point for the study of English legal history is taken to be 1066, just before the Conquest, to ascertain the legacy of the Anglo-Saxons rather than studying that period in its own right.

There is significant disagreement as to the emphasis that should be placed upon the importance of the Anglo-Saxon inheritance. Three differing perspectives can be identified: the minimalist, the maximalist and the cautionary. The view found in 'Pollock and Maitland' and the accounts inspired by it can be characterised as the minimalist perspective: this regards the Anglo-Saxon period as having little effect on the development of the common law, which it traces back to the Norman and Plantagenet era. In 'Pollock and Maitland', it was noted that the information about Anglo-Saxon laws and customs was 'so fragmentary and obscure that the only hope of understanding it is to work back to it from the fuller evidence of Norman and even later times'.[11] This is problematic since it means that the account is written with the experience of hindsight, leading to connections to be made that may not tally with reality. Wormald criticised Maitland for underplaying the importance of the Anglo-Saxon age. He wrote: 'Maitland was content that Anglo-Saxon law should be archaic. He deeply distrusted the motives of those who would make it relevant.'[12] Wormald criticised the way in which the account in 'Pollock and Maitland' presented Anglo-Saxon law as being 'archaic' and therefore of little relevance to those tracing the historical development of modern law. The minimalist view of 'Pollock and Maitland' and its successors regards the Anglo-Saxon period as being so far removed from what we today consider to be law that they regard it as a primitive first step in what they consider an evolutionary process. As Adekemi Odujirin has noted, the trend in such minimalist scholarship so far as it relates to Anglo-Saxon times 'has been to structure

---

Richard H Helmholz, *The Oxford History of the Laws of England Volume I: The Canon Law and Ecclesiastical Jurisdiction from 597 to 1640s* (Oxford University Press, 2004).

[9] Pollock and Maitland, *The History of English Law* 25.

[10] Frederic W Maitland *Doomsday and Beyond* (Fontana, 1960 [1897]). Though note his caution that 'we must not be in a hurry to get to the beginning of the long history of the law': ibid. 415.

[11] They contended that this was 'not due much for actual lack of materials as for want of any sure clue to their right interpretation at a certain number of critical points': Pollock and Maitland, *The History of English Law* 25, 29. See, further, HR Loyn, *The Governance of Anglo-Saxon England, 500–1087* (Edward Arnold, 1984) xiv.

[12] Patrick Wormald, *The Making of English Law: King Arthur to the Twelfth Century* (Blackwell, 1999) 17.

48   *The Anglo-Saxon Legacy*

and interpret the facts of legal history in a way that would ensure that the evolutionary assumptions of the investigators are invariably vindicated'.[13]

By contrast, writers since Maitland have contended that analysis of actual disputing in the Anglo-Saxon era has shown that much of what 'Pollock and Maitland' attributed to the Norman period can actually be dated to the Anglo-Saxon period. This is the maximalist view found in Wormald's work as well as that of James Campbell.[14] Wormald argued that the 'levers of power', the use of law by kings to ensure public order, can likely be traced back to Anglo-Saxon monarchs such as Cnut, Edward the Confessor and Harold II.[15] For Wormald, much of the 'raw energy' from which the common law emerged can be dated 'back to those who created the English kingdom'.[16]

Since Maitland wrote, there has been a significant increase in historical literature on the Anglo-Saxon era and of the analysing of primary sources. Yet not all agree with Wormald. Paul R Hyams has adopted what we might call the cautionary perspective.[17] He has argued that the 'historiographical trend to maximize the significance of state institutions during the century or so before the Norman Conquest' has 'swung the pendulum a mite too far'.[18] Hyams refers to the perspective taken by Wormald and James Campbell as 'maximalists', in that 'they tend to make more of our sparse and difficult evidence for kinship and royal government' than he felt able to do.[19]

Wormald himself suggested that the answer of the origins of the common law depended on whether you are looking at the history of law or the history of lawyers; that is, the history of the legal system or the history of law as experienced.[20] He argued that if you are looking for the history of 'the law as debated and applied in the sovereign's courts' (the history of law as system), then the Maitland thesis that focuses on events post-1066 and emphasised the role of Henry II is secure. By contrast, he noted that if by the origins of the common law 'you mean the principle whereby the ruler of England is answerable for the behaviour of and for the rights of English subjects' (the history of law as experience), then the roles of Norman and Plantagenet kings 'should be subordinated to that of their predecessors over the foregoing three centuries, the first kings of the English, who can most reasonably be described as the founders of the English state'.[21] Maitland's shadow has meant that the history of English law has been understood as being synonymous with the history of the civil courts. Maitland's influence has meant that the history of the common law has often neglected other forms of lawyering, not least the history of what we would call today criminal law. This is perhaps epitomised by Milsom's treatment of the subject, calling the history of crime 'miserable' and insisting that 'nothing 'worth-while was created'.[22]

---

[13] Adekemi Odujirin, *The Normative Basis of Fault in Criminal Law: History and Theory* (University of Toronto Press, 1998) 27.

[14] The term comes from Paul R Hyams and was first used in Paul R Hyams, 'Feud and the State in Late Anglo-Saxon England' (2001) 40(1) *Journal of British Studies* 1, which is an earlier version of chapter 3 of his *Rancor & Reconciliation in Medieval England* (Cornell University Press, 2003). Hyams notes that the title comes from a lecture given by Campbell: James Campbell, 'The Late Anglo-Saxon State: A Maximum View' (1995) 87 *Proceedings of the British Academy* 39, reprinted as James Campbell, *The Anglo-Saxon State* (Hambledon, 2000) chapter 1.

[15] Wormald, *The Making of English Law* 19.

[16] Patrick Wormald, *Lawyers and the State: The Varieties of Legal History* (Selden Society, 2006) 14.

[17] This label comes from his description of his views as leaning towards 'skeptical caution': Paul R Hyams, *Rancor & Reconciliation in Medieval England* (Cornell University Press, 2003) 72.

[18] Ibid. xvi.   [19] Ibid. 72.   [20] Wormald, *Lawyers and the State* 19.   [21] Ibid.

[22] Milsom, *Historical Foundations of the Common Law* 403.

From Feud to Compensation 49

He wrote that: 'So far as justice was done throughout the centuries it was done by jurors and in spite of savage laws. The lawyers contributed humane but shabby expedients, which did not develop into new approaches.'[23]

The influence of Maitland has meant that the historians following Maitland have underappreciated the importance of the earlier ways in which justice was dispensed through 'savage laws', largely because systems of justice developed by later reforms more closely resemble the legal system as it is today. The result is a partial history of the common law that focuses on the history of the legal system rather than the history of law. This approach traces the common law back only as far as it takes a form that remains identifiable today. It only looks for the orderly resolution of disputes by a centralised authority and dismisses anything before that as being primitive and, at best, a precursor to the common law. Yet, the wider environment that allowed for the common law to develop in this way can be dated further back.

While this chapter will generally follow Maitland's approach in focusing on the legacy of the Anglo-Saxon period, attention will be paid to how the development of lawyering and kingship during the Anglo-Saxon era laid the foundations upon which Norman and Plantagenet reforms built upon. Like 'Pollock and Maitland', our focus will largely be on the late Anglo-Saxon period: the situation immediately before the Norman Conquest. This is because of two main reasons. First, it is a simplification to discuss the Anglo-Saxon era as one period. The 500-year period that historians designate as being Anglo-Saxon was actually a time of significant political uncertainty. It is wise to distinguish between the early and later Anglo-Saxon periods, and wiser still to acknowledge that no firm demarcation between the two can be made.[24] Second, talk of England is only possible very late in the Anglo-Saxon period. There were ten 'separate but not necessarily independent' kingdoms in the early Anglo-Saxon society and it was only over time that three of these kingdoms – Wessex, Mercia and Northumbria – established dominion over the others, and it was only in the tenth century under Alfred (871–99) that England became unified as one kingdom.[25] As Maitland noted, this meant that asking 'how much law there was common to the whole kingdom in the days before the Norman Conquest is a very difficult question'.[26] However, as we will see, it can be said that there was significant amount of law at this time, albeit law that looked different and was enforced differently than we might expect.

III   From Feud to Compensation

The land that was to become known as Anglo-Saxon England was a much invaded place. Following the withdrawal of the Romans from 440 and the settlement of the Angles, Saxons and Jutes in the late fifth and early sixth centuries, the native Britons were pushed

---

[23] Ibid.

[24] The reign of Alfred (871–99) can be seen as the end of the early Anglo-Saxon period and the beginning of the later Anglo-Saxon era: Loyn, *The Governance of Anglo-Saxon England*, 500–1087.

[25] See, further, James Campbell, 'The United Kingdom of England: The Anglo-Saxon Achievement' in Alexander Grant and Keith J Stringer (eds.), *Uniting the Kingdom? The Making of English History* (London, 1995) 31, reprinted as Campbell, *The Anglo-Saxon State* chapter 2.

[26] Frederic W Maitland, *The Constitutional History of England* (Cambridge University Press, 1941 [1908]) 3.

50   *The Anglo-Saxon Legacy*

to the Celtic fringes of Scotland, Wales and Cornwall. Viking raids were common, with areas and entire kingdoms falling under Danish control. This was not just a feature of the early Anglo-Saxon period. Danish kings, for instance, occupied the throne from 1017 to 1042.[27] The Norman conquest of 1066 was just one in a long line of invasion attempts, some of which had been successful. It is not surprising, therefore, that Anglo-Saxon kings were great warriors. It is more surprising that they were also great legislators. The land that was to become known as Anglo-Saxon England became a 'much-governed and on occasion a well-governed kingdom'.[28]

The word 'became' is important there. There is no doubt that a great deal of governance came to exist towards the end of the period. For maximalist writers, the strong centralised kinship often attributed to the Normans can be found in the late Anglo-Saxon period. Even if we do not go that far, it remains clear that the authority of kings – at least on paper – increased as the Anglo-Saxon period went on. The conventional account suggests that the same is true of the resolution of disputes: the centralisation of authority increased. However, both of these statements risk simplifying a pragmatic trend into a linear evolutionary process. As John Hudson noted in his introduction to his volume on *The Oxford History of the Laws of England*, there are many ways of resolving conflict, ranging from the legal to the extra-legal and the illegal.[29] This was particularly true of the Anglo-Saxon age. Commentators often refer to a shift in the Anglo-Saxon period from the resolving of disputes by violence to the resolving of disputes by a royally sanctioned system.[30] This is sometimes referred to as a shift from feud to compensation, for reasons that will become clear shortly. However, it is important not to see this shift as a linear process; as Hudson cautions, a 'combination of approaches' was taken to resolving disputes in the Anglo-Saxon period and beyond.[31] As Derek Roebuck noted that replacing tribal fighting with 'a criminal and civil justice, the same for all people of equal rank, administered eventually not by neighbours or families but by impartial outsiders' was 'a long time in coming'.[32] And this did not even exist until long after the Norman Conquest. The resolution of disputes by violence – the feud, sometimes referred to as the 'blood feud' – therefore cannot be dismissed as something that the Anglo-Saxons quickly grew out of. Rather, it informed and structured their whole approach to what we would call law and order.

1   *The Blood Feud*

As Hyams has noted, '[E]very student of the Anglo-Saxons accepts the existence of feud as a feature of society before the Norman Conquest.'[33] He commented that this can be seen by the fact that it appears in *Beowulf*, the sole surviving long poem from the era.[34] Feud was a feature for all parts of society up to and including the king.[35] This raises the question of

---

[27] Cnut (1017–35); Harold I (1035–40); Harthacnut (1040–2).
[28] Loyn, *The Governance of Anglo-Saxon England, 500–1087* 165.
[29] Hudson, *The Oxford History of the Laws of England Volume II* 5.
[30] Derek Roebuck, *The Background of the Common Law* (Oxford University Press, 1988) 20.
[31] Hudson, *The Oxford History of the Laws of England Volume II* 10.   [32] Roebuck, *The Background of the Common Law* 20.
[33] Hyams, *Rancor & Reconciliation in Medieval England* 71.   [34] Ibid. 74.   [35] Ibid. 77.

From Feud to Compensation   51

how feud operated. Feud was underpinned by the notion that 'responsibility for pursuing redress lay with the kin group rather than a state-sponsored apparatus of legal enforcement'.[36] Wrongs to the person or to their property were understood as violations against the individual and their family, often known as their kin or kindred. If a person was killed or maimed, if their property or produce was damaged, then this was seen as an attack upon the kindred as a whole, who then sought revenge, typically in the form of violence. Feud was as much about social duty as it was about emotional revenge.[37] The feud therefore was not only between the victim and the wrong-doer, it was also between the kindred of the victim and the kindred of the wrong-doer. Members of the wrong-doer's kindred could therefore be attacked in retaliation, not just the wrong-doer themselves. As Wormald put it, '[I]f a Smith kills a Jones, *any* Jones can kill *any* Smith.' It was a public act, not a secret killing.[38] The level of response was 'constrained by a notion of rough equivalence, requiring the keeping of a "score"'.[39] This would often result in 'tit-for-tat' retaliation between the two groups until something amounting to a peace settlement was reached between them. As Hyams pointed out: 'To the modern observer, feud constitutes personal relations conceived as international relations. These are conflicts whose resolution demands not the defeat of wrong-doers but a public declaration of the peace.'[40]

This differs from the way in which disturbances of the peace are dealt with in modern societies.[41] Although crime is still seen as an offence against the community, a wrong against what we would call the State, modern societies deal with it through the imposition of punishments. Yet, feud was not as barbaric as it is often assumed. It was not an 'open-ended vendetta'.[42] John D Miles has called for the term 'feud' not to be used since 'the evidence for open-ended feuding among rival kin groups' is very thin on the ground outside the realm of imaginative literature.[43] Feud was actually effective. As Hyams noted, 'one of the things feud could do in the right circumstance was to generate its own peace'.[44] Hyams also argued that the groups involved did not always correspond to blood ties, so chooses not to use the term 'blood feud'.[45] These 'support groups, although often described as kindreds, are neither magically available nor necessary constant in size and power'.[46] Rather, 'in a world of conscious political choices', people sought 'support proactively and in advance of any trouble'.[47] The feud was group justice; interference with property or with persons would effectively trigger war between the groups of the victim and perpetrator.

Accounts of the history of English law have often downplayed the importance of feud. This is true of both minimalistic and maximalist accounts. Minimalist accounts have seen

---

[36] Andrew Rabin, *Crime and Punishment in Anglo-Saxon England* (Cambridge University Press, 2020) 4.

[37] Patrick Wormald, *The First Code of English Law* (Canterbury Commemoration Society, 2005) 13.

[38] Paul R Hyams, 'Was There Really Such a Thing as Feud in the High Middle Ages'? in Susanna A Throop and Paul R Hyams (eds.), *Vengeance in the Middle Ages: Emotion, Religion and Feud* (Ashgate, 2010) 151, 160.

[39] Wormald, *The First Code of English Law* 13; ibid., see also Hyams, *Rancor & Reconciliation in Medieval England* 9.

[40] Ibid. 13.

[41] As Philip Rawlings has noted, 'The reliance we in the twenty-first century appear to place on the modern police to deal with a mixed bag of wrongs rather arbitrarily labelled as crimes would seem very odd to our ancestors. If someone steals from me or attacks me, they might have said, it is up to me to decide on my response, if any (Philip Rawlings, *Policing: A Short History* (Routledge, 2014 [2002]) 8).

[42] John D Miles, 'The Myth of the Feud in Anglo-Saxon England' (2015) 114(2) *Journal of English and Germanic Philology* 163, 199–200.

[43] Ibid.   [44] Hyams, *Rancor & Reconciliation in Medieval England* 14.   [45] Ibid. xvi.   [46] Ibid. 9.   [47] Ibid. xvi.

52   *The Anglo-Saxon Legacy*

feud and law as being separate processes, and typically regarded feud as a Continental phenomenon and contrasted with the centralisation and order found in England, especially after the Conquest.[48] As Wormald put it, 'Maitland naturally lacked an ear for the rhythms of blood-feud.'[49] Yet, maximalist writers like Wormald have also been accused of underplaying feud. Though they devote more time to discussing it, they are also quick to see its demise. Their portrayal of Anglo-Saxon England as possessing State-like characteristics looks 'very different from the ones in which scholars have usually located, described and analyzed feuds'.[50] And so the tendency in most scholarship is to brand feud 'as archaic and barbaric, before hurrying on to more edifying forms of social and political arrangement'.[51] As Hyams asks: 'Why spoil the picture by seeking out the ugly creature –feud and violence – that may lurk beneath the fine stone paving of the common law?'[52]

There are two compelling reasons, however, for paying more attention to feud. First, as Hyams noted, feud becomes more important to the story of the development of English law if the focus shifts from a 'top-down' view of social order to seeing how legal change is 'at least partially demand-led and so related to patterns of grievance and the remedies that the aggrieved seek'.[53] Second, feud was not completely separate from law. Feud co-existed with law.[54] As royal authority grew, it continued to operate in a culture informed by the feud. Moreover, in the words of Hyams, '[T]his feud culture was a prime target for much legislative activity.'[55] Ideas of and norms surrounding compensation, which were to prove to be so important to the common law, initially arose in relation to the extra-legal feuds. Rather than responding violently when a wrong had been committed against the group, compensation was sought in order to restore the peace.

2   *Compensating Wrongs*

Late Anglo-Saxon laws encouraged feuding parties to agree a sum of money to be paid by the wrong-doer in compensation to restore the peace, and stipulated in considerable detail the system of compensation that applied. The amounts of compensation varied according to the status of the victim (the *wer* or *wergild*) and the nature of the act (this compensation was known as the *bot*).[56] For instance, under the Laws of Æthelbert (who reigned between c.589 and 616), if a man lay with a commoner's serving maid, he would pay six shillings compensation, if it was a nobleman's serving maid, then the compensation was twelve shillings, and if it was a maiden belonging to the king, then it was fifty shillings.[57] The wrongs covered included 'any injury or harm which in any significant way detracted from individual honour and dignity', including seizing a man by his hair or punching him on the

---

[48] Ibid. 7, x.
[49] Patrick Wormald, 'Maitland and Anglo-Saxon Law: Beyond Doomsday Book in John Hudson (ed.), *The History of English Law: Centenary Essays on 'Pollock and Maitland'* (Oxford University Press, 1996) 1, 16.
[50] Hyams, *Rancor & Reconciliation in Medieval England* 71.   [51] Ibid. x.   [52] Ibid.   [53] Ibid. xi.   [54] Ibid. 4.
[55] Ibid. 72.   [56] On status generally, see Hudson, *The Oxford History of the Laws of England Volume II* chapter 8.
[57] For the texts, see Frederick L Attenborough (ed.), *The Laws of the Earliest Kings* (Cambridge University Press 1922) or Lisi Oliver, *The Beginnings of English Law* (University of Toronto Press, 2002).

From Feud to Compensation 53

nose.[58] Indeed, each tooth had its own price. Protection was afforded not only in the case of wrongs against the person but also wrongs against property including livestock and wrongs against the authority of the king or Church.[59] The fine paid to the king for the breach of the peace was the *wite*.

The late Anglo-Saxon kings therefore provided supervision of the customary feud process by clarifying standards of conduct.[60] This intensified further thorough the introduction of a range of punishments.[61] For instance, under the reign of Æthelstan (924–39), wrong-doers could be excluded from their kindred and region as well as from Christian burial.[62] This was amplified towards the end of the era with the development of the idea of the *botless* wrong: a breach of the king's peace was *botless* when it could not be redeemed by compensation at all but only by the mercy of the king.[63] This was also known as 'unemendable' wrongs – that is, they could not be remedied by compensation to the kin.[64] This was radical in that it meant in principle that victims had no claim of their own against the wrong-doer and their kindred.[65] Wormald suggested that payment of *bot* to the king or the Church rather than to the victim or their family had become the norm by the tenth century.[66] He suggested that it was appropriate at this point, if not before, to think in terms of crime and punishment. He argued against the conventional account inspired by 'Pollock and Maitland' that saw the dominant notion of being that of tort law (private wrongs enforceable by victims) rather than of criminal law (public wrongs enforceable by public authorities).[67] He said that Maitland had missed the 'pronounced switch in later Anglo-Saxon law'.[68] This, however, has proved contentious. Odujirin has argued that there was no criminal law as such because the conception was still one of wrongs and nothing else.[69] Anglo-Saxons did not classify wrongs into civil and criminal offences and did not distinguish between compensation, fine and punishment.[70] There were distinctions between different types of wrong but there was no 'sharp classification with strict procedural and other legal consequences' as would later be developed between crime and tort.[71] That distinction would only develop much later on in the Plantagenet era.

3   *Fault*

There is also controversy as to whether the Anglo-Saxons regulation of wrongs paid attention to what we would call the question of fault and distinguished between intentional

---

[58] Odujirin, *The Normative Basis of Fault in Criminal Law* 20–1.
[59] Indeed, it is thought that Christianity had considerable influence upon the composition of the list of wrongs (ibid. 15). For discussion of the range of offences, see Rabin, *Crime and Punishment in Anglo-Saxon England* 26–39.
[60] Hyams, *Rancor & Reconciliation in Medieval England* 19.
[61] See Hudson, *The Oxford History of the Laws of England Volume II* 180 96.
[62] Hyams, *Rancor & Reconciliation in Medieval England* 81.
[63] Ibid. 80; Hostettler, *A History of Criminal Justice in England and Wales* 17.
[64] Thomas A Green, 'The Jury and the English Law of Homicide, 1200–1600' (1976) 74 *Michigan Law Review* 413, 417.
[65] Hyams, *Rancor & Reconciliation in Medieval England* 85.   [66] Wormald, *The First Code of English Law* 14–15.
[67] Wormald, 'Maitland and Anglo-Saxon Law' 13.   [68] Ibid. 14
[69] Odujirin, *The Normative Basis of Fault in Criminal Law* 33.
[70] Ibid. 38. They also did not distinguish between what would become known as felony and misdemeanour (Rabin, *Crime and Punishment in Anglo-Saxon England* 4).
[71] Hudson, *The Oxford History of the Laws of England Volume II* 161.

54   *The Anglo-Saxon Legacy*

and non-intentional acts. Odujirin has identified three main schools of thought on the topic.[72] The first coincides with the minimalist approach identified earlier. Odujirin noted that many legal historians have been 'obsessed with the idea that modern legal concepts and categories represent not just a phase but the ultimate or final step in an evolutionary process that started from a complete lack of morality'. This has meant that they saw early law generally and Anglo-Saxon law in particular as being characterised by what we would call 'strict' or 'absolute' liability: the idea that the wrong-doer is liable for their actions even if they are not at fault. Odujirin attributed this view point to 'Pollock and Maitland', stating that they maintained that 'Anglo-Saxon society had neither the means nor the inclination to distinguish between intentional and non-intentional wrongs', and that all that was required was that the wrong-doer had caused the wrong.[73] There is evidence to support this. Maitland did write that '[O]nce it be granted that a man's death was caused by the act of another, then that other is liable, no matter what may have been his intentions of motives.'[74] He also suggested that a wrong-doer would be equally culpable even if their actions were a mere accident: 'in the case of harm ensuring from a pure accident from a distinct voluntary act, we find that the actor, however innocent his intention, is liable'.[75] However, passages in 'Pollock and Maitland' also recognised that, although questions of fault did not determine questions of liability, they did determine questions of sentencing and punishment. Maitland wrote that '[E]arly age law begins to treat intentional as worse than unintentional homicide. In either case the *wer* is due; but in the one there can, in the other there can not be a legitimate feud; intentional homicide must be paid for by *wite* as well as *wer*, unintentional by *wer* without *wite*.'[76]

This sounds similar to Odujirin's second school, which 'see traces of the beginning of the idea of responsibility based on the presence or absence of intention in Anglo-Saxon law but do not go as far as saying that this was in any way determinative'.[77] Members of this school of thought regard intention as an 'intensifier of punishment'.[78] The third and final approach identified by Odujirin is the one to which he himself subscribed. This approach suggests that we have been asking the wrong question and it is inappropriate to apply modern legal ideas of fault onto the Anglo-Saxon period.[79] He attributes this view to John McLaren[80], G MacCormack[81] and Sally Moore.[82] Under this perspective, it is accepted that Anglo-Saxon law 'did not make any subtle analysis of the mental liability in liability' but it is also recognised that 'some attention was paid to the actor's state of mind'.[83] As MacCormack argued, in the Anglo-Saxon period 'an injury is considered in the context of all the circumstances in which it is inflicted and it is this combination of circumstances

---

[72] Odujirin, *The Normative Basis of Fault in Criminal Law* 30.   [73] Ibid. 29.
[74] Pollock and Maitland, *The History of English Law* 471.   [75] Ibid. 54.   [76] Ibid. 471.
[77] Odujirin, *The Normative Basis of Fault in Criminal Law* 32.
[78] E Levitt, 'The Origins of the Doctrine of Mens Rea' (1922–3) 17 *Illinois Law Review* 116, 135.
[79] Odujirin, *The Normative Basis of Fault in Criminal Law* 32.
[80] John PS McLaren, 'The Origins of Tortuous Liability: Insights from Contemporary Tribal Societies' (1975) 25(1) *University of Toronto Law Journal* 42.
[81] G MacCormack, 'Standards of Liability in Early Law' (1985–6) *Juridical Review* 166.
[82] Sally Moore, 'Legal Liability and Evolutionary Interpretation' in Max Gluckman (ed.), The *Allocation of Responsibility* (Manchester University Press, 1972) 32.
[83] Odujirin, *The Normative Basis of Fault in Criminal Law* 35.

which determines the response or penalty. Embedded in the circumstances is the offender's state of mind'.[84] Fault was part of the circumstances taken into account rather than a separate test.

The interplay between feud and law sowed many seeds that were to develop later on. There was no abrupt shift from feud to compensation or later on from compensation to kin to compensation to king. However, these rough directions of travel – though never complete – provided the foundations upon which the common law would be built. This is particularly true of the idea of the king's peace, which has been hailed as 'the most important contribution made by the Anglo-Saxon law to the common law of crimes'.[85] Originally, there were various different forms of peace: 'every determinate legal authority had its own peace, breach of which entitled the owner to compensation or fine'. The king's peace was originally 'not universal but particular': originally it just referred to the special sanctity of the king's own house and of his attendants and servants.[86] However, the Anglo-Saxon period saw the 'rapid expansion' of the term so much so that after the Conquest it became 'the normal and general safeguard of public order'. Seeds planted in the Anglo-Saxon era often did not flower until much later, and some, of course, never flowered at all. Moreover, many of the practices that we see as being Anglo-Saxon continued after the Conquest and for much longer still. There is some debate as for how long feud continued. However, it was not until the Statute of Marlborough in 1267 that it was established that all persons 'shall receive Justice in the King's Court, and none from henceforth shall take such Revenge or Distress of his own Authority without Award of the King's Court' and would be fined for doing so, a provision that remains part of English law today.

IV   The Late Anglo-Saxon Legal System

The fact that Anglo-Saxon society was much invaded explains why it also became much governed. The rise in governance came not from any desire to create a system of law for its own sake but rather from the need to maintain order. Over the Anglo-Saxon period and the Norman and Plantagenet centuries that followed it, the centralisation of justice that produced the common law was a side effect of the need to maintain order. Developments that hindsight suggests were important precursors of and first steps towards the common law were typically pragmatic experiments – and legal historians have only tended to focus on those that proved successful. Moreover, there are varying interpretations and opinions as to how important these experiments were. Again, it is possible to distinguish between minimalist, maximalist and cautionary commentators. Minimalist accounts tend to identify emergent institutions and developments but stress how ill-formed they were compared to those that followed the Conquest. Maximalists, by contrast, have developed the notion of the late Anglo-Saxon State. For them, the century before 1066 saw a high degree of central control over law and order, which was higher than not only its Continental comparators but also its Anglo-Norman successors.[87] The cautionary view stresses the lack of definitive evidence on the

---

[84] MacCormack, 'Standards of Liability in Early Law' 167.   [85] Odujirin, *The Normative Basis of Fault in Criminal Law* 41.
[86] Pollock and Maitland, *The History of English Law* 45.   [87] Hyams, *Rancor & Reconciliation in Medieval England* 98.

56   *The Anglo-Saxon Legacy*

matter. Hyams has noted that 'the sparseness of the documentary foundations on which all tenth- and eleventh-century arguments rest precludes finality'.[88] As he also pointed out, the two successful foreign invasions in the eleventh century also questions the picture of England as 'allegedly the most powerfully organized "state" of its time'. Andrew Rabin has similarly warned that the 'pre-Conquest notions of law and justice were not necessarily objective, widely recognized, and with communally agreed upon standards, even if – indeed, especially if – they were often portrayed as such'.[89] There is always a difference between law and practice: re-constructing past practices based on surviving documentation will never quite capture how things operated at the time. Things will always appear more formal, more fixed and more regular than they probably were. With these warnings in mind, the following section will seek to describe the main claims about the institutions that developed that to modern eyes can be seen to represent the Anglo-Saxon legal system.

1   Laws

Although it was beyond question that Anglo-Saxon England was 'a highly segmented society',[90] with a focus on the local, the powers of kings increased throughout the period.[91] As HR Loyn pointed out, Anglo-Saxon kings exercised 'a jurisdiction that was exceedingly powerful'.[92] They issued royal proclamations or decrees (known as dooms), and in the later Anglo-Saxon period these took the form of codes of law.[93] Phrases that were to be become part and parcel of the English common law can be found in these codes, often in embryonic form such as the 'king's peace'. More legal texts survive from Anglo-Saxon England than any other contemporaneous European community.[94] However, Anglo-Saxon codes were not intended to be comprehensive but were rather often sought to make a particular declaration, being directed at those who were aware of existing customs. Brian Simpson referred to the laws of Æthelbert as 'an expression of aspirations, not a compulsory and enforceable set of regulations'.[95] As Maitland noted, royal proclamations constituted a 'small part of the whole field of law'.[96] They existed alongside and assumed the existence of a body of customs that varied from place to place.[97] Anglo-Saxon law consisted of both 'royal initiative' and 'folkright', the customary law common to the community: 'there existed for every ordered community a body of law to which the term folkright may properly be given and from time to time was clarified by royal decree'.[98]

---

[88] Ibid. 101.   [89] Rabin, *Crime and Punishment in Anglo-Saxon England* 5.
[90] Hyams, *Rancor & Reconciliation in Medieval England* 101, 88.
[91] See Hudson, *The Oxford History of the Laws of England Volume II* chapter 2 for a full account.
[92] Loyn, *The Governance of Anglo-Saxon England, 500–1087* 16542. At least towards the end of the era, 'Kingship was hereditary in the sense that it was confined to a member of the ruling house' (George W Keeton, *The Norman Conquest and the Common Law* (Ernest Benn, 1966) 11).
[93] See Agnes J Robertson, *The Laws of Kings of England from Edmund to Henry I* (Cambridge University Press, 1925); Attenborough, *The Laws of the Earliest Kings* or Oliver, *The Beginnings of English Law* for original sources.
[94] Rabin, *Crime and Punishment in Anglo-Saxon England* 52.
[95] AW Brian Simpson, 'The Laws of Ethelbert' in Morris S Arnold, Thomas A Green and Dally A Scully (eds.), On *the Laws and Customs of England: Essays in Honor of Samuel E Throne* (University of North Carolina Press, 1981) 3), reprinted as chapter 1 of AW Brian Simpson, *Legal Theory and Legal History: Essays on the Common Law* (Hambledon Press, 1987).
[96] Maitland, *The Constitutional History of England* 4.
[97] In some places, this would include Danelaw, the customary law of the Danes.
[98] Loyn, *The Governance of Anglo-Saxon England, 500–1087* 42, 43.

The Late Anglo-Saxon Legal System 57

The development of such royal initiative grew and was bolstered by the conversion of Christianity following the arrival of St Augustine in 597.[99] The development of some written records meant that literate servants were required and churchmen took on such roles in return for the legal protection of the Church and her property.[100] For Loyn, Biblical notions of kingship began to influence ideas that were to become instrumental to the development of the common law. He wrote that '[T]he suggestion of a just king with responsibility for the proper government and administration of the people committed to his care was implicit if not fully formulated or always understood.' For example, Cnut's proclamation of 1020 declared that he would 'be a gracious lord and will not fail to support the rights of the church and just secular law', and his ordinance to the people stated that 'above all else they would ever love and honour one God and unanimously uphold Christian faith, and love King [Cnut] with due fidelity'.[101] However, it is important not to overplay this trend, being seduced by the benefit of hindsight. Local custom remained all important, with codes of law just amending and supplementing those customs. England had barely become a common kingdom, so it is not surprising that it did not boast a common law.

2   *Courts*

The enforcement and adjudication of law was also a local rather than a national matter. There was no separation of powers in the Anglo-Saxon age.[102] Local customs were applied, administered and created in local assemblies. These assemblies were called moots or folk-moots. These were decision-making bodies that were focused on making a decision on the matter before them influenced by local custom, tradition and the guidance of those held in esteem locally. Over time, these decision-making bodies became known as the shire and hundred courts. Each village or group of small villages had its own hundred court.[103] An Ordinance of King Edgar (959–75) recognised that the hundred courts were well-known and had already been in existence for some time, confirming pre-existing practice.[104] Such courts met once every four weeks, often, but not always, in the open air and, although they were presided over by the town reeve and the parish priest, the judgments were given by ordinary town members.[105] Although according to a law of Cnut every free man over the age of twelve was to be in a hundred, it is not likely that all free men attended

---

[99] Kings sometimes claimed 'to be acting in accordance with Biblical and Christian law' (Hudson, *The Oxford History of the Laws of England Volume II* 21).

[100] Loyn, *The Governance of Anglo-Saxon England, 500–1087* 44.

[101] Robertson, *The Laws of Kings of England from Edmund to Henry I* 141, 155.

[102] The separation of powers is a doctrine of political theory whereby the legislative (which makes laws), executive (which implements laws and makes policy) and judicial (which apply the law) branches of government are operated by different sets of people, so each can provide a check on the other.

[103] It usually corresponded to either a hundred households or a hundred acres of land, but this varied from shire to shire. Harding contended that it corresponded to 'a hundred hides, and the hides was reckoned as the amount of land which supported a family'. This meant that the size of hundreds varied from region to region and boundaries 'changed continually' (Alan Harding, *The Law Courts of Medieval England* (George Allen & Unwin, 1973) 17). Keeton, *The Norman Conquest and the Common Law* 14, who noted that 'The origin of the term [hundred] is unknown.'

[104] Robertson, *The Laws of Kings of England from Edmund to Henry I* 27. For discussion of their earlier origins, see Loyn, *The Governance of Anglo-Saxon England, 500–1087* 141.

[105] Pollock and Maitland, *The History of English Law* 42.

58   *The Anglo-Saxon Legacy*

every hundred meeting.[106] This reference to 'free men' underscores how 'slaves were an integral and numerically important part of English society in the Anglo-Saxon period'.[107] As Loyn noted, '[T]he sources of supply of slaves were maintained throughout the Anglo-Saxon period, to some extent by warfare, but much more significantly by legal penalties and economic pressures.'[108] Slavery could result from defeat in battle, failure to full obligations as a freeman or default of payment of a due legal penalty, and it was possible and common for people to sell themselves during troubled times.

The main governing body, however, was not the hundred court but the shire court, which operated at the county level.[109] Although the Ordinance of King Edgar stated that the shire court would meet twice a year, as time went on, they sat more regularly.[110] The shire courts were presided over by the king's *ealdorman*, a regional lieutenant who was both a local magnate and the king's representative. The *ealdorman* was joined by the bishop and also often by a deputy or 'shire-reeve', who was also the king's representative for matters of taxation and the collection of fines, and whose title would become known as the 'sheriff' by the time of Cnut.[111] While originally attendance at the shire court had been the privilege or obligation of all freemen, as time went on, the obligation to attend (as distinct from the right to attend) become narrowed to representatives of the hundred.

Alan Harding noted that the case load of the shire courts comprised of both cases that were brought up from 'the hundred by the initiative of complainants or the king's order' and those that had been 'sent down from the witan [King's Council] by the king for effective settlement in the shire'.[112] Although the shire court had a wide range of business including the witnessing of land transactions and the deciding of land disputes,[113] they dealt mainly with offences of violence and thefts, usually of cattle.[114] Their focus was more upon compensating the victim than punishing the offender.[115] These moots or assemblies did not resemble modern courts of law. There was 'no body of professional lawyers', no judge nor jury.[116] The records were not written down. They were basically places where people met to resolve local business.

Four further points need to be kept in mind regarding the local courts of Anglo-Saxon England.[117] First, although there were also large Church gatherings or synods that dealt with a variety of matters including disputes,[118] the day-to-day affairs of the Church were dealt with in the hundred and shire courts. These included ecclesiastical issues, such as the

---

[106] Robertson, *The Laws of Kings of England from Edmund to Henry I* 185; Hudson, *The Oxford History of the Laws of England Volume II* 53.

[107] David Pelteret, 'Slave Raiding and Slave Trading in Early England' (2008) 9 *Anglo-Saxon England* 99.

[108] HR Loyn, *Anglo-Saxon England and the Norman Conquest* (Longman 1962) 87.

[109] Keeton, *The Norman Conquest and the Common Law* 15. For Loyn, the shire court was 'apart from the monarchy perhaps the most important institution in Anglo-Saxon England' (Loyn, *The Governance of Anglo-Saxon England, 500–1087* 138).

[110] This was recognised in the laws of Cnut; Robertson, *The Laws of Kings of England from Edmund to Henry I* 183. Watkin noted that the shire-moot met monthly; Watkin, *The Legal History of Wales* 76.

[111] For discussion of reeves and sheriffs, see Hudson, *The Oxford History of the Laws of England Volume II* 37–40.

[112] Harding, *The Law Courts of Medieval England* 23. Hudson, however, has contended that evidence for cases passing from hundred to shire is 'exceptional' (Hudson, *The Oxford History of the Laws of England Volume II* 64).

[113] Ibid. 49–50.

[114] Hudson noted that, although both hundred and shire courts dealt with land cases, the shire court 'probably dealt with more serious criminal cases' (Ibid. 64).

[115] Hostettler, *A History of Criminal Justice in England and Wales* 14.

[116] Maitland, *The Constitutional History of England* 4–5.

[117] For a detailed account see Hudson, *The Oxford History of the Laws of England Volume II* chapter 2.   [118] Ibid. 63.

The Late Anglo-Saxon Legal System   59

governance and discipline of clerics, attacks on clerics and matrimonial matters.[119] What later generations would refer to as secular and ecclesiastical jurisdictions were 'hardly distinguished'.[120] This did not weaken the integrity of the Church, because, where relevant, ecclesiastical punishments were ordered in addition to lay ones.[121] Moreover, the role of the priest in the hundred court and bishop in the shire court was by no means reserved to the affairs of the Church. Harding noted that the bishop served as 'the interpreter of God's judgment upon society; and therefore its critic'.[122] As Loyn noted, 'The prominence of the Church and churchmen in royal government and general administration is one of the outstanding features of late Old-English society.'[123] Indeed, it has been a characteristic of most of English legal history.

Second, in addition to the 'public' courts described earlier, there also existed 'private' courts presided over by lords or their reeves.[124] These institutions, often referred to as seigniorial courts or courts of private jurisdiction, developed particularly in the last century of Anglo-Saxon England.[125] According to Hudson, two types of jurisdiction can be distinguished: the 'Lord's courts', where authority derived from a lord's relationship to his men and land, and the 'franchisal courts', where authority from a grant of powers was normally exercised by the king or his officials.[126] In either case, the result was that of 'lords of various degrees, from the king himself downwards, holding courts on their lands at which their tenants were entitled to seek justice in their own local affairs, and bound to attend that justice might be done to their fellows'.[127] Anglo-Saxon landowners enjoyed 'considerable powers of peace-keeping':[128] lords were responsible for the good behaviour of their household and immediate followers and this involved the settlement of disputes in at least an informal manner.[129] This was recognised in a law of Cnut, which stated that 'every lord shall be personally responsible as surety for the men of his own household'; however, that law went on to say that 'if any accusation is brought against one of them he shall answer, in accordance with the law, within the hundred in which he is accused'.[130] This did not mean, however, that there remained a clear demarcation between the hundred courts and the private jurisdiction of lords. Indeed, over time, many hundred courts came into private hands.[131] The lord would achieve 'sake' and 'soke' of the hundred, 'sake' denoting the right to hear cases, and 'soke' the right to require attendance.[132] Elsewhere, such private jurisdictions ran parallel to and sometimes overlapped with the 'public'

---

[119] Harding, *The Law Courts of Medieval England* 22.   [120] Pollock and Maitland, *The History of English Law* 40
[121] Loyn, *The Governance of Anglo-Saxon England, 500–1087* 157.
[122] Moreover, 'While the king's protection covered land-holding and the status and privileges of the great, God's protection covered the whole of society and all His people' (Harding, *The Law Courts of Medieval England* 21).
[123] Loyn, *The Governance of Anglo-Saxon England, 500–1087* 154.
[124] Hudson, *The Oxford History of the Laws of England Volume II* 56.
[125] Pollock and Maitland, *The History of English Law* 43; Loyn, *The Governance of Anglo-Saxon England, 500–1087* 161.
[126] Hudson, *The Oxford History of the Laws of England Volume II* 56.
[127] Pollock and Maitland, *The History of English Law* 43.   [128] Harding, *The Law Courts of Medieval England* 15.
[129] Hudson, *The Oxford History of the Laws of England Volume II* 56; Loyn, *The Governance of Anglo-Saxon England, 500–1087* 162. Maitland observed that the 'greatest of the Anglo-Saxon lords had enjoyed wide and high justiciary rights' (Maitland, *Doomsday and Beyond* 117).
[130] Robertson, *The Laws of Kings of England from Edmund to Henry I* 193.
[131] Helen Cam, 'The "Private" Hundred in England before the Norman Conquest' in James Conway-Davies (ed.), *Studies Presented to Sir Hilary Jenkinson* (Oxford University Press, 1957), reprinted as Helen Cam, *Law-finders and Law-makers in Medieval England* (Merlin Press, 1962) chapter 3.
[132] Harding, *The Law Courts of Medieval England* 18.

The Anglo-Saxon Legacy

jurisdiction of the hundred courts.[133] There remains 'much room for differences of opinion' concerning how the extent and existence of private jurisdiction in Anglo-Saxon England.[134] Roebuck observed that the key shift in Anglo-Saxon law was 'from kin responsibility to lord's responsibility'.[135] However, Wormald argued that Maitland's over-emphasis upon the private jurisdiction of Lords led him to downplay the role of the Anglo-Saxon kings.[136]

Third, there is a lack of evidence as to whether courts were held at a level below that of the hundred in the Anglo-Saxon period.[137] 'Pollock and Maitland' stated that there may have been a smaller unit comprising of 'some sort of township meeting' but there is no evidence to suggest it exercised judicial functions.[138] Yet, as we have seen, kindred connections were important in this era and feud rested upon such informal ties. There is some evidence to suggest that these ties were formalised. All free men over the age of twelve were not only members of the hundred but also of a tithing. A tithing referred to a group of ten men or possibly a distinct of ten hides or all the men of one village.[139] Tithings took on both social and legal roles.[140] A system of surety developed whereby all members of the tithing took responsibility for the actions of each other, and if one committed a wrong, then the others were obliged to present him for punishment, otherwise they would all be held responsible for the wrong. There is some debate as to whether this system, known as *Frankpledge*, pre-dated the Norman Conquest. The conventional account is that it was a post-Conquest development.[141] However, Hudson – though noting that it was perhaps geographically limited – came to the conclusion that it is likely that 'frankpledge was a pre- rather than post-Conquest creation'.[142] Wormald saw the frankpledge as reflecting the principle that there was not only a duty to avoid breaches of the king's law but also to publicise breaches by neighbours.[143] He noted that '[T]o take an oath not to cover up for criminals is not a lot different from swearing to denounce them.'[144] For Wormald, this 'came close' to the system that is accredited to Henry II, a century after the Anglo-Saxon period had come to a close.

Fourth, it should be noted that resort to the king and his royal advisers, known as the Witan, was rare. Rather than being regarded as the fountain of justice, recourse to the king was exceptional and tended to occur only where there was a failure in the usual local justice system that required royal interference in a manner that was 'barely distinguishable from that of combating an open rebellion'.[145] The King's Court, known as the *Witenagemot*,[146] was not a court of law but rather a gathering of the great and the good, the Witan.[147]

---

[133] Loyn, *The Governance of Anglo-Saxon England, 500–1087* 161.   [134] Maitland, *Doomsday and Beyond* 307.
[135] Roebuck, *The Background of the Common Law* 21.   [136] Wormald, *The Making of English Law* 19.
[137] Hudson, *The Oxford History of the Laws of England Volume II* 62.
[138] Pollock and Maitland, *The History of English Law* 42.
[139] Hudson, *The Oxford History of the Laws of England Volume II* 170.
[140] Loyn, *The Governance of Anglo-Saxon England, 500–1087* 146.   [141] Watkin, *The Legal History of Wales* 78.
[142] Hudson, *The Oxford History of the Laws of England Volume II* 171, 392.   [143] Wormald, *Lawyers and the State* 17.
[144] Wormald, 'Maitland and Anglo-Saxon Law' 11.
[145] Pollock and Maitland, *The History of English Law* 41. That said, some royal supervision did occur. The king and his advisers would tour the land, with the king taking the shire court when he visited that region.
[146] See, further, Loyn, *The Governance of Anglo-Saxon England, 500–1087* 100–6.
[147] Although offenders were sometimes accused before it; Keeton, *The Norman Conquest and the Common Law* 13. For further discussion, see Hudson, *The Oxford History of the Laws of England Volume II* 43–6.

The Late Anglo-Saxon Legal System   61

Neither its function nor composition was formalised.[148] Rather, it comprised of those bishops, abbots and warriors who happened to be guarding, drinking and advising the king at a particular time.[149] It travelled with the king as he progressed around the kingdom and 'dealt with the general business of the kingdom'.[150] Although the king often consulted the *Witan*, 'there does not appear to have been any constitutional necessity to do so', and the *Witan* seems to have played a small part in the preparation of Anglo-Saxon dooms.[151] Kings heard some cases in person, and towards the end of the Anglo-Saxon period, laws suggested that certain cases or rights were reserved to the king.[152] This included botless crimes and the 'king's pleas': namely, breaches of the king's peace, gifting at the King's Court, obstructing the king's officials, corrupting the processes of law and neglecting military service.[153] However, for the most part, Anglo-Saxon justice was very much a local affair. There was little attempt to achieve consistency from shire to shire. As Maitland noted, 'this localization of justice must have engendered a variety of local laws. Law was transmitted by oral tradition and the men of one shire would know nothing and care nothing for the tradition of another shire.'[154] In short, there was no such thing as a common law.

3   *Proof*

This localisation of justice was reflected in the procedure followed by the courts.[155] The Anglo-Saxons relied upon trial by compurgation and trial by ordeal. Trial by compurgation (also known as 'wager of law') required the accused to take an oath either alone or with others known as 'compurgators', 'oath-makers' or 'oath-helpers'. The oath had to be word perfect, the principle being 'fail in a syllable, fail in your case'.[156] Compurgation functioned effectively as a form of character reference: the accused was required to assemble the right number of compurgators who would testify to their claim or defence.[157] As Harding noted, its success 'depended on social reasons – the size and respectability of the following a litigant or his patron could call upon'. As he noted, '[A] false oath was reckoned to bring its own supernatural punishment.'[158] In trial by compurgation, justice was left in the hands of God rather than man.

This notion of divine justice was taken a stage further by trial by ordeal, an institution that was common globally in both the East and the West. Trial by ordeal applied where the accused failed in their oath or was disqualified from clearing themself by oath due to the severity of the allegation.[159] It took the form of a physical torment, which was regarded as a 'direct appeal to Heaven'.[160] Four ordeals were commonplace.[161] The first was ordeal by

---

[148] Keeton, *The Norman Conquest and the Common Law* 13.   [149] Harding, *The Law Courts of Medieval England* 16.
[150] Watkin, *The Legal History of Wales* 77.   [151] Keeton, *The Norman Conquest and the Common Law* 13.
[152] Hudson, *The Oxford History of the Laws of England Volume II* 43, 45.
[153] Harding, *The Law Courts of Medieval England* 22.   [154] Maitland, *The Constitutional History of England* 4.
[155] See, further, Hudson, *The Oxford History of the Laws of England Volume II* chapter 4 and Henry C Lea, *Superstition and Force* (University of Pennsylvania Press, 1866).
[156] Albert T Carter, *A History of the English Courts* (7th ed., Butterworths, 1944) 3.
[157] Pollock and Maitland, *The History of English Law* 39.   [158] Harding, *The Law Courts of Medieval England* 27.
[159] Pollock and Maitland, *The History of English Law* 39.   [160] Keeton, *The Norman Conquest and the Common Law* 16.
[161] See Attenborough, *The Laws of the Earliest Kings* 171–2.

62 *The Anglo-Saxon Legacy*

hot iron, whereby a hot bar would be put on the person's hands, which were then bandaged for three days; if the hand was scalded, then the wrong-doer was guilty. The second was ordeal by hot water, which was similar but the alleged wrong-doer was made to remove a coin from the bottom of a bucket of boiling water; depending on the accusation, they either had to plunge their hand in up to the wrist or to the elbow. The third, typically for persons without rank, was ordeal by cold water, whereby a person was bound onto a chair and lowered into a large bath, river or pond; if they floated, then they were seen as guilty. The fourth was trial by Corsnæd, where the accused had to swallow an ounce of consecrated barley bread, or an ounce of cheese, in which a feather had been placed. If the suspect choked, that was held to be proof form God of guilt. This ordeal tended to be used in relation to clerics but was sometimes used for non-clerics.[162]

All of the forms of ordeal operated on the same basis. They were means to determine the judgment of God. If the burns festered or the person floated or choked, then it was said that God had decided against them and the person was punished. The Church originally played a considerable role in proceedings. Those found guilty were then subject to a range of punishments, from death and mutilation to financial penalities. Many people opted for a confession rather than the endurance of physical agony, many endured the ordeal in a less severe form, and a surprising number not only survived the ordeal but were also found to be telling the truth, possibly due to the way in which they had been tied up. Pollock and Maitland's description of the forms of procedure as being 'complicated, always stiff and unbending' was clearly not an entirely accurate representation.[163]

V   Conclusions

Overall, it is clear that justice under the Anglo-Saxons was not as archaic and savage as it may at first appear. It is difficult to disagree with the judgment of Harding that the Anglo-Saxon era saw 'a great deal of the formation of the basic structure of English legal procedure'.[164] However, it is important not to over-state this legacy. Anglo-Saxon England was characterised by local justice rather than a common law. As Hudson has pointed out, since 'many of its ideas, rules, and practices were notably different from those of the common law' as it would emerge, this renders 'highly questionable the giving of a pre-eminent position to the Anglo-Saxon period in the making of English law'.[165] However, as Hudson conceded, the fact that distinctive features of the Anglo-Saxon era did not last does not mean that they did not influence what followed. The long and varied Anglo-Saxon era saw a number of significant social and political developments, not least the emergence of England as a kingdom, that were to be crucial to the future. That future, however, would be altered by a result of conquest. The next chapter, therefore, explores the extent to which the events of 1066 affected the Anglo-Saxon legacy and whether the Norman period can be said to be origin of the English common law.

---

[162] Hostettler, *A History of Criminal Justice in England and Wales* 20.
[163] Pollock and Maitland, *The History of English Law* 38.   [164] Harding, *The Law Courts of Medieval England* 29.
[165] Hudson, *The Oxford History of the Laws of England Volume II* 251.

'The Norman Conquest is a catastrophe which determines the whole future history of English law'.

Frederick Pollock and Frederic W Maitland,
The History of English Law (2nd ed, vol 1,
Cambridge University Press, 1968 [1898]) 79.

4

The Norman Conquest (c.1066–1154)

I   Introduction

Before he became known as William the Conqueror, William of Normandy was referred to as William the Bastard. However, the question that haunted William was not that of his own illegitimate birth but rather the legitimacy of the reign of Harold I. The year 1066 was the year of three kings: Edward the Confessor, Harold Godwinson and William the Conqueror.[1] At the start of 1066, King Edward the Confessor lay dying and the question of succession remained disputed. At his deathbed, Harold claimed that Edward had promised the throne to him. However, there were also allegations that both Edward and Harold had promised the throne to others, most notably William of Normandy. On Edward's death, Harold became king but then William sought to claim the throne that he considered rightfully his. With the support of the Pope, William and his army invaded England, successfully dethroning Harold the oath-breaker. Anglo-Saxon England became Norman England.

However, it is easy to over-estimate the effect that the Norman Conquest had upon the development of English law. Even Frederic W Maitland who saw 1066 as being cata-strophic,[2] wrote that Anglo-Saxon laws and customs were not 'swept away or superseded by Norman law'.[3] He noted that the system of law and government found by the Normans was more sophisticated than the one that they had left in Normandy.[4] The Normans had 'little, if any, written law to bring with them', and the Norman kings did not become great legislators once they had arrived in England.[5] There was no Norman code and Norman law did not 'exist in a portable, transplantable shape'.[6] Indeed, the first of the very few legislative actions of William I was to confirm the old laws of Edward the Confessor.[7] The London Charter stated that the bishop and mayor 'shall be entitled to all the rights

---

[1] Edgar Æteling was elected king by the Witenagemot but never crowned.
[2] Frederick Pollock and Fredric W Maitland, *The History of English Law*, vol. 1 (2nd ed., Cambridge University Press, 1968 [1898]) 79.
[3] Frederic W Maitland, *The Constitutional History of England* (Cambridge University Press, 1941 [1908]) 6–7.
[4] Pollock and Maitland, *The History of English Law* 64–5.   [5] Maitland, *The Constitutional History of England* 9.
[6] Pollock and Maitland, *The History of English Law* 79.   [7] Maitland, *The Constitutional History of England* 6–7.

66 *The Norman Conquest (c.1066–1154)*

which you had at the time of King Edward'.[8] Although it is clear that the invaded English men were harshly and brutally treated by the Normans,[9] the chief consequence of the Conquest was not the subjection of England to a foreign law but the development of a strong kingship that would in time allow for national unity and moves towards centralised governance and justice.[10]

The Norman Conquest saw the sudden replacement of an entire ruling class. However, the changes in terms of what we would call law and order were not immediately visible in 1066. Rather, they occurred throughout the Norman period as a whole as a means to secure and consolidate order. The changes that did occur were clearly built upon the Anglo-Saxon foundation. Indeed, an argument can be made that they simply continued where the Anglo-Saxons left off – or to be more precise, where Edward the Confessor ended. As in the Anglo-Saxon period, the law-and-order developments under the Normans focused more on order than law. Legal developments – further seeds of what was to become the common law – were merely the side effect of trying to keep control over a violent and recently invaded kingdom.

This chapter explores the effect of the Norman Conquest as well as looking at the developments during the Norman period as a whole during the reigns of William I (1066–87), William II (1087–100), Henry I (1100–35) and Stephen (1135–54).[11] It falls into three sections. Section II provides an overview of the main effects of 1066 in terms of law and order. Section III then discusses in detail what is often considered to be the most significant development under the Normans, the feudal system, and how this impacted upon law and order. Section IV then focuses upon two aspects that are often overlooked in accounts of the effect of the Conquest: the effect of the Norman era upon the position of slaves and women. The importance of the later Norman kings will be the focus of the Conclusion. Overall, the chapter will not seek to judge Maitland's claim that the Conquest was catastrophic, but it will substantiate and evaluate his claim that it had an effect upon English law.[12]

II   What Have the Normans Ever Done for Us?

Periodisation – the separating out of history into set periods – tends to over-emphasise the amount of change and downplays the degree of continuity.[13] It is also inherently artificial. Everyday life does not completely change suddenly the day after a big event such as an invasion or the coronation of a new monarch. Periodisation is by its very nature 'a

---

[8] Agnes J Robertson, *The Laws of Kings of England from Edmund to Henry I* (Cambridge University Press, 1925) 231. Also, the seventh of ten articles attributed to William stated that 'all men shall keep and observe the law of King Edward ..., with the additions which I have decreed for the benefit of the English nation' (ibid. 241). Although these texts were probably produced much later (Judith A Green, *The Government of England under Henry I* (Cambridge University Press, 1986) 97), they nevertheless were intended to be a reconstruction of the law of the earlier age.

[9] Pollock and Maitland, *The History of English Law* 92.   [10] Ibid. 94.

[11] However, as we will see, the kingship was contested during the final part of this period in what is known as the Anarchy.

[12] Cf. Pollock and Maitland, *The History of English Law* 79. For a detailed account of how the Norman Conquest has been viewed throughout English histories, see George Garnett, *The Norman Conquest in English History* (Oxford University Press, 2021), vol. 1.

[13] See further Russell Sandberg, *Subversive Legal History: A Manifesto for the Future of Legal Education* (Routledge, 2021) chapter 5.

simplifying, consolidating and universalising process'.[14] But this is also what makes it useful and necessary. It prevents the whole of history happening at once. As Jeanne Boydston noted, its purpose 'is to bring order and meaning to an otherwise unruly tangle of data and permit us to hold steady the otherwise constant flurry of difference and change'.[15]

Traditionally, talk of the Norman period has emphasised the impact of 1066 and the Norman changes and has downplayed the Anglo-Saxon legacy. This is the minimalist account that is discussed in the previous chapter. However, since the time of Maitland, the pendulum has swung the other way. Interpretations now constantly downplay the importance of 1066 itself and employ maximalist accounts of the Anglo-Saxon State. Again, there is a need for a cautionary perspective. The Norman Conquest was a genuine turning point in history and, although the changing of a king and of a ruling class did not result in sudden changes to what we would call law and order, changes developed over time. However, determining what these changes were is not straightforward. As Maitland observed, the precise legal effects of the Norman Conquest were shaped by a plethora of factors, meaning that English law cannot be understood merely as 'a mixture, or a compound, of two old national laws'.[16] He gave the analogy of a river, arguing that the Norman Conquest did not lead to the merging of existing Anglo-Saxon law with the law from Normandy as if they were two streams:

The picture of two rivulets of law meeting to form one river would deceive us, even could we measure the volume and analyze the waters of each of these fancied streams. The law which prevails in the England of the twelfth century – this one thing we may say with some certainty – cannot be called a mixture of the law which prevailed in England on the day when the Confessor was alive and dead, with the law which prevailed in Normandy on the day when William set sail from Saint Valery.[17]

While it is tempting to envisage a gradual process of Norman ideas building upon existing Anglo-Saxon customs, this would be a simplification. This is underscored by the question of language. One of the main effects of the Conquest is often taken to be the introduction of Latin and 'the popular hybrid tongue known as Anglo-Norman or Norman-French'.[18] It is true, that the number of legal terms that are of French descent may point to the Normans having a clear linguistic inheritance over the development of law in England. As Maitland noted:

Contract, agreement, covenant, obligation, debt, condition, bill, note, master, servant, partner, guarantee, tort, trespass, assault, battery, slander, damage, crime, treason, felony, misdemeanour, arson, robbery, burglary, larceny, property, possession, pledge, lien, payment, money, grant, purchase, devise, descent, heir, easement, marriage, guardian, infant, ward, all are French ... We enter a court of justice: court, justices, judges, jurors, counsel, attorneys, clerks, parties, plaintiff, defendant, action, suit, claim, demand, indictment, count, declaration, pleadings, evidence, verdict, conviction,

---

[14] Jeanne Boydston, 'Gender as a Question of Historical Analysis' (2008) 20(3) *Gender & History* 558, 560.   [15] Ibid.
[16] Pollock and Maitland, *The History of English Law* 80.   [17] Ibid. 80.
[18] Harold Potter, *An Historical Introduction to English Law and Its Institutions* (Sweet & Maxwell, 1932) 11.

68   *The Norman Conquest (c.1066–1154)*

judgment, sentence, appeal, reprieve, pardon, execution, every one and every thing, save the witnesses, writs and oaths, have French names.[19]

However, these French words were not immediately introduced and did not replace the Anglo-Saxon terms. Indeed, it was not until a century after the Conquest that the use of legal French became commonplace.[20] This underscores Maitland's warning that the question of the effect of the Norman Conquest cannot be 'stated as though it were a simple ethnical question between what is English and what is French'.[21] This is not to say, however, that new ideas often introduced from abroad did not influence the infant legal system. Indeed, they often provided a new meaning or importance to an older institution.[22]

There were three distinctively Norman innovations that were to prove to be important.[23] The first was the separation of the ecclesiastical courts from the courts of the shire and the hundred.[24] Church affairs were now to be judged according to Church law and not according to the laws of the hundred.[25] Church courts (which were to become also known as the 'Courts Christian') operated on the same levels as the other local courts:[26] the equivalent to the hundred levels was the parish; the diocese was analogous to the shire; whilst the provinces of archbishops acted on a level loosely parallel to that of the kingdom. These courts were part of a European system subject to the pope, and as SFC Milsom pointed out, they were the earliest court in England that looked like a court of law.[27] A single judge considered and compared the evidence of witnesses and applied the rules of law to the facts. The Courts Christian continued to exercise an extensive jurisdiction, not only including ecclesiastical affairs such as the law of status of clerics, spiritual functions and the property of the Church including tithes, but also a wide range of matters that to modern eyes would seem to be matters for the State not for the Church. The Courts Christian dealt with a range of matters such as the law of marriage, divorce and legitimacy, the validity and interpretation of wills, defamation and the general correction of sinners. As Maitland observed 'the whole province of sexual morality is annexed by the church; she punishes fornication, adultery, incest'.[28] The Courts Christian often competed with the lay courts for business, and while the power of the bishop in the shire courts decreased after 1066, the influence of the Church and of Church figures continued to be important. The Courts Christian continued to have authority over many of these areas for centuries and clerics were often in positions or close to positions of authority. Some of this continues in the present day, with bishops sill sitting in the House of Lords and with ecclesiastical courts and laws still operating as part of the law of the land.[29]

---

[19] Pollock and Maitland, *The History of English Law* 80–1.

[20] Under the Assize of Novel Dissesin, discussed in the next chapter (ibid. 82–4.   [21] Ibid. 79.

[22] Maitland, *The Constitutional History of England* 9.

[23] Another important development was the designation of a third of England as 'forest', which was subject to its own 'forest law'.

[24] An ordinance on this was drawn up between 1072 and 1085, not as a code but as a writ that was distributed to the shire courts; JR Maddicott, *The Origins of the English Parliament 924–1327* (Oxford University Press, 2010) 61; Pollock and Maitland, *The History of English Law* 88.

[25] See the Episcopal laws translated in Robertson, *The Laws of Kings of England from Edmund to Henry I* 235.

[26] Such courts were formalised in 1077 under Archbishop Lanfranc; John Hostettler, *A History of Criminal Justice in England and Wales* (Waterside Press, 2009) 40.

[27] SFC Milsom, *Historical Foundations of the Common Law* (2nd ed., Butterworths, 1981) 25.

[28] Pollock and Maitland, *The History of English Law* 124–5.

[29] For a discussion, see Russell Sandberg, *Law and Religion* (Cambridge University Press, 2011).

The second Norman import was trial by battle (also known as trial by combat). This became a third form of trial alongside compurgation and the ordeal.[30] Trial by battle was considered to be foreign, unpopular and likely to favour the Normans, as they were good fighters. An ordinance from William I gave Englishmen permission to defend themselves by ordeal of iron if this was preferred to combat.[31] However, as Thomas Watkin noted, this procedure was 'not as maverick as might at first appear', given that conflict was common place, it made sense that lords wanted their lands to be held by the best fighting men.[32] This meant that using trial by battle as the mode of trial was 'far from irrational'. There were other minor but significant changes to the existing courts.[33] Sheriffs became appointed by the king, meaning, in the words of Watkin, that 'there was in effect royal supervision if not control of the shire court'.[34] The sheriff would provide account for his shire to the king and would tour each of the hundreds twice a year. While doing so, the sheriff would enforce frankpledge and the obligations of the tithing. As we noted in the last chapter, there is debate as to whether frankpledge was a pre- or post-Norman innovation.[35]

A third development was the inquest whereby locals were summoned to advise the king. This built upon the Anglo-Saxon idea that the community was responsible to the central government for the behaviour of its individuals.[36] However, in the Norman period, such inquests were typically used to determine questions of fact and their use in lawsuits were exceptional.[37] Other concepts that appeared in embryonic form before the Conquest grew after it, most notably the notion of the king's peace.[38] All serious wrongs became a breach of the king's peace and became known as felonies.[39] Other Anglo-Saxon creations such as compurgation declined and gave way to the appeal.[40] The word 'appeal' is used here not in its modern meaning (where it refers to the review of a decision by a senior court) but simply meant asking for a decision. It was 'a stylized and tamed alternative feud'.[41] An allegation of wrong was made by the victim or 'approvers', so called because 'they had to prove their accusations by doing battle'.[42] Where the appeal was successful, two things followed, the wrong-doer was punished for the wrong and was required to pay compensation to the victim. The distinction between crime and tort, therefore, remained undistinguished. Again, whether this was a pre- or post-Conquest innovation is not clear. Although the appeal has been described as 'the regular method under the Normans of dealing with crime',[43] Paul Hyams has argued that 'appeals, in everything except their (French) name and their characteristic denouement of trial by battle, undoubtedly figured prominently in pre-Conquest law'.[44] He noted, however, that 'we have no way to know

---

[30] Pollock and Maitland, *The History of English Law* 39.
[31] Robertson, *The Laws of Kings of England from Edmund to Henry I* 233.
[32] Thomas G Watkin, *The Legal History of Wales* (University of Wales Press, 2007) 78.
[33] For full discussion of courts and procedure, see John Hudson, *The Oxford History of the Laws of England Volume II: 871–1216* (Oxford University Press, 2012) chapters 12 and 13
[34] Watkin, *The Legal History of Wales* 78.   [35] Hudson, *The Oxford History of the Laws of England Volume II* 391.
[36] Derek Roebuck, *The Background of the Common Law* (Oxford University Press, 1988) 20.
[37] Chares H Haskins, 'The Early Norman Jury' (1903) 8(4) *American Historical Review* 613.
[38] Hudson, *The Oxford History of the Laws of England Volume II* 386.
[39] Adekemi Odujirin, *The Normative Basis of Fault in Criminal Law: History and Theory* (University of Toronto Press, 1998) 43.
[40] Albert T Carter, *A History of the English Courts* (7th ed., Butterworths, 1944) 126.
[41] Paul R Hyams, *Rancor & Reconciliation in Medieval England* (Cornell University Press, 2003) 147.
[42] John H Baker, *An Introduction to English Legal History* (5th ed., Oxford University Press, 2019) 543.
[43] Carter, *A History of the English Courts* 127.   [44] Hyams, *Rancor & Reconciliation in Medieval England* 103.

70   *The Norman Conquest (c.1066–1154)*

what proportion of the "wrong" market they covered'. It is clearer, however, that the appeal of felony 'continued to be a regular method of initiating criminal prosecutions throughout the medieval period and beyond'; though in time it would be overtaken and replaced by indictment.[45] The third Norman import was feudalism, which will be explored in detail in the next section.[46]

III   Feudalism

The extent to which Norman England could be described as being 'feudal' and what that meant is controversial. Eric John argued that it was possible to call Anglo-Saxon society feudal because the kinship network was reinforced by the institution of lordship.[47] However, he noted that scholars have traditionally agreed that 'feudalism was introduced by William the Conqueror in 1066, although they have totally failed to agree about what this entailed'.[48] For current purposes, feudalism can be understood as the means by which a lord gave his immediate social inferiors land in return for their loyalty and services. The conventional depiction is that of a 'feudal pyramid' (Figure 4.1).[49] At each level, in exchange for holding land, each group had to give services to the group above. The only person who did not give services was, of course, the king, who sat at the top of the pyramid. Where the services under which the land was held were fixed, it was said that the landholder had 'free tenure' and was a 'freeholder'.

The caricatured version of the feudal system is shown in Figure 4.1. At the top, the king gave land to his tenants in chief and in return they gave him their loyalty, including the promise of a number of knights to secure the kingdom for a fixed period. The tenants in chief then portioned this land, giving some to the knights, and in return the knights would provide forty days a year of military service. The knights in turn obtained food and other services by giving some of their land to tenants in socage, while the rest of the land was worked by villeins who provided services to the lord. Feudalism was a quasi-contractual arrangement that used land rather than money as the method of exchange.

However, talk of the feudalism as a distinct system and of a neat feudal pyramid is a simplification. The term feudalism is the invention of historians.[50] Although the root of the word ('feudum') was used in medieval times to describe 'a proportion of land held in return for the performance of military service', the phrase feudal system was not used until the eighteenth century and the word feudalism was not used until the nineteenth century. Since then, the terms have been put to a variety of different uses, with historians often meaning

---

[45] Baker, *An Introduction to English Legal History* 543. As Margaret Kerr noted, 'A specialized form of the appeal also existed, one that may or may not have been known before Henry II's reign: the approver's appeal, which permitted an accused person who had confessed to a crime to accuse others and prove the accusation by battle. If the approver won, he was allowed to evade execution by going into exile' (Margaret H Kerr, 'Angevin Reform of the Appeal of Felony' (1995) 13(2) *Law and History Review* 351, 353). Approvers had to give evidence that led to the conviction of ten felons in order to escape hanging: John Briggs, Christopher Harrison, Angus McInnes and David Vincent, *Crime and Punishment in England: An Introductory History* (UCL Press, 1996) 8, 10.

[46] See George Garnett, *Conquered England: Kingship, Succession and Tenure, 1066–1166* (Oxford University Press, 2007).

[47] Eric John, 'The Age of Edgar' in James Campbell (ed.), *The Anglo-Saxons* (Penguin, 1991 [1982]) 168.   [48] Ibid. 169.

[49] Milsom, *Historical Foundations of the Common Law* 19; Watkin, *The Legal History of Wales* 77.

[50] JWM Bean, *The Decline of English Feudalism* (Manchester University Press, 1968) 1.

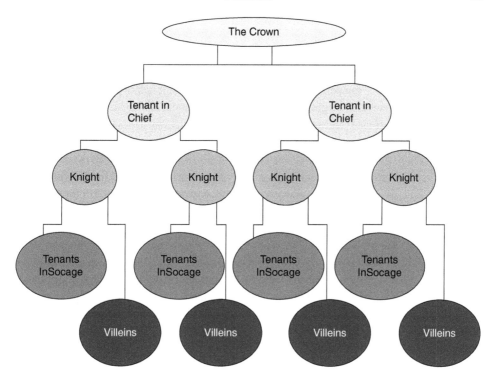

Figure 4.1 Feudal pyramid

different things. As Milsom asserted, 'feudalism was not a system, or even an ideal, having fixed properties'.[51] Such talk of a system 'are the creation of lawyers and historians seeking to systematise certain features that the facts of power may produce in medieval society'. These concerns have led some commentators to argue that the term should be avoided or at least caution is required.[52] Susan Reynolds has argued that the study of both political relations and property rights has 'been hampered by the use of naive concepts and naive assumptions about the relation between concepts, words, and phenomena'.[53] For Reynolds, concepts of feudalism were constructed by post-medieval scholars based on legal records that may not reflect the realities of medieval society. This has meant that the 'Middle Ages have been taken as a time of feudalism, and so what does not form part of that image of feudalism is flittered out of the view of adapted to fit into the background'.[54] As Kathleen Davis has argued, this assumption that we can talk of a feudal medieval period as a meaningful entity incorrectly promotes a linear grand narrative of 'progress'.[55]

---

[51] Milsom, *Historical Foundations of the Common Law* 19.
[52] Elizabeth AR Brown, 'The Tyranny of a Construct: Feudalism and Historians of Medieval Europe' (1974) 79 *American Historical Review* 1077.
[53] Susan Reynolds, *Fiefs and Vassals* (Oxford University Press, 1994) 480–1. See also Susan Reynolds, *Kingdoms and Communities in Western Europe* (2nd ed, Oxford University Press, 1997) and Susan Reynolds, *The Middle Ages without Feudalism* (Ashgate, 2012).
[54] Reynolds, *Fiefs and Vassals* 9.
[55] Kathleen Davis, *Periodization & Sovereignty* (University of Pennsylvania Press, 2008) 134.

The Norman Conquest (c.1066–1154)

However, this does not necessarily mean that the term feudalism should be abandoned. Rather, as Maitland noted, it should simply be accepted that feudalism was never 'complete'.[56] Maitland defined feudalism as 'a state of society in which all or a great part of public rights and duties are inextricably interwoven with the tenure of land, in which the whole governmental system – financial, military, judicial – is part of the law of private property'.[57] It is clear that this was true of England in the period following the Norman Conquest. Land was given in return for services and a rough feudal pyramid can be said to have existed whereby at each level, land was given in exchange for particular services and the tenant was granted some protection in the courts of their feudal lord. A distinction developed between freehold and leasehold estates. Freehold estates exist where the property is granted for the tenant's life (the 'fee'), for as long as the tenant and any of his descendants lived ('in tail') or for as long as the tenant and any of his heirs, whether descendants or not, lived ('in fee simple'). Leasehold estates, where property is held for a fixed term, by contrast came to be recognised. In the feudal pyramid, the tenants in chief, knights and tenants in socage were all freeholders. They all held land from the knights in return for fixed services. The villeins, however, were not freeholders. They simply worked the land. Over time, however, they became leaseholders when the knights began to give them land for a fixed term of years in return for money.

Recognising this should not mean that we should over-emphasise the degree of conformity found in the feudal system. In practice, the feudal pyramid was much more disjointed and complex. There are two main reasons for this. First, it should be noted that the Norman Conquest did not lead to a 'process of wholesale eviction' but rather 'a system of parasitism' whereby, although the tenants in chief were new, those at lower levels continued to do what they had done prior to the events of the Battle of Hastings.[58] Peasants continued to work the land as they had during Anglo-Saxon times, and certain characteristics of feudalism such as the increased tendency of peasants to be reliant upon the local lord and the practice of loaning land preceded the Conquest.[59] The second reason is the practice of subinfeudation: the process whereby those who held land under tenure would give a part or the whole of that land to a third party, making a new bargain between those two that did not affect the original lord.[60] This meant that new relationships were created, extending the feudal pyramid to create new shapes and making a greater gap between the feudal lord and the actual land. Subinfeudation was controversial, however, in that it undermined feudalism. It undid the feudal bargain between the tenant and his lord. It stopped lords from benefitting from the economic and political advantages that feudalism gave them. These were known as the feudal tenures and feudal incidents.

1   *Feudal Tenures*

Although feudalism is often characterised as the bargain whereby the lord gives land to a tenant in return for military service, the provision of an army was just one of a number of

---

[56] Maitland, *The Constitutional History of England* 24.   [57] Ibid. 23–4.
[58] AW Brian Simpson, *A History of the Land Law* (2nd ed., Oxford University Press 1986) 4.
[59] Ibid. 2; Milsom, *Historical Foundations of the Common Law* 19.   [60] Simpson, *A History of the Land Law* 5.

Feudalism 73

types of tenure that existed. As Milsom noted, the holding of land under tenure by a freeholder always 'was in some sense conditional upon his performance of the services due'.[61] Brian Simpson, drawing upon Thomas Blount,[62] wrote that the absence of fixed rules governing the type or nature of services meant that they ranged 'from the ludicrous to the obscene and from the onerous to the nominal', and so included such preposterous feudal services, including holding the king's seasick head during trips across the channel, making a leap, a whistle and a fart on Christmas day, and caring for falcons and hounds.[63] Overtime, however, standardisation gradually developed. Littleton in the fifteenth century classified the tenures that existed under a number of heads and his scheme has become the authoritative account.[64] Three groups of tenure can be broadly identified.[65]

The first group of tenures comprised of military services to the king. These chivalric tenures can be divided into three. The first, knight service, was originally the most important and the most self-explanatory. In the years that followed the Norman Conquest, this amounted to an obligation to fight as a knight in the royal army either in person or by providing other people to fight.[66] However, by the twelfth and thirteenth centuries it became common for those who had knight tenure not to do the actual military service themselves but to simply give money to the king so that he could recruit a professional army. This payment was known as scutage/escuage.[67] The second, castle guard, was also self-explanatory: here, the tenure was providing defence of the castles and borders of the kingdom. This tenure also became commuted to a money payment known as ward money.[68] The third chivalric tenure, grand sergeanty, was not a military service at all. It was rather a personal honorific to the king. This was typically the military tenure owed by the tenant in chief and sometimes would only need to be performed once during the king's reign, such as at the coronation. However, the tenant was obliged to perform the service themselves.[69]

The second group comprises of religious services. Tenure in frankalmoign was said to exist where land was given to churches and monasteries. The gift was said to have been given in free alms, meaning that no secular services had to be provided, and the obligation was to pray for the souls of those named in grant to and their ancestors.[70] Where the obligation was to provide divine services for the lord on certain days, such as a mass for the lord's family, this was known as the tenure by divine service. These tenures were problematic in terms of feudal theory, given that it meant that religious tenants were not obliged to provide homage (discussed later).[71] Corporations such as churches were known as a mortmain corporations; the word 'mortmain' literally meant 'dead hand', signifying how the land was in the same position as if it had been owned by the dead, since taxes and

---

[61] Milsom noted that a medieval freeholder had 'tenure in the same sense as a professor or judge today' (Milsom, *Historical Foundations of the Common Law* 104). This analogy is explored further in SFC Milsom, *A Natural History of the Common Law* (Columbia University Press, 2003) chapter 3.

[62] Thomas Blount, *Fragmenta Antiquitas: Ancient Tenures of Land and Jocular Customs of Manors* (enlarged ed., Butterworths, 1815 [1679]).

[63] Simpson, *A History of the Land Law* 6.   [64] Eugene Wambaug (ed.), *Littleton's Tenures* (John Byrne, 1903).

[65] Following Simpson, *A History of the Land Law* 7–15.   [66] Ibid. 7.

[67] There is some controversy as to whether tenure by scutage/escuage constituted a separate tenure; ibid. 8–9.   [68] Ibid. 9.

[69] Ibid. 10.   [70] Ibid. 11

[71] David Postles, 'Gifts in Frankalmoign, Warranty of Land, and Feudal Society' (1991) 50 *Cambridge Law Journal* 330, 331.

74   *The Norman Conquest (c.1066–1154)*

feudal incidents could no longer arise. As time went on, gifts in frankalmoign were simply seen as a gift to God, this could be reconciled with feudal theory in that these tenures concerned a different relationship – that between God and man.[72] Associated with frankalmoign was frankmarriage.[73] This covers gifts of land by fathers to one of his children on the occasion of their marriage. As with frankalmoign, no secular services were to be performed, at least not for a number of generations. This too was anomalous from a feudal point of view, as once again the feudal structure was forced to incorporate giving.

The final group consisted of socage tenure and its variants. These can be defined negatively as being all secular tenures other than military ones.[74] At first, socage tenures were typically agricultural. The land was given in exchange for a fixed amount of produce. However, overtime these services were exchanged for money and became an annual payment as gradually socage tenures became 'the great residual category of tenure'.[75] Other forms of tenure that may or may not be subsumed under the general heading of socage tenures included petty sergeanty, the providing of some article or equipment to the king to help with warfare, and burgage tenure, which applied in ancient boroughs where a number of 'special customs' existed, such as traders being given land under the obligation that they had to form part of a cooperation of the borough, providing its government.[76] Following the Tenures Abolition Act of 1660, all of the tenures bar grand sergeanty had been converted into socage tenures.

2   *Feudal Incidents*

The feudal tenures gave birth to the feudal incidents. Whereas the tenure services owed were frequent, the incidents were occasional. As Milsom wrote, it is important not to be misled by the word incident because 'they were as regular as death'.[77] They were triggered by certain social events and happenings and had a significant impact. The incidents were of considerable financial value to the lords and 'formed a body of legal rights enjoyed by the lord over the lands held by him, giving him on a number of occasions a share of the revenues of the lands of his tenant'.[78] The feudal incidents increased in value as time went by. Five incidents were common.[79]

The first were the ceremony of homage and the swearing of fealty, which were due when the tenant was first admitted to the land.[80] If the tenure was chivalric, then homage was taken, if the tenancy was not chivalric, then only a declaration of fealty was made. It has been suggested that oaths of fealty took place long before the Conquest.[81] The second, aids, were monetary payments from the tenant to the lord to assist him on some special occasion. Clause 12 of Magna Carta in 1215 later laid out the three occasions when this

---

[72] Ibid. 331–2.
[73] Again, there is controversy regarding whether this is a separate form of tenure; Simpson, *A History of the Land Law* 11.
[74] Wambaug, *Littleton's Tenures* 58.   [75] Simpson, *A History of the Land Law* 11.   [76] Ibid. 14.
[77] Milsom, *Historical Foundations of the Common Law* 110.   [78] Bean, *The Decline of English Feudalism* 7–8.
[79] Simpson, *A History of the Land Law* 15–20.
[80] For detailed discussion, see John Hudson, *Land, Law, and Lordship in Anglo-Norman England* (Oxford University Press, 1994) chapter 2.
[81] John, 'The Age of Edgar' 168.

Feudalism 75

could take place: the knighting of the lord's eldest son, the marriage of the lord's eldest daughter and if the lord was taken prisoner in war time. The third incident was known as relief and *primer seisin*. Relief referred to the sum of money that the tenant paid to the lord when he inherited the land.[82] *Primer seisin* was the paying of a year's income to the king when the tenant inherits from a tenant in chief who held land directly from the king.

The fourth incident, wardship and marriage, arose when the tenant in a chivalric tenure[83] died but where the heir is not of age to take over the tenure.[84] The incident of wardship saw the lord take possession of the land until the heir came of age, keeping the profits for himself.[85] The incident of marriage occurred in the same scenario, when the lord had the additional right to arrange the marriage of an underage female heir, with the effect that he could pick an acceptable tenant.[86] The fifth and final typical incident was that of escheat and forfeiture, these provided means by which the land could revert back to the lord in specified situations. Escheat *propter defectum sanguinis* applied when there was a 'defect of blood'. When the tenant died without any heirs, the land went back to the lord from whom it was held.[87] Escheat *propter delictum tenentis* covered the situation when a tenant was convicted of felony (a serious wrong), in which case it was part of the punishment that the land be taken away from him and his family and given back to the lord. Similar to this was forfeiture; this applied where the crime was treason, since this a wrong directed against the king personally, the convicted tenant lost his land, not to his immediate feudal lord but to the king.[88]

3   *Feudal Courts*

Feudalism also affected the court system, building upon the 'private' courts of the late-Anglo-Saxon period. It became understood that at each level of the pyramid, the lord was obligated to hold a court for his tenants, and that tenants were obligated to attend this court as the keepers of the customs. The King's Court, the *curia regis*, provided protection for the tenants in chief; at the county level, the tenants in chief provided protection for knights; at the level of the hundred, a manor court was operated by the knight for his tenants; and there was also a separate court for the villeins. These courts operated alongside the courts of the shire and hundred, though many of these courts had already fallen into private hands.[89]

As Maitland put it, this meant that by the beginning of the twelfth century, 'England was covered by an intricate network of local courts', each of which had a very limited sphere of jurisdiction. Each court was concerned only with the affairs of the lord's immediate social

---

[82] Simpson, *A History of the Land Law* 16.

[83] If a tenant in socage tenure died leaving an heir under age, the land would pass into the guardianship of the nearest relative, who would render all profits to the heir who would take over as lord when he came of age.

[84] The necessary ages for chivalric tenures was that sons must be 21 and that daughters must be 14 if married or 16 if unmarried; ibid. 18.

[85] Wardship was affirmed at the Assize of Northampton in 1176; Bean, *The Decline of English Feudalism* 8.

[86] Milsom, *Historical Foundations of the Common Law* 108.   [87] Simpson, *A History of the Land Law* 19.

[88] Ibid. 20. The Statute of Treason of 1353 defined 'treason' specifically in order to draw a distinction between when the land was returned to the king by forfeiture and when it was returned to the lord by escheat *propter delictum tenentis*.

[89] Frederic W Maitland, *The Forms of Action at Common Law* (Cambridge University Press, 1965 [1909]) 12.

76   *The Norman Conquest (c.1066–1154)*

inferiors. This was also true of the *curia regis*, which was composed of those summoned by the king and those who owned compulsory membership of it due to their tenure.[90] As Simpson pointed out, the role of the king was to hold court for his tenants (the tenants in chief) only and not to meddle further down the feudal ladder.[91] The scope of the royal jurisdiction and therefore the common law was 'extremely narrow' in the period immediately following 1066. As Simpson noted, 'Had this theory (if one can call it such) been maintained there could be no common law, as we know it.' The development of the common law therefore came about as a result of the rejection (or at least relaxation) of the feudal system. This was to result from the growing centralisation that was to occur in the later Norman and Angevin periods. However, the seed of what was to come was planted by William the Conqueror in 1086 on a hill top two miles north of the modern city of Salisbury.

4   *The Sarum Oath*

An important date in the development of the common law was 1 August 1086. At Sarum, William I summoned 170 of his tenants in chief and other landowning men from across England.[92] For general historians, the meeting at Sarum is of importance since it is probably where the Domesday Book was presented. The Domesday Book was an administrative triumph, cataloguing in minute detail the kingdom that William had invaded twenty years previously.[93] In many ways, the catalogue represented a second conquest. The Domesday Book was important legally. Maitland hailed it as the 'greatest legal monument of the Conqueror's reign', and as evidence that 'the Norman landowners were conceived as stepping into the exact place of the English owners whose forfeited lands had come to their hands'.[94] However, this should not be taken as evidence of a calm and peaceful transfer, given the increasingly arbitrary and oppressive nature of the Conqueror's reign.

For legal historians, however, there was a further event at Sarum that day that is of even more importance. On Salisbury Plain, the attendees all swore oaths of fealty to William that they would be faithful to him against all other men.[95] As Maitland noted, the Sarum Oath (sometimes also known as the Salisbury Oath) was taken not only from the king's 'own tenants, but from all the possessors of the land, no matter whose men they were; they were to be faithful to him against all other men, even against their lords'.[96] The Sarum Oath provided an unambiguous declaration that, despite the divided loyalties sustained by the feudal pyramid, all free men also owed allegiance to their king. The king became the 'immediate sovereign and immediate lord of every man'.[97] As Watkin has noted, 'The

---

[90] The Witan had been converted into a royal council and was slowly superseded by the *curia regis*; Hostettler, *A History of Criminal Justice in England* 41.

[91] Simpson, *A History of the Land Law* 25.

[92] Michael Swanton (ed.), *The Anglo-Saxon Chronicles* (Phoenix, 2000) 217. The event is sometimes referred to as the 'Gemōt of Sainsbury'; see, e.g., Edward A Freeman, *The History of the Norman Conquest of England* (Cambridge University Press, 2011 [1876]) vol. 4, 694.

[93] For the text, see Ann Williams and Geoffrey H Martin (eds.), *Domesday Book* (Penguin, 2002).

[94] Maitland, *The Constitutional History of England* 8–9.   [95] Pollock and Maitland, *The History of English Law* 88.

[96] Maitland, *The Constitutional History of England* 161.   [97] Freeman, *The History of the Norman Conquest of England* 695.

The Position of Slaves and Women 77

Sarum Oath may not have been intended to challenge the feudal order, but it did transverse it, for the free men of England were no longer linked to their king by a series of feudal bonds...; they now bore him direct allegiance.'[98] Maitland said that the Sarum Oath 'became fundamental law'. In the future when oaths of fealty or homage were given to any lord, it was also accepted that the tenant also owed allegiance to the king.[99]

As with many events that later generations hail as being constitutionally important, the motives behind the Sarum Oath were utterly practical. At the time, it was little more than a pragmatic attempt to keep the peace in the face of a rebellion led by William's half-bother, Odo of Bayeux. Yet, the Sarum Oath articulated (or possibly re-articulated)[100] an understanding that was to allow the common law to develop. As Simpson pointed out, the advent of the common law was to be based upon two key notions: one, the 'idea that in some sense all free tenants were the king's tenants', and second, the 'idea that the king is the fount of all justice'.[101] The first idea was formulated formally at Sarum and would become entrenched over time, with later kings routinely demanding the same oath. Simpson saw signs of the second idea in the way in which William I undertook to maintain the laws of his Anglo-Saxon predecessors. Yet, even at Sarum, this second idea was not fully articulated. The king took the loyalty of all freemen but did not offer anything in return. It was only over time that it would be fully understood that loyalty to the king would be rewarded with protection under the king's justice. For Watkin, '[T]he seeds of enhanced royal jurisdiction were sown on Salisbury Plain.'[102]

IV   The Position of Slaves and Women

Feudalism also had some unexpected effects. It improved the position of slaves but worsened the position of women. The Norman Conquest did not result in the ending of slavery but over a couple of generations the practice declined significantly.[103] John Hudson has asserted that 'slavery seems to have disappeared by 1135' but that this 'may simply have been a change in terminology'.[104] Slavery was effectively replaced with unfree peasants becoming villeins.[105] Slavery was no longer necessary where feudal discipline was strong. It no longer made economic sense; while slaves had their food provided for them by their lords, under the feudal system, the emphasis was 'squarely on the peasant's obligation to the lord'. Although it may be questioned whether villeins were in a markedly different position to slaves, John Baker argued that the popular saying that villeins owned only what they had in their bellies was a 'coarse exaggeration', in that villeins could own property at the will of the lord and have assets.[106] 'The bonds which tied them to their lords

---

[98] Watkin, *The Legal History of Wales* 89.   [99] Maitland, *The Constitutional History of England* 161.
[100] See, for instance, the second of the ten articles questionably attributed to William: 'we have decreed that all freemen shall affirm by covenant and oath, that, both in and out of England, they will be loyal to King William' (Robertson, *The Laws of Kings of England from Edmund to Henry I* 239).
[101] Simpson, *A History of the Land Law* 25–6.   [102] Watkin, *The Legal History of Wales* 89.
[103] HR Loyn, *Anglo-Saxon England and the Norman Conquest* (Longman, 1962) 326.
[104] Hudson, *The Oxford History of the Laws of England Volume II* 424.
[105] The term 'villein' originally 'bore no unpleasing connotation' and was translated as 'inhabitant of a vill' or 'villager' but as the Norman period went on, it took on an increasingly pejorative meaning.
[106] Baker, *An Introduction to English Legal History* 503.

78   *The Norman Conquest (c.1066–1154)*

were little different in practice from those which bound low-born free men to lords and masters.'[107] The decline in slavery was not only attributable to feudalism, however. Opposition from the Church also proved influential and, as David Pelteret noted, the achievement and maintenance of peace also played a significant role: '[T]he risk of enslavement through captivity and of sale into foreign hands, which had for so many centuries been a constant hazard of English life, was finally removed only when the Normans had brought the neighbouring Scots, Welsh and Irish under their hegemony and had gained control of the seas round the coast.'[108] He noted that, although slavery was not completely prohibited, there was a significant shift in moral values, with the Westminster Council of 1102 declaring that 'no one is henceforth to presume to carry on that shameful trading whereby heretofore men used in England to be sold like brute beasts'.[109]

Changes in Church teachings and the feudal changes also impacted upon the position of women.[110] However, in this context, the change was clearly retrogressive: the legal position of women worsened after 1066. Although rules differed by region, time and class throughout Anglo-Saxon England,[111] the general picture was that women (or at least those of the upper classes) could hold, inherit and sell land.[112] On marriage, land remained in their possession even if in practice it was maintained by the husband.[113] The husband paid a 'morning gift', giving part of his property to the wife, which was 'intended to guarantee her financial security and independence within marriage'.[114] Where there were children, this 'morning gift' was 'superseded by a principle of community: the wife became co-possessor with the husband of family property'.[115] There was not complete equality between the sexes: women remained 'subordinate to the guardianship and undue influence of their male relatives'.[116] However, overall, women 'were recognized – and in cases of wrongdoing penalized – as autonomous adults fully responsible for their actions'. While marriage was 'most likely the preferred state for Anglo-Saxon women', there were various occupations that could be pursued instead of or alongside married life.[117] Women had the same *wergild* (the monetary value placed on a person's life) as men of their rank, and were just as eligible to receive *wergild* payments as men.[118] Anglo-Saxon women could be litigants and oath-givers and were held accountable for their own crimes: they 'were their own creatures and not merely appendages to their husbands'.[119]

As Doris Stenton noted, the Norman Conquest changed all this:

The evidence which has survived from Anglo-Saxon England indicates that women were then more nearly the equal companions of their husbands and brothers than at any other period before the

---

[107] Ibid.   [108] David Pelteret, 'Slave Raiding and Slave Trading in Early England' (2008) 9 *Anglo-Saxon England* 99, 114.

[109] Ibid. 113.   [110] See Christine Fell, *Women in Anglo Saxon England and the Impact of 1066* (Wiley-Blackwell, 1986).

[111] Shelia C Dietrich, 'An Introduction to Women in Anglo-Saxon Society' in Barbara Kanner (ed.), *The Women of England: From Anglo-Saxon Times to the Present* (Mansell Publishing, 1980) 32.

[112] Christine G Clark, 'Women's Rights in Early England' (1995) *Brigham Young University Law Review* 205.

[113] Marc A Meyer, 'Land Charters and the Legal Position of Anglo-Saxon Women' in Kanner, *The Women of England: From Anglo-Saxon Times to the Present* 57, 61–2.

[114] Fell, *Women in Anglo Saxon England and the Impact of 1066* 16.

[115] Maeve E Doggett, *Marriage, Wife-Beating and the Law in Victorian England* (Weidenfeld and Nicolson, 1992) 71.

[116] Andrew Rabin, *Crime and Punishment in Anglo-Saxon England* (Cambridge University Press, 2020) 41.

[117] Clark, 'Women's Rights in Early England' 217.   [118] Ibid. 220.   [119] Ibid. 221.

modern age. In the higher ranges of society this rough and ready partnership was ended by the Norman Conquest, which introduced into England a military society relegating women to a position honourable but essentially unimportant.[120]

This occurred not only because Norman society was 'a society organized for war' and so 'was essentially a man's world', but also because the Normans brought with them the principle that on marriage the guardianship and legal control of the wife was vested in the husband.[121] Land ownership became a male prerogative, with the principle of primogeniture meaning that land was passed on to male heirs.[122] A woman became either the responsibility of her father or her husband, with heiresses and widows being freely sold to the highest bidders or friends of the lord.[123] The doctrine of coverture or 'marital unity' developed as the centuries went on: on marriage, husband and wife became one person (or one flesh) and this meant that 'a woman's property and income became her husband's on marriage'.[124] Under coverture, a married woman's legal rights and property became invested in her husband. A married woman was unable to bring litigation, plead in the courts or control land. This doctrine of coverture was to exert a considerable influence over centuries, disadvantaging and excluding women.

V   Conclusions

Determining cause and effect in legal history is a complex matter. There is unlikely to be a singular straight line of cause and effect moving forwards in a measured and considered way. Yet, the benefit of hindsight tempts us into drawing such straight lines because we know what the end point is (or at least what the current position is, which we assume is the end point). One way of overcoming this risk of adopting an evolutionary functionalist approach is to adopt a counterfactual analysis.[125] Counterfactual legal history asks the 'what if' question; it traces what would have been the outcome if a different path had been taken. Comparison of this alternative timeline with what actually happened can shed light upon the effect of the variable in question. So, a counterfactual approach to the question of the origins of common law could return to Maitland's comment about the Norman Conquest being 'a catastrophe which determines the whole future history of English law',[126] and could ask what would have happened to English law had the Norman Conquest not taken place. This could involve asking, for instance: whether the private courts that emerged at the end of the Anglo-Saxon period would had resulted in a feudal system anyway, how would that feudal system have differed in a realm that did not focus as much on military power, and what consequences might that have had upon the position of slaves, women's rights and the growing powers of the king? Such questions would at least make us rethink the relationship between cause and effect, highlight that other possibilities could have happened and show that what did happen was by no means inevitable.

---

[120] Doris M Stenton, *The English Woman in History* (Allen and Unwin, 1987) 28.
[121] Doggett, *Marriage, Wife-Beating and the Law in Victorian England* 72.
[122] Clark, 'Women's Rights in Early England' 227.   [123] Ibid. 232, 227.
[124] Sharon Thompson, *Prenuptial Agreements and the Presumption of Free Choice* (Hart, 2015) 40.
[125] See Sandberg, *Subversive Legal History* chapter 6.   [126] Pollock and Maitland, *The History of English Law* 79.

The Norman Conquest (c.1066–1154)

Whether or not a counterfactual analysis is used, answering the question of the effect of William the Conqueror upon law and order in England is by no means straightforward. On the one hand, the reign of William I simply saw the continuation of the moves towards centralisation found in the late Anglo-Saxon period. Feudalism ensured that justice remained mostly a local affair. As Maitland put it, 'The king's own court was but a court for the protection of royal rights, a court for the causes of the king's barons, and an ultimate tribunal at which a persistent litigant might perhaps arrive when justice had failed him everything else.'[127] Although there were some innovations, most notably those that occurred at Sarum, William I was a great administrator rather than a great legislator. William's reign focused on order rather than law. His focus was on keeping control of the country that he had conquered. The way in which he did that was to make England more of a military country, as shown by trial by battle and the close control provided by feudalism. A major act of centralisation came with the Sarum Oath, but perhaps this was little more than a symbol, reflecting an idea that had long persisted in the idea of the king's peace.

Ironically, having received the allegiance of the English people at Sarum, William left to Normandy never to return. He died the following year, leaving an England that had been in many respects transformed, with a new ruling class that was now firmly in place. However, in many respects, the centralisation that William's reign advanced was already a characteristic of the late Anglo-Saxon period, and the feudal focus on local justice prevented rather than caused the development of a truly common law.

The reigns of the Norman kings that followed William had a mixed impact upon the development of the common law. On the Conqueror's death, William's eldest son, Robert, took Normandy, while the English crown found itself on the head of William Rufus, the Conqueror's second eldest son. The reign of William II was characterised by rebellions, with the only real innovation in governance being the appointment of Ranulf Flambard as his agent in legal and financial affairs.[128] The role played by Flambard was effectively that of the Chief Justiciar, a role roughly equivalent to that later played by the prime minister. This position of Chief Justiciar became formalised during the reign of Henry I, William Rufus' younger brother.

In addition to reuniting England and Normandy, the reign of Henry I saw a number of important developments in the governance of England.[129] On his accession, Henry again purchased the support of the people by means of a charter.[130] The Coronation Charter stated that 'I restore to you the law of King Edward with all the reforms which my father introduced with the consent of the Barons.'[131] Henry's reign saw the formalisation of the financial system: written record became kept and sheriffs rendered the shire accounts twice a year at an 'Exchequer', which became fixed at Westminster.[132] The Exchequer became

---

[127] Frederic W Maitland and Francis C Montague, *A Sketch of English Law* (GP Putnam's Sons, 1915 [1899]) 30.
[128] Ann Lyon, *Constitutional History of the United Kingdom* (2nd ed., Routledge, 2016) 35.
[129] For a full discussion, see Green, *The Government of England under Henry I.*
[130] Maitland, *The Constitutional History of England* 9.
[131] Robertson, *The Laws of Kings of England from Edmund to Henry I* 283.
[132] The earliest surviving pipe rolls, records of the crown's revenue, dates from this time, 1131; Maitland, *The Constitutional History of England* 9–10.

Conclusions 81

one of the two major administrative offices alongside the chancellor. The origins of the role of chancellor are disputed, but it is thought that the role came into existence before the Norman Conquest, with the chancellor playing a key role on the King's Council as the keeper of the king's conscience. The Royal Chancery, comprising the chancellor and a small group of scribes, issued royal orders, authenticated with the king's seal.[133] These were known as writs and, in the words of Hudson, this 'practice was an important if limited precursor to the more precise writs introduced in the Angevin period'. Royal justice also became more formalised. A permanent tribunal, a group of justiciars presided over by a Chief Justiciar, became apparent and from time to time members of this tribunal were sent to the counties to hear cases.[134] As royal justice became mobile, litigants began to see the attractions of bringing their disputes before this tribunal. The mechanisms whereby a common law could eventually develop had been tentatively put in place.

Yet, these developments were not complete and the direction of travel was not linear. This is shown in the text *Leges Henrici Primi*, which claimed to be a collection of laws in effect in England at this time.[135] Thought to be written in around 1115–18,[136] the text is a disorderly hodgepodge of rules from the Anglo-Saxon and Norman periods. As Hyams noted, although this as a 'royalist legal treatise', written 'in a society in which total authority proclaimed itself the guardian of order and the prime dispenser of royal justice', nevertheless it 'is striking to find that the author, despite a persistent effort to put royal justice first, nevertheless felt that feud persisted and still required regulation by the law and some extended and not unsympathetic treatment from him'.[137]

The *Leges* paints an uncertain picture of how far English law had advanced. Most well-known is the appearance in the *Leges* of the Latin maxim *'reum non facit nisi mens rea'*, translated by Downer as 'a person is not to be considered guilty unless he has a guilty intention'.[138] This principle, commonly dated to St Augustine and found in canon law, was to become the cornerstone of English criminal law: the notion that for a person to be found liable for a crime, it needed to be proven that they had not only committed the prohibited act (the *actus reus*) but also had the guilty mind prescribed for the offence (*mens rea*). However, Maitland has argued that this was not a statement of general application in the *Leges* but rather related only to perjury.[139] This is supported by the numbering: this rule is found at 5.28b, while 5.28 and 5.28a are concerned with perjury, as are the surrounding provisions. Indeed, the *Leges* include a number of contradictory statements about legal responsibility. Some suggest that people were culpable for accidents. According to 88.6: 'If a person in the course of a game of archery or of some exercise kills anyone with a spear or as the result of some accident of this king, he shall pay compensation for him'; while 88.6a recasts this as a general principle, stating: 'For it is a rule of law that a person who unwittingly commits a wrong shall consciously make amends.'[140] Yet, 90.11 reads: 'There

---

[133] Hudson, *The Oxford History of the Laws of England Volume II* 270–1.
[134] Pollock and Maitland, *The History of English Law* 108–9.
[135] The modern translation is LJ Downer (ed.), *Leges Henrici Primi* (Oxford University Press, 1972).
[136] LJ Downer, 'Introduction' in Downer, *Leges Henrici Primi* 1, 9.
[137] Hyams, *Rancor & Reconciliation in Medieval England* 137.   [138] Downer, *Leges Henrici Primi* 95.
[139] Pollock and Maitland, *The History of English Law* 476.   [140] Downer, *Leges Henrici Primi* 271.

82 — The Norman Conquest (c.1066–1154)

are very many kinds of misfortune which occur by accident rather than by design and which should be dealt with by the application of mercy rather than by formal judgement.'[141] Again, seeds had been sown and the benefit of hindsight seduces us into interpreting such provisions as being more important than they may have been at the time.

What is more certain is that Henry's death put all developments on hold. The absence of a male heir had meant that Henry had named his daughter Matilda as his heir and had required his tenants in chief to recognise this.[142] However, on Henry's death, these pre-emptive moves proved futile. Henry's nephew Stephen rushed to Westminster to seize the throne. The next nineteen years saw civil war erupt between Stephen and Matilda, a period known as the Anarchy. Unsurprisingly, little evidence survives of royal government during the constantly disputed reign of Stephen. However, the compromise that was eventually reached was to have momentous ramifications for English law. In 1153, the Treaty of Wallingford was agreed that stipulated that Stephen could keep the crown for his lifetime, but on his death, it was to pass to Matilda's son, Henry. Within a year, Stephen was dead and the English crown had passed to a new dynasty, known to historians as the Plantagenets, who were to rule the realm until the death of Richard II on Bosworth Field in 1485. It has been customary for historians to divide the Plantagenet dynasty into smaller groups. The first such group, labelled the Angevins, comprised of the first three Plantagenet kingships. It was the reign of the first Angevin king, Henry II (1154–89), that would prove particularly important to the development of English law. It was under Henry Plantagenet that the common law fully emerged, developing the centralising mechanisms put in place under the Normans, especially the short-lived developments under his namesake Henry I. The next chapter will turn to the reign of Henry II, who is often regarded as the father of the common law.

---

[141] Ibid. 283. [142] Lyon, *Constitutional History of the United Kingdom* 39.

'Under Henry II the exceptional becomes normal. He places royal justice at the disposal of anyone who can bring his case within a certain formula'.

Frederic W Maitland, *The Forms of Action at Common Law* (Cambridge University Press, 1965 [1909]) 21.

5

The Father of the Common Law (c.1154–1215)

I Introduction

Henry II (1154–89) is often hailed as the father of the common law. However, he was neither its biological parent nor its creator. Under his reign, the ideas and structures that had already emerged during the Anglo-Saxon and Norman periods were cultivated and adapted in order to develop a common law that was systematic, universal, seemingly autonomous and self-perpetuating. Through marriage and diplomacy, Henry became head of an empire that ranged all the way down from Scotland to Spain. And the context of the civil war in the years prior to his reign meant that, like William the Conqueror before him, the new king's main purpose was to maintain order. However, unlike William, the way in which Henry II sought to maintain such order was through law. It was his reign that saw the opening up of the royal courts to all free men. These courts were to become common to all and their law was to become the common law. Henry II should be hailed as the nurturer of the common law.

Frederic W Maitland's account of legal history emphasised the importance of the reign of Henry II. He stated that it was 'of supreme importance in the history of our law'.[1] Indeed, it has been suggested that the 'presentation of Henry II as founder of the common law' was Maitland's 'chief impact upon the teaching of history'.[2] However, although Maitland referred to Henry II as 'a great legislator and a great administrator', he conceded that Henry followed his Norman predecessors in not being a prolific legislator.[3] Like William the Conqueror before him, it was 'as an organizer and governor rather than as a legislator that Henry was active'.[4] The 'supreme importance' of his reign lay in the reforms enacted that further centralised power. Henry was concerned with creating 'new devices for enforcing the law', and this was achieved 'in an informal fashion without the pomp of legislation'. Changes in procedure were experimented with, often introduced by just a few words written or spoken by the king to his justices, meaning that there is now a 'lamentable

---

[1] Frederick Pollock and Frederic W Maitland, *The History of English Law* (2nd ed., Cambridge University Press, 1968 [1898]) vol. 1, 136.
[2] James R Cameron, *Frederick William Maitland and the History of English Law* (University of Oklahoma, 1961) 19.
[3] Frederic W Maitland, *The Constitutional History of England* (Cambridge University Press, 1941 [1908]) 10.
[4] Pollock and Maitland, *The History of English Law* 136.

86   *The Father of the Common Law (c.1154–1215)*

lack of documentary evidence'. What is clear, however, is that several of the king's experiments worked and proved durable, becoming part and parcel of the common law for centuries to come.

The reign was characterised by piecemeal and pragmatic developments. One of Henry II's first actions was to issue a Charter of Liberties to confirm the law and customs of his grandfather Henry I. And many of Henry II's innovations built upon those of his grandfather. As Maitland put it, what was once exceptional, now became normal.[5] However, it would be wrong to paint Henry Plantagenet as being satisfied with simply retaining the status quo. The order achieved under the Normans had been lost during the Anarchy. In particular, the Church and its courts system had become increasingly powerful, filling the vacuum left by the weakened State.[6] This meant that Henry II now sought to curb the Church's power, resurrecting the old boundaries between the courts of the Church and the courts of the king. This led to the event for which Henry II is probably best remembered: the Becket controversy.

This chapter will begin by examining the Becket controversy but will then move on to argue that it is for other developments that Henry Plantagenet's reign should be remembered. Section III will explore the developments to the legal system that occurred during this reign and that allowed for a common law to develop and be regularised. Doris Stenton referred to this and the development of the writ system as the 'Angevin leap forward'.[7] Section IV will explore in detail the origins of the writ system, following Maitland's legendary account of *The Forms of Action*, as well as the revisions and criticisms put forward by SFC Milsom in one of the major contributions to legal history in recent times. The importance of Henry II's reign will be assessed in the Conclusion, which will also briefly examine the reigns of his sons, Richard I (1189–99) and John (1199–216), although Magna Carta in 1215 will be left to the next chapter. The focus here is to assess the extent and significance of the 'Angevin leap forward', to determine the extent to which Henry II really was the father of the common law and whether Maitland's account of the origins of the common law still stands up.

II   The Becket Controversy

In 1162, when appointing a new Archbishop of Canterbury, Henry appointed his then chancellor Thomas Becket, with the intention of turning 'his faithful chancellor into his faithful archbishop'.[8] However, this intention was thwarted as the new archbishop clashed with the king over the payment of debts from Church lands, the perceived 'inordinate and irregular prosecution of the laity for moral offences' and the problem of the treatment of 'criminous clerks', that is, priests and others accused of committing serious felonies who claimed 'benefit of clergy' so that they could be tried in the Church courts rather than in the

---

[5] Frederic W Maitland, *The Forms of Action at Common Law* (Cambridge University Press, 1965 [1909]) 21.
[6] Maitland, *The Constitutional History of England* 10–11; Frank Barlow, *Thomas Becket* (Phoenix, 1986) 68.
[7] Doris M Stenton, *English Justice between the Norman Conquest and the Great Charter* (Allen & Unwin, 1965) chapter 2.
[8] Barlow, *Thomas Becket* 67. Becket was not even an ordained priest: Ann Lyon, *Constitutional History of the United Kingdom* (2nd ed., Routledge, 2016) 46.

The Becket Controversy 87

common law courts. This was to provoke a famous controversy between Church and State, which would have ramifications for centuries to come.

The dispute eventually culminated in the Constitutions of Clarendon, issued by Henry in 1164. These constitutions, confirmed by the bishops and the barons, curbed the powers of the Church and restored much of the distinction between ecclesiastical and civil courts that had been introduced by William the Conqueror. For instance, most disputes about land were not to be heard in the Church courts and judicial appeals to the papacy were to be limited.[9] In relation to 'criminous clerks', clause 3 was interpreted by Maitland as follows:[10] every serious felony was both a breach of the king's law and also a breach of the law of the Church. A criminous clerk would be summoned before the King's Court and was to answer there for the breach of the King's peace and for the felony. If they proved their clerical status, then they would be sent to the Church court without any trial. At the Church court, the clerk would answer to the breach of Church law and there would be a trial. If the Church court found the clerk guilty, then they would degrade him and the Church would no longer protect him. This would mean that he would be brought back to the King's Court but as a layman and so would be punished. As Maitland put it, the system was 'accusation and plea in the temporal court; trial, conviction and degradation in the ecclesiastical court; sentence in the temporal court to the layman's punishment'.[11]

The Constitutions of Clarendon were not the end of the conflict between the king and his archbishop, however, with Becket refusing to accept this compromise.[12] The clash eventually culminated in 1170 with the murder of Becket in Canterbury Cathedral, apparently on the instructions from Henry: 'Will no man rid me of this turbulent priest!' This murder shocked both the kingdom and the king, with a repentant Henry flagellating himself before the Church and surrendering several points achieved at Clarendon.[13] Yet, as Maitland concluded, Henry was generally successful in that a 'steady and vigorous ... line was drawn between the temporal and the spiritual spheres'. A 'debateable border land' still existed between Church and State but the line between the two came to be policed by writs of prohibition issued by the King's Court against the exercise of jurisdiction in a particular case by a Church court, bringing the matter to the common law courts.[14]

The Becket controversy showed the tensions between Church and State, with the Catholic Church seeking its authority from the Pope in Rome rather than the king of England. These tensions existed and were largely successfully managed in the Norman and Plantagenet eras but, as we will see, would come to a head under the Tudors. However, the controversy is also important because not only did it curb the growth of the Church courts, which had taken advantage of the Anarchy, but it also showed how far what we would call the criminal justice system had come. The Becket controversy typically overshadows Henry II's other achievements. The image of the repentant king wearing a hair shirt lingers. Yet, the controversy only came about and was only resolved largely in the favour of the

---

[9] Barlow, *Thomas Becket* 101.
[10] Frederic W Maitland, *Roman Canon Law in the Church of England* (Methuen & Co., 1898) 135.   [11] Ibid.
[12] See Harold Berman, *Law and Revolution* (Harvard University Press, 1983) chapter 7.
[13] Maitland, *The Constitutional History of England* 10–11
[14] Russell Sandberg, *Law and Religion* (Cambridge University Press, 2011) 22.

88 The Father of the Common Law (c.1154–1215)

king's system of justice because of the advances in the administration of royal justice achieved by the first Plantagenet king.

III   The Angevin Advance

Henry II is often referred to as the father of the common law because his reign saw the completion of the process whereby the king's peace covered the whole of England. By the end of his reign, there was a common law and, as RC van Caenegem noted, 'royal justice functioned in two ways: either the country came to it or it went to the country'.[15] Although both methods had existed prior to Henry II's reign, it was during this period that they stabilised and became the norm. Henry II's reign saw the revitalisation of the sending of justices around the kingdom to preside over courts. In Henry I's reign, the justices had from time to time been sent to the counties to hear cases. However, such visitations had ceased under the reign of Stephen. Under Henry II, this system of itinerant royal justices became embedded. At the same time, the King's Court became more centralised and professional. As the next section will explore, the development of the writ system gave people access to justice in the feudal courts and also increasingly in the King's Court.

The sending of royal justices to the localities, variously known as the 'justices in eyre', itinerant royal justices and most amusingly the 'wandering eyre', was a practice that dated back at least as far as the Conquest. However, at first, their role was not distinctively judicial. They provided an 'inquest' of what was happening at the local level. This is the process by which the Doomsday Book was written. However, there were two important landmarks that consolidated the process: the Assize of Clarendon of 1166 and the Assize of Northampton of 1176. The meaning of the word 'assize' seems to have shifted during this period: it was used variously to describe the particular sitting of the king and his barons at a particular place, the ordinance agreed at such a session, and institutions created by such an ordinance.[16] Here, the term has its second meaning: the two Assizes of Clarendon and Northampton were ordinances; indeed, today, we would call them legislation.

Henry held an assize at Clarendon, probably in early 1166, assembling together the barons to issue an ordinance that became known as the Assize of Clarendon. As Maitland noted, it is unclear whether the terms of this ordinance was 'intended to be a permanent measure ... but it was sufficiently new and stringent to require the consent of the magnates'.[17] It established a mechanism so that an inquest to would carried out whereby 'twelve of the most lawful men of the hundred' would declare under oath whether 'there had been an man who, since the lord king had been king, had been charged or published as being a robber, a murder or thief; or anyone who is harbourer or robbers or murderers or thieves'.[18] Those found to be robbers, murders or thieves were then to undergo the ordeal of cold water. The Assize also made it clear that the justices were present to 'do their law', and that no defence is to be permitted to those of whose guilt there is direct proof.[19]

---

[15] RC van Caenegem, *Royal Writs in England from the Conquest to Glanvill* (Selden Society, 1959) 19.
[16] Maitland, *The Constitutional History of England* 12.   [17] Pollock and Maitland, *The History of English Law* 137.   [18] Ibid.
[19] Naomi D Hurnard, 'The Jury of Presentment and the Assize of Clarendon' (1941) 56(223) *The English Historical Review* 374, 396.

The Assize of Clarendon is therefore often taken to have established three main developments. First, it abolished compurgation in the case of the serious offences mentioned and replaced it with ordeal of cold water.[20] Second, it established or re-established the practice whereby in cases of serious wrongs, justices went into the locality to try defendants.[21] Justices were to check that the sheriffs were appropriately administering royal justice. Sheriffs and county justices now had to hold inquiries into all serious wrongs (murders, thefts and robberies), naming the criminals. Third, it established what is known as the 'accusing jury', 'jury of presentment' or 'the recognition', whereby a group of twelve was required to name individuals who had committed serious offences and answered a set of questions (later to be known as the articles of eyre because it was given to the presenting jury by the justices in eyre) on specific serious offences that had been committed.[22] Margaret Kerr commented that this 'instituted a form of public prosecution'.[23] The system had two aspects: the reporting of crimes that have been committed and the prosecution of the suspected criminals.[24] The role of these presenting juries was to determine whether the accused person should be released or proceed to trial by ordeal. As Maitland noted, this development introduced the 'germs of trial by jury: the old modes of trial, the ordeals and the judicial combat, begin to yield before the oath of a body of witnesses'.[25] However, this still differed from the modern jury since the presenting jury members 'were asked to swear, at least ostensibly, on what they knew to be true, rather than what they judged to be true after weighing up the evidence presented to them'.[26] Moreover, the presenting juries did not issue final verdicts.[27] This would only begin to occur after 1215, when the Church stopped supporting the ordeals leading to the development of the trial jury (or 'petty jury').

As Naomi D Hurnard has noted, it is commonly assumed that 'the jury of presentment was introduced into England by the Assize of Clarendon in 1166' but this assumption is 'due to the influence of Maitland'.[28] A different interpretation is to see the assize as at most institutionalising the concept of neighbourhood reputation, used in England since at least the eleventh century.[29] Indeed, there are references to the role of twelve local men playing a role in the administrative of justice in the laws of Æthelred,[30] and the Constitutions of

---

[20] John Hostettler, *A History of Criminal Justice in England and Wales* (Waterside Press, 2009) 19.

[21] John Briggs, Christopher Harrison, Angus McInnes and David Vincent, *Crime and Punishment in England: An Introductory History* (UCL Press, 1996) 8.

[22] Paul R Hyams, *Rancor & Reconciliation in Medieval England* (Cornell University Press, 2003).

[23] However, trial by ordeal under the Assize of Clarendon 'could not be imposed on offenders who were appealed; the appeal took precedence and appellees were entitled to all the benefits of inefficiency that the appeal conferred'. This meant that Henry took steps to reform the appeal, largely though fines: this included 'fining appellors for abandoning their appeals (from 1165 to 1166, in various forms), requiring appellors to obtain sureties for prosecution (from 1167 to 1168), and fining appellors for settling appeals without permission of the royal court (from 1182–83)' (Margaret H Kerr, 'Angevin Reform of the Appeal of Felony' (1995) 13(2) *Law and History Review* 351, 352, 382, 383).

[24] Hurnard, 'The Jury of Presentment and the Assize of Clarendon' 378.

[25] Maitland, *The Constitutional History of England* 13.

[26] William Eves, 'Justice Delayed: Absent Recognitors and the Angevin Legal Reforms, c1200' in Travis R Baker (ed.), *Law and Society in Later Medieval England and Ireland* (Routledge, 2018) 1, 1.

[27] Ibid. 22. [28] Hurnard, 'The Jury of Presentment and the Assize of Clarendon' 374.

[29] Hyams, *Rancor & Reconciliation in Medieval England* 159.

[30] 'And a court shall be held in every wapentake, and the twelve leading thegns along with the reeve shall go out and swear on the relics ... that they will not accuse any innocent man or shield any guilty one' (Agnes J Robertson, *The Laws of Kings of England from Edmund to Henry I* (Cambridge University Press, 1925) 65).

Clarendon provided that where a layman was so powerful that 'no one wishes of dares to accuse them, the sheriff, being requested by the bishop, shall cause twelve lawful men of the neighbourhood or town to swear in the presence of the bishop that they will make manifest the truth in this matter, according to their conscience'. Seen in this light, the presenting jury built upon the communal responsibility found in tithing units and frankpledge.[31] Indeed, 'Pollock and Maitland' actually states that 'in 1166 the accusing jury becomes prominent'.[32] This suggests that it was not a totally new phenomenon. Moreover, the 1166 Assize did not result in the development of a public prosecution system immediately. As Paul Hyams noted, '[A] royal monopoly of illicit violence and response to wrong remained at least a distant goal in 1166.'[33] Yet, the Assize of Clarendon 'marked a significant procedural change' by entrenching the presenting jury and cementing further the role of wandering justices.[34]

This was built upon by the Assize of Northampton of 1176. This reinstated the contents of the Assize of Clarendon on a permanent basis.[35] It provided that those 'charged before the justices of the lord king' would be tried 'by the oath of twelve knights of the hundred, and if knights are not present, by the oath of twelve free, legal men'. The list of serious offences was expanded to also include forgery and arson. As Hyams noted, the Northampton Assize 'groups its offenses under the general heading of *felonia*, although the word had not figured at all in the received text of the 1166 assize'.[36] The king's peace came to cover all felonies. As Thomas A Green has noted: 'No longer were there botless and emendable felonies; all were capital.'[37] By the fourteenth century, the word 'indictment' referred to the written accusation that had come from a public enquiry into recent crimes.[38] Indictment by presentment of a jury became the normal way of prosecuting criminals, rather than the appeal initiated by the victim. The presenting body became known as the 'grand jury'.

The Assize of Northampton of 1176 also divided the land into six circuits of justices in eyre. The realm was split into six circuits, with six groups of three justices travelling the country.[39] The justices took all of the disputes that arose in a shire when they were there, dealing with all pleas. This gave people an experience of and an appetite for royal justice. As time went on, the king's wandering eyre ensured that justice became common throughout the land. This system became consolidated in the thirteenth century into a single system known as the assizes, the assize courts or the county assizes. This assize system lasted until 1971. Its immediate consequence, however, was to weaken the influence of the local elite by removing their influence in criminal justice. For Hyams, they represented 'the most important royal intervention of the whole Angevin reform into English social arrangements' and 'through them Henry and his advisers made a firm bid for the mastery of the public sphere of his realm'.[40]

---

[31] Elizabeth Papp Kamali, *Felony and the Guilty Mind in Medieval England* (Cambridge University Press, 2019) 20.
[32] Pollock and Maitland, *The History of English Law* 152. [33] Hyams, *Rancor & Reconciliation in Medieval England* 161.
[34] Kamali, *Felony and the Guilty Mind in Medieval England* 21. [35] Pollock and Maitland, *The History of English Law* 149.
[36] Hyams, *Rancor & Reconciliation in Medieval England* 157.
[37] Thomas A Green, 'The Jury and the English Law of Homicide, 1200–1600' (1976) 74 *Michigan Law Review* 413, 418.
[38] See John H Baker, *An Introduction to English Legal History* (5th ed., Oxford University Press, 2019) 545.
[39] Van Caenegem, *Royal Writs in England from the Conquest to Glanvill* 29.
[40] Hyams, *Rancor & Reconciliation in Medieval England* 157.

The Angevin Advance 91

These developments collectively saw the centralisation of justice: for Maitland, law became common to the whole land as local variations were gradually suppressed and 'the king's own court became ever more and more a court of first instance for all men and all causes'.[41] In addition to royal justice being throughout the country, the King's Court also became centralised, sitting at Westminster. The Court of Exchequer was also strengthened and the office of justiciar was re-established.[42] However, it is important not to overplay this trend towards centralisation. Maitland warned that given the king's penchant for experimenting and the informal way in which such experiments were made, it is difficult to define the structural changes that took place, not least because the benefit of hindsight means that 'we are tempted to use terms which are more precise than those that were current in the twelfth century'.[43] For instance, talk of *the* King's Court as a definite article is inaccurate given that at this time any court held in the king's name would take this title. Yet, by the end of Henry's reign, it is clear that there was indeed 'a permanent central tribunal of persons expert in the administration of justice'.[44] As Maitland put it, '[I]n addition to each court held by itinerant justices, known as a *curia Regis,* there now exists a centralised permanent court, a *capitalis curia Regis.*'[45]

A professional judiciary also emerged, headed by the Chief Justiciar, 'the great permanent dignity with vice-regal powers and the responsibility – after the king – for the functioning of royal justice, with the right to preside at every court'.[46] The increase in judicial business soon proved too much for the traditional King's Court of the king and his barons. And so, in 1178, a permanent deputation from the King's Court of five justices, two clerks and three laymen was appointed to deal with the mass of the ordinary litigation: the birth of the Court of Common Pleas.[47] As time went on, a division occurred: the King's Bench would deal with pleas where there was a royal interest, where the action was 'against the peace of our lord the king'; while the Court of Common Pleas would deal with everything else – those pleas not concerning royal rights. By the thirteenth century, the justices of the King's Court were no longer politicians but were judges.[48]

However, as Maitland warned, it is important to note that this was a piecemeal process: there was still no general principle that the King's Courts were there 'to provide a remedy for every wrong'.[49] These processes were not linear. The developments often seen as consolidating the common law were experiments focused on maintaining order. The fact that many developments were administrative changes, the fact that many of the texts of the relatively few legislative changes were lost, and the gradual and ad hoc nature of reform all mean that dating the developments in this era is difficult.[50] Moreover, while accounts often focus separately on developments in land law and wider changes to the administration of justice,[51] this is to apply modern distinctions that did not apply at the time, since many disputes and suggestions of wrongdoing were frequently caused by competition for land.[52]

---

[41] Maitland, *The Constitutional History of England* 13.   [42] Briggs et al., *Crime and Punishment in England* 8.
[43] Pollock and Maitland, *The History of English Law* 153.   [44] Ibid.   [45] Ibid. 154.
[46] Van Caenegem, *Royal Writs in England from the Conquest to Glanvill* 29.   [47] Ibid. 30.
[48] Maitland, *The Forms of Action at Common Law* 16–17.   [49] Ibid. 10.
[50] John Hudson, *The Oxford History of the Laws of England Volume II: 871–1216* (Oxford University Press, 2012) 509.
[51] Hostettler, *A History of Criminal Justice in England and Wales* 43.
[52] Hyams, *Rancor & Reconciliation in Medieval England* 156.

Yet, by the end of Henry II's reign, the common law had been transformed. Private compensation or even feud violence had given way to the public prosecution of serious offences.[53] And as Hyams has noted, Henry and his advisers had won 'the battle of ideas':

> They made a serious attempt to redefine actionable wrongs in such a way as to extend royal control over more local conflict than before. One important consequence was to initiate a move towards that equation of royal justice with public justice, which lies at the core of our Anglo-American notion of the common law.[54]

A decisive step in this direction was made by the development of the writ system in Henry's reign. The people from the shires had no right to be tried at Westminster and so had to obtain special permission. They achieved such permission in the form of a royal writ. These writs provided what Milsom has referred to as a 'ticket' to royal justice:[55] the writ allowed litigants to go to the royal court. If a claimant could make their case fit one of the writs, then they could seek royal justice. As Maitland put it, Henry II had placed 'royal justice at the disposal of anyone who can bring his case within a certain formula'.[56] The settlement of disputes resolved 'not upon the application of rules but upon making an acceptable claim by means of the correct writ'.[57] As the next section will discuss, a multitude of writs came to exist, each relating to a distinct factual scenario. Each writ would begin a particular 'form of action', a particular legal claim. This writ system would become the 'key-stone' of the 'system of centralised justice'.[58] It would also give rise the rules of the common law, though for now, substantive rules of the common law existed only implicitly in the writ formula.

IV   The Writ System

The origins of the common law are to be found in the development of what we now call land law. Land is, of course, important to most societies throughout history. It was, however, particularly important in medieval England. In the early medieval period, land rather than money was the currency of the realm. This was shown by the fact that the Norman invasion was based in part on the promise of land for William the Conqueror's supporters. It is therefore unsurprising that the first developments of the common law were in relation to landholding.[59] Questions about landholding were to prove crucial to the development of the common law in two ways. First, as we saw in the previous chapter, the Normans introduced into England the feudal system that defined social ties and obligations, and was based on the giving of land in return for services and loyalty. This mutual obligation led to the development of feudal courts. Second, as we have just mentioned, one of the key ways in which the common law developed was through the writ system, which developed in the

---

[53] Ibid. 229–30.   [54] Ibid. 185.

[55] SFC Milsom, 'Trespass from Henry III to Edward III: Part 2: Special Writs' (1958) 74 *Law Quarterly Review* 407, 435.

[56] Maitland, *The Forms of Action at Common Law* 21.

[57] Norman Doe, *Fundamental Authority in Late Medieval English Law* (Cambridge University Press, 1990) 1.

[58] Florence E Harmer, *Anglo-Saxon Writs* (Manchester University Press, 1952) 3.

[59] Hudson has noted that this prominence also 'reflects in part the concerns of post-medieval lawyers and also political thinkers' interest in the nature of "property"' (John Hudson, *The Formation of the English Common Law* (2nd ed., Routledge 2018) 73).

reign of Henry II. It allowed people to enforce their rights at the royal courts. Maitland's legendary account of the writ system – outlined in his lectures on *The Forms of Action at Common Law*,[60] which were published after his death – showed that the first of these writs concerned the legal ownership of land.[61]

Both the feudal system and the writ system exerted significant influence upon the development of English law, and not only in relation to land law. Maitland noted since under feudalism 'a great part of public rights and duties are inextricably interwoven with the tenure of land', it followed that 'it is utterly impossible to speak of our medieval constitution except in terms of our medieval land law'.[62] He also commented that the full history of the writ system would be 'a full history of English private law'.[63] Indeed, although both systems have now been abolished in whole or in part, they continue to exert influence over English law today. Although most of the feudal pyramid was demolished by the Tenures Abolition Act of 1660, the top two layers continue to survive. Owners of property today are tenants in chief; they continue to hold the land from the crown.[64] And, although the writ system was abolished by the Common Law Procedure Act 1852, we still think in terms of legal actions. As Maitland famously commented in his lectures: 'The forms of action we have buried, but they still rule us from their graves.'[65]

However, these two systems – the feudal system and the writ system – were at odds with each other. Put simply, the development of a common law fostered by the centralised writ system was contrary to the promotion of local justice under feudalism. In the twentieth century, Maitland's account of the writ system was criticised by Milsom for underplaying the importance of the feudal aspect. Milsom, in a new introduction to 'Pollock and Maitland' – and a raft of other publications[66] – outlined what he referred to as his 'heresy' that Maitland had not placed sufficient emphasis upon the continuing importance of the feudal courts and the localisation of justice, and suggested that the early writs did little to replace this.[67] Therefore, the question may be posed as to which of these systems were most important to the development of the medieval land law. Maitland's account of the writ system and its emphasis upon centralisation can be contrasted by Milsom's work that stresses the on-going importance of feudalism and the focus upon localisation.

However, this question is a simplification for two reasons. First, it should be noted that the labels we have given these systems were retrospectively applied: medieval litigants would not have spoken of systems in theoretical terms (including speaking of the 'legal system') and systems do not exist in pure forms; talk of a feudal (or indeed capitalist) system is 'a paradigm rather than a social reality'.[68] Second, it should be noted that a

---

[60] Maitland, *The Forms of Action at Common Law*.
[61] Other writs concerned what we would now call the law of obligations (the law of contract and tort) as we will discuss in chapter 7.
[62] Maitland, *The Constitutional History of England* 23–4.   [63] Ibid. 10.
[64] Land that is in the crown's own occupation is referred to as 'demesne land' under the Land Registration Act 2002. Note Simpson's warning that the modern doctrine that all land is 'owned' (rather than 'held') by the crown is misleading; AW Brian Simpson, *A History of the Land Law* (2nd ed., Oxford University Press, 1986) 1.
[65] Maitland, *The Forms of Action at Common Law* 2.
[66] See especially SFC Milsom, *The Legal Framework of English Feudalism* (Cambridge University Press, 1976). These insights are integrated within SFC Milsom, *Historical Foundations of the Common Law* (2nd ed., Butterworths, 1981 [1969]).
[67] S F C Milsom, 'Introduction' in Pollock and Maitland, *The History of English Law* xxiii, xxv.
[68] Thomas G Watkin, 'Feudal Theory, Social Needs and the Rise of the Heritable Fee' (1979) 10 *Cambrian Law Review* 39, 39.

94 *The Father of the Common Law (c.1154–1215)*

choice between the two systems does not need to be made. Both were clearly important. The question is rather how the two systems interacted; the relationship between the two. It is a question of emphasis. While some accounts (most notably that of Maitland) emphasise the importance of the writ system, others (most notably Milsom) stress the significance of the feudal system. This section explores that question by examining Maitland's elucidation of the writ system before concluding by analysing what may be styled the Maitland-Milsom debate.

1 *Maitland and* **The Forms of Action**

A strong claim can be made that Maitland's posthumously published undergraduate lectures on *The Forms of Action* represent a, if not the, most important work on the development of the common law.[69] Over the course of seven lectures, Maitland explained the procedural law, exploring the various writs, or forms of action,[70] that those who wanted to bring a case had to ensure that their complaint fitted. Writs had been used since at least the Anglo-Saxon period. A royal writ was generally 'a sealed governmental document, drafted in a crisp businesslike manner, by which the king conveys notifications or orders'.[71] However, according to the orthodox account authored by Maitland, the reign of Henry II saw the creation and use of particular writs that were used where there was a dispute as to land. This is the story of how 'certain royal writs, dealing with redress of private wrongs in extra-judicial executive ways, became, via a process of judicialisation . . . the originating writs of the common law'.

A complaint could only be brought to the royal court if the facts fitted the formula of a particular writ. The rules would be different for each writ: the writ would dictate the court that would hear the dispute, the mechanisms by which the other party is made to appear in court, the mode of trial, the rules of pleading and court procedure, and the potential remedy or punishment.[72] In short, the writ chosen would provide the 'rules of the game', and once a writ was chosen, that choice was irreversible.[73] Whether a claim could be heard rested entirely upon whether there was a writ and whether the writ was made correctly. Sometimes, the facts of the dispute would leave litigants with a choice of writs, other times, the facts might not fit any writ, and so royal justice would be denied.[74]

This focus on procedural law appears at first glance to be rather odd. As Maitland noted at the start of his first lecture, the scholarly study of law usually focuses upon substantive law (the body of abstract rules) rather than procedural law (the rules under which litigation is begun and pursued), which tends to be learnt afterwards, whether as part of a vocational

---

[69] Maitland, *The Forms of Action at Common Law.*

[70] Bracton defined an action as 'nothing other than the right of pursuing in a judicial proceeding what is due to one' (Samuel E Thorne, *Bracton on the Laws and Customs of England* (Harvard University Press, 1968) vol. 2, 282).

[71] Van Caenegem, *Royal Writs in England from the Conquest to Glanvill* v.

[72] Maitland, *The Forms of Action at Common Law* 2–3. The writs were collected in registers of writs and the compliant was first made to the Chancery, who served as a secretariat; Milsom, *Historical Foundations of the Common Law* 37, 34.

[73] Maitland, *The Forms of Action at Common Law* 4.

[74] Ibid. 4–5. Though there were some procedures without writ: on which, see HG Richardson and GO Sayles, *Select Cases of Procedure without Writ under Henry III* (Selden Society, 1941) vol. 60.

course or at the workplace.[75] Maitland rebutted this objection on the basis that the infant common law was not a system of substantive rules of prohibitions and permissions, rights and duties. Rather, substantive law only existed to the extent that it was implicit within the procedural law.[76] Each distinctive writ had its 'own rules of substantive law'; as Maitland put it, each 'procedural pigeon-hole' had' its own precedents'.[77] The seeds of the substantive law were to be found in the detail of the procedural law. As Maitland noted, the writ system was 'the most important characteristic of English medieval law'.[78] The following will therefore follow Maitland's outline on how the early writs concerning landholding provided the foundations of the common law of real property.[79]

2   The Writ of Right

The first writ described by Maitland was the writ of right. This stated that a royal writ was required when there was a dispute as to freehold land. Where A claims land that B holds, then B would not need to answer that claim unless A brought a writ of right. Maitland dated this writ to the reign of Henry II, speculating that the king 'in some ordinance lost to us, laid down the broad principle that no man need answer for his freehold without royal writ'.[80] This is known as the first principle of the common law.[81] For Maitland, it appeared to be 'a new principle; we have little cause to believe that it was in force before Henry's day or that it ever was law in Normandy'.[82] It is important, however, not to over-emphasise the importance of this development. The principle that royal writ was required for disputes concerning freehold land did not lead to all land disputes being heard in the King's Court, since this would have undermined feudal principles.[83] Rather, the principle simply required that such disputes be heard in the feudal courts. The writ was sent from the king to the feudal (or other) lord of the land.[84] The writ would require the feudal lord to do 'full right', meaning to do full justice, stating that if the lord did not deal with the dispute, the sheriff would. This would usually mean that the feudal lord would hold a feudal court that would then determine the dispute.[85] It was therefore a remedy to enforce feudal customs. The writ therefore did not lead to centralisation; rather, it led to more business at the feudal courts,

---

[75] Maitland, *The Forms of Action at Common Law* 1.

[76] This meant that 'substantive rules existed only latently within claims that a litigant could put (in his count) before a court, within the writs (those instruments initiating suits in the royal courts) which facilitated those claims, and within the remedies which the writs embodied' (Doe, *Fundamental Authority in Late Medieval English Law* 1).

[77] Maitland, *The Forms of Action at Common Law* 4.   [78] Ibid. 1, 10.

[79] The account given by Maitland could just be the tip of the iceberg. Hudson has noted that 'there are writs dealing with a greater variety of situations' than often assumed, and that 'procedure had not entirely hardened into a finite number of writs and procedures' (Hudson, *The Oxford History of the Laws of England Volume II* 577–8).

[80] Maitland, *The Forms of Action at Common Law* 21.

[81] There is disagreement as to the origins of the rule but 'there is no disagreement that it was a rule by 1189 and that its effect was to ensure that any litigation about title to free land brought in lords' courts had to be initiated by royal writ' (Paul Brand, '*Multis Vigiliis Excogitatam et Inventam*: Henry II and the Creation of the English Common Law' (1990) 2 *Haskins Society Journal* 197, reprinted in Paul Brand, *The Making of the Common Law* (Hambledon Press, 1992) 97–8).

[82] Maitland, *The Forms of Action at Common Law* 21.   [83] Ibid. 22.

[84] It 'was a royal writ ordering someone, who held or presided over a non-royal court, to see that in that court right was done'. It was normally addressed to lords who were presidents of feudal courts but could also be directed to bishops in ecclesiastical courts and sheriffs in communal courts as well; van Caenegem, *Royal Writs in England from the Conquest to Glanvill* 207.

[85] Maitland, *The Forms of Action at Common Law* 23.

The Father of the Common Law (c.1154–1215)

rather than centralising business at the King's Court. The writ addressed to the feudal lord was known as a writ of right *breve de recto*.[86]

Such a writ was lacking, however, where the dispute arose at the top of the feudal pyramid, where the king himself was the feudal lord. At the top, the king gave land to his tenants in chief. Where a third party challenged the title of the tenant in chief, the writ *breve de recto* would mean that the king would be sending a writ to himself because he was the tenant in chief's feudal lord. To cover this situation, the writ of *praecipe* (also known as *praecipe quod reddat* or *praecipe in capite*) was used.[87] This was named after its opening word 'command' and was addressed not to the lord (who would in this instance be the king) but to the sheriff.[88] It instructed the sheriff to order the tenant in chief to either give back the land in question or appear before the justices on a set day.[89] The *praecipe* writ meant that the dispute would always be heard in the King's Court.[90] In this scenario, this was logical. The writ belonged in the court of the king because the king was the tenant in chief's feudal lord. However, the king frequently sent a *praecipe* as opposed to a *breve de recto* purely at whim.[91] Rather than allow feudal courts to try land disputes, Henry II would simply 'summon the disputants to his court with a *praecipe* to have the issue tried more efficiently and with greater despatch'.[92] This did lead to centralisation and the eclipse of the feudal courts.

The writ of *praecipe* was especially favoured in the reigns of Richard and John. Maitland's account regarded this as a 'deliberate poaching by the king's courts, part of the supposed royal policy of undermining feudal jurisdiction'.[93] As Maitland observed, this 'was regarded as a tyrannical abuse and was struck at by a clause of the Great Charter'.[94] Clause 34 of Magna Carta decreed that in the future, a *praecipe* writ was not to 'be issued to anyone in respect of any holding of land, if a free man could thereby be deprived of the right of trial in his own lord's court'.[95] This decree that a propriety action for land must begin in the court of the feudal lord has often been seen as a protection of the rights of the lords but, as Brian Simpson noted, it is also possible that 'the intention was to protect tenants, as well as lords, or even instead of lords, from the inconveniences of the centralised state'.[96] Moreover, Milsom questioned Maitland's assertion that the king's motive was centralisation. Milsom argued that his motive was more practical. The Anarchy had meant that land had often changed hands. The victorious had taken the land of the vanquished and granted it to their supporters, and when the vanquished themselves became victorious, they had done the same. The writ of

---

[86] For discussion of the origins of the term, see van Caenegem, *Royal Writs in England from the Conquest to Glanvill* 206–7.

[87] This had its 'roots in the old executive writs' (ibid. 239). Although not called so in the early sources, it has often been assumed that this was a 'writ or right' too. However, Milsom has argued that there is no reason for this; Milsom, *Historical Foundations of the Common Law* 125, 126.

[88] At least in its classic form, see van Caenegem, *Royal Writs in England from the Conquest to Glanvill* 234.

[89] Maitland, *The Forms of Action at Common Law* 23.

[90] However, as Milsom has noted, 'there is no way of telling' how many claims were first made under a *praecipe* writ or whether they actually began in the lord's courts and were moved to the king's court. Cases could be moved by *tolt* from the lord's court to the county court and then by *pone* to the king's court; Milsom, *The Legal Framework of English Feudalism* 67.

[91] Maitland, *The Forms of Action at Common Law* 23.

[92] Watkin, 'Feudal Theory, Social Needs and the Rise of the Heritable Fee' 41.

[93] Milsom, *Historical Foundations of the Common Law* 125.   [94] Maitland, *The Forms of Action at Common Law* 23.

[95] MT Clanchy, 'Magna Carta, Clause Thirty-Four' (1964) 79 *English Historical Review* 542.

[96] Simpson, *A History of the Land Law* 35.

The Writ System 97

right, therefore, argued Milsom, 'reaches back to undo things done in the past'.[97] It had the particular motive of returning the land to those who had held it at the death of Henry I.[98]

However, regardless of the motive, from 1215 onwards, claimants had to begin with a writ against their lord.[99] *Praecipe* writs were only given where they contained a clause 'explaining why the matter could come directly to the King's Court' without depriving the lord of his jurisdiction.[100] This meant that they tended only to be issued in two scenarios: where the dispute arose at the top of the feudal pyramid or where the lord did not hold a court for his tenants, in which case, a writ of *praecipe* would not deprive him of anything.[101] For Milsom, these were 'definite exceptions' to the general rule.[102] Therefore, although for a time the widespread use of the writ of *praecipe* had threatened to replace the feudal courts, overall, the extent of centralisation was limited.

3   *The Possessory Assizes*

In Maitland's words, '[T]he action commenced by the Writ of Right was an extremely slow and solemn affair.'[103] The mode of trial was trial by battle.[104] And this led to delays, especially where the landowner was sick and so could not defend his oath.[105] A new mode of trial was therefore introduced by the Assize of Windsor of 1179: the Grand Assize.[106] Here the word assize is being used in its third meaning to describe an institution that had been created;[107] in this case, a new mode of proof designed as an alternative to trial by battle. This was applied to both writs of right, *breve de recto* and *praecipe*. The Grand Assize required four knights of the county to summon twelve other knights who were sworn to 'recognise' who had the greater right to land. Maitland stressed that although the grand assize was an important stage in the development of trial by jury, it is best not to refer to the twelve knights as a jury.[108] They were still witnesses as opposed to deciders of fact, and what was important was not their sense of justice but their memory.

The crucial thing about the Grand Assize was that it was only available in the King's Court, and it was the sitting tenant now had a choice between either trial by battle in the lord's court or trial by grand assize in the King's Court. This was because the sitting tenant had 'seisin' (possession of the land).[109] This put the sitting tenant at an advantage and it did not take long for this fact to be realised. Consequentially, third parties began to simply take the land so that they would be the sitting tenant. This was known as deseising the tenant, since the third party was putting him out of seisin. The deseised tenant still had a claim and

---

[97] Milsom, *Historical Foundations of the Common Law* 129.   [98] Milsom, *The Legal Framework of English Feudalism* 179.
[99] Ibid. 69.   [100] Ibid. 102; Milsom, *Historical Foundations of the Common Law* 133.
[101] Watkin, 'Feudal Theory, Social Needs and the Rise of the Heritable Fee' 41.
[102] Milsom, *The Legal Framework of English Feudalism* 69.   [103] Maitland, *The Forms of Action at Common Law* 25.
[104] Ibid. 26.   [105] Watkin, 'Feudal Theory, Social Needs and the Rise of the Heritable Fee' 40.
[106] Maitland, *The Forms of Action at Common Law* 26. Milsom notes that this provision allowing the choice of the Grand Assize is attributed to 1179; Milsom, *Historical Foundations of the Common Law* 130.
[107] Maitland, *The Constitutional History of England* 12.   [108] Maitland, *The Forms of Action at Common Law* 26.
[109] Milsom has argued against Maitland's equation of seisin with possession, arguing that the term refers to 'a relationship between two persons about the thing, not just an abstract relationship between the thing and one person'. It was only the later 'superimposition of royal jurisdiction that turned seisin into a kind of abstract possession' (SFC Milsom, *A Natural History of the Common Law* (Columbia University Press, 2003) 91, 92). See, further, Simpson, *A History of the Land Law* 40–4.

could go the king for a writ but now the third party, as sitting tenant, had the advantage in terms of choice over the mode of trial and would invariably decide on trial by battle.

Maitland noted that to overcome this, a range of new assizes were introduced.[110] These are known as the 'possessory assizes' because these protected seisin/possession in contrast to the writ of right, which protected proprietary rights.[111] These were also known as the 'petty assizes' because they produced a speedier enquiry by sworn neighbours into questions of fact than the Grand Assize did.[112]

Maitland's account began with the Assize of *Novel Disseisin* (meaning 'recent act of taking someone out of seisin').[113] This led to what has often been referred to as the second principle of the common law: namely, that no free tenant should be deseised unjustly and without a judgment. Under the Assize of *Novel Disseisin*, where A had unjustly and without a judgment disseised B of his land and B had at once complained to the king, then B would be put back into seisin by the judgment of the King's Court.[114] The writ would be sent to the sheriff of the county, ordering him to empanel an assize of twelve to answer from their local knowledge two questions of fact: whether A had been deseised without a judgment and whether that had taken place within a relatively recent period of time.[115] If the assize answered in the affirmative to these questions, then the sheriff put the tenant back into seisin. If the third party still wished to possess the land, then he had to take his claim to the king, and in such a case the tenant will now have the choice as to the mode of trial. The remedies therefore complemented each other.

The origins of *Novel Disseisin* are disputed. Milsom referred to this as 'the greatest enigma in the history of the common law'.[116] While traditionally *Novel Disseisin* has been dated back to the Assize of Clarendon in 1166, Milsom has questioned this on the basis that the Assize of Clarendon only created a 'criminal' offence 'casting upon local people a duty to present recent disseisins to the justices in eyre' and not what we would call a 'modern civil process'.[117] John Baker pointed out that a procedure for investigating disseisins can be dated back to the late 1150s.[118] Milsom has suggested that chronologically *Novel Disseisin* was not the first of the possessory assizes, while Thomas G Watkin has asserted that the most recent 'evidence tends to support the view that the civil aspect of *Novel Disseisin* emerged after 1176'.[119]

Milsom further argued that at first *Novel Disseisin* was used by tenants to recover land that had been taken back by the feudal lord.[120] It was only over time that the assize became

---

[110] Maitland, *The Forms of Action at Common Law* 27.

[111] For further discussion of the proprietary-possessory distinction, see AW Brian Simpson, *An Introduction to the History of Land Law* (2nd ed., Oxford University Press, 1986) 36–44 and Milsom, *Historical Foundations of the Common Law* 119 *et seq.*

[112] Baker, *An Introduction to English Legal History* 253.

[113] See also Donald W Sutherland, The Assize of *Novel Disseisin* (Clarendon Press, 1973).

[114] Maitland, *The Forms of Action at Common Law* 27.

[115] Maitland noted that this term was fixed from time to time by royal ordinance and at the time of Glanvill, the limitation period was defined as since the king's last crossing to Normandy, an event that took place around once every two years (ibid. 28).

[116] Milsom, 'Introduction' xxxix.

[117] Milsom, *Historical Foundations of the Common Law* 138–9; Milsom, 'Introduction' xxxix.

[118] Baker, *An Introduction to English Legal History* 253.

[119] Watkin, 'Feudal Theory, Social Needs and the Rise of the Heritable Fee' 55.

[120] Milsom, *The Legal Framework of English Feudalism* 11; Milsom, *Historical Foundations of the Common Law* 140; Milsom, 'Introduction' xli.

The Writ System   99

used against third parties who had taken the land.[121] As Milsom observed, 'Without the backing of Maitland's authority, it would take an unalterable faith in coincidence still to see generalized protection of abstract possession as the aim of the *Novel Disseisin* writ.'[122] However, Milsom's revision has been questioned. Thomas Gallanis has argued that Milsom regarded the word 'disseisin' as referring to the undoing of seisin and so referred only to the undoing of the feudal bond between lord and tenant.[123] Gallanis, by contrast, found evidence that 'disseisin' had a broader meaning than that and that the writ was a remedy not only for dispossession but also for substantial interference with the land. Regardless of the differing interpretations, it is clear that the Assize of *Novel Disseisin* came to be advantageous to disseised tenants. It provided 'a quick and efficient means of legal redress offered by the king's justices'.[124] It therefore marked the growth of royal centralised justice, but this was often to support the feudal localised justice.

However, the writ of *Novel Disseisin* only covered very limited circumstances.[125] Different possessory actions dealt with other circumstances. The Assize of *Novel Disseisin* was of no help in the situation where on the death of the tenant, a third party took possession of the land before the agreed heir could do so. The agreed heir would not have been deseised. The Assize of *Mort D'Ancestor* ('death of ancestor'), introduced in at the Assize of Northampton in 1176,[126] filled this gap. A writ was sent to the sheriff to empanel an assize of twelve to answer on oath whether the tenant on the day he died was seised of land that could be inherited and whether the claimant was the nearest heir.[127] If these questions were answered in the affirmative, the heir was given seisin of the land.

The Assize of *Mort D'Ancestor* was only effective for a limited number of relatives: the father, mother, brother, sister, uncle or aunt of the deceased. In 1237, the writs of aiel, besaiel and coinsage were invented to recover land left by the grandfather, great-grandfather and other kinsmen respectively.[128] Other possessory actions were also created, for example, to deal with Church property. The Assize of *Darrein Presentment* ('last presentation') provided that where a church was vacant, it was for the person who last presented a parson (or their heir) to do so unless an action is brought by another who thought that they had a better right.[129] The Assize of *Utrum* concerned the dispute where one party says that the piece of land has been given in free alms to the Church. The Constitutions of Clarendon of 1164 stated that in such disputes, it was to be decided by a panel of twelve whether the land was given as a gift to God (known as a gift in free alms) or not.[130] If it was, then the plea was to continue in the ecclesiastical courts if it was not, then the case would continue in the King's Court (or other feudal court). Later on, the Assize of *Utrum* was to become 'the parson's writ of right'. It was understood that where the land was in free alms, then it followed that it was the parson of the parish's land.[131]

---

[121] Milsom noted that this had occurred by the time of Glanvill given that Glanvill contemplated the assize being used by neighbour against neighbour: Milsom, *The Legal Framework of English Feudalism* 13.

[122] Milsom, *A Natural History of the Common Law* 87.

[123] Thomas P Gallanis, 'The Evolution of the Common Law' in Troy L Harris (ed.), *Studies in Canon Law and Common Law in Honor of R H Helmholz* (The Robbins Collection, 2015) 61, 67.

[124] Van Caenegem, *Royal Writs in England from the Conquest to Glanvill* 262.   [125] Simpson, *A History of the Land Law* 29.

[126] Milsom, *Historical Foundations of the Common Law* 135.

[127] Watkin, 'Feudal Theory, Social Needs and the Rise of the Heritable Fee' 40.

[128] Ibid.; Maitland, *The Forms of Action at Common Law* 31.   [129] Ibid. 32.   [130] Ibid. 33.

[131] Simpson, *A History of the Land Law* 32.

100 *The Father of the Common Law (c.1154–1215)*

For Maitland, this underscored how 'an action instituted for one purpose in one age comes to be used for another purpose in another age'.[132]

Milsom argued that this also applied to Assize of *Mort D'Ancestor* itself. He argued that, as with the Assize of *Novel Disseisin*, the original aim of *Mort D'Ancestor* was 'to protect the heirs of tenants against their lords', as opposed to against third parties.[133] For Milsom, neither action was aimed at 'simple disorder' but was rather intended as additional sanctions for feudal custom; by preventing tenants vulnerable to abuse by their lord.[134] Although over time these writs led to more litigation at the royal courts at the expense of the feudal courts, at first, they were used to enforce rather than to superseded feudal justice. As Milsom argued, it was only as time went on that 'the assize came to be used as a remedy in a wider range of situations than that first envisaged'.[135] William Eves has shown that *Mort D'Ancestor* became used to transfer land.[136] He noted that although these common law writs were 'designed to adjudicate contentious disputes, parties could reach an agreement during the course of litigation', known as a final concord. These 'final concords, also known as "fines", soon became popular for conveyancing purposes'. As Eves noted, '[P]arties to a sale of land would bring a fictitious suit to court simply to obtain a final concord in which the terms of the transaction were recorded.'[137] His research showed that the principal use of *Mort D'Ancestor* during the period 1198–230 'was clearly still that of bringing contentious disputes to court', nevertheless 'a significant number of actions brought before the justices of eyre were quite possibly intended to facilitate conveyancing'.[138] This and other wider uses of *Mort D'Ancestor* came to represent a move towards centralisation. As Milsom noted, over time, this 'caused, or at least precipitated' structural changes, which resulted in the emasculation of the 'disciplinary' jurisdiction of lords.[139]

4   The Writs of Entry

There was another flaw with the Assize of *Novel Disseisin*, however. It did not cover the situation where a tenant for life (A) was deseised by a third party (B) who promptly passed the land on to another party (C) before A could use the Assize of *Novel Disseisin* against B. The Assize of *Novel Disseisin* was not effective against C, since C did not deseise A. This gap was again filled by new writs: the writs of entry. These writs of entry were part of a 'rapid growth' of the writ system that occurred during the reigns of Richard I (1189–99), John (1199–1216) and Henry III (1216–72).[140] For Maitland, these writs of entry constituted a 'large and popular group'.[141] They followed the form of the *praecipe in*

---

[132] Maitland, *The Forms of Action at Common Law* 33.

[133] Milsom, 'Introduction' xxxvii. Milsom noted that this 'is conclusively shown only by the Assize of Northampton which created it' (Milsom, *Historical Foundations of the Common Law* 138); Milsom, *The Legal Framework of English Feudalism* 164–7.

[134] Milsom, *Historical Foundations of the Common Law* 140.   [135] Milsom, *The Legal Framework of English Feudalism* 166.

[136] William Eves, 'Collusive Litigation in the Early Years of the English Common Law: The Use of *Mort D'Ancestor* for Conveyancing Purposes c. 1198–1230' (2020) 41(3) *The Journal of Legal History* 227.

[137] Ibid. 228.   [138] Ibid. 255.   [139] Milsom, *Historical Foundations of the Common Law* 142–3.

[140] Maitland, *The Forms of Action at Common Law* 41. The dating of this development is unknown. Milsom has cautioned that 'they are probably later than we have thought' (Milsom, *The Legal Framework of English Feudalism* 101).

[141] Maitland, *The Forms of Action at Common Law* 41–2. See also Joseph Biancalana, 'The Origin and Early History of the Writs of Entry' (2007) 25(3) *Law and History Review* 513.

capite writ, in that they ordered that either the land was to be given back or the matter was to be brought to the King's Court. However, the writs of entry went further than the *praecipe in capite* writ in that they explicitly stated that there was a flaw in the defendant's title, which would justify the hearing of the dispute in the King's Court. The writ of entry in the *per* covered the situation where a tenant (A) was deseised by a third party (B) who promptly passed the land on to another party (C). The flaw in C's title was that he only had entry through – or *per* – the third party. The writ of entry in *cu* dealt with the matter where A was deseised by B who passed the land to C who then died, passing it on to D. Originally, the writs of entry were limited to relatively recent flaws in the title. The reason behind this was that to go further would go beyond the memory of the assize. In Richard I's reign, however, court records began to be kept and the reliance placed upon memory diminished. The Statute of Malborough of 1267 removed the limitation.[142] Writs could now be framed 'in the *post*'. This writ would contend that E only had entry *post* (after) a disseisin committed by someone without showing how the land had passed.[143]

These writs of entry led to an increase in cases at the king's courts.[144] However, Milsom questioned the conventional view that regarded the writs of entry as 'possessory' actions descending from *Novel Disseisin*.[145] He pointed out that the records of cases in the year books do not speak of 'rights' of entry but rather *entre congeable*, permissible entry. Milsom queried the assumption that 'entry' denoted a physical event, suggesting that 'it was not the physical tenement that you entered but the fee of the lord'.[146] He therefore suggested that, at least originally, the writs were used not against a third party, rather, the writs were used by lords to question whether the tenant was entitled to be the tenant or not. For Milsom, this queries the 'assumption' that the writs of entry were a creation fundamentally distinct from writs of right.[147] It was simply 'a general way of asserting title'.[148] This, indeed, may explain its popularity.

For Maitland, the proliferation of writs caused by the writs of entry led to a 'hopeless tangle' and a system that became 'so very complex and unintelligible'.[149] The writs of entry clearly enabled centralisation, allowing disputes to be dealt with in the King's Court rather than the court of the feudal lord.[150] As Milsom noted, 'The result of the whole development, intended or not, has been seen as bringing virtually all litigation about freehold land into the King's Court.'[151] This had also occurred under Henry II's reign and until Magna Carta limited the use of the *praecipe* writ. That provision and the short periods of limitation found in the possessory assizes meant that most actions were still brought in the feudal courts. By contrast, the later writs of entry provided a writ of *praecipe* that effectively took the law back to the situation prior to Magna Carta. Overall, therefore, it would appear that these early actions did see the King's Court supplant feudal jurisdictions.

---

[142] Simpson, *A History of the Land Law* 35.
[143] Maitland, *The Forms of Action at Common Law* 42. See Paul Brand, *Kings, Barons and Justices: The Making and Enforcement of Legislation in Thirteenth century England* (Cambridge University Press, 2006) 336–9.
[144] Milsom, *A Natural History of the Common Law* 99.   [145] Ibid. 98.   [146] Ibid.
[147] Milsom, *The Legal Framework of English Feudalism* 99.   [148] Milsom, *A Natural History of the Common Law* 100.
[149] Maitland, *The Forms of Action at Common Law* 43, 44.
[150] This did not necessarily mean at Westminster. The majority of the assizes 'were probably heard locally, during visitations to the counties undertaken by the itinerant justices' (Eves, 'Justice Delayed' 8).
[151] Milsom, *Historical Foundations of the Common Law* 145.

102 *The Father of the Common Law (c.1154–1215)*

In Maitland's account, it is suggested that this result was deliberate. For Maitland, the object of the writs of entry was to 'evade feudal jurisdiction',[152] especially once limitations had been removed by Statute of Marlborough of 1267, which allowed writs of entry 'in the *post*'.[153] For Maitland, this 'in many ways marks the end of feudalism'.[154] This interpretation has, however, been rejected by Milsom, who suggested that the consequences of the Statute of Marlborough were 'certainly approved and probably promoted by the baronage', leading him to suggest that 'the writs of entry were still thought of in 1267 as essentially remedies for lords'.[155] This conflict of opinion is symptomatic of a wider debate that pitches the Maitland account of the centralisation brought about by the writ system with Milsom's response that highlighted the continued localisation of justice resulting from the feudal system. The next section will explore this in more detail, examining the Maitland-Milsom debate.

5   *The Maitland–Milsom Debate*

It is undeniable that the growth of royal justice undermined feudalism not only by providing an alternative to the feudal courts but also enabling land to change hands outside the feudal system. This undermining of feudalism was controversial given how the feudal bargain underlined social and economic relations. The decline of feudalism meant that feudal lords began losing feudal revenues and services. The Maitland-Milsom debate, then, is not a dispute as to the direction of the process: it is uncontested that the increased centralisation of justice led to a common law. However, there are questions in relation to the speed and extent of this process. This is the basis of what may be styled the 'Maitland-Milsom debate' or, as Ralph V Turner has characterised it, the debate between the 'royalist' and 'feudalist' approaches.[156] The disagreement can be summarised as follows.

The 'royalist' account attributed to Maitland assumed that 'feudal ties of personal loyalty and performance of military service had rapidly lost their significance after their introduction to England after 1066'.[157] According to this view, Henry II and his advisers 'took steps to protect tenants' proprietary interest, providing procedures that reduced lords' jurisdictional rights.[158]

The feudalist account provided by Milsom pointed out that 'Maitland did not sufficiently reckon with the feudal dimension'.[159] For Milsom, the growth of the royal courts and writ system under Henry II aimed not to replace the feudal jurisdiction of the lords but to make those feudal courts function more effectively.[160] The feudal relationship between

---

[152] Maitland, *The Forms of Action at Common Law* 44.
[153] See Ashley Hannay, '"By Fraud and Collusion": Feudal Revenue and Enforcement of the Statute of Marlborough, 1267–1526' (2021) 42 *Journal of Legal History* 65.
[154] Maitland, *The Forms of Action at Common Law* 42.   [155] Milsom, *Historical Foundations of the Common Law* 149.
[156] Ralph V Turner, 'Henry II's Aims in Reforming England's Land Law: Feudal or Royalist' in EB King and SJ Ridyard (eds.), *Law in Medieval Life and Thought* (University of the South Press, 1990) 121, reprinted in Ralph V Turner, *Judges, Administrators and the Common Law in Angevin England* (Hambledon Press, 1994) 1 (all subsequent references are to the reprint).
[157] Turner, *Judges, Administrators and the Common Law in Angevin England* x–xi.   [158] Ibid.
[159] Milsom, *The Legal Framework of English Feudalism* 104.
[160] Turner, *Judges, Administrators and the Common Law in Angevin England* xi.

The Writ System 103

lord and tenant had an 'insignificant position' in Maitland's account in *The Forms of Action*. Milsom commented that Maitland had 'ousted a great deal of legalistic history: perhaps too much'.[161] It was only over time that the courts of the king eclipsed the courts of the lord, and this was an unintended consequence. This account was established in Milsom's 'anti-creed of disbeliefs' in his introduction to the reissued 'Pollock and Maitland'.[162] It raised Milsom's concern that Maitland's account had 'beguiled us into a too easy dependence'.[163]

Milsom's heresy was based on four main criticisms of Maitland's account in *The Forms of Action*. The first criticism was that Maitland misunderstood the role of the feudal courts. For Milsom, 'Maitland did not sufficiently reckon with the laws of courts other than the King's Court.'[164] Milsom conceded that this criticism might seem to be 'deeply unjust' given that Maitland had focused on such courts more than anyone, not only in his books but in his edited work for the Selden Society. However, for Milsom, the point was not that Maitland ignored feudal courts but rather that he had misunderstood their role, assuming that they were 'doing the same kind of thing as the King's Court but less important, and doing it less effectively'.[165]

Maitland did not mention and probably did not know about the evidence about what lord's courts could properly do without writ, and the evidence of early plea rolls about that they actually did.[166] Milsom's account, by contrast, stressed that the feudal courts had until a generation before 1200 been the 'only relevant legal system'.[167] He stressed that England in 1200 was 'a world in three dimensions', which included not just 'a dispute between two persons with rights generated or evidence by an abstract possession' but also the role of the lord, what Milsom styled the 'seigniorial dimension'.[168] For Milsom, words such as 'seisin' and 'entry' showed that what tenants were entering was 'not just the property of an equal' but was rather a feudal tenure.[169] Disputes were of a 'contractual rather than the proprietary nature', essentially concerning the bargain between the lord and the tenant.[170]

On the surface, this appears to be an unfair criticism of Maitland who discussed the ways in which feudalism shaped the law albeit in his other works, particularly in 'Pollock and Maitland'. Indeed, there Maitland stressed that medieval proprietary rights in land could be understood not only in a 'private law' sense by reference to the development of the writ system but also in a 'public law' sense in terms of duties owed as a result of the feudal scheme.[171] However, even there, Maitland suggested that by the thirteenth century, the 'public law' dimension had decayed: '[H]omage and fealty and seignorial justice no longer mean what they once meant.'

The second criticism by Milsom was that Maitland's account misunderstood the relationship between the feudal and the common law courts. Maitland's understanding of

---

[161] Milsom, 'Introduction' xxviii.   [162] Ibid.; Milsom, *A Natural History of the Common Law* xxiii.
[163] Milsom, 'Introduction' xxv.   [164] Ibid. xxvii.   [165] Milsom, *The Legal Framework of English Feudalism* 8.
[166] Milsom, *A Natural History of the Common Law* xxvi.
[167] Milsom, *The Legal Framework of English Feudalism* 11; Paul Brand, 'The Origins of English Land Law: Milsom and After' in Brand, *The Making of the Common Law* 203–4.
[168] Milsom, 'Introduction' xxxiii; Milsom, *The Legal Framework of English Feudalism* 7.
[169] Milsom, *Historical Foundations of the Common Law* 143.
[170] Turner, *Judges, Administrators and the Common Law in Angevin England* 3.
[171] Pollock and Maitland, *The History of English Law* 1.

feudal jurisdiction was that of jurisdiction in a modern sense, simply the question of 'should a dispute go to this court or to that?'[172] Milsom argued that the growth of royal writs did not result in a rivalry between the king's and lord's courts 'as parallel institutions making little direct contact with each other'.[173] Rather, the writ system actually provided a means of supervision: rather than providing an alternative form of justice, the writ system sought to ensure that feudal jurisdictions functioned effectively. Rather than regarding them as 'a straightforward attempt by the Crown to steal jurisdiction',[174] Milsom saw the writs as ensuing that feudal justice was 'made to work according to its own rules'.[175] The forms of action provided 'additional safeguards for a framework in which all parties believed'.[176] For Milsom, feudal lordship had not simply 'been reduced to a puppet part'.[177] The growth in royal control should be understood as 'compelling a proper exercise of power rather than compelling particular result'.[178] Milsom stressed that:

> The actions came into being in a framework in which lords were still in control of their lordships, and in which therefore the King's Court could seek only to control the doings of lords. The purpose of this control was not, and could not be, in any sense 'anti-feudal': it was to present and correct departures by lords' courts from the accepted body of feudal custom.[179]

Many of the writs were directed to lords, requiring them to do feudal justice. Even in the case of writs that led to actions in the king's courts, Milsom argued that these were designed to ensure that feudal bargains were kept. As we have seen, he argued that Maitland was wrong to understand the *Novel Disseisin* and *Mort D'Ancestor* as providing general remedies for third parties.[180] This is the role that they came to play, but they began as remedies against the lord and again can be seen as ways in which the feudal bargain was made to work in practice. For Milsom, '[T]he only intention behind the writ of right *Mort D'Ancestor* and *Novel Disseisin* was to make the seigniorial structure work according to its on assumptions.' At first, it was all 'about the feudal relationship rather than about ownership and possession'.[181]

Developing this argument, the third criticism was that Maitland's account presented the development of the writ system as being part of an intentional move towards the centralisation of justice, whereas in reality it was a mere accident. In Maitland's account, he suggests that this result was deliberate. According to this view, Henry II and his advisers 'took steps to protect tenants' proprietary interest, providing procedures that reduced lords' jurisdictional rights'.[182] For Milsom, however, this was a 'juristic accident, altogether beyond foresight'.[183] It was ironic that regulation that sought to supervise and improve the effectiveness of feudal justice had the eventual result of supplanting it. This 'unintended effect' came about because as the lord's courts powers became reduced to applying 'externally fixed rules', litigants began to prefer to go directly to the courts of the king.[184]

---

[172] Milsom, 'Introduction' xxviii.   [173] Milsom, *The Legal Framework of English Feudalism* 36.
[174] Milsom, 'Introduction' xxx.   [175] Milsom, *The Legal Framework of English Feudalism* 37.
[176] Milsom, *Historical Foundations of the Common Law* 151.
[177] Milsom, *The Legal Framework of English Feudalism* 174–5.   [178] Ibid. 175.
[179] Milsom, *Historical Foundations of the Common Law* 124.   [180] Milsom, 'Introduction' xxxvii.   [181] Ibid.
[182] Turner, *Judges, Administrators and the Common Law in Angevin England* x–xi.
[183] Milsom, *The Legal Framework of English Feudalism* 37.   [184] Milsom, *Historical Foundations of the Common Law* 124.

The Writ System 105

This has been supported by the work of Robert Palmer, which has shown that a number of developments under Henry II could not be anti-feudal since they 'assumed the necessity and desirability of strong feudal relationships'.[185] Milsom argued that the forms of action were not part of any deliberate plan by Henry II and his advisers to centralise justice. The actions were not intended to depart from the feudal framework of their world.[186] There was 'no intention to change the framework at all, not even to take jurisdiction'.[187]

The fourth criticism provided the reason why Milsom thought that Maitland got it wrong. Milsom maintained that Maitland's account was influenced by the benefit of hindsight: Maitland knew that the common law courts would rise and the feudal jurisdiction would decrease, and so he read this further back than it actually happened. Milsom argued that Maitland has been influenced by the work that he had carried out on *Bracton's Note Book*,[188] a collection of cases decided in the King's Court during the reign of Henry III (1216–72).[189] For Milsom, Maitland's familiarity with the work of Bracton led him to suppose 'too great a degree of general sophistication' in his interpretation of the early land law assuming 'highly abstract notions of property too early'.[190] By contrast, Maitland's much later work on editing year books of the early fourteenth century, which were chronologically later than Bracton but 'centuries earlier in spirit', led Maitland to suddenly realise 'that the common law began from something more primitive than he had supposed'.[191] For Milsom, this insight of Maitland came too late since it came after he had published 'Pollock and Maitland' and given his lectures on *The Forms of Action*, which in any case had not been intended for publication.[192]

The Maitland-Milsom debate is, at heart, an argument about timings and intention.[193] Milsom did not argue that Maitland's picture of the rise of royal justice and the decline of feudal justice was incorrect; his argument is simply that it occurred later than Maitland suggested and that it was not intended.[194] Milsom's aim was to 'try to reconstruct what may be called the feudal component in the framework of English society in the year around 1200'.[195] Milsom contended that Maitland's picture only came to exist by the late thirteenth century. Milsom conceded that the royal actions were 'largely instrumental in destroying' the feudal framework but denied that they were 'the prime cause of its destruction'.[196] For Milsom, Maitland's account was readily accepted because it fitted the legal assumptions and legal culture at the time in which Maitland was writing, and which continue to this day.[197] Maitland's account of the early common law actions for land provided the template for how he saw the common law as developing. The writ system developed in a pragmatic manner, with each development simply filling the gap or dealing

---

[185] Robert C Palmer 'The Origins of Property in England' (1985) 3 *Law and History Review* 1, 8.
[186] Milsom, *The Legal Framework of English Feudalism* 3, 186.   [187] Ibid. 185.
[188] Frederic W Maitland, *Bracton's Note Book* (Cambridge University Press, 2010 [1887]).
[189] Milsom, *Historical Foundations of the Common Law* vi; Milsom, *A Natural History of the Common Law* xxii.
[190] Milsom, 'Introduction' ixxii.   [191] Milsom, *Historical Foundations of the Common Law* vi–vii.
[192] Milsom, *A Natural History of the Common Law* xiv; Milsom, *Historical Foundations of the Common Law* vi–vii.
[193] This reflects in part the different focuses of Maitland and Milsom. Maitland's focus was on the period 1154–272, while Milsom was seeking to reconstruct the years around 1200; John Hudson, *Land, Law, and Lordship in Anglo-Norman England* (Oxford University Press, 1994) 7.
[194] Milsom, 'Introduction' xxix, ixxii, xlvii.   [195] Milsom, *The Legal Framework of English Feudalism* 1.
[196] Milsom, *Historical Foundations of the Common Law* 151.   [197] Milsom, *The Legal Framework of English Feudalism* 65.

106   *The Father of the Common Law (c.1154–1215)*

with the unforeseen effects of the previous development. For Maitland, it was an organic process – one of evolution. In 'Pollock and Maitland', he noted that the forms of action were 'living things' and that 'the struggle for life is keen among them and only the fittest survive'.[198] Milsom's critique can therefore be interpreted more generally as an attack upon the evolutionary assumptions that underpin Maitland's account. As Milsom put it:

Maitland saw England as a legal Galapagos insulating native evolution from Roman contamination. We now know that he pressed the Darwinian analogy too far, seeing the whole development of English law in terms of monstrous species, the 'forms of action'.[199]

Today, it is Milsom's heresies that have become accepted. Turner asserted that '[I]t is unfashionable today to see behind this shift in Henry II's time any deliberate plan by the king, any great legislative vision.'[200] However, this does not mean that Milsom's account has escaped criticism itself. Robert Palmer concluded that, although if we have to choose between the accounts of Maitland and Milsom, we should accept Milsom, 'it may be that we should not accept either completely'.[201] Three main concerns can be made of Milsom's account. First, Milsom's account had been criticised for its vagueness. Palmer criticised it on the basis that, although it was 'carefully written', it was 'almost impossible to understand', in that it 'raised allusion, hint and obscure suggestion to an art'.[202] He added that Milsom failed to 'provide a clear chronology for the development of the law'.[203]

The second concern is that Milsom underplayed the extent to which English society was already beginning to move beyond feudalism during the reign of Henry II. Palmer suggested that Milsom overestimated the degree of feudalism in 1200.[204] Turner pointed out that evidence of frequent intervention by Anglo-Norman kings in the courts of the lords casts doubt on 'on Milsom's picture of independent feudal lordships'.[205] And Watkin saw 'the period 1176–9' as 'acquiring great significance', contending that it was after the Assize of *Novel Disseisin* that 'royal activity in relation to land-holding becomes regular'.[206] Later research has questioned some of Milsom's assumptions. Relying upon the work of Samuel E Thorne,[207] Milsom assumed that the heirs of tenants had no property right to inherit before 1200, but Turner asserted that more recent research[208] has shown that 'strong norms of inheritance' were at work earlier than this.[209] These criticisms led Turner to ask of Milsom: 'Is he attempting to force the king to fit into a feudal framework?'[210]

Turner's question underlines the third concern relating to Milsom's account, namely that Milsom's 'presentation of Henry II's aims appear inadequate'.[211] Turner has argued that Milsom overplayed the extent to which Henry II endorsed feudalism, pointing out that the

---

[198] Pollock and Maitland, *The History of English Law* 561.
[199] SFC Milsom, 'Maitland' (2001) 60 *Cambridge Law Journal* 265, 268.
[200] Turner, *Judges, Administrators and the Common Law in Angevin England* 1.
[201] Robert C Palmer, 'The Feudal Framework of English Law' (1981) 79 *Michigan Law Review* 1130, 1140.   [202] Ibid. 1130–1.
[203] Palmer 'The Origins of Property in England' 3.   [204] Palmer, 'The Feudal Framework of English Law' 1141.
[205] Turner, *Judges, Administrators and the Common Law in Angevin England* 10.
[206] Watkin, 'Feudal Theory, Social Needs and the Rise of the Heritable Fee' 55.
[207] Samuel E Thorne, 'English Feudalism and Estates in Land' (1959) *Cambridge Law Journal* 193.
[208] Joseph Biancalana, 'For Want of Justice: Legal Reforms of Henry II' (1988) 88 *Columbia Law Review* 433, 495; John Hudson, 'Life-Grants of Land and the Development of Inheritance in Anglo-Norman England' (1990) 12 *Anglo-Norman Studies* 67; van Caenegem, *Royal Writs in England from the Conquest to Glanvill.*
[209] Turner, *Judges, Administrators and the Common Law in Angevin England* xii.   [210] Ibid. 1, 6.   [211] Ibid. 5.

The Writ System 107

king's relations with his own tenants 'did not show any great respect for feudal custom'.[212] Moreover, by providing tenants with a royal court protection against their lords, Henry II and his advisers would appear to 'have had an anti-lord, or perhaps better a pro-tenant bias, if not an anti-feudal one'. Subsequent work seems to support this, questioning Milsom's suggestion that the centralisation of justice under Henry II was unplanned and accidental. Joseph Biancalana found that Henry II and his counsellors 'imagined an organized central power' to overcome the failures of justice in the lords' court.[213] David Crouch argued that while the twelfth century was one of feudal honours, it was also 'a society in which public authority, whether stemming from the king or the concerns of the local community, underlay, or existed side-by-side with, such aristocratic groupings'.[214] Paul Brand argued that the developments during the reign of Henry II 'were in many cases the result of careful and deliberate changes made by the king and those who advised him'.[215] For instance, as Thomas P Gallanis has pointed out, the Assize of *Novel Disseisin* 'was not an organic development within the common law but instead a decision of royal policy'.[216] Bracton described it as being 'devised and invented after many watchful nights'.[217]

Although this does not necessarily mean that the centralisation of justice was intended, the context would suggest that this it was far from accidental. Paul Brand has argued that 'Henry II and his advisers were indeed "reaching out" from their own world and consciously attempting to create something quite new', including the creation of 'a system of regular countrywide judicial visitation and a central royal court for the hearing of civil litigation'.[218] The advance of the writ system needs to be placed in the context of the changes within the reign of Henry II generally that point to a tendency towards centralisation.[219] Henry II became king after civil war and 'saw himself very much in the [mould] of Henry I: a strong king who would restore order and centralized control'.[220] Similarly, Turner has debunked any suggestion that the growth of the writ system was a judicial development opposed by the king. He argues that the justices whose work caused the decline of the feudal courts 'were royal appointees, removable by the king, owing their fortunes to his patronage, striving to do his will' and so it 'will not do to depict Henry II as a perfect feudal overlord, served by anti-feudal royalist judges'.[221]

Milsom was not the heretic that he thought he was. Although his heresies have had a considerable impact upon the work of legal historians (as opposed to general historians of medieval England), with legal scholars taking them as their starting point to 'either confirming or challenging them',[222] Milsom's work is now seen as a refinement rather than as a rejection of Maitland's account. Moreover, it is not the last word on the topic. Milsom 'almost certainly overestimated the degree of independence actually enjoyed by

---

[212] Ibid. 11.   [213] Biancalana, 'For Want of Justice' 446, 483, 534.

[214] David Crouch, 'Debate: Bastard Feudalism Revised' (1991) 131 *Past and Present* 166.

[215] Paul Brand, 'Multis Vigiliis Excogitatam et Inventam: Henry II and the Creation of the English Common Law' in Brand, *The Making of the Common Law* 101.

[216] Gallanis, 'The Evolution of the Common Law' 61, 67.   [217] Ibid. 68.   [218] Brand, *The Making of the Common Law* 101.

[219] Turner, *Judges, Administrators and the Common Law in Angevin England* 11.

[220] Gallanis, 'The Evolution of the Common Law' 69.

[221] Turner, *Judges, Administrators and the Common Law in Angevin England* 15.

[222] Ibid. 2. Brand asserted that Milsom's account represents 'a new orthodoxy to which all English legal historians interested in the beginnings of the common law must now subscribe' (Brand, *The Making of the Common Law* 225).

108   *The Father of the Common Law (c.1154–1215)*

feudal courts prior to the reign of Henry II'.[223] And he was unconvincing in his argument that the replacement of the feudal court's jurisdiction by royal justice was unplanned and accidental.[224] Milsom himself conceded that his modifications were 'not important when compared to the original picture'.[225] This was too modest an assessment. However, it underscores that no real heresy took place. Milsom's work developed rather than discarded the account given by Maitland.[226] Turner is correct to conclude that the development of the early land law should be understood as being both feudal and royalist.[227]

In a sense, whether the erosion of feudal jurisdictions was deliberate or not does not matter.[228] What matters is not so much the intent than the effect of the early forms of action. Both Milsom and Maitland were clear as to what the effects eventually was: it was, in Milsom's words, that 'of a different society ... taking away from lords the ultimate control over lands within their lordships, leaving them with the fixed economic rights of our picture. Tenants became owners, subject only to these fixed rights, because lords and their courts lost their power of final decision.'[229] Milsom's concern was with the dating of the movement from feudal justice to the royal common law, from personal bargains to property rights – not that such a movement had taken place. John Hudson contended that the transformation of these ideas should be seen as marking 'the two poles of a continuum, rather than opposites'.[230] These legal ideas transformed slowly over time, meaning that while in 1166 the world was largely as Milsom saw it, by 1272 the world was largely as Maitland saw it. In between these dates, it was a combination of the two visions. This shows the danger of legal historians trying to impose order upon times where no such neatness existed.

The Maitland-Milsom debate also highlights wider concerns about the relationship between legal change and social change. One answer to Milsom's criticism is that feudal dimension was underplayed in *The Forms of Action* because that was not the focus of those lectures: Maitland was seeking to explain how legal ideas and legal institutions developed, not the wider social context. The equivalent of Milsom's criticism today would be to chide a series of lectures on modern land law for not including enough coverage of the capitalist system. Yet, such a criticism would not be completely misplaced. An argument can be made that law should always be studied within its social context. Indeed, it has been argued that the legal and the social cannot be completely distinguished.[231]

---

[223] Brand, 'The Origins of English Land Law' 219.

[224] Turner, *Judges, Administrators and the Common Law in Angevin England* 14.   [225] Milsom, 'Introduction' ixxii.

[226] To be compared with the view that Maitland's account has been 'somewhat superseded' (Simpson, *A History of the Land Law* 25).

[227] Turner, *Judges, Administrators and the Common Law in Angevin England* 14. Though he later added that 'Angevin reforms in English law were basically "royalist" in nature and intent and that characterization of Anglo-Norman and Angevin England as a "feudal monarchy" or searches for purely feudal sources of the legal innovations contribute little to historical understanding' (ibid. x).

[228] Turner, however, has cautioned that: 'Although Milsom's chief concern was with the results of Henry's legal reforms and not his aims, certain assumptions lay behind his findings' (ibid. 5).

[229] Milsom, *The Legal Framework of English Feudalism* 66.

[230] John Hudson, 'Milsom's Legal Structure: Interpreting Twelfth-Century Law' (1991) 59 *Tijdschrift voor Rechtsgeschiedenis* 47, 61.

[231] Roger Cotterrell, 'Why Must Legal Ideas Be Interpreted Sociologically?' (1998) 25 *Journal of Law and Society* 171, reprinted as Roger Cotterrell, *Law, Culture and Society* (Ashgate, 2006) chapter 3.

V   Conclusions

Identifying the precise origins of the common law is difficult. Ancient ideas and customs were developed in a pragmatic and piecemeal way over the course of many centuries. Developments were the complex result of a cocktail of change and continuity. The Anglo-Saxon period was itself diverse but important strides were made. Glimmers of what were to become the common law were there but in a very different guise. The Norman Conquest of 1066 then had an earth-shattering impact upon England as a whole, but the death of a ruling class had more impact upon order than law, with key changes taking some time to be felt. These crystallised in the reign of Henry II, but the so-called father of the common law was to some extent simply nurturing and experimenting with what had happened before. By the end of his reign a common law had developed through the development of the King's Court, the wandering justices and the writ system, but much of what underpinned that system had been there for long before. As William Holdsworth pointed out, although the 'definite beginnings' of the common law can only be found in the twelfth century, the legal historian needs to examine the earlier Anglo-Saxon and Norman periods, since it was under the Norman kings that earlier rules were 'administered and shaped'.[232]

The development of the common law was not a linear, singular, natural or inevitable process. There was not one development, one event or one day that resulted in vengeance being replaced by justice. The rise of the common law was a pragmatic consequence of the need to maintain order and developments were responses to the particular needs and tensions of those times. It was the result of strong centralised kingships combined with the local administration of justice to prioritise the pragmatic protection of public order, often invoking and drawing upon the traditions of the past (particularly idealised notions of Anglo-Saxon kingship) but without affording too much, if any, concern as to laying a legacy or precedent for the future. The Anglo-Saxon, Norman and Angevin periods were all crucial to the development of common law. Different authors have different emphases because they are telling different stories based on different assumptions. Moreover, the reign of Henry II does not present the end of the story. The common law did not exist in its finalised form. Much was left to develop and this would be shaped by external factors such as the rise of Parliamentary statute and disorderly reigns characterised by rebellions.

The end of Henry II's reign can nevertheless be seen as a decisive moment. This is reflected in the fact that 1189 (the date of the end of his reign and of Richard I's coronation) has become the age of legal memory:[233] references to 'time immemorial' are references to that date. As Maitland noted, it is appropriate that the age of legal memory is 1189, given that at this time Henry's reforms were taking effect: '[A] strong central court was doing justice term after term on a large scale; [and] it was beginning to have a written memory which would endure for all ages in the form of a magnificent series of judicial records.'[234]

This was underscored in the publication at around this time of *On the Laws and Customs of England,* a book based the work of the royal court and 'questionably' attributed

---

[232] William S Holdsworth, *A History of English Law* (3rd ed., Methuen & Co., 1923) vol. 2, 12
[233] Statute of Westminster 1275.   [234] Pollock and Maitland, *The History of English Law* 168.

110   *The Father of the Common Law (c.1154–1215)*

to Glanvill, the Chief Justiciar of England from 1180 to 1189.[235] This was the first text book of the common law and showed that, although local customs remained important, the fixed customs of the King's Court were beginning to lead to a truly common law. The opening words of the prologue of *Glanvill* underscore the centrality and importance of law by the reign of Henry II:

> Not only must royal power be furnished with arms against rebels and nations which rise up against the king and the realm, but it is also fitting that it should be adorned with laws for the governance of subject and peaceful peoples; so that in time of both peace and war our glorious king may so successfully perform his office that, crushing the pride of the unbridled and ungovernable with the right hand of strength and tempering justice for the humble and meek with the rod of equity, he may both be always victorious in wars with his enemies and also show himself continually impartial in dealing with his subjects.[236]

In short, the Sarum Oath had been taken to its logical conclusion. In return for their loyalty, the king provided his people with justice. *Glanvill* stated that although the laws of England were 'not written, it does not seem to be absurd to call them laws' and that while it was 'utterly impossible for the laws and legal rules of the realm to be reduced to writing, …there are some general rules frequently observed in court'.[237] *Glanvill* also distinguished between criminal and civil pleas and noted the offences that belonged to the court of the king. It stated: 'Pleas are either criminal or civil. Some criminal pleas belong to the crown of the lord king, and some to the sheriffs of countries.' However, as Milsom pointed out, *Glanvill*'s 'distinction is not ours': in *Glanvill*, civil pleas refer to the personal actions such as those concerning land, while all wrongs are criminal.[238] Wrongs were not yet divided into categories such as 'offences against society to be punished, and injuries to victims who must be civilly compensated'.[239] The category, therefore, covered not only what we would today call crimes but also some of what we would today call torts. The key concept that did appear in *Glanvill* was 'pleas of the crown', used to denote matters that belonged to the king. However, as Hudson has noted, 'for *Glanvill* not all crimes – in his terms or our – were crown pleas', and pleas of the crown included certain non-criminal scenarios where there was a royal interest expressed as a breach of the peace of the king.[240]

It is clear, then, that much had been achieved by the end of Henry II's reign, but it is possible to overstate the extent to which the developments were part of an intentional plan. Rather, the common law developed in an ad hoc fashion. As van Caenegem noted, '[T]he king's court never became competent for all pleas.'[241] Rather, '[O]ne by one the various pleas were admitted and by the time the ambition germinated to make it a refuge for all civil complaints, the existing common law actions with their procedure were already too established to make away with them altogether.'[242] Moreover, the extent to which these

---

[235] See further Ralph V Turner, 'Who Was the Author of Glanvill? Reflections on the Education of Henry II's Common Lawyers' (1990) 8 *Law and History Review* 97.

[236] GDG Hall (ed.), *The Treatise on the Laws and Customs of the Realm of England and Commonly Called Glanvill* (Clarendon Press, 1993 [1965]) 1.

[237] Ibid. 2–3.   [238] Milsom, *Historical Foundations of the Common Law* 285.   [239] Ibid. 403–4.

[240] Hudson, *The Formation of the English Common Law*.

[241] Van Caenegem, *Royal Writs in England from the Conquest to Glanvill* 46–7.   [242] Ibid.

Conclusions 111

developments were felt on the ground is debatable. Hyams has suggested that 'local power equations may in fact have changed rather little under the new common-law regime'.[243] And Nicholas Karn has argued more generally that the influence of nineteenth-century historians has meant that the literature remains overly concerned with the central institutions that directly served the kings, and misunderstands governance in terms of institutions and bureaucratic relationships that fail to correspond to the shakier realities of medieval government.[244]

It should also be noted that the developments under Henry II did not continue unbroken under the reigns of his Plantagenet successors. For instance, from 1209 to 1214, the Bench at Westminster was suspended. Indeed, the same mixed pattern that was seen in relation to the Norman kings can also be witnessed in relation to the second and third Angevin kings. The reign of Richard I largely saw the continuation of the orderly administration and centralisation of justice that had characterised his father's reign.[245] Indeed, as Richard was an absentee king, visiting England just twice, the common law took on a life of its own at this time.[246] The country was now governed by the justiciars and official records of the business of the king's courts began to be kept.[247] Knights and other local dignities were appointed as 'keepers of the peace' in order to maintain order and record pleas of the crown.[248] Coroners were now appointed who, along with a jury, looked into sudden and unnatural deaths, reporting these to the visiting justices.[249]

Things changed, however, in the second half of the reign of John.[250] A series of disasters at home and abroad, including the loss of Normandy, an increase in taxation and the exploitation of feudal revenues, led to the king being excommunicated by the Pope in 1208 and the surrender of the realm to the Pope in 1213 to be held by the king only as a feudatory.[251] John was nick-named 'lack land' and 'soft sword', and from around 1207, the king's administration of justice became 'particularly oppressive and arbitrary' as the conflict between the king and his barons intensified.[252] This would culminate in 1215 to a royal concession of profound constitutional significance that we will examine in the next chapter: Magna Carta.

---

[243] Hyams, *Rancor & Reconciliation in Medieval England* 156.

[244] Nicholas Karn, 'Centralism and Local Government in Medieval England: Constitutional History and Assembly Politics, 950–1300' (2012) 10 *History Compass* 742.

[245] Maitland, *The Constitutional History of England* 14. See Ralph V Turner and Richard R Heiser, *The Reign of Richard the Lionheart* (Longman, 2000).

[246] Though it is important to note that Henry II was himself absent from England for twenty-one years of his thirty-five-year reign; Lyon, *Constitutional History of the United Kingdom* 53.

[247] See Ralph V Turner, *The English Judiciary in the Age of Glanvill and Bracton, c 1176–1239* (Cambridge University Press, 1985) chapter 3.

[248] They would later become known as justices of the peace, as will be discussed in Chapter 8.

[249] Briggs et al., *Crime and Punishment in England* 9. Their role was refocused under the Tudors: see KJ Kesselring, *Making Murder Public: Homicide in Early Modern England, 1480–1680* (Oxford University Press, 2019) chapter 2.

[250] See Ralph V Turner, *The English Judiciary in the Age of Glanvill and Bracton, c 1176–1239* (Cambridge University Press, 1985) chapter 4 and Ralph V Turner, *King John* (The History Press, 2015).

[251] Hudson, *The Oxford History of the Laws of England Volume II* 847.

[252] Ibid. 848; JR Maddicott, *The Origins of the English Parliament 924–1327* (Oxford University Press, 2010) 111.

'The great charter, from whatever point of view we regard it, is of course a document of the utmost importance ... It is intensely practical; it is no declaration in mere general terms of the rights of Englishmen, still less the rights of men; it goes through the grievances of the time one by one and promises redress. It is a definitive statement of law upon a great number of miscellaneous points. In many cases, so far as we can now judge, the law that it states is not new law; it represents the practice of Henry II's reign. The cry has not been that the law should be altered, but that it should be observed, in particular, that it should be observed by the king. Henceforward matters are not to be left to vague promises; the king's rights and their limits are to be set down ... [The] issue of so long, so detailed, so practical a document means that there is to be a reign of law'.

Frederic W Maitland, *The Constitutional History of England* (Cambridge University Press, 1941 [1908]) 14–15.

6

The Myth of Magna Carta (c.1215–1272)

I   Introduction

There is no document in the history of English law as well-known as Magna Carta. Even Frederic W Maitland was not immune to its charms. He wrote that Magna Carta has rightly become 'a sacred text, the nearest approach to an irrepealable "fundamental statute" that England has ever had'.[1] For Maitland, Magna Carta meant 'that the king is and shall be below the law'. Yet, there is also no document in the history of English law as misunderstood as Magna Carta. The leading commentator on the charter, JC Holt, wrote that:

In 1215 Magna Carta was a failure. It was intended as a peace and it provoked war. It pretended to state customary law and it prompted disagreement and contention. It was legally valid for no more than three months and even within that period is terms were never properly executed.[2]

In several respects, the Great Charter is much more mundane than its reputation suggests. Maitland conceded that the charter contained 'little that is absolutely new', and in the main accepted the reforms of Henry II.[3] It provided little resolution to baronial grievances relating to the king's exploitation of taxation and other feudal privileges. As Maitland noted, the charter was 'restorative': 'in the main the reforms of Henry II's day are accepted and are made a basis for the treaty'. Magna Carta was a response to King John's actions and was an explicit setting of standards: it established that 'the law must be defined and set in writing'. It is for this approach that Magna Carta was to prove important, not for the minute details of its contents. As Maitland put it, many of its clauses 'at least in their original meaning, have become hopelessly antiquated' but Magna Carta has remained a potent symbol that underlied that 'the king is and shall be below the law'.[4]

It was the existence of Magna Carta itself, rather than its contents, that was radical. Maitland notes that in some clauses there was 'even retrogression'.[5] He singled out clause 34, discussed in the last chapter, which decreed that a *praecipe* writ was not to 'be issued to anyone in respect of any holding of land, if a free man could thereby be deprived of the

---

[1] Frederick Pollock and Frederic W Maitland, *The History of English Law* (2nd ed., Cambridge University Press, 1968 [1898]) vol. 1, 173.

[2] JC Holt, *Magna Carta* (3rd ed., Cambridge University Press, 2015) 33.

[3] Pollock and Maitland, *The History of English Law* 172.   [4] Ibid. 173.   [5] Ibid. 172.

114 *The Myth of Magna Carta (c.1215–1272)*

right of trial in his own lord's court'. Maitland commented that this amounted to a recognition of the 'exclusive competence in proprietary actions' of feudal lords and their courts, and that 'Henry II would hardly have been forced into such an acknowledgment, and it does immeasurable harm to the form of English law, for lawyers and royal justices will soon be inventing elaborate devices for circumventing a principle which they cannot openly attack'.[6] The developments that we explored in the last chapter, which Maitland referred to as 'the horrible tangle of our "real actions, our "writs of entry" and so forth', were, in his opinion, the effect of clause 34 of Magna Carta.

Magna Carta was also not unique. As Maitland noted, although it 'came to be reckoned as the beginning of English statute law' and 'was printed as the first of the statutes of the realm', the truth is more complicated than that.[7] There was actually more than one Magna Carta: versions of the charter were issued in 1215, 1216, 1217 and 1225, and it was the 1225 charter that became considered to be the beginning of English statute law, being confirmed in 1237 and 1297. It was also quickly followed by other legislative documents that further clarified the law, most notably the Charter of the Forest in 1217 and the Statute of Merton in 1235. Magna Carta, then, was just one of a number of kingly compromises during this period which slowly began to establish the idea that the monarch ruled by consent. Most notably, the Provisions of Oxford 1258 was arguably as important in this regard as the Great Charter and yet is far less well known.

This chapter examines the legal importance of Magna Carta and places it in the context of the period that followed it. It surveys the period from the end of the reign of King John (1199–216) up to the end the reign of Henry III (1216–72).[8] This period, together with the reign of Edward I (1272–307), which will be the focus of the next chapter, was a bloody era, with strong-minded kings battling with their barons and turning their sights to Wales, Scotland and Ireland. The long reign of Henry III is perhaps best known for culminating in a long and protracted dispute with the barons, which led to civil war and a short period where the barons were victorious and their leader Simon de Montfort effectively became the uncrowned king of England. His reign was characterised by conflict but not by lawlessness. Indeed, as Maitland observed, 'Henry's tyranny was the tyranny of one who had a legal system under his control; it was enforced by legal processes, by judgments that the courts delivered, by writs that the courts upheld.'[9] If Magna Carta was largely 'restorative' of the rights and freedoms consolidated under Henry II,[10] the reign of Henry III saw the common law take 'definite shape'.[11] The end of the ordeal from 1215 onwards provided a significant move towards the modern jury system and the role of the common law courts became well established, as Maitland documented:

The King's Court has been steadily at work evolving common law; that law is carried through the length and breadth of the kingdom by the itinerant justices. As yet the judges have a free hand – they can create new remedies to meet new cases … English law, we see, is already becoming what we

---

[6] Ibid.   [7] Frederic W Maitland, *The Constitutional History of England* (Cambridge University Press, 1941 [1908]) 15.
[8] For discussion of the legal system under John, see Doris M Stenton, *English Justice between the Norman Conquest and the Great Charter* (Allen & Unwin, 1965) chapter 4.
[9] Pollock and Maitland, *The History of English Law* 174.   [10] Ibid. 172.
[11] Maitland, *The Constitutional History of England* 17.

now call 'case law' – a decided case is an 'authority' which ought to be followed when a similar case arises ... We may indeed regard the reign of Henry III as a golden age of judge-made law: the King's Court is rapidly becoming the regular court of all causes of great importance ... Also we now hear very little of local customs deviating from the common law; as the old local courts give way to the rising power of the King's Court so local customs give way to the common law.[12]

While attention usually focuses on the tensions with the barons and the growth of a body that will be known as Parliament, Henry III's reign was also characterised by the 'rapid, but steady and permanent growth' of the common law.[13] Indeed, Maitland went as far as to say that by the end of that period 'most of the major outlines of medieval law have been drawn for good and all; the subsequent centuries will be able to do little more than to fill in the details of a scheme which is set before them as unalterable'.[14]

The chapter explores how the common law continued to develop in this period. It falls into three sections. Section II discusses the importance and effect of Magna Carta. It explores what Magna Carta said and what effect it had upon feudalism, the operation of courts, governance and upon immigration. Section III will then explore the debate concerning the role the charter played in the development of Parliament, examining what Magna Carta said and also the importance of later developments during this period. Section IV will examine the impact of the charter upon the position of women.

II   The Great Charter?

Much has been written about the Great Charter that was sealed at Runnymede in 1215.[15] Yet, despite being hailed as a milestone that has been important for centuries, it needs to be remembered that in 1215 Magna Carta failed its main objective: It did not resolve the conflict between the king and the barons and its letter was not followed.[16] It was a political failure, at least in the short term. It was only in the medium to long term that Magna Carta became an important document in the constitutional development of England. The reputation and importance of Magna Carta rests on the fact that it provided a 'definitive statement of law upon a great number of miscellaneous points' of importance.[17] As Maitland put it, '[T]he issue of so long, so detailed, so practical a document, means that there is to be a reign of law.' It consolidated much of what had been achieved under Henry II. Magna Carta effectively restored the 'consensus which had marked the relationship between king and magnates for much of the twelfth century'.[18] Many provisions of Magna Carta had

---

[12] Ibid. 17–18.   [13] Pollock and Maitland, *The History of English Law* 174.   [14] Ibid.

[15] See, for instance, Holt, *Magna Carta*; AE Dick Howard, *Magna Carta: Text & Commentary* (University of Virginia Press, 1998); Clarie Breay, *Magna Carta: Manuscript and Myths* (The British Library, 2002); Danny Danziger and John Gillingham, *1215: The Year of Magna Carta* (Hodder and Stoughton, 2003); Katherine F Drew, *Magna Carta* (Greenwood Press, 2004); Randy J Holland (ed.), *Magna Carta: Muse & Mentor* (Thomson Reuters, 2014), Anthony Arlidge and Igor Judge, *Magna Carta Uncovered* (Hart, 2014); Robin Griffith-Jones and Mark Hill QC (eds.), *Magna Carta, Religion and The Rule of Law* (Cambridge University Press, 2015) and John Baker, *The Reinvention of Magna Carta 1216–1616* (Cambridge University Press, 2017).

[16] A papal bull annulled the charter and civil war resumed; John Hudson, *The Oxford History of the Laws of England Volume II: 871–1216* (Oxford University Press, 2012) 852.

[17] Maitland, *The Constitutional History of England* 15.

[18] JR Maddicott, *The Origins of the English Parliament 924–1327* (Oxford University Press, 2010) 106.

116   *The Myth of Magna Carta (c.1215–1272)*

their precedents in previous royal concessions, particularly Henry I's coronation decree.[19] That said, as John Hudson noted, Magna Carta contained a 'much wider and more detailed range of liberties' than previous concessions and so had 'continental parallels'.[20] As Anthony Musson has argued:

> Magna Carta yielded a new and (shifting) perspective, both in terms of the prevailing concepts of 'law' and 'justice' and with regard to political life in general. It can be seen to have reached beyond the purely legal content of its chapters, becoming ... the touchstone of all good governance and symbolising a body of 'rights' applicable to all. Magna Carta evolved from certain deeply held options and beliefs about law and government and, in turn, creates in people's minds expectations concerning royal justice and the king's authority.[21]

Bryce Lyon opined that there came to be two versions of Magna Carta: In addition to the real charter of the thirteenth century, there came to exist a fictitious version that served as a symbol.[22] Both served their purpose, in the medieval period[23] and beyond.[24] Magna Carta was and became contested, controversial and paradoxical. The way in which the charter innovated in the tone and generality of its language whilst simultaneously being conservative and even at times retrogressive in terms of the meanings of its provisions is shown clearly by its first clause, which stated that '[T]he English church shall be free, and shall have its rights diminished and its liberties unimpaired.'[25] This is a 'vague large promise' that arouses hopes that cannot be fulfilled.[26] Yet, in practical terms, it provided nothing that was new, making no concessions that had not already been conceded by previous kings and indeed by John himself.[27] While that first clause was granted to God, the remainder of the clauses were addressed to all free men in the kingdom and their heirs forever. The following sections examine the clauses of Magna Carta, organised into four themes (feudalism, courts, governance and immigration), while later sections will examine how the charter and later developments shaped the development of Parliament and the role of women.[28]

1   *Feudalism*

Much of Magna Carta was actually dedicated to maintaining the feudal status quo. Several clauses dealt with abuses in feudal relationships such as limiting the 'relief' to be paid by

---

[19] Hudson, *The Oxford History of the Laws of England Volume II* 848.   [20] Ibid. 849.

[21] Anthony Musson, *Medieval Law in Context* (Manchester University Press, 2001) 2.

[22] Bryce Lyon, *A Constitutional and Legal History of Medieval England* (2nd ed., Norton, 1980) 324.

[23] Lyon noted that: 'Between 1215 and the end of the Middle Ages Magna Carta acquired three roles. It was cited as legal precedent in the pleadings and sentencings of the common law courts it was adopted by barons as part of their political program in the numerous struggles to curb the royal prerogative and is came to be confirmed by the kings at the openings of Parliament' (ibid. 310).

[24] For comprehensive discussion of the legacy of Magna Carta up to the seventeenth century, see Baker, *The Reinvention of Magna Carta 1216–1616*. Lyon observed that while seventeenth- and eighteenth-century writers often hailed Magna Carta as 'a potent weapon in the struggle for constitutional government', late nineteenth-century scholars reacted against this 'myth of Magna Carta', denigrating it as a 'feudal reaction and a block in the road towards progress'. Lyon cautions that the truth lies somewhere between these two interpretations; Lyon, *A Constitutional and Legal History of Medieval England* 321, 311.

[25] Although the original charter was not divided into clauses, all recent editions and translations have divided it into paragraphs that are variously referred to as clauses, chapters and articles.

[26] Pollock and Maitland, *The History of English Law* 172.

[27] Lyon, *A Constitutional and Legal History of Medieval England* 315.

[28] For a clause-by-clause account of Magna Carta, see Howard, *Magna Carta* and Breay, *Magna Carta* on which the following sections rely upon. It therefore uses their numbering of the original 1215 charter, while others tend to use the 1225 charter.

The Great Charter? 117

heirs (clauses 2 and 3), allowing guardians to take only reasonable profits from the land and imposing an obligation on guardians to maintain the land (clauses 4 and 5). The situations where the crown could take guardianship were limited (clause 37). As we noted in Chapter 4, feudal aids were limited to three kinds: ransom of the king or lord, the knighting of the king or lord's eldest son, and the marriage of the king or lord's eldest daughter, and even then, there needed to be a reasonable 'aid' (clauses 12 and 15). The levying of other aids required the general consent of the realm through a specially summoned council of archbishops, bishops, abbots, earls and greater barons (clause 14). The services that were to be performed for a knight's fee or other freeholding of land were limited so that the no more service was to be given than was due from it (clause 16). The land of convicted felons was to be returned to the lord within a year and a day (clause 32).[29]

Moreover, as we have seen, Magna Carta also protected the rights of feudal courts to hear certain actions.[30] It dictated that trials concerning the writs of *Novel Disseisin, Mort D'Ancestor* and *Darrein Presentment* were to be held in the county where the property was situated (clause 18). Furthermore, praecipe writs were not to be issued to anyone in respect of landholding if that deprived a free man of the right to trial in his own lord's court (clause 34). However, Magna Carta's feudal focus did not mean that the charter sought to undo the reforms of Henry II and the growth of royal justice that had begun to eclipse the local feudal courts. Indeed, Lyon noted that Magna Carta strengthened the reforms of Henry II by preventing the abuses that had occurred under John whereby justice had become arbitrary and the king had 'denied the royal court to numerous causes and he sold his justice at exorbitant prices to others'.[31]

2   Courts

Several provisions of Magna Carta consolidated the operation of both royal and feudal courts. In terms of royal justice, the Great Charter centralised royal justice, declaring that Common Pleas (ordinary lawsuits) were no longer to follow the royal court geographically but were to be held in a fixed place, which turned out to be Westminster (clause 17).[32] This confirmed a judicial custom that had evolved gradually before the tyranny of King John.[33] Similarly, Magna Carta strengthened and regulated the assize procedure that had been established under Henry II.[34] Two justices were to be sent to each county four times a year and these with four knights of the county were to hold the assizes on a given day but were

---

[29] Similar provision was made for the holding of escheats (clause 43) and the guardianship of abbeys (clause 46).

[30] Clause 34 prevented *Praecipe* writs from being 'issued to anyone in respect of any holding whereby a free man may lose his court'. *Praecipe* writs will be discussed in the next chapter.

[31] Lyon, *A Constitutional and Legal History of Medieval England* 313. There was also concern aroused by 'John's predilection for "familiar counsel" and his general "disingenuous" and "evasive" character in the extent to which and the manner in how he consulted magnate councils' (Maddicott, *The Origins of the English Parliament 924–1327* 112–13).

[32] Hudson noted that the phrase 'Common Pleas' was 'probably not yet a technical term, rather indicating pleas arising from the general royal jurisdiction' (Hudson, *The Oxford History of the Laws of England Volume II* 851).

[33] Lyon, *A Constitutional and Legal History of Medieval England* 318; Hudson, *The Oxford History of the Laws of England Volume II* 851.

[34] Lyon, *A Constitutional and Legal History of Medieval England* 318; Pollock and Maitland, *The History of English Law* 172.

to stay behind if necessary (clauses 18 and 19). Only men who knew the law of the land and would keep it well were to be appointed as justices, constables, sheriffs or bailiffs (clause 45). But such sheriffs, constables, coroners or bailiffs were not to hear pleas of the crown (clause 24).

The charter also included some safeguards about the administration of justice. It decreed that fines should be in proportion to the offence and should only be imposed by an oath of peers (clauses 20, 21 and 22). There was to be no arbitrary seizing of property without consent (clauses 28, 29, 30 and 31). A person was not to be put to trial without producing credible witnesses to the truth of the allegation (clause 38).[35] No right or justice was to be sold, denied or delayed (clause 40).

One of the, if not the, most famous clause of the charter provided that no free person was to be taken, imprisoned, disseised, outlawed or banished except by the lawful judgment of peers or by the law of the land, and the same was to apply to proceedings against or prosecutions of any free man (clause 39). It is often thought that the germ of the idea of 'due process of law' can be found here: The idea that the legal rights owed to a person must be respected by what we would call the State. However, it is important not to read too much into this provision. It simply guaranteed a judgment given in court; the reference to 'lawful judgment of his peers' referred to a judgment given in a court composed of the magnates.[36] The reference to peers referred simply to communal justice.

The word 'or' in the clause has proved especially controversial: The provision mentions trial according to lawful judgment of peers or by the law of the land. Thomas J McSweeney has argued that this presents two alternative ways in which a free man could be tried.[37] The reference to 'law of the land', he suggested, could refer to an oath. He concluded that 'Magna Carta guaranteed a trial, but not a trial by jury.'[38] The catalyst for that was the other momentous event of 1215: the Fourth Lateran Council of the Western church that forbade clerics to bless judicial ordeals. Juries or their equivalent had long been used to declare local customs and to find facts (often referred to as the inquest).[39] By 1221, however, trial by jury had replaced the ordeal as the means to try felons in the royal courts.[40] As time went on, the effects of the two events of 1215 became blurred: people 'came to think of trial by jury as a protection against royal tyranny and, over time, they began to associate it with Magna Carta'.[41]

---

[35] Similar rules applied in relation to the harsher 'forest law' that was applied in districts set aside by the monarch for sport and hunting (clauses 44, 47 and 48).

[36] Maddicott, *The Origins of the English Parliament 924–1327* 117.

[37] Thomas J McSweeney, 'Magna Carta and the Right to Trial by Jury' in Holland, *Magna Carta* 139, 146.   [38] Ibid. 149.

[39] The writs of *Novel Disseisin* and *Mort D'Ancestor* used juries as a matter of fact to decide land disputes, while the juries of presentment in criminal cases served as a further precursor for this. As Briggs et al. noted: 'It was not a difficult or a large jump, therefore, to adapt the civil juries in land cases to criminal cases' (John Briggs, Christopher Harrison, Angus McInnes and David Vincent, *Crime and Punishment in England: An Introductory History* (UCL Press, 1996) 10).

[40] McSweeney, 'Magna Carta and the Right to Trial by Jury' 153. Trial by battle, however, remained possible in an appeal of felony, but over time such actions 'ceased to be a significant component of the criminal justice system' (Margaret H Kerr, 'Angevin Reform of the Appeal of Felony' (1995) 13(2) *Law and History Review* 351, 352).

[41] For detailed discussion of this, see Baker, *The Reinvention of Magna Carta 1216–1616* 32–42 and chapters 2 and 7. In Baker's numbering, this clause is chapter 29.

3   *Governance*

Several provisions in Magna Carta dealt with issues of governance. Several provisions concerned local government. The ancient liberties and free customs of local government were protected (clause 13), and this was manifested in the specific but at the time important provision that localities were not to be obliged to build bridges over rivers (clause 23).[42] Most provisions, however, involved the central government of the king. As might be expected from what was effectively a peace treaty of a conflict won by the barons and lost by the king, a number of provisions sought to correct the king's past wrongs, including requiring the return of hostages (clause 49) and the remission of unlawful fines (clause 55). Anyone dissiesed or deprived without legal judgment of land, castles, liberties or rights were to have them restored, with some exceptions such as if the king went on a crusade (clauses 52 and 53).[43] Mercenaries were to be expelled (clause 51) and certain persons were specified to be prevented from holding any office (clause 50). All ill will, wrath and malice that had arisen during the disputes between the king and his barons were to be wholly remitted and pardoned (clause 62).

The most important provisions, however, related to the enforcement of the charter. The customs and liberties granted by the charter were said to apply to all subjects whether clerics or laymen and should be observed by all (clause 60). A committee of twenty-five barons were to be elected by the barons to enforce the charter, to swear to keep faithfully the provisions and to cause them to be kept by others (clause 61). The charter concluded by repeating that the English Church shall be free and that all men in the kingdom shall have and hold the liberties, rights and concessions laid out in the charter, and that they and their heirs should enjoy them peaceably, freely, quietly and fully (clause 63). In short, the charter sought to bring an end to what has been referred to as 'Angevin absolutism'.[44] In doing so, Maitland noted that its main achievement was its iteration that 'the king is and shall be below the law'.[45] Magna Carta was important, in that defined limitations to royal rights were established in written law. However, it is important to note that 'Magna Carta did not initiative effective limited monarchy'; its letter was not followed and even if it had been, the terms of the charter 'did not prevent the king from misgovernment it merely punished him for it'.[46] Although Magna Carta was largely a rearticulating of ideas previously assumed,[47] it gave legal force to them, including the possibility of legal and extra-legal enforcement. As DA Carpenter has put it, the charter 'set a standard by which the activities of kings might be judged, making absolutism more difficult and protest more legitimate'.[48]

---

[42] Local rent charges were also to remain at their ancient levels (clause 25).
[43] Similar provisions applied to Scottish hostages (clause 59) and Welsh rights and hostages (clauses 56, 57 and 58).
[44] Lyon, *A Constitutional and Legal History of Medieval England* 314.
[45] Pollock and Maitland, *The History of English Law* 173.
[46] Lyon, *A Constitutional and Legal History of Medieval England* 322.
[47] Coronation oaths requiring the king to judge with justice and mercy dated back to the late Anglo-Saxon period, and the idea that the king could rule without restating such an oath is fanciful given the possibility of rebellion; Maddicott, *The Origins of the English Parliament 924–1327* 34, 97.
[48] DA Carpenter, *The Minority of Henry III* (University of California Press, 1990) 404.

4   Immigration

A number of provisions in Magna Carta dealt with free trade. Obstacles to free trade were removed, such as the fishweirs that clogged up rivers (clause 33). Standard weights and measures were to be established (clause 35). All merchants were to have free movement out of and into England, and to stay in and travel through England in accordance with ancient and just customs except in time of war (clause 41). The same right applied to all except prisoners and outlaws (clause 42). These last two clauses laid important foundations for the law on immigration. Before this point, there was no special regulation of 'aliens', those of foreign birth who were resident in England.[49] This was despite the fact that by the late medieval era, 'England was a temporary or permanent home to hundreds of thousands of people of foreign birth' who came from other parts of the British isles, from more or less all regions of continental Europe, and as time went on from the wider world of Africa and Asia.[50] The reason for this lack of special regulation was that England has been ruled by those of Scandinavian or French birth or descent for centuries, and so 'since many of these had interests outside England, it was impossible to have a legal system limited only to defending the rights of native-born "English"'.[51] The result was that generally English law from the Conquest to the twelfth century 'tended to be inclusive in its approach to English and Normans'.[52] This meant that those from outside the Norman and Plantagenet dominions who were resident in England 'were effectively ignored by the law, and had no observable rights within the realm'.[53]

Mark Ormrod et al. suggested that the expansion of commercial activity during the thirteenth century 'put pressure upon the crown to provide foreign merchants with a clearer sense of the rights they enjoyed while they remained within England's borders'.[54] This was behind the securities and freedoms provided in Magna Carta, which 'acknowledged that such men were an integral part of the English economy'. This conflicted with a much more restrictive approach taken by the City of London, which limited their visits to forty days.[55] Their important economic role was also in tension with the consequence of the realm's foreign policy.[56] War and the loss of overseas land such as Normandy under King John resulted in 'a very significant change of attitude towards people born outside the realm'.[57] This is, for Maitland, where 'our law of aliens finds its starting point'.[58] During the conflict with the barons in the reign of Henry III, 'his opponents picked up the idea that the king's "natural" (that is, native-born advisers among the political elite) ought to have a greater say'.

---

[49] W Mark Ormrod, Bart Lambert and Jonathan Mackman, *Immigrant England 1300–1550* (Manchester University Press, 2019) 19, 12. The terms 'alien', 'foreigner' and 'stranger' were in frequent use in later medieval England; the term 'immigrant' was not used until the eighteenth century (ibid. 8, 7). See also Joanna Story, W Mark Ormrod and Elizabeth M Tyler, 'Framing Migration in Medieval England' in W Mark Ormrod, Joanna Story and Elizabeth M Tyler (eds.), *Migrants in Medieval England, c500–1500* (Oxford University Press, 2021) 1.

[50] Ormrod, Lambert and Mackman, *Immigrant England 1300–1550* 1.   [51] Ibid. 12.

[52] There were exceptions, most notably in relation to the murdrum fine that applied where the murder victim was a Norman: ibid. 12.

[53] Ibid. 19.   [54] Ibid.   [55] Other towns followed the London example; ibid. 20.

[56] See Jenny Kermode, *Medieval Merchants: York, Beverley and Hull in the Later Middle Ages* (Cambridge University Press, 2002) and the essays in Caroline M Barron and Anne F Sutton (eds.), *The Medieval Merchant* (Paul Watkins Publishing, 2014).

[57] Ormrod, Lambert and Mackman, *Immigrant England 1300–1550* 12.

[58] Pollock and Maitland, *The History of English Law* 461.

The Great Charter? 121

Wars with Scotland and France 'reinforced those trends'. This culminated in legislation that stated that 'the realm of England should in future be governed by native-born men'.[59]

Legislation under Edward I built upon Magna Carta so as to allow aliens to recover outstanding debts in the royal courts with Carta Mercatoria ('the charter of the merchants') in 1303, providing that aliens had the right to a remedy in civil actions.[60] Moreover, in all pleas (except criminal cases punishable by death) in which the merchant was one of the parties, the 'half-tongue jury' was to apply. Provided that there was a sufficient number of merchants, half of the jury was to be selected from those merchants and the other half 'from reputable and law-abiding men of the place that the lawsuit happens to take place'. The 1303 charter also provided that a justice of the merchants was to be appointed so that merchants were 'able to bring their lawsuits and recover their debts speedily, in the event that the mayor and sheriffs do not provide them with full justice on a daily basis'. However, the access to the royal courts meant that separate tribunals were not necessary. Aliens were not permitted, however, to hold land in their own right, though this rule was circumvented by some urban jurisdictions that allowed aliens to become 'free men' or 'citizens of the place in question'.[61] These legal securities were also furthered by political actions. Most notably, in 1285, Edward I replaced the mayor of London with a royal warden, tasked with 'ensuring that merchants were able to trade more easily within the city'.[62]

However, as Magna Carta had stated, these rights and freedoms could be and were suspended during times of international conflict. A dispute between Henry III and the countess of Flanders in 1270–1 led to the arrest of all Flemish merchants, while Edward I's war with France led to the arrest of all of the subjects of the king of France found in England.[63] In both cases, belongings and assets were seized. Moreover, rights and freedoms were also suspended by exclusionary policies and ethnic cleansing directed at the Jewish communities. It is thought that the first Jews arrived in England as a result of the Norman Conquest:[64] a group of Jewish merchants from Normandy were invited in 1070. They played an important role as moneylenders and bankers, given that others could not fulfil such roles because the Catholic Church prohibited usury (the making of loans that enrich the lender).[65] Although Jewish communities were granted some rights, there was also evidence of violent anti-Semitism, most notably in the massacres at London and in York under Richard I.[66] They were also taxed heavily with the exchequer of the Jews

---

[59] This legislation was quashed the following year. See David A Carpenter, 'King Henry III's "Statute" against Aliens: July 1263' (1992) 107 *English Historical Review* 925, reprinted as David A Carpenter, *The Reign of Henry III* (Hambledon Press, 1996) chapter 14.

[60] Ormrod, Lambert and Mackman, *Immigrant England 1300–1550* 20. This was preceded by the Statute of Merchants of 1283 (also known as the Statute of Acton Brunell) and Statute of the Merchants of 1285.

[61] Ibid. 21.   [62] Tim Unwin, *Wine and Vine: An Historical Geography of Viticulture and the Wine Trade* (Routledge, 1996) 192.

[63] Ormrod, Lambert and Mackman, *Immigrant England 1300–1550* 21.

[64] Pollock and Maitland, *The History of English Law* 468.

[65] For discussion of the practice, see Richard Huscroft, *Expulsion: England's Jewish Solution* (The History Press, 2013) chapter 3 and Gwen Seabourne, *Royal Regulation of Loans and Sales in Medieval England* (Boydell Press, 2003) chapter 2.

[66] See the essays in Sarah Rees Jones and Seithina Watson (eds.), *Christians and Jews in Angevin England: The York Massacre of 1190, Narrative and Contexts* (York Medieval Press, 2016) and for the general background, see Joe Hillaby, 'Jewish Colonisation in the Twelfth Century' in Patricia Skinner (ed.), *Jews in Medieval England* (Boydell Press, 2003) 15.

122   *The Myth of Magna Carta (c.1215–1272)*

functioning as a division of the Court of Exchequer.[67] Although there had been previous legislation dealing with the financial activities of the Jews, the Statute of Jewry of 1253 broke new ground in being concerned with the threat that they were seen to pose to the Christian faith.[68] This statute was 'very much Henry's personal initiative' and was not agreed by 'common counsel' in parliament. The motive of gaining favour with the Church loomed large, and much of the provisions elucidated the teaching of the Catholic Church.[69]

Although it mostly restated past decrees and its effectiveness is largely unknown,[70] the Statute of Jewry set the scene for the horrors that were to come. The statute insisted that the Jewish community were in England due to the king's bidding: they were only to remain if they would 'serve us in some way'. It prevented the building of any further synagogues and declared that Jews should lower their voices during worship so that they could not be heard.[71] 'Secret familiarity' between Jews and Christians was prohibited, and Jews were obliged to pay to their local Christian church. Jews were to wear badges and had to obtain a licence if they wished to live in a town that did not already have a Jewish community. The Statute of the Jewry 1275 under Edward I went further again, outlawing usury and writing off certain debts owed to Jews.[72] All Jews now had to wear a yellow felt badge and pay a special tax annually. They were only allowed to live in towns and cities where there was a Jewish settlement. The outlawing of money-lending effectively prevented them from earning a living, and the illicit money-lending that continued to occur was to prompt even more drastic actions.[73] On his return to England in July 1290, Edward issued a decree that all Jews should leave England before the November of that year, issuing the sheriffs of all English counties to enforce this.[74] Tens of thousands of Jews were expelled in this act of ethnic cleansing and, as Ormrod et al. noted, this action would have significant long term effects:

Edward I's decision to expel all Jews from England in 1290, and the official upholding of this ordinance until the seventeenth century, meant that England was marked by deep cultural and institutional discrimination against racial minorities. Muslims from southern Europe, North Africa and the Middle East – usually referred to as 'Saracens' in medieval Christendom – were not subject to an official ban, but the presumption was that they, like the Jews, were only officially acknowledged in England if they accepted conversion to Christianity.[75]

This added a further dimension to Magna Carta's pledge that the English Church would be free. The safeguarding of the freedom of the Catholic religion did not extend to protecting other faiths. The reverse was true. Showing support and favour for the Church and getting

---

[67] Pollock and Maitland, *The History of English Law* 470. On the exchequer, see Paul Brand, 'The Jewish Community of England in the Records of English Royal Government' in Skinner, *Jews in Medieval England* 15. On the position under Henry III generally, see Robert C Stacey, 'The English Jews under Henry III' in Skinner, *Jews in Medieval England* 41.

[68] David Carpenter, *Henry III: The Rise to Power and Personal Rule* (Yale University Press, 2020) 563.

[69] John Edwards, 'The Church and Jews in Medieval England' in Skinner, *Jews in Medieval England* 85, 94.

[70] Darren Baker, *Henry III: The Great King England Never Knew It Had* (The History Press, 2019) 215.

[71] Carpenter, *Henry III* 563.

[72] For discussion of the period of Edward I generally see Robin R Mundill, 'Edward I and the Final Phase of Anglo-Jewry' in Skinner, *Jews in Medieval England* 55.

[73] Though it has also been argued that some Jews had adapted; Robin R Mundill, *England's Jewish Solution, Experiment and Expulsion, 1262–1290* (Cambridge University Press, 1998) 25–7.

[74] For discussion, see Huscroft, *Expulsion* chapter 6.   [75] Ormrod, Lambert and Mackman, *Immigrant England 1300–1550* 3.

The Origins of Parliament 123

the Pope on side required Catholicism to be seen as the only true faith, which justified horrific acts of discrimination and exclusion that would have long-term ramifications.[76]

III   The Origins of Parliament

There is much debate as to the origins of Parliament. Magna Carta is often considered to be part of this story. The origins of Parliament are sometimes attributed to the establishment of the council described in clauses 14 and 12, which stated that feudal aids or scutage (the money paid in lieu of knight service) were to be levied by 'common counsel of our Kingdom'.[77] Clause 12 is often interpreted as saying that 'no taxation could be imposed without the consent of Parliament'. Yet, as Lyon pointed out, this is to misunderstand the role of the counsel, which 'was not a parliament, it was a royal feudal court exercising a traditional feudal right – the consent to extraordinary feudal taxes'.[78] This means that 'Magna Carta did not, it must be emphasized create Parliament; it only regularized the summoning of a great council'. Similar misconceptions exist regarding the role of the barons. While this provision was important in that it provided a check on kingly powers, it was also ineffective. Dick Howard has retorted that 'a greater invitation to quarrels between the king and the barons could hardly be imagined'.[79] Magna Carta did not provide for the origin of Parliament but it was an important precursor to its development. As John Maddicott put it, the charter 'marked a significant stride in the transformation of the old council, the lineal descendent of the witan, into the Parliament of the 13th century'.[80]

Most conventional accounts have regarded the reign of John's successor, Henry III (1216–72), as being the formative period that laid the seeds for Parliament to truly develop in the reign of Edward I (1272–1307). Although the term had been used before then, it was the period from Magna Carta to the death of Edward I that saw the term Parliament being 'used for the special occasional meetings of the King's Council to which a larger group of the king's subjects were summoned'.[81] It was also this period 'when representatives of the counties, of towns and cities, and of the lower clergy were first summoned to attend such meetings' and when petitions started to be submitted to the king and council in Parliament, with the first official surviving records of Parliament dating back to this time.[82] Commentators have often distinguished different periods. The period of 1215–72 has been referred to as the 'pre-history of parliament'[83] or its 'prelude',[84] while the years 1272–1377 have been considered to be the 'formation'[85] of Parliament, or its

---

[76] Cf. 'Whether the sojourn of the Jews in England left any permanent marks upon the body of our law is a question that we dare not debate' (Pollock and Maitland, *The History of English Law* 475).
[77] Except for the three exceptions in clause 12. Clause 14 dealt with how the 'common counsel' was to be summoned.
[78] Lyon, *A Constitutional and Legal History of Medieval England* 317, 322.   [79] Howard, *Magna Carta* 21.
[80] John Maddicott, 'Origins and Beginnings to 1215' in Clyve Jones (ed.), *A Short History of Parliament* (Boydell Press, 2009) 3, 7.
[81] Paul Brand, 'The Development of Parliament 1215–1307' in Jones, *A Short History of Parliament* 10.
[82] David A Carpenter suggested that the first official use of the term was the adjournment of a law case in 1236; Carpenter, *The Reign of Henry III* 382.
[83] JC Holt, 'The Prehistory of Parliament' in RG Davies and JH Denton (eds.), *The English Parliament in the Middle Ages* (Manchester University Press, 1981) 1.
[84] R Butt, *A History of Parliament: The Middle Ages* (Constable, 1989) chapter 1.
[85] GL Harriss, 'The Formation of Parliament, 1272–1377' in Davies and Denton, *The English Parliament in the Middle Ages* 29.

124   *The Myth of Magna Carta (c.1215–1272)*

'emergence'.[86] However, regardless of the terminology used, the origins of Parliament are typically attributed to the thirteenth century. It was then when the word Parliament moved into common usage and 'the thing itself acquired its later constitution of king, lords, and commons'.[87]

However, some commentators, most notably Maddicott,[88] trace the origins much further back. For Maddicott, the origins of the English Parliament lay in the 'simple and primitive practice' of 'a leader, usually a king, taking counsel within his great men'.[89] Its genesis can therefore be traced back to the witan,[90] which emerged in the late Anglo-Saxon period and, though described variously,[91] remained common during the reigns of the Norman kings (except under Stephen) and the Angevin kings. Although the frequency, form and duration of gatherings became shaped by each king's 'own policies, habits and preferences',[92] the role of such gatherings became strengthened by the way in which feudal tenure began to determine and oblige attendance at such gatherings, in that 'summons to the King's Council was generally determined by status as a tenant-in-chief'.[93] Coronation charters had long 'created a closer link between assemblies and restraints on kingship'.[94] The Great Council 'attained an unprecedented prominence' during the reign of Richard, given the King's absence and it developed 'a growing claim to represent the real interests of the king and kingdom'.[95]

Maddicott argued that this memory helped to shape views for the future, setting expectations that were not met during the reign of John and which led in part to Magna Carta. He claimed that the origins of popular representation can be dated back to the reigns of Richard and John. At this time, local government became more important and counties took on a new role, rather than 'simply responding to direction from above' each county 'became a more overtly political community'.[96] The financial pressures brought about by war meant that counties began to process 'a corporate will and a voice through which grievances could be expressed, and with the capacity to be represented at the centre of government'. Leading knights became seen more formally as heads of their community and represented their country in bargaining with the crown.[97] For Maddicott, the 'principle that the magnates could represent the realm had begun to be turned against the king' prior to 1215 but the regulation provided by Magna Carta 'was adventitiously to shape the way in parliament evolved', albeit as part of a wider European shift 'from assemblies to proto-Parliaments'.[98]

Indeed, Maddicott's account stated that it was the reign of Henry III that was to prove crucial, refuting conventional views that stressed the importance of reigns of later

---

[86] Butt, *A History of Parliament* chapter 2.   [87] Maddicott, *The Origins of the English Parliament 924–1327* 440.

[88] He notes that the argument that 'the start of the story comes much earlier … revive[s] what may seem to be an archaic and outdated orthodoxy', as found in the work of Stubbs; ibid. vii. See further Carpenter, *The Reign of Henry III* chapter 19.

[89] Maddicott, *The Origins of the English Parliament 924–1327* 1. This is based on the notion that the king's need for council as acknowledged by kings themselves in charters 'was a concomitant if oblique emphasis on the need for assemblies' (ibid. 36).

[90] Though he asked, 'do we have here an institution, a capitalized "Witan", as it were, or merely a lower-case ad hoc gathering of the wise men?' (ibid. 4).

[91] Ibid. 74.   [92] For instance, in relation to crown-wearing; ibid. 73.

[93] Ibid. 79. Carpenter, however, has cautioned that 'much remains obscure about the history of the council, notably its composition and the formality and regularity of its sessions' (Carpenter, *The Reign of Henry III* 388).

[94] Maddicott, *The Origins of the English Parliament 924–1327* 99.   [95] Ibid. 109, 111.   [96] Ibid. 134.   [97] Ibid. 135, 139.

[98] Ibid. 107, 142, 106.

The Origins of Parliament

Plantagenet kings. Henry was nine years of age when he came to the throne, and so it is customary to separate his reign into two periods: his 'minority' of 1216–27, in which the affairs of the realm were placed in the hands of a group of regents, and his 'majority' after 1227, when Henry began issuing charters.[99] However, Maddicott instead distinguished three periods within Henry's reign: the 'transformation' of Parliament prior to 1227; the 'establishment' of Parliament in the years 1227–58; and the 'consolidation' of Parliament from 1258 to 1272. The following develops this to identify the four main pieces of what modern eyes would call legislation: (1) Magna Carta and the Charter of the Forest; (2) the Statute of Merton 1235; (3) the Provisions of Oxford 1258 and the Provisions of Westminster 1259; and (4) the Statute of Marlborough 1267. The first and second of these pieces of legislation respectively map upon the first two periods identified by Maddicott. The third and fourth pieces of legislation can both be found within his third period of the 'consolidation' of Parliament.

1   *Magna Carta and the Charter of the Forest*

Maddicot's first period covered Henry's minority, which he referred to as the 'transformation' of Parliament prior to 1227.[100] The early years of Henry's reign was dominated by the continued fallout from his father's reign. When he came to the throne, half the country was controlled by Louis, the eldest son of King Phillip of France, who had been offered the throne by the barons.[101] Although Louis had been defeated within a year, civil war erupted in 1217, which led to the re-issuing of Magna Carta and the Charter of the Forest, which imposed tighter restrictions on kingship.[102] For the first time, the forest land was not simply subject to the king's will. The bench of justices and the exchequer was reinstated and 'the government moved with speed'.[103] This was followed by a decade in which 'magnate assemblies were especially prominent' to such a degree that it was 'in effect a period of proto-parliamentary government'.[104] The kingdom was governed by 'small and shifting combination of magnates, ministers, and churchmen' and by means of numerous councils and assemblies though 'there was no temporal or locational pattern to their meetings'.[105] These associations sanctioned taxes and made ministerial appointments.[106] Notably, in February 1225, a week-long Great Council was held in light of conflict with the French, which led to agreement for a general tax on moveable goods if the king would confirm and reissue Magna Carta.[107]

For Maddicott, this Great Council of 1225 provided a paradigm for the later parliaments of the thirteenth and fourteenth centuries. It was 'summoned in advance of a foreign campaign and in order to finance that campaign, as well as to provide more generally for the kingdom's defence'.[108] It led to the reissuing of Magna Carta and the Charter of the Forest in what was to be their final form, with a new preamble that stated that they had been

---

[99] Ibid. 148.   [100] See ibid. 147–56.   [101] Carpenter, *The Minority of Henry III* 1.   [102] Ibid. 62   [103] Ibid. 65.
[104] Maddicott, *The Origins of the English Parliament 924–1327* 148.   [105] Ibid. 148, 149.   [106] Ibid. 150.
[107] Ibid. 107, 108.   [108] Ibid.

126 *The Myth of Magna Carta (c.1215–1272)*

issued by the king's 'spontaneous and free will'.[109] From now on, no new versions of these charters were to be made, rather, kings would confirm those of 1225.[110]

2   *The Statute of Merton 1235*

Maddicott's second period was the 'establishment' of Parliament in the years 1227–58,[111] in which 'constitutional practices which had solidified during the minority were confirmed'.[112] The word Parliament began to be commonly used to describe large assemblies and the English Parliament took 'the shape which, with some variations, it was to maintain for the rest of the middle ages'[113]: it acquired a core and more varied membership, including smaller landholders of the knightly class and was summoned fairly regularly at fixed times at Westminster, and had 'generally recognized if loosely defined functions', including the dispending of justice.[114] Maddicott suggested, however, that the assembly was not primarily a judicial occasion. Although justice was often dispensed during the time that Parliament was assembled, 'relatively few judicial cases' were heard in Parliament, and those that were related to matters that had been 'staple fare for earlier councils': state trials and disputes between magnates over land and other rights.[115] Much of the judicial work associated with Parliament simply consisted 'of cases deferred until Parliament met, so that they could be dealt with by the appropriate judges and officials and by the courts then in session'.[116]

In this second period, Parliament had become 'a platform from which the king's actions could be publicly examined and opposed': between 1237 and 1258, Henry asked and was refused a general tax on at least ten occasions, though 'he secured consolation prizes in the form of the less valuable feudal aids'.[117] The vagueness of the charters, underlined by the omission of clause 63 in the reissued versions, proved problematic once the period of Henry's minority finished.[118] Now, the king could choose his own ministers and used the opportunity to decrease the importance of positions such as chancellor and justiciar.[119] While the minority councils were 'both small gatherings of ministers and large assemblies of ministers and magnates', Henry sought advice from a small council that became formalised from 1236. Such developments proved controversial and resulted in a backlash.

This resulted in the Statute of Merton 1235 (also known as the Provisions of Merton), which is sometimes considered to be the first English statute (depending on whether Magna Carta is considered as a statute prior to its confirmation in 1297). Like Magna Carta, it was the result of a further struggle between the king and his barons. It provided a range of provisions, including giving further rights to widows and minors and providing that

---

[109] Carpenter, *The Minority of Henry III* 383. As Matthew Lewis has noted: 'This was, crucially, the first ever granting of the Charters by the truly free will of the king and they were given a new level of force, authority and meaning in that subtle alteration' (Matthew Lewis, *Henry III: The Son of Magna Carta* (Amberley, 2018) 102).

[110] David Carpenter, *The Struggle for Mastery* (Penguin, 2004) 307.

[111] See Maddicott, *The Origins of the English Parliament 924–1327* chapter 4.

[112] There were some exceptions but the way in which reference was made to Magna Carta to resolve them indicated that kingship resting on 'force and will' was 'no longer possible'; ibid. 166, 168.

[113] Ibid.   [114] Ibid. 198, 156, 182, 184.   [115] Ibid. 185.   [116] Ibid. 186.   [117] Ibid. 175, 173.

[118] Carpenter, *The Minority of Henry III* 406, 407–8.

[119] The office of justiciar was allowed to lapse after 1234 and the title of chancellor was frequently left in abeyance from 1244; ibid. 409.

The Origins of Parliament

freemen were represented by an attorney in the county court. A crucial provision gave the right for lords to enclose commons and waste land, provided that sufficient pasture for tenants was available. Given that most land was common land, this provision clearly benefitted lords as well as mortmain corporations such as monasteries. The statute also provided a remedy for redissessin: where A had legally secured possession of the land but B dispossessed him for a second time, the sheriff was to hold a meeting with the twelve knights or free men and an inquest with the coroner, and if they found that the second repossession had taken place, then the land was returned to A and B was imprisoned. The provisions on enclosure and common land were to reverberate through the centuries, but perhaps the most important thing about the Statute of Merton 1235 was that it showed that the actions of 1215 were no longer an exceptional one-off. The statute was the product of the Great Council meeting at Merton at which kingly concessions were sought by barons who were fearful of being sidelined. And like the Great Charter, the events at Merton did not end the conflict between the king and the barons. Indeed, by the end of Maddicott's second period, Henry had been overtaken 'by schemes of political reform more radical than the Charters; schemes which both took control of central government out of his hands and regulated in detail the running of local government'.[120] This resulted in the Provisions of Oxford 1258.

3 The Provisions of Oxford 1258 and the Provisions of Westminster 1259

The third and final period identified by Maddicott was the 'consolidation' of Parliament from 1258 to 1272.[121] The year 1258 proved to be a turning point, marking what GO Sayles described as 'the date of the conception of organised parliaments in England'.[122] Discontent caused by Henry III's foreign policy pursuits and his governing style (not only the constant tension over 'whether the King alone had the power to choose his ministers'[123] but also his wider 'failure to consult, his exploitation of the church, his thriftlessness, his fiscal harassment of the localities [and] his unwillingness or inability to discipline his local officials according to the supposed terms of Magna Carta')[124] bolstered a reform movement that 'gave parliament a formal place in the country's government for the first time'.[125] This was achieved by the Provisions of Oxford, which the king was asked to sign but not discuss.[126]

The Provisions of Oxford, it has been argued, should be understood more as a programme of reform rather than a document, partly because a single original text does not survive.[127] It was a series of minuted decisions.[128] The effect was to shift control of government from the king alone to the king acting with a council of fifteen. These fifteen

---

[120] Ibid. 405.   [121] See Maddicott, *The Origins of the English Parliament 924–1327* chapter 5.

[122] Sayles wrote that 'there is no room for doubt that the year 1258' (GO Sayles, *The King's Parliament of England* (Norton, 1974) 48).

[123] Ann Lyon, *Constitutional History of the United Kingdom* (2nd ed., Routledge, 2016) 67.

[124] Maddicott, *The Origins of the English Parliament 924–1327* 233.

[125] Ibid. 234. See also David A Carpenter, 'What Happened in 1258?' in J Gillingham and JC Holt (eds.), *War and Government in the Middle Ages* (Boydell and Brewer, 1984) 106, reprinted as Carpenter, *The Reign of Henry III* chapter 9.

[126] For a copy of the text, see Lewis, *Henry III* appendix III.

[127] H Rothewell, *English Historical Documents 1189–1327* (Oxford University Press, 1975) 356.

[128] Maddicott, *The Origins of the English Parliament 924–1327* 237.

128 *The Myth of Magna Carta (c.1215–1272)*

members were to be chosen by twenty-four men, twelve of which were nominated by the king and twelve of which by the reformers. This King's Council was to function permanently, having authority to advise the king on all things and authority, 'to amend and to redress all the things they see need to be redressed and amended'.[129] For Maddicott, 'precision, system and practicality were the keynotes of that regulation' and in the long term, 'legislation proved to be the most important item on the business agenda'.[130] The council had authority over the Chief Justiciar and all other people. The office of Chief Justiciar was revived and that office and offices of treasurer and chancellor were to be appointed annually rather than indefinitely.[131] The Chief Justiciar had the power to amend wrongs committed by all other justices and by bailiffs, and earls and barons and all other men. The powers of the Chancery to create new writs ended: it was stated of the chancellor that 'merely by the king's will he shall seal nothing out of course'. There were to be three parliaments a year, which the chosen councillors of the king were to meet without being summoned by the king. They could also be summoned at other times by the king.

Like Magna Carta, the Provisions of Oxford 1258 reflected the concerns of their time and failed to stick.[132] They were followed by even further-reaching reforms in the Provisions of Westminster 1259.[133] These provisions 'were particularly important in providing remedies for some of the main abuses associated with Henry's misgovernment of the localities; they curtailed the sheriff's power and improved the efficiency of the royal courts'.[134] Provisions dealt with the fines and mechanisms concerning the obligation of attendance at courts and 'distraint', the seizure of property in order to obtain the payment of money owed.[135] It was stipulated that no judgment of murder should be rendered in a case that is adjudged to be one of accident: the *murdrum* fine paid by the community whenever a murdered body was found was not to be 'adjudged as due before the justices where only death by misadventure has been adjudged but is to apply only to those killed feloniously'. And all cases in which litigants alleged that a court had given them a 'false judgment' (a wrongful judgment) were reserved to the crown. The Provisions of Westminster were to prove a step too far. Several reissues of the provisions were to follow in subsequent years as the pendulum of power swung between the supporters of the provisions and the king, eventually leading to civil war.[136]

4   The Statute of Marlborough 1267

While Maddicott regarded the period from 1258 to 1272 as collectively constituting the 'consolidation' of Parliament, it may be argued that the civil war can be seen as dividing this period in two. The Battle of Lewes in 1264 provided a watershed moment. The barons headed by Simon de Montfort were victorious. The terms of the Mise of Lewes settlement

---

[129] Ibid.   [130] Ibid. 238, 248.   [131] Lyon, *Constitutional History of the United Kingdom* 69.   [132] Ibid. 70.

[133] For detailed discussion, see Paul Brand, *Kings, Barons and Justices: The Making and Enforcement of Legislation in Thirteenth Century England* (Cambridge University Press, 2006) chapters 1–6.

[134] Maddicott, *The Origins of the English Parliament 924–1327* 243–5.

[135] For details, see Brand, *Kings, Barons and Justices* chapter 3 and appendix I (or Lewis, *Henry III* appendix IV).

[136] Lyon, *Constitutional History of the United Kingdom* 70.

The Origins of Parliament 129

are unknown but Henry was forced to accept the Provisions of Oxford and Prince Edward remained hostage of the barons. Simon de Montfort became the uncrowned king of England, the closest the county had come to being a republic. His summoning of the knights to Parliament in June 1264 and of the knights and burgesses in January 1265 has often been regarded as the 'foundations of Parliament', or more specifically 'the birth of local representation'.[137]

However, the idea that the foundations of Parliament were laid by the civil war has been debunked by Maddicott as 'a popular myth which is astonishingly difficult to dispel' on the basis that evidence 'points to the presence of knights in most of the parliaments of the early reform period'.[138] Maddicott concluded that what was unique was not that the knights were summoned but that they were summoned when taxation was not an issue.[139] Montfort's achievement, therefore, was 'to extend their parliamentary role beyond taxation and to encourage their participation in the larger world of politics and government'. However, this was the extent of his achievement, since de Montfort's unpopularity meant that he was unable to consolidate his victory. He was defeated (by Prince Edward who had escaped from captivity) at Battle of Evesham in 1265. More of a massacre than a battle, at Evesham, Simon de Montfort was killed and royal authority restored.[140]

The king's focus then shifted to securing peace, at first in brutal ways but then through a settlement known as the Dictum of Kenilworth.[141] The product of the work of a commission created by Parliament, the dictum re-established royal authority, declaring that the 'illustrious king of England, shall have, fully receive, and freely exercise his dominion, authority, and royal power without impediment or contradiction of anyone'. The appointment of minsters was once more a matter for the royal prerogative. The dictum reconfirmed Magna Carta and the Charter of the Forest, while all bonds, deeds and instruments drawn up by reason of the Provisions of Oxford or at the instance of de Montfort and his accomplices were 'absolutely nullified and destroyed'. It stated that 'henceforward all shall keep a firm peace', and that anyone who committed 'murder, arson, robbery or any other violation of the peace ... shall have judgement and law according to the custom of the realm'. It also said that the king would 'confirm on a permanent basis other necessary measures devised by his men with his agreement'. In November 1267, Parliament met at Marlborough and passed the Statute of Marlborough, which achieved this objective.

Only four of the clauses of the Statute of Marlborough 1267 were new.[142] The first four clauses were 'in effect an expanded version of the opening clause of the Dictum of Kenilworth', while clauses 9–29 represented the final revision of the text of the Provisions of Westminster.[143] After a new preamble that emphasised the king's role in the making of the legislation, the first clauses restated and affirmed 'some of the basic rules of the English thirteenth-century legal system relating to the exercise of royal and private jurisdiction and the need to follow due process in seeking compensation for

---

[137] Maddicott, *The Origins of the English Parliament 924–1327* 234.   [138] Ibid. 234, 246.   [139] Ibid. 260.
[140] Carpenter, *The Struggle for Mastery* 380.   [141] For a copy of the test see Lewis, *Henry III* appendix V.
[142] For details, see Brand, *Kings, Barons and Justices* chapter 6 and appendix II.
[143] Ibid. 192, 188. These included the reissued versions that had included new provisions such as the new writs of entry in the post, described in the last chapter, on which see ibid. 336–9.

130 *The Myth of Magna Carta (c.1215–1272)*

alleged wrongs'.[144] Clause 1 declared that 'both great and lesser men are to do and receive justice in the court of the lord king and that no one in future is to take revenge or make distraints at their own pleasure without a judgment of the court of the lord king'. As Paul Brand noted, the 'failure even to mention the possibility of seeking redress in other courts (county, hundred or seignorial) may not be deliberate but simply the result of attempting to keep the clause as simple and short as possible'.[145] However, clause 2 'recognised the possibility, if only indirectly, that it might be perfectly proper in the right circumstances to seek redress for wrongs in other courts'. Clause 2 provided that 'no one was to make distraints outside his fee or outside the area of his jurisdiction'.[146] Clause 4 underscored that distraints were to be reasonable.[147]

The first of the new provisions, clause 5, confirmed Magna Carta, and stated that it was to be enforced 'both by the justices in eyre on their circuits and by individual sheriffs within their counties whenever necessary'.[148] For Brand, the most 'obviously innovative' of the new clauses were clauses 6 and 7, which provided ways of overcoming collusions that occurred in relation to wardship that frustrated the rights of feudal lords.[149] Clause 8 provided that those who had been 'arrested and imprisoned for redisseisin are not to be released without the specific order of the king obtained in return for a fine agreed with the lord king for their offence'. For Brand, this seemed 'in effect to be no more than a confirmation or reaffirmation of the existing law' found in the Statute of Merton 1235.[150] This was typical of the Statute of Marlborough 1267 as a whole: it consolidated and confirmed a raft of pieces of legislation from the fifty-year period following Magna Carta. A strong thread can be identified from the Great Charter to the 1267 statute.

Declaring the rights and liberties of the land – a rule of law that bound all including the king – was no longer novel. But what had changed is that these rules were no longer found in one-off peace treaties made by specially gathered groups. Now, these rules were routinely made by Parliament. As Maddicott noted, by the end of Henry's reign, parliament had become 'an integral part of government': Parliament was no longer 'the embodiment of a national community set against the crown, but instead a reinvigorated part of the consensual apparatus of the state'.[151] This meant that '[T]he reform movement had, in a manner of speaking, already helped to create the parliaments of Edward I.'[152] This rebuts the conventional understanding that regarded Henry's reign as a mere prelude to the development of Parliament under the Edward. For Maddicott, the reign of Edward I simply saw the 'expansion' of parliament.[153] The reign of Henry III laid the groundwork not only for the institution of Parliament itself to function but also for the relationship between Parliament and the king. The ambition of Magna Carta had eventually become realised.

---

[144] Ibid. 187, 192.   [145] Ibid.   [146] Ibid. 193.   [147] Chapter 3 dealt with punishment; ibid. 194.

[148] Brand noted that later copies of the statute added a sentence confirming the Charter of the Forest. However, 'although this was also something requested in the Dictum of Kenilworth, the manuscript evidence suggests that it formed no part of the Statute as originally enacted' (ibid. 195).

[149] Ibid. 196.   [150] Ibid. 195.   [151] Maddicott, *The Origins of the English Parliament 924–1327* 273, 235.   [152] Ibid. 276.

[153] See Maddicott, *The Origins of the English Parliament 924–1327* chapter 6. Madicott saw the period 1324–7 as seeing 'some dramatic changes in the organization of assemblies, but they were subsumed within an essential continuity of composition, work and purpose' and stressed the 'continuity of function' (ibid. xii, 440–1). For discussion of the position towards the end of Edward's reign, see Frederic William Maitland (ed.), *Records of the Parliament Holden at Westminster* (Cambridge University Press, 2012 [1893]).

IV   Women under Medieval Law

While Magna Carta is conventionally included and perhaps overstated in discussions about the origin of Parliament, it usually plays less of a role in consideration of the role of women. This perhaps reflects the fact that, until fairly recently, legal historians have paid little attention to the role of women. Yet, the developing literature on the role of women suggests that Magna Carta is part of that story too. This is despite the surface impression that Magna Carta was not particularly concerned with the rights of women.[154] It has been suggested that the Great Charter was largely concerned with the rights of the king and the barons with neither promoting 'any concept of "equal rights for all' (beyond themselves)'.[155] It is noticeable that wherever women are mentioned, it is through their relationships with men: 'as with heiresses, wards or widows, and the Scots' King's daughters – John's hostages'.[156] None of the signatories were women.

Most of the provisions affecting women in Magna Carta were incidental. Magna Carta's focus on dealing with feudal rules and grievances meant that several of its provisions affected widows and heirs. Heirs could be given in marriage but not to someone of lower social status and the next of kin should be informed (clause 6). Widows were to have their dower[157] and inheritance at once (clause 7), and were not to be compelled to marry but were to require the lord's consent if they were to re-marry (clause 8). If the widow did remarry without consent, then she would typically recover any land confiscated by the lord on payment of a fine.[158] Further provisions of the Great Charter dealt with arrangements of debts. Heirs and widows were not to pay interest of debts owed to Jews (clauses 10 and 11). Debts owed by the dead were to be dealt with differently, depending on whether the debt was due to the crown or not (clause 26). If a free man died intestate (without a will), then his chattels (moveable goods) were to be distributed by his next of kin and friends under supervision by the Church, except in the case of any debts owed that were to be repaid (clause 27).

However, possibly the most notable provision was clause 54, which stated that no one was to be arrested or imprisoned on the appeal of a woman for the death of any person except her husband. This severely limited women's ability to bring appeals.[159] Women's actions were limited to the prosecution of her husband.[160] A woman who killed her husband would be accused of petty treason since it was an attack upon a social superior.[161] Clause 54 was intended to end 'what was thought to be the unfair disadvantage enjoyed by

---

[154] It is notably not included as a landmark in Erika Rackley and Rosemary Auchmuty (eds.), *Women's Legal Landmarks: Celebrating the History of Women and Law in the UK and Ireland* (Hart, 2018).

[155] Jocellynne A Scutt, *Women and Magna Carta: A Treaty for Rights or Wrongs* (Palgrave, 2016) 2.   [156] Ibid. 3.

[157] This referred to the common law entitlement of a widow to a portion of her husband's estate in the absence of a will. It was recoverable by writ: see Frederic W Maitland, *The Forms of Action at Common Law* (Cambridge University Press, 1965 [1909]) 36–7. Later changes dealt further with the law on dower. The 1217 and 1225 versions of Magna Carta stated that the wife's dower was to be one-third of the land that the husband had had. Chapter 1 of the Statute of Merton 1235 provided that women could recover damages in a writ of dower, giving a widow a share of her late husband's estate, and chapter 2 provided that widows could 'bequeath the crop of their lands'; Jennifer C Ward, *English Noblewomen in the Later Middle Ages* (Longman, 1992) 27.

[158] Ibid. 40.   [159] Gwen Seabourne, *Women in the Medieval Common Law c.1200–1500* (Routledge, 2021) 15.

[160] Lynda Telford, *Women in Medieval England* (Amberely Publishing, 2018) 88.

[161] See further the discussion of treason in Chapter 8.

132   *The Myth of Magna Carta (c.1215–1272)*

women litigants, who could appoint a champion to fight for them in the trial by combat, while the unfortunate accused man had to do his own fighting'.[162]

The extent to which the general provisions of the charter applied to women is also open to debate. This has been most debated in relation to clause 39, which provided that no free person was to be taken, imprisoned, disseised, outlawed or banished except by the lawful judgment of peers. The phrase 'no free person' is translated from '*nullus liber homo*' and John Baker has maintained that 'it was always clear that *homo* included women'.[163] However, Gwen Seabourne has argued that '[W]hile it is clear that the orthodox view among later common lawyers came to be that women were covered by *liber homo* in this provision, however, it appears less clear that this as unequivocally the case throughout the medieval period.'[164] Other legislation was clearer about whether it referred to men and women. The Statute of Merton 1236 discussed wardship with only reference to the male age of majority, while the Statute of the Jewry 1275 provided that the taxation of every Jew was to apply to women as well as to men.[165]

Seabourne's work has made the convincing argument that the charter's 'implications for medieval ideas about sex, gender and law are yet to be given full consideration', and that equally attention needs to be afforded to 'the inclusion, explicit or implicit of women, or their exclusion, from legislative and quasi-legislative materials more widely'.[166] This includes the changing interpretations over time with regard to the categorisation of women.[167] Seaborne gave the example of clause 13 of the Statute of Westminster 1275,[168] which stated that 'none do ravish, no take away by force' any women against her will. Seabourne suggested that, despite not mentioning servants, this provision became referred to as the foundation of actions concerning servants.

Seabourne's work has also suggested that many of the concepts and distinctions made by legal historians in relation to how the law regulated women are simplifications that are in need of revision. She noted that 'Maitland was at times content with summaries of the area of women and the law which were elegant in style but did not measure up to the level of insight he displayed on other matters.'[169] In Maitland's account, two distinctions were important to understanding the position between women and the law: the first was between private law and public law rights, and the second was between unmarried and married women. Maitland's first distinction described how 'private law with few exceptions puts women on a par with men', while 'public law gives a woman no rights and no exacts from her no duties'.[170] His second distinction then revealed that women who had husbands were in a different position to those who were unmarried or widowed.[171] Married women lacked most legal rights, not only public rights but also private ones. As we have noted, this is commonly referred to as the doctrine of coverture or 'marital unity', that 'a woman's property and income became her husband's on marriage'.[172] However, Maitland preferred

---

[162] Howard, *Magna Carta* 16.   [163] Baker, *The Reinvention of Magna Carta 1216–1616* 34.
[164] Seabourne, *Women in the Medieval Common Law c.1200–1500* 22.   [165] Ibid. 27.   [166] Ibid. 21.   [167] Ibid. 33.
[168] This statute will be discussed in more detail in the next chapter.
[169] Seabourne, *Women in the Medieval Common Law c.1200–1500* 3.
[170] Pollock and Maitland, *The History of English Law* 482.   [171] Ibid. 485.
[172] Sharon Thompson, *Prenuptial Agreements and the Presumption of Free Choice* (Hart, 2015) 40.

Women under Medieval Law

to refer to it as a 'guardianship ... that the husband has over the wife and over her property'.[173] Regardless of the terminology used, the basic and blunt point in Maitland's analysis was clear: All women mostly lacked public law rights and married women mostly lacked private law rights too.

Yet, Maitland's account has been criticised. Seabourne has criticised his presentation as emphasising the less common position of unmarried women. She argued that this provided 'an unbalanced description of the legal picture, for example, positing a "rule" of women's full rights in private law, with the considerable disabilities of the married women diminished as an "exception", however extensive the impact of those "exceptional" disabilities may have been'.[174] Seabourne was equally as critical of the doctrine of coverture or marital unity. Seabourne's critique painted coverture as a 'familiar metaphor' and a legal fiction rather than a dogma to be ignored, and recast it as 'something which could be used if desired, as an origin story for particular rules, but which did not necessarily indicate a clear response in the practical world of common law'.[175] Her work underscored that there 'was not, in the medieval common law, a unified and coherent "doctrine of coverture" of the later model'.[176] As with the changed interpretation of clause 39 of Magna Carta, the explanatory principle of coverture was retrospectively applied and did not fit the facts of the time: the doctrine of coverture for Seabourne was 'an explanation after the facts, itself a "cover" for a fairly disparate and sometimes inconsistent body of rules, liabilities and disabilities relating to married women'.[177]

Seabourne also argued that commentators following Maitland had simply accepted his simplified account and had not paid enough attention to the law applying to unmarried women. Seabourne questioned Maitland's neat distinction between the position of unmarried women in private and in public law a being drawn on Roman law and as not mapping 'well onto medieval legal practice'.[178] Through three case studies, her work illustrated 'the range of medieval women's participation in common law cases, in both "criminal" and "civil" actions, accusing or being accused or wrongdoing, claiming and defending rights, alone or with a husband, having a case brought by another with regard to a wrong to them and experiencing a variety of different outcomes'.[179] For Seabourne, this meant that a comprehensive answer to the legal position of women in the late medieval period could not be provided 'given the dissonances and inconsistencies seen in much learned medieval discourse relating to women' and because the developing body of law did not stand entirely part from other common law rules.[180] She concluded that 'in undertaking studies of women and the common law, legal historians should be prepared to embrace complexity and nuance rather than seeing attention given to women (or other groups other than the stand free, non-"foreign" male) as a distraction likely to produce regrettable derogation from neat narratives, such as those of the "rises" of centralisation and professionalization of the common law'.[181] A focus on women subverts our understanding of the medieval legal system. As Seabourne noted, it underscores that 'medieval common law did not always

---

[173] Pollock and Maitland, *The History of English Law* 485. For a detailed discussion, see volume 2 of ibid. at 403 *et seq.*
[174] Seabourne, *Women in the Medieval Common Law c.1200–1500* 12. [175] Ibid. 36. [176] Ibid. 38. [177] Ibid. 43.
[178] Ibid. 53. [179] Ibid. 83. See also W Mark Ormrod, *Women and Parliament in Later Medieval England* (Palgrave, 2020).
[180] Seabourne, *Women in the Medieval Common Law c.1200–1500* 159. [181] Ibid. 158–9.

134 *The Myth of Magna Carta (c.1215–1272)*

provide a clear and straightforward body of strict rules against which "practice" can be measured and exceptions identified'. This underscores the risk of an evolutionary functionalist mindset that uncritically embraces narratives and expectations of progress.

V   Conclusions

As Matthew Lewis commented, 'Magna Carta owes its place to those who followed John'.[182] It was the reign of Henry III that saw the rule of law presented in the Great Charter become a reality. As Maitland put it, '[T]he reign of Henry III is the time when a great part of the common law takes a definite shape.'[183] It was 'an age of rapid, but steady and permanent growth'.[184] Magna Carta's insistence that the king was subject to the law and that constitutional matters be written down as law proved influential throughout the reign of Henry III and proved crucial to the development the English legal system as a whole, building upon the Angevin reforms. Magna Carta, therefore, was not the only significant legal development of this period.

Magna Carta was also not the only important legal text of this period. Many of the changes during this time were precise and technical and the common law became increasingly complex as a result. This created a need for further books upon the law, known as treatises.[185] The most well-known of these is *De Legibus et Consuetudinibus,* dated to the 1220s and attributed to Henry Bracton.[186] Bracton's book painted a much more technical and detailed account of the common law than that found in Glanvill, which we discussed in the last chapter. However, Bracton drew heavily upon Roman law thinking, and so it is open to question whether it summarised the common law practice or whether it derived from and inspired the acceptance of Roman law ideas and conceptualisations into the common law. This was true of its treatment of criminal law, where it 'seems to have put down the final seal of acceptance upon the mental element in criminal law' by emphasising 'to a high degree the mental requisites of criminality' in a way that 'marked the beginning of a moral mens rea concept in criminal law'.[187] For instance, Bracton stated that 'a crime is not committed unless the intention to injure exists'.[188]

Bracton also recognised that what modern eyes would regard as the rule of law had been cemented in this era, asserting that 'whatever has been rightly decided and approved with the counsel and consent of the magnates and the general agreement of the public, the authority of the king or prince having first been added thereto, has the force of law'.[189] Bracton's statement that laws 'cannot be changed without the common consent of all those whose counsel and consent they were promulgated' underscored how law making and

---

[182] Lewis, *Henry III* 11.   [183] Maitland, *The Constitutional History of England* 17.

[184] Pollock and Maitland, *The History of English Law* 174.

[185] This need increased during the reign of Edward I, as explored in the next chapter, with treatises such as *Placita Corone*, dated to 1274, *Fleta* and *Britton* in the 1290s, and the *Mirror of Justices* in the 1300s.

[186] On which, see Paul Brand, 'The Age of Bracton' in John Hudson (ed.), *The History of English Law: Centenary Essays on 'Pollock and Maitland'* (Oxford University Press, 1996) 65.

[187] Eugene J Chesney, 'Concept of Mens Rea in the Criminal Law' (1938–9) 29 *American Institute of Criminal Law and Criminology* 627, 632.

[188] Samuel E Thorne (ed.), *Bracton on the Laws and Customs of England* (Harvard University Press, 1968) vol. 2, 384.

[189] Ibid. 19.

Conclusions 135

governance had become an issue for king and Parliament in concert.[190] Parliament had become 'regarded as an organ of state both beneficent and venerable existing almost time out of mind'.[191] The same could be said for the common law. Most of the building blocks were now in place. By this time, the principle that courts were open to all litigants had become admitted.[192] However, it is important not to be swept away by this narrative of completion and of progress. The cementing of the common law was an incidental effect of the need to preserve order, as indicated by the regular reissuing of Magna Carta. Indeed, this re-issuing represented a development that only came to the fore during the next period. It was the reign of Edward I that cemented the use of statute law. If the common law had taken shape under Henry III, it was the reign of Edward I during which passing laws by means of statutes became normalised. The next chapter tells that story.

---

[190] Ibid. 21.   [191] Maddicott, *The Origins of the English Parliament 924–1327* 277.
[192] Maitland, *The Forms of Action at Common Law* 14.

'Edward's reign is an unique period in the history of our law ... The legislative activity of [his first] thirteen years remains unique until the reign of William IV [in 1830]. The main characteristic of Edward's statutes is that they interfere at countless points with the ordinary course of law between subject and subject. They do more than this – many clauses of the greatest importance deal with what we should call public law – but the characteristic that makes them unique is that they enter the domain of private law and make vast changes in it'.

Frederic W Maitland, *The Constitutional History of England* (Cambridge University Press, 1941 [1908]) 19.

7

The English Justinian (c.1272–1307)

I   Introduction

By the reign of Edward I (1272–307), the foundations of the common law had been laid and occasional provisions following Magna Carta had made it plain that the king was subject to the law and that rules of law could be articulated in statute form. However, such statutes were exceptional and tended to deal with what we would today call public or constitutional law. This changed under the reign of Edward I, a period that was also to prove pivotal in the development of English legal history. Edward Coke, the leading jurist of the late Tudor and early Stuart period, called Edward I the 'English Justinian' after the Roman Emperor Justinian I who codified Roman law.[1] Frederic W Maitland argued that this the comparison was not entirely convincing: 'Justinian, we may say, did his best to give final immutable form to a system which had already seen its best days', while Edward 'legislated for a nation that was only just beginning to have a great legal system of its own'.[2] Yet, this nickname was apt given that Edward was England's first prolific legislator.[3]

It has been suggested that Edward was 'the first monarch fully to understand the value of statute in effecting change and created one of the most comprehensive bodies of legislation seen in any medieval European realm'.[4] His reign was a golden age of statute law and, as Maitland opined, what made it noteworthy was how statute law not only dealt with matters of public law but also made 'vast changes' in private law.[5] This was exceptional compared not only to the periods that came before but also the periods that followed it. Maitland wrote that 'for ages after Edward's day King and parliament left private law and civil procedure, criminal law and criminal procedure, pretty much all to themselves'.[6]

The Edwardian legislation was designed to satisfy a growing 'hunger for royal justice'.[7] But it also led to some curtailment of the role of judges. As we discussed in the previous chapter, the Provisions of Oxford 1258, a major concession by Henry III, limited the

---

[1] Edward Coke, *The First Part of the Institutes of the Laws of England* (19th ed., Butterworth, 1832) vol. 1. L2, C11. Sect188 123b.
[2] Frederic W Maitland, *The Constitutional History of England* (Cambridge University Press, 1941 [1908]) 18–19.
[3] See, generally, Theodore FT Plucknett, *Legislation of Edward I* (Clarendon Press, 1949).
[4] Caroline Burt, *Edward I and the Governance of England, 1272–1307* (Cambridge University Press, 2013) 1.
[5] Maitland, *The Constitutional History of England* 19.   [6] Ibid.
[7] Burt, *Edward I and the Governance of England, 1272–1307* 28.

137

development of royal justice by decreeing that no new writs be created. Under Edward I, this prohibition was removed under the Statute of Westminster II 1285, but this did not result in the Chancery being again free to create whatever new writs it wanted. Rather, clause 24 of the statute allowed new writs to be created, provided that they were 'very similar', '*in consimili casu*', to existing writs.[8] This allowed the common law to grow again, provided that there was a similar precedent was required. This focus on finding a similar precedent was to become one of the main and distinctive skills of common law lawyers. The growth of statute law under Edward I also cemented that the interpretation of statutes was to become the other central pursuit of lawyers.

The development of statute law imposed a further straitjacket on the development of the common law. The role of judges shifted to become interpreters of statute law, applying rather than making the law (though the distinction between the two at times remained more a matter of constitutional theory than actual practice, with interpretations of statute law and previous judicial precedents being used to generate legal change). As Maitland explained, the effect was to slow the pace of legal change in the common law system from Edward I's reign onwards:

Henceforward the common law grows much more slowly than under Henry III. Its growth is hampered at every turn by statute – the judges are checked by the now admitted principle that changes in the law are not to be made without the consent of parliament. Law continues to grow, but it can grow but slowly; the judges are forced to have recourse of fictions and evasions because the highroad of judge-made law has been barred.[9]

It is fitting that the term 'common law' came to be used either in or shortly after Edward's reign,[10] since his reign saw the establishment of the main methodology of English lawyers. From now on, the role of counsel and judges alike was to dispute and determine the legal position by reference to the rules laid out in statute law and in previous judicial decisions. Statutory interpretation and the study of judicial precedent were to become central to English law, with justice and legal change being determined by whether loopholes could be found in how statutes could be interpreted and whether previous decisions had to be followed or could be distinguished from the facts of the case in question.

This chapter will focus on the 'English Justinian' and will survey how the statutes of the reign of Edward I affected both feudal and royal justice. It will fall into three sections. Section II will discuss the main statutes of Edward I, focusing on the Statute of Westminster 1275, the Statute of Wales 1284 and the Statute of Westminster II 1285. Section III will examine statutes that had a particular effect upon feudalism: the Statute of Mortmain 1279 and *Quia Emptores* 1290 (also known as the Statute of Westminster III). Section IV will explore a development in the common law that began before this time but blossomed in this period: the origins of what is now known as the law of obligations, or the law of contract and tort. This discussion underlines that, although the English Justinian is known for the growth of statute law, the era also saw the continued development of the

---

[8] Thomas G Watkin, 'The Significance of "In Consimili Casu"' (1979) 23 *American Journal of Legal History* 283.
[9] Maitland, *The Constitutional History of England* 21.   [10] Ibid. 22.

common law. Moreover, what was most noticeable was the way in which the growing statute law dealt with matters of what we would call private law that were usually regulated only at common law. The English Justinian not only increased the frequency of statute law but also its importance.

II   The Statutes of Edward I

The reign of Edward I is often hailed. For Ann Lyon, 'Edward I may be bracketed with his great-grandfather Henry II, as the greatest of England's medieval kings';[11] while for Caroline Burt, Edward 'was without a doubt one of the greatest kings to rule England'.[12] Central to this is Edward's reputation as a law-maker, as Burt put it: 'He was the first monarch fully to understand the value of statute in effecting change and created one of the most comprehensive bodies of legislation seen in any medieval realm.' However, Edward I was not only known as the English Justinian, he was also known as 'longshanks' and the Hammer of the Scots on account of the fact that he was also 'the first king to attempt to unify the isles under one ruler, an attempt that partly succeeded'. He was his father's son: his ambitions were manifest in military fights. The great codifier of English law was no mere wordsmith. Moreover, his effectiveness as a legislator depended upon his military success. As Lyon pointed out, his was a reign of 'two halves. The first half (until the early 1290s) was one of success; consolidation of royal power through strengthening royal justice.'[13] By contrast, the second half of his reign (until 1307) was characterised by war with France, Scotland and domestic opposition. It was the first half of the reign that saw Edward act as the English Justinian. However, even then, his militaristic thinking came to the fore. For Edward, legislation was employed to achieve specific results. Technical, particular provisions were enacted that sought to achieve tactical advantages for the crown, and Edward was not afraid to go further and deeper than ever before into areas of life and of law that statute had previously not touched. As Theodore Plucknett observed, Edward's 'policy was not to refashion the framework of government, but to get better results, if that could be done, from the machinery with which he and his people had been familiar for generations'.[14] In his legislative and military endeavours alike, Edward sought to improve the performance of his apparatus. However, this did not rule out radical and repulsive moves such as the expulsion of the Jews, discussed in the last chapter.

Edward's reputation as the English Justinian rests upon the fact that during the first half of his reign a number of important statutes were enacted. These included the Statute of Westminster 1275, the Statute of Jewry 1275, the Ragman Statute 1276, the Statute of Gloucester 1278, the Statute of Mortmain 1279, the Statute of Merchants (also known as the Statute of Acton Brunell) 1283, the Statute of Wales 1284 (also known as the Statute of Rhuddlan), the Statute of Westminster II 1285 (the first clause of which, *De Donis Conditionalibus*, came to acquire statute status itself) , the Statute of Winchester 1285,

---

[11] Ann Lyon, *Constitutional History of the United Kingdom* (2nd ed., Routledge, 2016) 78.
[12] Burt, *Edward I and the Governance of England, 1272–1307* 1.   [13] Lyon, *Constitutional History of the United Kingdom* 79.
[14] Theodore FT Plucknett, *Edward I and Criminal Law* (Cambridge University Press, 1960) 43.

The Statute of Merchants 1285, the Statute of Westminster III 1290 (also known as *Quia Emptores*) and the Statute of *Quo Warranto* 1290.[15] As HR Loyn noted, these statutes covered a significant range of activities: 'land law, the relationship between lord and tenants, the problems of merchants facing the payment or non-payment of commercial debit, usury, the status of the Jews' and amendments to criminal law.[16] They dealt with many of the same matters as Magna Carta and its successors had dealt with and represented a marked change from governance by peace treaty to governance by specific statutes. Though the precedent set was not followed by Edward's immediate successors, during which statute law was used more lightly, it set the model for reigns to come, showing that the technical reform of English law could be achieved through legislation.

Yet, it is important not to overstate the importance of statute law reform in Edward's reign. As Maitland noted, 'Edward was not merely a great legislator, he was a great administrator also, a great organizer.'[17] Statute was just one of three means by which the government of Edward I brought about legal changes, alongside informal changes that left 'no direct trace in the public records' and 'administrative documents that were used merely for the purpose of communicating the government's intentions to the judges of the officials immediately concerned'.[18] Edward's reign was 'notable for the scale and frequency into the way the country was governed',[19] including the Hundred Rolls, which effectively served as a secondary Doomsday Book.[20] The system of general eyres was reformed, in that now two permanent circuits were set up to provide 'what was designed to be a continuous visitation of the whole country'.[21] Other important measures included the Ordinance of London 1285, which attempted to ensure that the City of London was in the king's hand,[22] and *Circumspecte Agatis* 1286, which clarified the jurisdiction of ecclesiastical courts in relation to marriage and testamentary issues.[23]

Moreover, there was no grand plan to increase the role of statute law; rather statute law just happened to be the means used to provide Edward and his ministers with tactical advantage. As Loyn has stressed: 'The statutes were the produce of the reforming zeal of the King's Council, anxious to learn from the dangers and disasters of the Barons' War of the 1260s and anxious to safeguard the future. Much of their content was the product of immediate troubles and at times personal plaints.'[24] This description sounds very similar to Magna Carta and underscores that legislation that historians regard as ground-breaking and seminal was not thought of in such terms at the time. They were enacted to attempt to deal with particular problems. As ever, the centralisation of power arose from a need to maintain order, not some blueprint to advance the development of English law. The need for law in

---

[15] HR Loyn, *The Making of the English Nation* (Thames and Hudson, 1991) 167.   [16] Ibid.

[17] Maitland, *The Constitutional History of England* 20.

[18] Plucknett, *Legislation of Edward I* 10. There was also a significant change in personnel – including most local officials – early in Edward's reign; Michael Prestwich, *Edward I* (new ed., Yale University Press, 1997) 93.

[19] Ibid. 92.

[20] See Helen Cam, *Studies in the Hundred Rolls* (Clarendon Press, 1921) and Helen Cam, *The Hundred and the Hundred Rolls* (Methuen, 1930).

[21] Anthony Musson, *Medieval Law in Context* (Manchester University Press, 2001) 139.

[22] Edward Jenks, *Edward Plantagenet (Edward I) the English Justinian* (Knickerbocker Press, 1902) 224.

[23] David Millon, '*Circumspecte Agatis* Revisited' (1984) 2(1) *Law and History Review* 105.

[24] Loyn, *The Making of the English Nation* 167.

The Statutes of Edward I   141

Edward I's reign once came from the particular problem that he had inherited a divided kingdom from his father.

1   The Statute of Westminster 1275

It is perhaps the Statute of Westminster 1275 and the Statute of Westminster II 1285 that are to be credited for Edward's reputation as the English Justinian. These were both codifying pieces of legislation that covered, reviewed and reformed a range of legal areas. As Plucknett noted, much of the Statute of Westminster 1275 was concerned with criminal law and focused on the crown and feudalism.[25] The statute in part re-enacted elements of the Statute of Marlborough.[26] Clause 1 stated that 'the King willeth and commandeth that the peace of Holy Church and of the Land, be well kept and maintained in all points, and that common Right be done to all, as well Poor as Rich'. As Plucknett pointed out, following this statement, clauses 'succeed one another in no discernable order'.[27] Like Magna Carta, the Statute of Westminster 1275 was a pragmatic and practical document that dealt with the grievances and problems at the time.

Provisions ranged from how to determine what was a 'wreck of the sea' (clause 4), to stating that there was no disturbance of free elections (clause 5), to stipulating that all men should be ready to pursue felons (clause 9) and to outlining the punishment of those 'that doth ravish a woman' (clause 13). Several provisions concerned the administration of justice and underlined the rule of law. Clause 6, for instance, declared that financial penalties (amecriaments) should not be imposed without reasonable cause, and that they should be according to the quantity of the offence, while clause 23 declared that no one should be 'distrained for a debt that he oweth not'. Some provisions dealt with the standards expected of those who administer justice. Clause 27 stated that clerks and officers shall not commit extortion, while clause 29 said that a serjeant or pleader should not commit deceit. Anthony Musson considered this an early example of the regulation of the nascent legal profession.[28]

One of the most well-known clauses was clause 39, which provided a limitation clause, providing that in an action of the writ of right, no one should presume to declare the seisin of his ancestor further or beyond the time of King Richard. This stopped actions being brought in relation to anything before that date. The date of 1189 became the date of legal memory: proving that something had happened since 'time immemorial' would require the claimant to prove that it had happened since 1189.[29] This cast the whole period up until the reforms of Henry II as the pre-history of the common law. The first major legislative act of the English Justinian therefore helped to establish the reputation of Henry II as the father of the common law.

---

[25] Plucknett, *Legislation of Edward I* 30.   [26] Clause 16 re-enacted clauses 2 and 4 of the Statute of Marlborough; ibid. 59.
[27] Plucknett, *Edward I and Criminal Law* 84.   [28] Musson, *Medieval Law in Context* 48.
[29] Clause 39 included different limitation periods for different actions. John H Baker has contended that it was the Statute of *Quo Warranto* 1290 that set 1189 as the date of time immemorial; John H Baker, *An Introduction to English Legal History* (5th ed., Oxford University Press, 2019) 155.

142 *The English Justinian (c.1272–1307)*

Several statutes were enacted during the decade between the Statute of Westminster 1275 and the Statute of Westminster II 1285. The Ragman Statute, usually dated to 1276, provided for justices to hear offences committed by the king's officials and private officials that had been unearthed as part of the Hundred Rolls.[30] The same year saw *Officium Coronatoris* (Office of the Coroner), which dealt with what a coroner should inquire into, and the Statute of Bigamy, which stated that men who had married twice were not to be left to be tried by the ecclesiastical courts but also dealt with other matters such as land law. The Statute of Gloucester 1278 was a more detailed collection of provisions, though Plucknett commented that it was 'comparable to a government statement read at a press conference rather than a statute'.[31] A number of reforms to the legal system were introduced or re-stated. The statute provided for an increase of the writ *quo warranto*, which could challenge those claimant jurisdiction or territory by summoning them to show by what authority (*quo warranto*) they exercised it. Clause 8 also underscored that actions were to be brought in the local courts, and stipulated that an action should not be brought to the King's Court unless it was for goods worth forty shillings or more. Clause 9 regulated the law on the criminal appeal and provided that pardons would be allowed for self-defence and for deaths by misadventure. Other statutes in this period dealt with the position of Jews and merchants, as discussed in the last chapter.

2   The Statute of Wales 1284

Of particular note was the Statute of Wales 1284, which was also known as the Statute of Rhuddlan, after Rhuddlan Castle where it was first promulgated. It was a royal ordinance rather than an Act of Parliament. It was enacted following the conquest of Wales and further violence that followed the refusal of the Prince of Wales Llywelyn ap Gruffudd to travel to Parliament to do homage to the new king, which culminated in Llywelyn's severed head being sent to Edward at Rhuddlan.[32] The statute intended to settle the government of Wales through an act of colonisation. As its first clause recognised, some of the existing Welsh laws were abolished, some were allowed and some were corrected. However, this was no overall statement of Welsh law. Rather, much of the English common law was introduced. As Plucknett noted, the 'statute is so long that it almost amounts to a short treatise on the state of the law in 1284; its practical interest to historians is therefore considerable, for it contains information which is difficult to find elsewhere'.[33] As Paul Brand has commented:

What one expects to follow in the text is a revised restatement of the whole of Welsh law in Latin or perhaps just of some of its main rules, with a limited number of deliberate omissions, amendments and additions. What one finds instead is, at least for the most part, something very different, a blue print for the transplanting to the king's territories in Wales of what is perhaps best described as a simplified, though also in some respects improved, version of many of the main institutions and

---

[30] Prestwich, *Edward I* 96.   [31] Plucknett, *Legislation of Edward I* 39.
[32] Lyon, *Constitutional History of the United Kingdom* 83. The head was later sent to London and put in the city pillory adorned with a crown of ivy.
[33] Theodore FT Plucknett, *A Concise History of the Common Law* (Little Brown and Co., 1956 [1929]) 27.

The Statutes of Edward I 143

procedures of contemporary English law, with no more than a relatively small input from existing Welsh legal custom and institutions and procedures.[34]

English structures of government such as the division into shires were introduced, with these shires becoming effectively provinces of the English crown under the king's will. The entirety of English criminal law was introduced, with the concept of felonies and une-mendable offences (those for which amends could not be made by compensation).[35] The English methods of prosecuting wrongs by presentment and by appeal were introduced, as were several of the most important civil pleas such as the writ of right and the assizes of *Novel Disseisin* and *Mort D'Ancestor*, with the definition of 'novel' being since Wales had been annexed to the English crown.[36] As Watkin has noted, it was recognised that *Mort D'Ancestor* could be extended to remote degrees of relationship, and so there was no need of the extensions provided by the writs of aiel, besaiel and cosinage in England.[37] Instead, 'such extensions were to be allowed to litigants in Wales "upon their Case"', providing that the 'forms of the writs shall be changed according to the Diversities of the Case'. For Watkin, 'this in effect anticipated the solution' to the problem caused in England by the Provisions of Oxford 1258, which had prohibited the development of new writs. The following year, the Statute of Westminster II 1285 gave a similar power to the Chancery clerks to create new forms of writs in cases that were similar to existing ones, and so, for Watkin, 'the Welsh provision appears to have anticipated the English solution'.[38]

There were some limits to the transplanting of the English common law in Wales: total uniformity was not achieved. The courts at Westminster did not exercise any jurisdiction in error over the courts in Wales. Welsh customs and law were to operate in some civil matters such as in respect of proof in civil litigation other than that relating to land,[39] a state of affairs that continued until the Law in Wales Acts 1535 and 1542, often known as the Acts of Union.[40] As Lyon has commented, the statute was 'seen in very different lights by English and Welsh commentators':

To the English, the terms were merciful, the acts of English administration no more than appropriate to ensure peace and good order among a hostile people. To the Welsh, 1284 brought the end of their independence, destruction of the traditions and imposition of an alien and harsh system of rule.[41]

3   The Statute of Westminster II 1285

Turning to the Statute of Westminster II 1285, this statute, like its namesake from 1275, provided a code of miscellaneous provisions. Its best-known provision, clause 1, *De Donis*

---

[34] Paul Brand, 'An English Legal Historian Looks at the Statute of Wales' in Thomas G Watkin (ed.), *Y Cyfraniad Cymreig: Welsh Contributions to Legal Development* (Welsh Legal History Society, 2003) 20, 37.
[35] Thomas G Watkin, *The Legal History of Wales* (University of Wales Press, 2007) 107.
[36] Ibid. 108. The penalties payable to the king for defaults by defendants in civil process were 'to be in accordance with "Welsh law and Custom"' (Brand, 'An English Legal Historian Looks at the Statute of Wales' 37).
[37] Watkin, *The Legal History of Wales* 108.   [38] Ibid.
[39] Brand, 'An English Legal Historian Looks at the Statute of Wales' 38.
[40] Carol Howells, 'Cyfriath Hywel (The Laws of Hywel Dda) c.940' in Erika Rackley and Rosemary Auchmuty (eds.), *Women's Legal Landmarks: Celebrating the History of Women and Law in the UK and Ireland* (Hart, 2018) 25, 29.
[41] Lyon, *Constitutional History of the United Kingdom* 83.

144 *The English Justinian (c.1272–1307)*

Conditionalibus, became key to the development of land law.[42] This concerned the making of conditional gifts of land. It stipulated 'the will of the donor' was to be followed, including conditions attached to a gift of land. It provided a new writ – the writ of formedon in the descender – which allowed land to be recovered where the conditions had not been met.[43] Other provisions dealt with the problems of unreliable bailiffs (clause 11), and strengthened further the law on rape by stating that it was a serious felony, making it clear that the offence covered all women, not just virgins (clause 34).[44] Much of the statute was technical, dealing with the administration of justice, feudal abuses and particular areas of law. As we have seen, clause 24 was a seminal provision, in that it allowed the Chancery clarks to create new writs, provided that they were 'very similar', '*in consimili casu*', to existing writs. This enabled the common law to grow once again, albeit in a more restrained way than it had prior to the Provisions of Oxford 1258. Moreover, it was stated that if there was no similar parallel to an existing writ, then the matter was to be adjourned to Parliament.[45] For Plucknett, this unambiguous acceptance that it was for Parliament to create new remedies was the real importance of clause 24.[46] The importance and effect of the provision has been debated by legal historians over the centuries. However, Milsom underplayed its significance, stating that the clause was an afterthought and 'had only minor and more or less immediate effects, all in land law'.[47]

As Michael Prestwich noted, the major changes in criminal law during 1285 came not from the Statute of Westminster II but from the Statute of Winchester.[48] However, as Plucknett observed it was 'concerned with the urban rather than the rural aspects of crime'.[49] The statute began by noting that robberies, murders, burnings and theft were more frequent than they had been before, and then proceeded to reform law enforcement. It stipulated that the local community would need to produce the criminals before the authorities within forty days, and that the whole of the hundred would be liable for the loss and damage caused by robbery. This provision for collective responsibility recognised existing practices and harked back to an earlier age: in the words of Plucknett, it was 'a principle strongly reminiscent of Anglo-Saxon law'.[50] Provision was also made for security in towns and cities, with town gates being closes from sunset to sunrise, weekly inquiries by the bailiffs and the reinforcement of a night watch with powers to arrest strangers. It stipulated the armour that each man who was aged between fifteen and sixty should have in the house in order to keep the peace. It is probably best known for the requirement to raise 'hue and cry': anyone who witnessed a crime should assist in the apprehension of the criminal and should shout and cry to summon others to assist; this shouting was to continue from place to place, town to town, county to country, until the felon was apprehended. It was a formal duty to follow the hue and cry. If the felon escaped,

---

[42] AW Brian Simpson, *A History of the Land Law* (2nd ed., Oxford University Press,1986) 81.

[43] Prestwich, *Edward I* 96. This writ was provided together with other remedies to protect others who might succeed to the land from actions 'which went against the form of the gift, *forma doni*, hence formedon' (Thomas G Watkin, 'Efficacy, Impact and English Legal History' (2020) 91 *Acta Universitastis Lodziensis Folia Juridica* 83, 95–6).

[44] Prestwich, *Edward I* 275, 280.   [45] Ibid. 276.

[46] Theodore FT Plucknett, 'Case and the Statute of Westminster III' (1931) 31 *Columbia Law Review* 778.

[47] SFC Milsom, *Historical Foundations of the Common Law* (2nd ed., Butterworths, 1981) 284.   [48] Prestwich, *Edward I* 280.

[49] Plucknett, *Edward I and Criminal Law* 89.   [50] Ibid.

The Decline of Feudalism 145

then they would become an outlaw. They would be declared an outlaw after being summoned five times by the county court.[51] According to a legal text of the time, *The Mirror of Justice*, the outlaw had the same status as a wolf, 'a beast hated of all folk; and from that time forward it is lawful for anyone to slay him like a wolf'.[52]

Although many of these practices pre-dated it, the Statute of Winchester 1285 'rapidly became a symbol of communal self-policing'.[53] However, Philip Rawlings has noted that, although greater emphasis was placed on the role of the community',[54] practices such as the hue and cry system 'quickly acquired a production of officials with overlapping duties and mechanisms of review to check and re-recheck whether appropriate actions had been taken'.[55] From 1331, it was stated in legislation that the constable had primary responsibility for raising the hue.[56] Overall responsibility rested with the sheriffs and increasingly with coroners who were tasked to track the progress of crown pleas and could arrest witnesses and suspects.[57] The hundred court and the royal justices inquired into every raising of the hue, with fines being imposed in relation to hues improperly raised or not properly pursued. What had been created, or at least now recognised in statute, 'was not just a means of apprehending offenders, but also a way of rendering the community and particular individuals accountable for their actions'.[58] The Statute of Winchester 1285, therefore, largely focused on the enforcement rather than the content of the criminal law, and formalised much of what was already practiced. As Plucknett commented:

All these provisions are more directed to the general problem of enforcement than to the actual content of criminal law. The passages in which they more nearly concern themselves with the substance of the law are few and are comparatively unimportant. We do not find under Edward I precise and technical definitions of crimes; the most his statutes contain is procedural details and very occasionally, the specification of penalties.[59]

This focus on procedure and enforcement meant that the work of the English Justinian did have a considerable effect upon feudalism – through the Statute of Mortmain 1279 and *Quia Emptores* of 1290 (which is sometimes referred to as the Statute of Westminster III).

III   The Decline of Feudalism

As we saw in Chapter 4, feudal tenures and incidents were lucrative to feudal lords. Over time, the incidents of tenure became 'viewed essentially as a form of taxation'.[60] While Brian Simpson used the term 'fiscal feudalism' to describe this practice, the label more generally used is that of 'bastard feudalism'.[61] Bastard feudalism denoted the illegitimate

---

[51] Philip Rawlings, *Policing: A Short History* (Routledge, 2014 [2002]) 17.
[52] William J Whittaker, *The Mirror of Justices* (Selden Society, 1895) vol. 7, 125. However, see Maitland's introduction to the volume for discussion of why this text is to 'be used with some circumspection'.
[53] Rawlings, *Policing* 24.   [54] Ibid. 15.   [55] Ibid. 17.
[56] Ibid. 24; see DA Crowley, 'The Later History of Frankpledge' (1975) 48 *Bulletin of the Institute of Historical Research* 1.
[57] Ibid. 17–18.   [58] Ibid. 17.   [59] Plucknett, *Edward I and Criminal Law* 90.   [60] Simpson, *A History of the Land Law* 22.
[61] It is thought that the term was first used by Charles Plummer in 1885. See KB McFarlane, 'Bastard Feudalism' (1943–5) 20 *Bulletin of the Institute of Historical Research* 162 and KB MacFarlane, *England in the Fifteenth Century* (Hambledon, 1981); Michael Hicks, *Bastard Feudalism* (Longman, 1995); and John Bellamy, *Bastard Feudalism and the Law* (Routledge, 2013 [1989]).

146   *The English Justinian (c.1272–1307)*

development of feudalism from a bargain based on service to an agreement based on periodic payment. While feudalism can be defined 'as the bond between lord and vassal based on the hereditary tenure of land and its use for military service', bastard feudalism can be defined as 'periodic payment for service'.[62] Michael Hicks observed that from 1150 to 1300, feudal bonds 'co-existed and interacted with other types of bastard feudal relationship'. The development of bastard feudalism also meant that a conflict further developed between those who sought to evade feudal payments and those who sought to profit from them.[63] Lords became opposed to subinfeudation, whereby their tenants made new bargains with their land with third parties. This was especially the case where the subinfeudation was to a church of similar body (known as a mortmain corporation), where no secular services or incidents would therefore arise, and there would be no chance of the land returning to the crown because of lack of heirs.

Several attempts were made to overcome subinfeudation and to restore the feudal benefits to the feudal lords, including to the king himself.[64] In 1260, while he was earl of Chester, Edward himself successfully sought a ruling from the county court that prevented subinfeudation, and when he became king, he sought to extend such provision to the whole of the kingdom.[65] This was achieved by the Statute of Mortmain 1279 and *Quia Emptores* 1290, which Milsom referred to as 'legislation as radical as any the common law has known'.[66] The Statute of Mortmain, officially known by its opening words *de Viris Relgiosis*, took the form of a writ addressed by the king to the justices of the Common Pleas.[67] It was a response to the practice whereby subinfeudation took place to give property to the Church. After first explaining 'the damage to the lord's services and incidents' that had been caused by this ecclesiastical scandal, the statute stipulated that grants to mortmain corporations were forbidden.

However, as JWM Bean noted, a 'considerable gulf' developed between the language of the statute and 'the policies that were feasible and in the long run followed by the Crown'.[68] The rule was relaxed, 'very soon, apparently'.[69] In 1280, a system was introduced whereby gifts to mortmain corporations were allowed provided that a royal licence had been given. This need for a royal licence meant that, although 'the flow of property to the church continued much as before, now 'from every gift the king (now) took such toll as he could get'.[70] This favoured feudal lords since before a royal licence was granted, an inquiry took place to see what the potential effect would be, and often the tenant was required to pay the lord a sum of money, effectively as a means of compensation. This successfully overcame the problem of tenants making gifts to mortmain corporations, but it did not stop tenants from passing the land onto new real persons by subinfeudation.[71]

The wider problems of the transfer of land by subinfeudation was dealt with by *Quia Emptores* ('because the buyers') in 1290. It said that land could not be alienated by

---

[62] Hicks, *Bastard Feudalism* 3–4.   [63] Simpson, *A History of the Land Law* 22.

[64] Milsom noted that in the thirteenth century, 'a considerable apparatus of royal actions grew up for the protection of wardship, marriage and escheat' (SFC Milsom, *The Legal Framework of English Feudalism* (Cambridge University Press, 1976) 155).

[65] Plucknett, *Legislation of Edward I* 5.   [66] Milsom, *Historical Foundations of the Common Law* 112.

[67] JWM Bean, *The Decline of English Feudalism* (Manchester University Press, 1968) 52–3.   [68] Ibid. 53.

[69] Plucknett, *Legislation of Edward I* 99.   [70] Ibid. 99–100

[71] The Statute of Mortmain remained on the statute books until 1960, when the Charities Act repealed what was left of it.

subinfeudation and new sub-grants could not be made. Any new owner must replace the original tenant either in whole or in part. In other words, subinfeudation was replaced by substitution.[72] As Milsom has noted, these were 'different kinds of arrangement': whereas subinfeudation was 'a "vertical" transaction by which the original tenant remains in place as the lord's tenant and creates a new tenure so that the grantee will hold of him', substitution was 'a "horizontal" transaction by which the grantee is substituted as the lord's tenant and the original tenant just drops out of the picture'.[73] The passing of *Quia Emptores* is usually considered a seminal moment in the history of land law, recognising that land was now sold for money rather than services, and that the transaction was no longer between tenant and sub-tenant, but rather between vendor and purchaser.[74] As Milsom put it: 'A social structure depending upon obligations between lord and tenant has been flattened out into technical rules about property.'[75]

Quia Emptores marked the 'virtual end' of feudal jurisdiction.[76] It meant that the feudal system could no longer expand, rather its only option was to decrease.[77] Milsom described it as 'as acknowledging the end of an age':[78] the lord 'has finally lost any control over who is to be his tenant' and the 'feudal relationship is recognized as dead, but his actual economic interests are saved'.[79] Yet, because some of the economic benefits of feudalism remained, feudalism was not completely dead.[80] Milsom agreed that following *Quia Emptores*, 'tenure and its incidents were to have a long life yet'.[81] As Hicks argued, 'Bastard feudalism was very much alive in Tudor and Early Stuart England up to and beyond the English Civil War.'[82] It was only the 'the rise of alternative sources of capitalist wealth, the emergence of the middle class and the class system, the relative and absolute decline of the aristocracy, and the constitutional monarchy and parliamentary democracy' that curtailed the importance of feudalism and, even then, 'some bastard feudal relationships and results persisted, persist today'.

It was the monarch themselves who became 'increasingly the one who gained from the feudal incidents and increasingly the loser from their evasion'.[83] Feudal revenue became increasingly important for the crown and it was that revenue that afforded kings a level of autonomy and control. The decline of that revenue scheme would, in time, have drastic effects for the powers and position of the monarchy. The fall in feudal income would make kings increasingly beholden to Parliament, who could raise taxes. A fuse had been lit that, as we will see, would explode centuries later in events that led to the Civil War. The fire that began with *Quia Emptores* would also have a significant effect upon English law. The desire to evade feudal incidents and the inability to dispose of land by a will led tenants to substitute their land before their death to friends, giving them instructions on how the land was then to be dealt. As we will discuss later, from these practices grew the law of uses, the

---

[72] Milsom has warned that the distinction between subinfeudation and substitution has often 'either reduced it to a lawyer's technicality or assumed the early possibility of substitution without the lord's consent': (Milsom, *The Legal Framework of English Feudalism* 103).

[73] Milsom, *Historical Foundations of the Common Law* 110. [74] Milsom, *The Legal Framework of English Feudalism* 112.

[75] Milsom, *Historical Foundations of the Common Law* 116. [76] Ibid. 100. [77] Ibid. 118. [78] Ibid. 116. [79] Ibid. 115.

[80] Plucknett argued that this did not occur until the Administration of Estates Act 1925, section 45, which 'robbed feudalism of its last surviving legal importance' (Plucknett, *Legislation of Edward I* 23).

[81] Milsom, *Historical Foundations of the Common Law* 118. [82] Hicks, *Bastard Feudalism* 4.

[83] Milsom, *Historical Foundations of the Common Law* 118.

148 *The English Justinian (c.1272–1307)*

forerunner to the modern law of trusts.[84] These, however, were concerns for the future. At the time, *Quia Emptores* was an effective way for lords to retain some of the financial benefits of feudalism whilst admitting that the feudal system itself was no longer needed.

Quia Emptores also represented the high point of the legislative activities of the English Justinian. Other statutes would follow but the second half of Edward's reign from the 1290s onwards was dominated by military matters. This would lead to echoes of the reign of his father Henry III, with the growth of Parliamentary opposition. The 'Model Parliament' of 1295 was comparable to the Montfort Parliaments in terms of the range of its members and the way in which Parliament became 'the cockpit of conflict' during the later stages of Edward's reign, providing 'a common stage of which the king confronted prelates, magnates, and increasingly, elected local representatives'.[85] The sense of déjà vu even extended to the reissuing of Magna Carta in 1297. Yet, much had changed in the hundred years after the Great Charter was sealed at Runnymede. By the end of Edward's reign, the rule of law was well established: the roles of both Parliament and the courts were now clear and set. The term 'common law' was now used and from 1292, law reports existed in the form of the Year Books that provided 'reports of discussions which took place in court – of the arguments of counsel and the opinions of the judges'.[86] Yet, it can be debated whether all this constituted progress and whether it was intentional. Perhaps Edward was just another king who unwittingly developed this common law out of a need to impose and keep order after inheriting a fractured kingdom. Indeed, MT Clanchy has argued that the expansion of royal justice may have actually increased disorder:

It might even be argued that royal power contributed to disorder and that the judicial authority of the crown was a public nuisance. In the thirteenth century the justices in eyre came into a county at infrequent intervals of six or seven years. On the criminal side the system of indictment encouraged secret accusations by neighbour against neighbour. On the civil side the availability of writs may have increased litigiousness. When the royal justices had departed, local communities were left to pick up the pieces.[87]

IV   The Origins of the Law of Obligations

The century following Magna Carta also saw the development of what modern-day lawyers refer to as the law of obligations, or the laws of contract and tort. Central to this was the development of the writ of trespass, which Maitland referred to as 'that fertile mother of actions'.[88] In the twelfth century, the royal courts were little concerned with personal obligations, as shown by the way in which the work of Glanvill focuses on personal status and land law.[89] An action for nuisance – the interference with the

---

[84] See Chapter 9.
[85] JR Maddicott, *The Origins of the English Parliament 924–1327* (Oxford University Press, 2010) 304, 305.
[86] Maitland, *The Constitutional History of England* 22. On which see Thomas Lund, *The Creation of the Common Law: The Medieval Year Books Deciphered* (Talbot Publishing, 2015).
[87] MT Clanchy, 'Law and, Government and Society in Medieval England' (1974) 59(195) *History* 73, 78.
[88] Frederic W Maitland, *The Forms of Action at Common Law* (Cambridge University Press, 1965 [1909]) 48.
[89] David J Ibbetson, *A Historical Introduction to the Law of Obligations* (Oxford University Press, 1999) 13.

The Origins of Obligations   149

enjoyment of freehold land – developed but this and other actions were 'concerned more or less with the incidents of property'.[90] There were also a number of contractual remedies: the actions for covenant, debt, detinue and account.[91] This section will discuss this medieval law of contracts before exploring the rise of trespass (which may be seen as the medieval law of tort) and the dispute concerning its origins.

1   *Covenant*

Actions for covenant were simply actions to enforce agreements. Milsom has noted that 'we are wrong to use the definite article and write of "the" actions in covenant'.[92] Actions for covenant were originally actions taken by those at the foot of the feudal pyramid that did not have a freehold interest in their land.[93] As Maitland noted, at first it appeared that such actions would generally apply to all agreements, but as the thirteenth century developed, three limitations were imposed. First, covenant could only enforce formal contracts, written agreements under seal.[94] This excluded most of the lower strata of society who were illiterate, and in any case did not have their own seal, though the legislation relating to merchants extended the numbers who had seals. Second, the remedy changed from specific performance (whereby the defendant had to perform their side of the agreement) to damages. And third, covenant could not be brought in relation to a debt.[95] These three imitations meant that actions of covenant were never very common in the King's Court and that 'the action for covenant as a genuine remedy is almost unknown in the King's Court after the middle of the fourteenth century'.[96]

Other actions complemented covenant and enforced other promises. Actions for debt and detinue covered the return of a fixed amount in money or things, with the remedy being just the return of the fixed amount or thing.[97] This action also fell into disuse given its limited application and remedy, as well as the fact that where there was no written agreement, the mode of proof was compurgation, which was increasingly subject to abuse.[98] Moreover, later on in the fourteenth century, a further limitation was imposed when it became established that debt only applied where there had been something given in return, a *quid pro quo*. The action for account was created by the Statute of Westminster 1275 and covered the situation were a debt was owed but the amount was unknown. The action led to a court order that ordered the defendant to provide the claimant with a reasonable account of what was owed. Account was used, for example, by heirs who came

---

[90] CHS Fifoot, *History and Sources of the Common Law* (Stevens & Sons, 1949) 3.
[91] For detailed discussion, see, e.g., Milsom, *Historical Foundations of the Common Law* chapter 10 and AW Brian Simpson, *History of the Common Law of Contract* (Clarendon Press, 1987) part 1.
[92] Milsom, *Historical Foundations of the Common Law* 246.   [93] Maitland, *The Forms of Action at Common Law* 64.
[94] For further discussion of when and why royal officials adopted this requirement, see Joseph Biancalana, 'Actions of Covenant 1200–1300' (2002) 20 *Legal History Review* 1.
[95] AW Brian Simpson, *An Introduction to the History of Land Law* (2nd ed., Oxford University Press, 1986) 6.
[96] Milsom, *Historical Foundations of the Common Law* 249, 251.
[97] There has been significant debate as to whether detinue should be regarded as one of contract or one of tort; Fifoot, *History and Sources of the Common Law* chapter 2. There is also controversy as to whether debt and detinue are two separate actions. Glanvill treated them as one and Maitland wrote of 'debt-detinue', saying that the differentiation only occurred early in the thirteenth century; Maitland, *The Forms of Action at Common Law* 48.
[98] Ibid. 63.

150   *The English Justinian (c.1272–1307)*

of age and felt that they had been short-changed by the guardian. Milsom noted that the action was of 'great practical importance in the middle ages'.[99] However, it declined as it was eclipsed by the rise of the equitable jurisdiction of the chancellor.[100]

2   *Trespass*

In addition to actions of nuisance and these contractual remedies, there is some evidence of more general actions emerging from the beginning of the thirteenth century: writs of trespass were bought that alleged a wrong done in breach of the king's peace.[101] Such writs were a means by which the wealthy paid for the king's intervention. They became increasingly popular, and from 1258 onwards, the writ became available to anyone who asked for it.[102] The emergence of the writ of trespass, which provided what we today would call civil compensation for wrongs (in other words, tort law), would in time lead to a differentiation of the law of wrongs into the civil action of trespass and the criminal appeal of felony.[103] As Milsom noted, the medieval common law knew 'two kinds of legal claim: the demand for a right and a complaint of a wrong'.[104] A number of writs came to protect the demand for a right, including the actions in land law considered in Chapter 5 and the contractual writs discussed earlier. All praecipe writs constituted an order to do something. On the other hand, complaints of a wrong came to be 'split into two, the criminal law resulting from administrative changes in the handling of cases begun by public authority rather than by the victims. Proceedings begun by the victims became preoccupied with compensation rather than punishment, and hence the law of tort.'[105]

However, it is important not to get ahead of ourselves in two important respects. First, it is important not to erect firm distinctions between areas of law. Legal historians disagree on how to classify what was to become the law of tort. Some deal with the historical development of trespass alongside criminal law,[106] others deal with it alongside contract law,[107] while others again deal with the early development of tort alongside the early development of other writs concerning property.[108] As David Ibbetson has warned, '[L]egal categories are not real entities; different people might legitimately see things in different ways; abstract words can have a shifting range of meaning.'[109] These different approaches, therefore , reflect the ways in which there was a fusion of ideas and influences. Indeed, the modern law of both contract and tort can be dated back to trespass writ. As we will see in the next chapter, the rigidity of the medieval law of contracts – the actions for covenant, debt, detinue and account –meant that they fell into disuse and were superseded by the action on the case for assumpsit, a development of the action on the case that was

---

[99] Milsom, *Historical Foundations of the Common Law* 275.
[100] Maitland, *The Forms of Action at Common Law* 64. This will be discussed in Chapter 9.
[101] Ibbetson, *A Historical Introduction to the Law of Obligations* 13.
[102] Paul R Hyams, *Rancor & Reconciliation in Medieval England* (Cornell University Press, 2003) 233.   [103] Ibid. 231.
[104] Milsom, *Historical Foundations of the Common Law* 243.   [105] Ibid.
[106] E.g., Frederick Pollock and Frederic W Maitland, *The History of English Law* (2nd ed., Cambridge University Press, 1968 [1898]) vol. 2.
[107] E.g., Ibbetson, *A Historical Introduction to the Law of Obligations*; Milsom, *Historical Foundations of the Common Law*.
[108] E.g., Baker, *An Introduction to English Legal History*.
[109] Ibbetson, *A Historical Introduction to the Law of Obligations* 11.

The Origins of Obligations   151

itself a development from the action of trespass.[110] The second reason to be careful of firm distinctions is that such distinctions were unlikely to exist at the time. Indeed, at first, the choice for victims was not so much as between different forms of action but was rather about 'whether to seek a royal hearing at all or to content himself with seeking redress closer to home'.[111] As to the work of Milsom has underlined,[112] those who sought royal justice would exaggerate their injury if necessary and use the standard allegation of the trespass writ that the wrongdoer had committed the action 'by force and arms against the peace of the Lord King' in order to get into the King's Court.

This and similar allegations can be found in records from the time of King John, and there were references to trespass in a number of the legislative developments that we have examined so far.[113] Yet, there is a long-standing debate as to the origins of trespass, as CHS Fifoot noted:

The origin of trespass is to be sought among the dark places of the law, and the search is complicated by the ambiguity of the word ... It enjoys both a professional and a popular connotation. The Christian repeating the Lord's Prayer and a pleader conning the Register of Writs are not likely to attach the same meaning to the word and even the legal context varies with the period.[114]

Four main theories as to its origin can be identified. The first theory, put forward by nineteenth-century theorists like Maitland, Holmes and Ames, posited that trespass had simply derived as the successor of the appeal.[115] Whereas the appeal provided both criminal punishment and civil compensation, the increasingly used process of indictment only led to criminal punishment so the writ of trespass filled this gap in terms of providing civil compensation. This argument largely rested upon the linguistic similarity between the writs. This pointed to the 'semi-criminal character' of trespass, with standard allegation being similar to the language of the appeal, with the appeal allegation being that the wrongdoer had acted 'evilly and feloniously by force and with arms and against the peace of the Lord King'.[116] However, as the research of GE Woodbine has shown, this supposed standard allegation was nothing of the sort, and the phrase was rarely used in the early trespass writs.[117] For Fifoot, the evidence 'is more slender than its frequent repetition would suggest ... No legal inference is more dangerous than one based upon linguistic analogy.'[118] The second theory, put forward by Plucknett, stated that the writ of trespass

---

[110] Stoljar argued, however, that the medieval beginnings did have 'a direct influence upon the shape of things to some: the very emergence of the modern, so-called simple contract, with its characteristic octane of assumpsit and consideration, is essentially a tale of overcoming the special limitations of the medieval forms of action – those of contract, debt and detinue' (SJ Stoljar, *A History of Contract at Common Law* (Australian National University Press, 1975) 1).

[111] Hyams, *Rancor & Reconciliation in Medieval England* 231.

[112] SFC Milsom, 'Trespass From Henry III to Edward III: Part 1: General Writs' (1958) 74 *Law Quarterly Review* 195; SFC Milsom, 'Part 2: Special Writs' (1958) 74 *Law Quarterly Review* 407; SFC Milsom, 'Part 3: More Special Writs and Conclusions' (1958) 74 *Law Quarterly Review* 561.

[113] E.g., Magna Carta 1225; Statute of Westminster 1275; Statute of Gloucester 1278, clause 8.

[114] Fifoot, *History and Sources of the Common Law* 44. For discussion of the options (up to the work of Milsom), see ibid. 44–56.

[115] See e.g., Pollock and Maitland, *The History of English Law* 512, 526: 'The writs of trespass are closely connected with the appeals of felony. The action of trespass, we may say is an attenuated appeal.'

[116] Fifoot, *History and Sources of the Common Law* 45.

[117] GE Woodbine, 'Origins of the Action of Trespass' (1924) 33 *Yale Law Journal* 799; GE Woodbine, 'Origins of the Action of Trespass' (1925) 34 *Yale Law Journal* 343.

[118] Fifoot, *History and Sources of the Common Law* 44, 45.

152   *The English Justinian (c.1272–1307)*

came from the local courts.[119] However, this did not really solve the origins issue, and the evidence he used showing that the writs were used at the same time at both levels meant that the influence could have equally been the other way around.[120] The third theory, that of Woodbine, located the origin of trespass as the remedy that was used in situations where a third party had tried to take land from the claimant but had been unsuccessful.[121] Had the third party been successful, the writ of *Novel Disseisin* would have been available, but there was no such action where a disseisin had been attempted and damaged caused. However, this too suffers from causal problems. As Fifoot put it, to link up actions in land and trespass and to 'identify the one as a child of the other is to betray a too causal a view of childhood'.[122]

All three earlier theories were rebutted by the fourth: Milsom's revisionist account that was based in the careful reading of the writs used.[123] Milsom's work transformed the debate by discovering the word 'trespass' in the thirteenth and fourteenth centuries was not a technical legal word. His work showed that all of the previous participants in the debate had taken an anachronistic approach. They had assumed 'that it was from the beginning what is today' and 'that what came into being in the thirteenth century was a single entity, a definite tort with the essential ingredient of direct forcible injury'.[124] In contrast, Milsom discovered that the word 'trespass' simply came from the Latin *transgresso*, meaning 'wrong'. The term had the same meaning as it does in the Lord's Prayer: 'forgive us our trespasses' simply meant forgive us our wrongs. The word trespass covered all wrongs bar the most serious (which were known as felonies). It therefore covered 'the whole range of lesser wrongs'. For Milsom, historians had 'misunderstood the early developments by reading back a later and narrower meaning, and by imagining substantive ideas where contemporaries were concerned only with jurisdiction and proof.'[125] This mistake led to significant conceptual errors. Milsom wrote that had textbooks been written as the time, trespass 'would have been the title, not of a chapter, but of the book', because there was 'no entity equivalent to our tort of trespass, and that the only concept denoted by the word trespass was the elementary one of wrong. It was a generic term.'[126]

Milsom's contribution was to recast the debate.[127] He argued that 'the question was not whether a wrong qualified as a trespass, but whether it was the kind of trespass which the royal court could or would handle'. The only conceptual unity underpinning the various trespasses, he argued, was the fact that they belonged in the jurisdiction of the King's Court because: 'The allegation of breach of the king's peace makes it a plea for the Crown.'[128]

---

[119] Plucknett, *A Concise History of the Common Law* 349.   [120] Fifoot, *History and Sources of the Common Law* 47.
[121] Ibid. 113.   [122] Ibid. 54.
[123] Milsom, 'Trespass from Henry III to Edward III: Part 1: General Writs'; Milsom, 'Trespass from Henry III to Edward III: Part 2: Special Writs'; Milsom, 'Trespass from Henry III to Edward III: Part 3: More Special Writs and Conclusions' (all reprinted as SFC Milsom, *Studies in the History of the Common Law* (Hambledon Press, 1985) chapter 1 and integrated within Milsom, *Historical Foundations of the Common Law* chapter 11).
[124] Milsom, 'Trespass from Henry III to Edward III: Part 1: General Writs'.
[125] Milsom, *Historical Foundations of the Common Law* 285.
[126] Milsom, 'Trespass from Henry III to Edward III: Part 2: Special Writs'.
[127] It has not been unquestioned. Palmer has contended that 'the allegation of vi et armis was not fictional but was rather a low-threshold test' (Robert C Palmer, *English Law in the Age of the Black Death 1348–1381* (University of North Carolina Press, 1993) 166).
[128] Milsom, *Historical Foundations of the Common Law* 287.

Conclusions 153

Milsom argued that making the allegation provided a 'ticket of entry' to the royal courts. His research found that often there was no apparent royal interest at stake in an allegation of trespass, but that the allegation was used as mere window dressing. He noted that 'by about the end of the century it is reasonably clear that the allegation is being inserted not because of any element in the facts but because the plaintiff desires some consequence, presumably that of royal justice'.[129] While Milsom dated this increase to 1275, Watkin has suggested that the rise of trespass writs occurred post-1285 as a result of clause 24 of the Statute of Westminster II 1285, which, as we have seen, allowed the creation of new writs that were very similar to existing ones.[130] According to Watkin, this need to show similarity led to claimants making similar accusations to previous cases but using the same standard allegation. For Watkin, this explained the increase of trespass writs post-1285 and the increasingly common allegation. Like Milsom, he recognised that this allegation was a fiction but Watkin's account provided a reason why such a fiction became increasingly popular. The rise of trespass was actually the rise of a common allegation that came about from claimants overstating the wrong in order to get the action into the King's Court.

As Fifoot noted, the writ of trespass proved popular, and by the close of the thirteenth century, this abundance led to differentiation: from the standard trespass to land came trespass to the person and trespass to goods.[131] These trespass writs and those that grew from them were to dominate the common law. As Milsom has noted, by the eighteenth century, they were responsible for almost all litigation at common law: 'Although these writs covered various harms to persons, goods and lands, they were understood as representing a single entity: the essence of trespass was direct forcible injury.'[132] These judicial developments were to be as ground-breaking and long-lasting as any of the statutes passed under the English Justinian. Indeed, Fifoot noted that the early development of trespass fitted the timescale of Edward I's reign almost perfectly: '[T]he accession of Edward I saw the establishment of Trespass as a writ, his death its specifics distinct and its language set in a mould which was to endure.'[133]

V   Conclusions

Although other important developments were still to come, such as the use of English in court and the separation of the House of Commons and the House of Lords,[134] the reign of Edward I can be seen as a watershed in the history of English law. Though it is often remembered for the growth of statute law and the way in which such provisions dealt with private law matters that had hitherto been the preserve of the common law courts, the reign of the so-called English Justinian is notable not only for its legislative achievements. As Maitland pointed out, like William I and Henry II before him, Edward was also a great

---

[129] Ibid.   [130] Watkin, 'The Significance of "In Consimili Casu" 283.
[131] Fifoot, *History and Sources of the Common Law* 55.   [132] Milsom, *Historical Foundations of the Common Law* 283.
[133] Fifoot, *History and Sources of the Common Law* 56.
[134] The Pleading in English Act 1392 (commonly known as the statue of Pleading) did what the name of the Act suggests whilst by 1340 the Commons was meeting regularly and sitting in a separate chamber from the Lords and operating by 'common petition' to seek remedies.

154 *The English Justinian (c.1272–1307)*

organiser and his effect upon the institutions of government and justice was significant but often under appreciated.[135] In his lectures on constitutional history, Maitland turned to his students and said:

'Take any institution that exists at the end of the Middle Ages, any that exists in 1800 – be it parliament, or privy council, or any of the courts of law – we can trace it back through a series of definite changes as far as Edward's reign, but if we go further back the object that we have in view begins to disappear, its outlines begin to be blurred'.

Maitland argued that it was only during Edward's reign that 'all becomes definite' in terms of Parliament, the King's Council and the courts of the common law. He further noted that the language had become established. This included the term 'common law' itself which Maitland observed had come 'into use in or shortly after the reign of Edward I'.[136] Maitland further noted that while 'in older ages while the local courts were still powerful, law was really preserved by oral tradition among the free men', by the end of the reign of Edward I, 'as the King's Court throws open its doors wider and wider for more and more business, the knowledge of the law becomes more and more the possession of a learned class of professional lawyers'.[137] This has crucially meant that the development of the common law became more fixed, through the developing idea of precedent. As Maitland noted, 'common law is gradually evolved as ever new cases arise; but the judges are not conceived as making new law – they have no right or power to do that – rather they are declaring what has always been law'.

This was also the result of the growth of and increased deference towards statute law. Maitland noted that further phrases that had become commonplace was referring to how 'the king in parliament can make statutes; the king in council can make ordinances'.[138] Yet, it would be incorrect to paint the reign of Edward I as the end of the story of the genesis of the common law and of where constitutional arrangements became fixed and non-contentious for all time. Although the reign Edward I was by no means peaceful, the relationship between the king and his council and Parliament was to become more volatile in the years to come. The century after Magna Carta was much more stable than the century that followed. As Lyon noted, 'Edward I was the last medieval English king to be completely secure on his throne. Nine reigned between 1307 and 1485, of whom four where disposed and murdered. A fifth lost his crown temporarily'.[139] The remainder of the Plantagenet period would be rocked not only by the civil war known as the War of the Roses but also the pandemic graphically but suitably described as the Black Death, which would have a significant impact upon English law, as the next chapter will discuss.

---

[135] Maitland, *The Constitutional History of England* 20. [136] Ibid 22. [137] Ibid 23. [138] Ibid. 20.
[139] Ann Lyon, *Constitutional History of the United Kingdom* (2nd ed., Routledge, 2016) 94.

'We have to remember the Black Death of 1349, one of the greatest economic catastrophes in all history; the guess has been made that it destroyed not much less than half the population. It utterly unsettled the medieval system of agriculture and industry'.

Frederic W Maitland, *The Constitutional History of England* (Cambridge University Press, 1941 [1908]) 208.

8

The Black Death (c.1307–1485)

I   Introduction

There have been several global pandemics throughout history. Many of these have affected England, including the Cyprian plague of 250, the leprosy pandemic of the early Middle Ages, the 1918 influenza pandemic, the HIV/AIDS pandemic of the 1980s and COVID-19 in the 2020s. However, the most fatal was the Black Death (also known as the Pestilence, the Great Mortality or the Plague),[1] which killed a third of the English population in the first outbreak in 1348–50 alone.[2] The bubonic plague first arrived in the fourteenth century but outbreaks were to sporadically occur in the centuries that followed, being responsible also for the Great Plague of 1665, for instance. In the fourteenth century, the Black Death provided a seismic shock socially and economically. Whole villages were deserted and labour became scarce.

Yet, the legal ramifications of the Black Death have often been underplayed or even ignored by legal historians. Those fortunate to live outside periods affected by pandemics often fail to appreciate the importance of such widespread diseases. Frederic W Maitland, for example, barely mentioned the Black Death. In part, this is unsurprising and comes from the structures he adopted for his works. 'Pollock and Maitland' stopped before the time of Edward I and his lectures on constitutional history were structured to avoid the fourteenth century, with his first period being up to the death of Edward I in 1307 and his second period being the legal position at the death of Henry VII in 1509. However, the fact that he made and used such periodisations is noteworthy and reflects how he saw the fourteenth century as being of comparatively little interest. As he saw it, much of the common law had already become settled before this time.[3] Indeed, his fleeting mentions of

---

[1] The term 'Black Death' was not applied to the outbreak until 200 years later, and became applied to the first outbreak of the plague, not to the subsequent epidemics of the same disease; Stephen Porter, *Black Death: A New History of the Bubonic Plagues of London* (Amberley Publishing, 2018) 21, 22.

[2] Robert C Palmer, *English Law in the Age of the Black Death 1348–1381: A Transformation of Governance and Law* (University of North Carolina Press, 1993) 3. One of the distinctive features of the disease was that 'it preferentially targeted men and women in the prime of life' (Frank M Snowden, *Epidemics and Society: From the Black Death to the Present* (Yale University Press, 2019) 29).

[3] W Mark Ormrod, 'The Politics of Pestilence: Government in England after the Black Death' in W Mark Ormrod and Philip Lindley (eds.), *The Black Death in England* (Stamford, 1996) 147.

157

158   *The Black Death (c.1307–1485)*

the Black Death relate to its economic and social effects, rather than to its legal effects. Its only mention in his constitutional history was to remind his student audience that it was 'one of the greatest economic catastrophes in all history' that 'utterly unsettled the medieval system of agriculture and industry'.[4] Similarly, elsewhere Maitland briefly referred to the Black Death as one of a list of 'great social catastrophes' alongside the Tudor dissolution of the monasteries.[5] No attention was given to the legal significance of the Black Death.

Maitland's influence, as ever, has been significant. Other legal historians have replicated this approach. John Baker asserted that while 'few would contend that English legal history should follow the Roman example by ending with its Justinian', it would not be 'a grave distortion to assert that much of what happened after his death, or at least after the death of his son Edward II, has been seriously neglected by historians of the law'.[6] However, in recent years, some historians have begun to reassess the legal importance of the fourteenth century and of the Black Death in particular;[7] most notable is Robert Palmer's treatment of the issue.[8] Palmer's thesis is that a whole host of legal changes that occurred in the fourteenth centuries can sensibly be understood as part of 'a transformation of law and governance in the wake of the Black Death'.[9] This contrasts with the conventional approach that regarded each of these changes separately as isolated examples of the common law reforming itself and working out existing inadequacies. Palmer denounced 'the fragmented, legally insular conceptualizations currently dominant that portray the change as gradual evolution with discrete non-interactive legal categories'.[10] However, the counter-risk that the importance of the Black Death can be over-played is as dangerous as the risk that it can be ignored or underplayed. As ever, the picture is one of both change and continuity, and of the common law struggling to adapt pragmatically to a new social and economic world.

This chapter explores the development of English law in the period that saw the fall of the Plantagenet period. It covers the period 1307–1485, which saw nine kings take the throne.[11] It focuses, however, on the impact of the Black Death, the defining event of this period that cast a long shadow. The chapter falls into three sections. Section II examines the most obvious direct effect of the Black Death: the rise of labour law. It will explore how the scarcity of labour caused by the pestilence led to legislation that resulted in an even more significant social and political shakeup. Section III then examines some of the other wider indirect effects that the Black Death had upon the legal system, looking at its effect upon

---

[4] Frederic W Maitland, *The Constitutional History of England* (Cambridge University Press, 1941 [1908]) 207–8.
[5] Frederic W Maitland, 'The Materials for English Legal History' in Frederic W Maitland (ed.), *The Collected Papers of Frederic William Maitland* (Cambridge University Press, 1911) vol. 2, 1, 56.
[6] John H Baker, 'The Dark Age of English Legal History 1500–1700' in D Jenkins (ed.), *Legal History Studies 1972* (University of Wales Press, 1975) 1–27, reprinted in John H Baker, *Collected Papers on English Legal History* (Cambridge University Press, 2013) 1446. Baker's own work has subsequently shed much light on the Tudor period.
[7] See, e.g., Ormrod and Lindley, *The Black Death in England*, which includes a chapter on government; Anthony Musson and Mark Ormod, *The Evolution of English Justice: Law, Politics and Society in the Fourteenth Century* (Palgrave, 1998); Anthony Musson, *Medieval Law in Context* (Manchester University Press, 2001).
[8] Palmer, *English Law in the Age of the Black Death 1348–1381*. See also Mark Bailey, *After the Black Death: Economy, Society and the Law in Fourteenth Century England* (Oxford University Press, 2021).
[9] Palmer, *English Law in the Age of the Black Death 1348–1381* 6.   [10] Ibid.
[11] Namely: Edward II (1307–27); Edward III (1327–77); Richard II (1377–99); Henry IV (1399–1413); Henry V (1413–22); Henry VI (1422–61); Edward IV (1461–3); Edward V (1483); and Richard III (1483–5).

courts and the legal profession. Section IV then examines the wider effect of the Black Death upon the substantive law (other than the immediate developments in labour law already discussed). This will begin by looking at how the law of obligations developed significantly in this period. Continuing the account began in the last chapter, this will examine how a moribund medieval law of contracts was replaced by a new law of contract that fed off developments from the law of trespass. As we will see, while Palmer attributes the Black Death a significant role in this transformation, other legal historians have disagreed, seeing changes in the law of obligations as purely legal developments. This reflects the two perspectives that we will see throughout this chapter: the orthodox position that regards each development as a separate evolutionary development, and the Palmer thesis that regards these changes as being the legacy of the Black Death. Section IV will also examine developments in criminal law in this era, most notably the Statute of Treasons 1352 and developments in the common law of murder, exploring the influence of the Black Death in that context. This chapter will explore why attention ought to be afforded to the final period of Plantagenet England, and to the impact and legacy of the Black Death in particular. Much of what follows will focus on developments in the fourteenth century, the descent into civil war during the fifteenth century will be the focus of the conclusion. The so-called War of the Roses drew a curtain on the long Plantagenet era, an era in which the common law had become firmly established but had also become increasingly rigid, complex and burdensome, leading lawyers to come up with creative circumventions.

II   The Origins of Labour Law

It is tempting to see the death of the English Justinian, Edward I, as also being the start of the death of the Plantagenet era. The conventional understanding is, as Ann Lyon put it, 'the rot set in with Edward II'.[12] Edward II (1307–27) is typically presented as 'worthless, incapable of any sustained policy, and influencing events only by sporadic displays of ill-directed energy or by a stubborn adherence to greedy and ambitious favourites'.[13] His reputation has been shaped by the fact that he lost the throne, though different stories exist as regards his demise: While the conventional story is that he was murdered possibly by having a red hot poker shoved up his rectum nine months after relinquishing his throne in favour of his fourteen-year-old son (who became Edward III), alternative tales include that he died of depression and natural causes or escaped to become a wandering hermit in Italy.[14] However, regardless of how it ended, his twenty-year reign was of some importance. As with other less talented or absent kings, his reign saw the developments of his predecessors run freely and autonomously. This was true of Parliament, for instance. Indeed, Edward II's coronation oath included for the first time a pledge 'to maintain and

---

[12] Ann Lyon, *Constitutional History of the United Kingdom* (2nd ed., Routledge, 2016) 94.
[13] Seymour Phillips, *Edward II* (Yale University Press, 2010) 1.
[14] See Ian Mortimer, 'The Death of Edward II in Berkeley Castle' (2005) 120(489) *English Historical Review* 1175.

160 *The Black Death (c.1307–1485)*

preserve the laws and rightful customs which the community of your realm shall have chosen'.[15] And as with so many Plantagenet kings, his reign was characterised by civil war and kingly concessions, most notably the Ordinances of 1311, which limited the king's right to go to war or to grant land without Parliament's approval.

These tensions continued during the long reign of Edward III (1327–77). Indeed, Lyon has argued that his reign was 'too long', in that, although initially the reign was an 'unprecedented success', with Edward becoming 'the archetype of a medieval monarch and the greatest patron of the cult of chivalry', from 1370, 'his glory faded' as he 'slide into senility' and 'became the pawn of others'.[16] Conventional accounts have seen his reign as sowing the seeds of what was to come, pointing to the state of public order and the cost of warfare during this reign.[17] Such problems escalated during the reign of Richard II (1377–99), leading to widespread civil unrest. Richard came to the throne at the age of just ten, and so for the first part of his reign, the kingdom was in the hands of a series of regency councils. These years were to prove tumultuous, with the so-called Hundred Years' War and the Peasants' Revolt dominating proceedings both abroad and at home.

Yet, despite these clear problems, the fourteenth century saw a number of significant legal developments, including the consolidation of Parliament; important legislation in the middle of his reign dealing with labour law, the powers of the Church and criminal law; and the emergence of State officials at the local level in the form of permanent justices of the peace. Conventional accounts understand these changes as just another in the 'series of steps' by which the common law developed; another instance of the 'short phrases of dramatic change interspersed with longer periods of comparative stability'.[18] Though Anthony Musson and Mark Ormrod note that war and plague were the 'two overriding influences at work upon English justice in the fourteenth century', they favour seeing the period within an evolutionary framework of 'punctuated equilibrium' whereby the long-term gradual process of change was occasionally punctured by events that caused the system to adapt, but only to restore balance and order.[19] They suggest that this scientific comparison can highlight how such events can include external or 'exogenous' forces for change that come from 'independent external triggers' as well as change from within, internal 'endogenous' changes that are ' a result of autonomous development rather than an reaction to external challenges'.[20] Musson and Ormrod, looking at the fourteenth century as a whole, see war, economic crisis, popular disturbances and constitutional conflict as external influences and 'consumer demand', the development of the judicial profession and the development of legislation as internal influences on the evolution of justice.

---

[15] Lyon, *Constitutional History of the United Kingdom* 96. For discussion of the different interpretations of the oath, see Roy Martin Haines, *King Edward II: His Life, His Reign and Its Aftermath, 1284–1330* (McGill-Queen's University Press, 2003) chapter 3.

[16] Lyon, *Constitutional History of the United Kingdom* 113.

[17] For a recent revisionist account see WM Ormerod, *Winner and Waster and Its Contexts: Chivalry, Law and Economics in Fourteenth Century England* (Boydell, 2021).

[18] Musson and Ormod, *The Evolution of English Justice* 2. See also W Mark Ormrod, *Political Life in Medieval England* (Palgrave, 1995).

[19] Musson and Ormod, *The Evolution of English Justice* 3, 4.   [20] Ibid. 6.

The Origins of Labour Law 161

Some historians, however, have seen the Black Death as the 'great catalyst' for legal change. This includes the work of Bertha Haven Putnam,[21] Michael Bennett,[22] Mark Bailey[23] and most notably Palmer.[24] This complements the work of economic, social, religious and cultural historians who often view the Black Death as a major turning point.[25] By contrast, conventional legal-historical accounts barely mention the Black Death; an omission that is problematic given that the population decline on the scale suffered in the middle of the fourteenth century must have had an impact upon all aspects of life.[26] Focusing upon the Black Death highlights the dating of the important changes usually attributed to the reign of Edward III or the fourteenth century generally.[27] Those who stress the importance of the Black Death often point out that the legal changes for which Edward III is renowned occurred in the middle of his reign, crucially in the aftermath of the Black Death. They also point out that the consolidation of the role of Parliament, the labour law legislation and the development of the justices of the peace were all related responses to the Black Death. They were all consequences of what Palmer described as 'vigorous action to preserve the status quo [that] in fact transformed both governance and law'.[28] His thesis can be summed up as follows:

After the Black Death and to preserve the status quo as far as possible, the upper orders of English society drew together into a cohesive government to facilitate or coerce the members of the upper orders to stand to their obligations, at the same time they were coercing the lower orders more punitively to stand by theirs. State authority increased greatly, although significant powers were to be exercised by delegation to the local level. Authority throughout society came to be more thoroughly to be exercised not by virtue of innate individual power but by virtue of state mandate, and the government took responsibility for the regulation and direction of the whole of society.[29]

Palmer's thesis was that as a result of the Black Death, government became more comprehensive and aggressive. He noted that while 'thirteenth century English government handled social needs as they arose', prior to the Black Death there was no need for government to 'meddle in a wide range of matters at the local level'.[30] The ability for government to be far reaching existed prior to the plague but was un-used: the common law regulated lives and fortunes and 'centralized bureaucratic governmental structures existed that could utilize that law to respond to an extraordinary demographic crisis'.[31] The Black Death proved to be such a crisis. The crisis led to an increase in the scope of government

---

[21] Bertha Haven Putnam, *The Enforcement of the Statute of Labourers, 1349–1359* (Columbia University, 1908); Bertha Haven Putnam, 'The Transformation of the Keepers of the Peace into the Justices of the Peace, 1327–1380' (1929) 12 *Transactions of the Royal Historical Society* 41.

[22] Michael Bennett, 'The Impact of the Black Death on English Legal History' (1995) 11 *Australian Journal of Law and Society* 191.

[23] Bailey, *After the Black Death.*   [24] Palmer, *English Law in the Age of the Black Death 1348–1381.*

[25] Bennett, 'The Impact of the Black Death on English Legal History' 191–2. Bailey has referred to the 'recent, extraordinary surge of interdisciplinary research' into the Black Death (Bailey, *After the Black Death* 6).

[26] Bennett, 'The Impact of the Black Death on English Legal History' 191.

[27] Ormrod saw Edward III's reign as being characterised by its stability in terms of politics: 'It is remarkable how little politics really changed under Edward III' (W Mark Ormrod, *The Reign of Edward III* (History Press, 2000) 202). However, more generally, he noted that 'Edward III lived and reigned too long to allow any easy generalizations about his personality, career and reign' (W Mark Ormrod, *Edward III* (Yale University Press, 2011) 603). Lyon suggested that Edward III 'lived too long' and that his glory faded from 1370, as he 'slid into senility' and became 'the pawn of others' (Lyon, *Constitutional History of the United Kingdom* 113).

[28] Palmer, *English Law in the Age of the Black Death 1348–1381* 1.   [29] Ibid.   [30] Ibid. 5.   [31] Ibid. 2–3.

162 *The Black Death (c.1307–1485)*

activity and also meant that 'Crown and Commons began to settle old disputes in a spirit of cooperation'.[32] For Palmer, the fact that there was no evidence of any form of economic crisis until the 1370s showed that the government had 'clearly made a major effort to counteract the plague'.[33] In the two decades following the Black Death, 'the government exerted itself to retain the old structure of society'.[34]

The main direct effect of the Black Death upon English law was the development of labour legislation. This was momentarily recognised by Maitland. The death of landowners and the scarcity of labour caused by the Black Death benefitted those at the bottom rung of the feudal ladder who remained fit and well. The villeins – those outside of the freehold legal bargain – suddenly found themselves in demand. They could now demand higher wages for their labour with the threat that they could easily go elsewhere. Maitland noted that 'an increased demand for hired labour and a consequent rise of wages may have been the forces which drove the peasantry to desert their holdings'.[35] This undermined the feudal system, which had rested on the labours of the villeins. Moreover, reversing this trend proved difficult. Villeins were understandably reluctant to return to their previous position. In his constitutional history, Maitland noted that the effect of the Black Death was that wages 'rose enormously' and this led Parliament to endeavour 'by statute after statute to keep them down, to fix a legal rate of wages'.[36]

The Ordinance of Labourers and Servants 1349 and the Statute of Labourers 1351[37] were drawn up in response to the shortages of labour caused by the plague.[38] Bennett has described this legislation as 'epoch-making both in the scope of its ambition and the manner of its enforcement'.[39] Prior to this legislation, the common law did not regulate labour relations.[40] Instead, the matter was dealt with under feudalism: where one worked and what one got in return was a matter of personal status and any regulation of this was a local affair, with feudal obligations being enforced by local courts and feudal abuses being subject to corrections by the common law courts. Fewer rights were held, however, by those outside the feudal pyramid – the villeins.[41] And it was this group that were to benefit from the after effects of the Black Death.[42]

---

[32] WM Ormrod, 'The English Government and the Black Death in the Fourteenth Century' in WM Ormrod (ed.), *England in the Fourteenth Century* (Boydell Press, 1986) 175, 187.

[33] Palmer, *English Law in the Age of the Black Death 1348–1381* 4. For a differing interpretation see Bailey, *After the Black Death* chapter 4.

[34] Palmer, *English Law in the Age of the Black Death 1348–1381* 4.

[35] Frederic W Maitland, 'History of a Cambridgeshire Manor' in Maitland, *The Collected Papers of Frederic William Maitland* vol. 2, 366, 379.

[36] Maitland, *The Constitutional History of England* 207–8.

[37] Though referred to as a statute, it was not formally enacted as such until later; Bennett, 'The Impact of the Black Death on English Legal History' 196.

[38] On which see the essays in James Bothwell, PJP Golderber and W Mark Ormrod (eds.), *The Problem of Labour in Fourteenth Century England* (York Medieval Press, 2000).

[39] Bennett, 'The Impact of the Black Death on English Legal History' 202. On its enforcement, see Haven Putnam, *The Enforcement of the Statute of Labourers*.

[40] Palmer, *English Law in the Age of the Black Death 1348–1381* 14.

[41] Ibid. 15. On which, see Paul R Hyams, *Kings, Lords and Peasants in Medieval England: The Common Law of Villeinage in the Twelfth and Thirteenth Centuries* (Oxford University Press, 1980).

[42] Bailey has, however, argued that villeinage was in retreat before this period and manorial lordship was not as dominant by this time. He contended that this gravely damages the credibility of the assumptions that underpin much work in this area; Bailey, *After the Black Death* 14, 12.

The Origins of Labour Law 163

This increase in the clout of those who worked the land troubled those who held the land. And as Bennett noted, this concern went all the way up the social order to the king himself: '[T]his decisive shift in the balance of bargaining power represented a major crisis for landed society and indeed for the Crown itself.'[43] This led to a 'rapid response' that united the upper social classes and resulted in legislation that not only took a radically different perspective on how labour was to be regulated but also transformed governance generally. As Palmer noted, labour became dictated not by personal status but by contract compulsory for all those not otherwise occupied and 'provision of a sufficient work force at acceptable wages became a matter of great concern to central government'.[44] Moreover, Palmer stressed how this legislation provided a clear example of how law was being used to attempt to reinstate the previous status quo and to put a lid upon class war. The two pieces of legislation merit examination in turn.

1   *The Ordinance of Labourers 1349*

Promulgated within a year of the outbreak of the Black Death, the Ordinance of Labourers 1349 dealt with the issue of the shortage of labour and the increase in prices of goods by attempting to freeze wages and levels at pre-plague levels.[45] It was addressed to sheriffs throughout England and began by stating that the measure was needed not only because of the deaths caused by the plague ('because a great part of the people, and especially of workmen and servants, late died of the pestilence') but also because those who were left 'will not serve unless they may receive excessive wages, and some [were] rather willing to beg in idleness, than by labour to get their living'. The ordinance's response was to decree that all able-bodied men and women under the age of sixty were to work. As Bennett noted, 'labourers without employment were to accept any position offered at the set rates'.[46]

Chapter 1 declared this with a number of exceptions: those who were self-sufficient, merchants, craftsmen and those who had sufficient land of their own to farm.[47] The lords of tenants retained priority of the tenants' service ('the lords be preferred before other') but this was subject to the provision that 'the said lords shall retain no more than be necessary for them'. Testimony by 'two true men before the sheriff or constable of the town' was sufficient to jail those who refused to work or to work at the accustomed wages. Chapter 2 provided that those who departed from service 'without reasonable cause of licence, before the term agreed' would be imprisoned. The same would apply to those who took on another's servant before that servant's term had expired.

Chapter 3 provided that those who offered or demanded excessive wages ('any more wages, liveries, meed or salary than was wont') were liable to a penalty of twice that offered or demanded, and that such claims could be brought by anyone at all in the Lord's Court. Chapter 4 stipulated that in actions against lords of the town or manor the penalties

---

[43] Bennett, 'The Impact of the Black Death on English Legal History' 196.
[44] Palmer, *English Law in the Age of the Black Death 1348–1381* 14–15.   [45] Ibid. 17.
[46] Bennett, 'The Impact of the Black Death on English Legal History' 197.
[47] Palmer, *English Law in the Age of the Black Death 1348–1381* 18.

164   *The Black Death (c.1307–1485)*

would be trebled. Further, the ordinance's rules applied to agreements for excessive wages made before the ordinance. Chapter 5 regulated craftsmen, listing a number of professions who 'shall not take for their labour and workmanship above the same' than before to the plague or would be imprisoned. Chapter 6 applied similar provisions to the sellers of food and made local officials liable 'to pay treble of the thing so sold'. Chapter 7 forbade under the threat of imprisonment giving alms to able-bodied beggars 'because that many valiant beggars, as long as they live of begging, do refuse to labour, giving themselves to idleness and vice, and sometimes to theft and other abominations'. As Palmer noted, the giving of alms was seen as aiding beggars to contravene the ordinance: 'The king in council thus forbade charitable giving to those who could work, explicitly to compel them to work for a living.'[48]

The ordinance from the king and his council concluded by commanding that it be publicly proclaimed out loud in important places within the sheriff's jurisdiction. Palmer noted that 'separate forceful "letters of request" were sent to the bishops' that asked them to follow similar wage restrictions, and the bishops had the ordinance proclaimed in churches. Yet, as he noted, 'ordaining and proclaiming are one thing; observing is another'. Although there were some prosecutions under its terms, for the most part, the ordinance was ineffective largely because, although some provision was made for public prosecution, it broadly rested on private enforcement.[49] This led to Parliament petitioning for what became the Statute of Labourers 1351.

2   *The Statute of Labourers 1351*

As Palmer noted, the 'tone of the statute was no different to that of the ordinance'.[50] The statute required servants to publicly swear 'to observe and perform these ordinances' and to stay in the same town, with those who refused to make such an oath or who did not perform as they had sworn were to be 'put in the stocks'.[51] It reinforced the ordinance by incorporating previous alterations, tightening the specification of wages and improving enforcement by extending 'local responsibilities to search out violators of the provisions' and providing for supervision by royal justices.[52] Palmer noted that 'the royal justices were to make their circuit at least four times a year in all the countries and to punish harshly anyone speaking or doing anything in their presence adverse to the provisions'.[53] Further pressure came from the recurrence of the plague in 1361, which led to wage increases and hundreds of prosecutions a year in the 1360s and 1370s.[54] The ordinance and statute were routinely confirmed in Parliament and buttressed by further regulations. In 1361, provision was made to brand fugitive labourers on the forehead, while in 1364, an attempt was made to specify the diet and apparel of servants.[55] In 1388, servants and prentices were mandated to

---

[48] Ibid. 19.   [49] Bennett, 'The Impact of the Black Death on English Legal History' 197.
[50] Palmer, *English Law in the Age of the Black Death 1348–1381* 21.
[51] Ibid. 20. The statute provided that 'stocks [were to] be made in every town for such occasion'.   [52] Ibid. 21.   [53] Ibid.
[54] Bennett, 'The Impact of the Black Death on English Legal History' 198.
[55] Palmer, *English Law in the Age of the Black Death 1348–1381* 22.

The Origins of Labour Law 165

help with the harvesting.[56] Palmer noted that, although these provisions, unlike the statute, lacked effective enforcement, 'the attempt shows the degree to which the central government had extended its concerns into the relatively mundane'.[57]

The overall effect of the ordinance and statute was far from trivial. Bennett noted that the 'assumption must be that the labour legislation acted in some measure as a brake on the upward movement of wages'.[58] As he went on to state, what was novel was 'the national scale of the enterprise'.[59] The labour legislation 'marked a spectacular expansion in the domain of statute law, bringing within its purview, first, wages and prices, but then, by extension, a whole range of other economic and social arrangements'. As Palmer proclaimed, although this new attitude would not be completed until Tudor times, the further changes that were to come can be traced back to 'the change in governmental approach and the great expansion of legal subject matter jurisdiction that began with the Black Death'.[60] The labour law legislation saw law used 'not only to regulate labour but, in some measure, to freeze the traditional social order'.[61] Indeed, Palmer went further to view this legislation as representing 'a newly responsible and newly intrusive' form of government.[62] Now, the king's government 'became responsible for the running of the whole society'.[63] As Bailey put it, there was a 'transformation of England from a "demesne" state, where the Crown was largely dependent upon its own financial resources, to a "fiscal" state in which the resources of the realm were mobilized through regular indirect and direct taxation'.[64] Such taxation was most burdensome in the 1370s 'when the government also experimented with new forms of direct taxation and when its management of the war with France was inept'.[65]

Bailey has, however, warned of the dangers of a 'narrative [that] imposes far too neat a pattern upon the events of the third quarter of the fourteenth century, when in reality this was a highly complex and contradictory period'.[66] There is a risk that this emphasis upon the effect of the Black Death presents a new evolutionary story that simplifies and constrains the developments that occurred. For Bailey, common law developments had already diluted feudal ties before the Black Death.[67] He rejected 'the notion that the lords had exercised considerable control over peasant labour' and argued instead that 'the pre-plague labour market was open, sizeable, and scarcely regulated by either manorial lordship or government'. For Bailey, '[T]he government's rapid intervention in the labour market in 1349 was a desperate and tardy attempt to exert some form of control, which heightened resentment.'[68] Bailey's 'alternative framework' sees the response to the Black Death as a belated and opportunistic correction on the part of government. It therefore arrives at the same position as the Palmer thesis (and the work of Bennett): while Bailey nuances the extent to which the new legislative framework was brought about by the Black Death, in particular by seeing the epidemic as an excuse for action, he nevertheless accepts

---

[56] Bennett, 'The Impact of the Black Death on English Legal History' 198.
[57] Palmer, *English Law in the Age of the Black Death 1348–1381* 22.
[58] Bennett, 'The Impact of the Black Death on English Legal History' 198.   [59] Ibid. 199.
[60] Palmer, *English Law in the Age of the Black Death 1348–1381* 30.
[61] Bennett, 'The Impact of the Black Death on English Legal History' 199.
[62] Palmer, *English Law in the Age of the Black Death 1348–1381* 6.   [63] Ibid. 5.   [64] Bailey, *After the Black Death* 218.
[65] Ibid.   [66] Ibid. 13.   [67] Ibid. 14.   [68] Ibid.

166   *The Black Death (c.1307–1485)*

that there were profound changes in the third quarter of the fourteenth century.[69] The Palmer thesis does not hinge so much upon the cause of this social and economic change bur rather its effect.

III   Effect upon the Legal System

Palmer's argument is that the labour legislation strengthened the social order by giving local figures power that was no longer based on status relationships but on delegated central authority. The authority given to local figures was 'a partial substitute for and in some ways stronger than' what they had previously enjoyed as a result of feudal status.[70] The enforcement of labour remained local but now 'local power was now more effectively exercised by lords representing central authority over all available workers instead of by lords exercising their own inherent authority over their unfree tenants'.[71]

The crown had previously been reluctant to make the keepers of the peace (the knights and other local dignities appointed to maintain order and record pleas of the crown) justices capable of hearing felonies and trespass claims.[72] However, once these keepers of justice were given the powers to deal with offences under the ordinance and statute, then the door was opened to more general judicial powers. There was a period of experimentation with separate commissions of justices of labourers trailed but by the 1360s, the re-emergence of plague caused these to be merged and the institution of justice of the peace acquired statutory definition by the Justices of the Peace Act 1361–2. This stated that in every county of England, there would be 'assigned for the keeping of the Peace, one Lord and with him three or four of the most worthy in the County, with some learned in the Law, and they shall have power to restrain the Offenders, Rioters, and all other Barators, and to pursue, arrest, take and chastise them according to their Trespass or Offence; and to cause them to be imprisoned and duly punished according to the Law and Customs of the Realm'. As Bennett noted:

What the gentry were losing as lords of the manor and employers, they were gaining on the peace commission as the agents of royal justice. From the start, and arising in some degree from the work with the labour laws, they not only assumed a range of administrative functions but also considerable scope for summary jurisdiction.[73]

For Bennett, the Black Death can therefore be seen as 'as a catalyst for the redefinition of feudal power'. Coercive power that had previously rested on personal status and enforced through local courts now 'increasingly began to operate through the agencies of the centralised state and the common law of the land'.[74] This new consistency and centralisation came at a cost, however. The move away from personal bonds coupled with the increased bargaining power that had been enjoyed at the start of the Black Death increased

---

[69] He regards it as a 'pivotal period characterised by complexity, volatility, uncertainty and opportunity' (ibid. 14–15).
[70] Palmer, *English Law in the Age of the Black Death 1348–1381* 17.   [71] Ibid. 15.
[72] Ibid. 23. See Haven Putnam, 'The Transformation of the Keepers of the Peace into the Justices of the Peace'.
[73] Bennett, 'The Impact of the Black Death on English Legal History' 200.   [74] Ibid.

Effect on the Legal System 167

the possibility of rebellion.[75] And such rebellious feelings were not without justification. As Bennett noted, the crisis of the Black Death had caused the establishment to 'close ranks'. The magnates and gentry, hit with a slump in their income, shifted that burden downwards using the fines imposed under the Statute of Labourers as well as increasing taxation. As Bennett noted, 'taxation, abuses of royal power, profiteering by government officials, judicial corruption, and the failings of the legal system represent the main grievances',[76] which grew in the decades that followed, reaching its peak with the Peasants' Revolt of 1381.

While the legal historians who mention the Black Death often just cite the labour law legislation and the rise of the justices of the peace,[77] Palmer and Bennett suggest that the pandemic had a much wider effect upon the law and upon legal institutions. As Palmer noted, it 'temporarily disrupted the institutions of central government'.[78] Some of these changes were immediate. The Parliament summoned for early in 1349 was cancelled; the courts were adjourned for a time during Trinity term in 1349.[79] However, the Black Death also had a longer-term impact, speeding up changes that were already underway. For instance, as Palmer noted, 'the King's Council, long an important but amorphous body vital to the running of the country, began to crystallize already prior to the Black Death into a much more professional institution involved in the day-to day operations of running the country'.[80] In terms of litigation, the picture is mixed, the number of criminal cases increased (possibly due to the conflict and the effect of the labour legislation), while civil litigation declined and recovered to 1348 levels only by 1365, though this may reflect the decline in population as a whole.[81]

A significant change arose through the bill procedure. In 1305–7, the King's Bench went on what is known as its 'trailbaston' sessions, named after the club-wielding gangsters known as 'trailbastons', and considered pleas of the crown, but also complaints brought by private companies in the form of a bill.[82] By 1350, similar bills were also considered by the King's Council and by the chancellor in his developing Court of Chancery.[83] And by 1420, the King's Bench had become settled at Westminster Hall, which was then in the county of Middlesex, and heard all first instance cases from the locality using this bill procedure rather than the traditional writ system. By contrast, cases from elsewhere that came to the King's Court still needed a writ.[84] Once persons were already present in the King's Court, then the King's Court had jurisdiction over them. This meant that it became the norm that claimants would 'piggy-back' actions on others that had already begun by writ or by combining procedures: for example, if a writ had been brought

---

[75] As Plucknett noted, 'the establishment of the justices of the peace mars the end of the practical importance of the old communal jurisdictions' (Theodore FT Plucknett, *A Concise History of the Common Law* (Little Brown and Co., 1956 [1929]) 169).

[76] Bennett, 'The Impact of the Black Death on English Legal History' 200.

[77] This is true of Maitland (*The Constitutional History of England* 208) and Plucknett (*A Concise History of the Common Law* 32).

[78] Palmer, *English Law in the Age of the Black Death 1348–1381* 17.

[79] Bennett, 'The Impact of the Black Death on English Legal History' 192.

[80] Palmer, *English Law in the Age of the Black Death 1348–1381* 2.

[81] Ibid. 3; Bennett, 'The Impact of the Black Death on English Legal History' 192.

[82] John H Baker, *An Introduction to English Legal History* (5th ed., Oxford University Press, 2019) 46.   [83] Ibid. 47.

[84] SFC Milsom, *Historical Foundations of the Common Law* (2nd ed., Butterworths, 1981) 62.

168   *The Black Death (c.1307–1485)*

against a defendant for trespass, bringing the defendant to the King's Court, then once he was arrested, bills could be brought against him that alleged (say) debt or detinue without having to seek separate writs or go to the Court of Common Pleas. Over time, the original writ of trespass in such cases became fictional, with the courts confirming that a bill could be brought against anyone in custody and the court would not enquire as to how that had come about.[85] This fictional allegation of trespass was usually of a trespass in Middlesex, where the court was sitting, and so became known as the bill of Middlesex. The allegation of trespass would be discontinued before the trial, and this enabled the King's Bench to take jurisdiction over Common Pleas such as debt.

By 1540, the King's Bench bill procedure had become well established and the pretence of getting the sheriff of Middlesex to confirm that he had failed to arrest the defendant there and the defendant 'lurks and roams about' elsewhere was dropped.[86] Litigation in the King's Bench rapidly increased, having an advantage over litigation in the court of Common Pleas, which continued to require a writ from the Chancery. The motive for this charade was to avoid 'the expense, delay and inconvenience of an original writ'.[87] It is difficult to determine, however, what impact the Black Death had upon this internal development since there is not a plague-free version of the fourteenth century for comparison.

The fourteenth century also saw the transformation of legal education and the legal profession. While informality still characterised legal education by the beginning of the century, by the 1380s, entry to the upper level of the legal profession was 'largely controlled by colleges of senior barristers, which became known as the Inns of Court'.[88] Bennett commented that the connection between this and the Black Death is open to question; he pondered whether it was 'an attempt to take advantage of the shortage to enforce more rigorously a monopoly of accreditation'.[89] The impact of the Black Death upon the legal profession was also not straightforward. Although lawyers were amongst the casualties of the Black Death, it is difficult to separate this from ongoing developments.[90] The roots of the modern division between barristers and solicitors can be found in the late thirteenth century, when the sergeants-at-law secured the exclusive right to represent at the Court of Common Pleas.[91] Bennett noted that while it might have been expected that the crisis caused by the Black Death would have led to the fusion of the two branches of lawyers, such fusion actually 'occurred at a different level', in that the leading barristers took on judicial work. As Bennett noted, '[T]he sudden depletion of the pool of suitable appointments to the bench doubtless strengthened the Crown's determination that the sergeants should undertake judicial responsibilities.'[92] This period therefore saw the

---

[85] Baker, *An Introduction to English Legal History* 49, citing *Kempe's Case* (1448) YB Mich. 27 Hen VI, fo 5 pl 35.
[86] Ibid. 50.   [87] Milsom, *Historical Foundations of the Common Law* 64.
[88] Bennett, 'The Impact of the Black Death on English Legal History' 194.   [89] Ibid. 194–5.
[90] Ibid. 193. See also John H Baker, *The Order of Serjeants at Law: A Chronicle of Creations, with related Texts and a Historical Introduction* (Selden Society, 1984); John H Baker, *The Legal Profession and the Common Law: Historical Essays* (Hambledon, 1986); and Paul Brand, *The Origins of the English Legal Profession* (Wiley Blackwell, 1992).
[91] Bennett, 'The Impact of the Black Death on English Legal History' 195–6. On the history of the 'lower branch of the legal profession', the ancestors of modern solicitors, see Christopher W Brooks, *Pettyfoggers and Vipers of the Commonwealth: The 'Lower Branch' of the Legal Profession in Early Modern England* (Cambridge University Press, 1986).
[92] Bennett, 'The Impact of the Black Death on English Legal History' 196.

Effect upon Substantive Law 169

fusion between the bar and the bench, with a convention developing that only sergeants-at-law could be appointed as judges. It is difficult, however, to determine whether this development was caused by the Black Death or merely accelerated by it. Indeed, it is difficult to assess whether developments in the legal profession would have happened anyway, and at the same pace, had the plague not paralysed the country.

IV   Effect upon Substantive Law

While there is some consensus that the labour law legislation and its effects were caused by the Black Death, it is more problematic to assert that other significant legal changes of the age were also attributable at least in part to the pestilence. This is where the Palmer thesis more sharply departs from conventional legal history accounts. The conventional accounts attribute late fourteenth-century changes in the common law largely to the working out of frustrations within the system, just more examples of the common law cleansing and improving itself in an evolutionary model of adaptation. Palmer, by contrast, sees the hurricane of the Black Death as challenging and uprooting everything and being a major cause of substantive legal changes. Regardless of which view is taken (or if a compromise between the two is preferred), there is agreement that the mid and late fourteenth century saw significant development in the substantive common law, especially in relation to what modern eyes would see as the law of obligations (contract and tort) and criminal law. As Palmer put it, '[T]he common law was entering an innovative and creative period.'[93] This can be seen in the law of obligations through the introduction of the action on the case as an offshoot from the writ of trespass and the later development of the action on the case of assumpsit, as well as in criminal law developments concerning treason and murder.

1   The Action on the Case

The fourteenth century saw a number of significant changes to the law of obligations. However, the significance of the Black Death upon these developments is open to debate. While Palmer attributes these changes to the aftermath of the Black Death, other legal historians conventionally understand them as organic developments within the common law.

By the fourteenth century, the writ of trespass had become increasingly popular, with its standard accusation that a wrong had been committed with force and arms and against the king's peace. An important shift occurred during the reign of Edward III (1327–77). Maitland noted that trespass writs began to omit some or all of the standard allegations but were still 'spoken of as writs of trespass, they appear in the Chancery Register as writs of trespass, mixed up with the writs which charge the defendant with violent assaults'.[94] As he noted, over time, the language shifted and the claimant was said to 'bring an action upon his case, or upon the special case, and gradually it becomes apparent that really a new and a

---

[93] Palmer, *English Law in the Age of the Black Death 1348–1381* 27.
[94] Frederic W Maitland, *The Forms of Action at Common Law* (Cambridge University Press, 1965 [1909]) 66.

170   *The Black Death (c.1307–1485)*

very elastic form of action has thus been created'.[95] Writs that were like actions of trespass but that did not make the standard allegation became known as the action on the case. The action on the case (sometimes called 'trespass on the case' and often abbreviated just to 'case') is said to be developed from the writ of trespass.[96] The conventional understanding was that the action on the case covered situations where the standard allegations of trespass did not apply: it covered situations where there had not been a direct application of unlawful physical force. However, the work of Milsom (discussed in the previous chapter) shattered previous understandings of the word trespass, showing that the standard allegation in writs of trespass was often fictitious. This has also rejected distinctions conventionally drawn between trespass and case. Previously, it was thought that the relaxation of the requirement that there be force led to the development of the action on the case. Milsom's work has shown that this requirement had already been relaxed and that the standard allegation had already become fictitious. The action on the case simply disregarded this fiction.

The question remains, however, of why the creation of the action on the case occurred. Given that the use of the standard allegation in trespass writs was usually fictitious, it may be asked why this 'formal relaxation' took place with the standard allegation being dropped entirely and replaced with a writ in which the claimant actually laid out his case.[97] As Fifoot has pointed out, the question of the origins of the action on the case 'has provoked a pretty a controversy as that of trespass itself'.[98] PA Landon identified three schools of thought amongst legal historians: the Modernist, Revolutionary and Traditionalist schools.[99]

The Modernist School comprised of the older generation of legal historians such as James Barr Ames,[100], Edward Jenks[101] and Ralph Sutton,[102] who were of the view that the action on the case 'originated in the Statute of Westminster II and it even received its name from the word *casu* in the phrase *in consimili casu*, contained in chapter 24 of that statute'.[103] They reasoned that the requirement that any new writs had to be very similar to existing ones created the possibility for the writ of the action on the case to develop from the writ of trespass. However, critics of this view have pointed out that the evidence does not support the modernists' proposition. Actions were not usually connected to statutes.[104] The name action on the case came not from *casu* but from the fact that the writ laid out the

---

[95] Ibid.

[96] There has been considerable debate too about the relationship between trespass and case. As Fifoot noted, by the 'end of the fourteenth century it was possible to contrast the old "general" trespass with the new "special" trespass framed on the individual facts of each case' (CHS Fifoot, *History and Sources of the Common Law* (Stevens & Sons, 1949) 75). However, Milsom has referred to this as the 'old theory: his work established a new theory that 'they were all just actions in tort': 'Trespass meant wrong, and trespass on the case meant the action on the case for a wrong' (SFC Milsom, 'Not Doing Is No Trespass: A View of the Boundaries of Case' (1954) 12(1) *Cambridge Law Journal* 105, 107). For a criticism of Milsom's theory, see Palmer, *English Law in the Age of the Black Death 1348–1381* chapters 21 and 26.

[97] Milsom, *Historical Foundations of the Common Law* 300.   [98] Fifoot, *History and Sources of the Common Law* 66.

[99] PA Landon, 'Action on the Case and the Statute of Westminster II' (1936) 52 *Law Quarterly Review* 68. See also Fifoot, *History and Sources of the Common Law* 66 et seq.

[100] James Barr Ames, *Lectures on Legal History and Miscellaneous Legal Essays* (Harvard University Press, 1913) 442.

[101] Edward Jenks, *A Short History of the English Law* (Little, Brown and Company, 1912) 137.

[102] Ralph Sutton, *Personal Actions at Common Law* (Butterworths, 1929) 24.

[103] Fifoot, *History and Sources of the Common Law* 66.

[104] Landon, 'Action on the Case and the Statute of Westminster II' 73. See, however, GDG Hall, 'Some Early Writs of Trespass' (1957) 73 *Law Quarterly Review* 6, which has demonstrated that there were actions produced under the terms of the 1285, statue and that the resulting actions did not mention the statute.

Effect upon Substantive Law

facts of claimant's case.[105] There was no chronological link between the statute and the popular use of the action: case-like actions have been identified well before the Statute of Westminster II in 1285,[106] but only became prevalent eighty years after the statute.[107]

The Revolutionary School, by contrast, 'would have nothing to do with the statute'.[108] Writers in this school, such as Theodore Plucknett[109] and Elizabeth Jean Dix,[110] provided much of the criticisms of the modernist view. They argued that the action on the case had nothing to do with the Statute of Westminster II 1285, and instead emphasised the role of the judges in the 1360s and 1370s. However, as Thomas Watkin has noted, the revolutionists do not provide an answer as to 'why the judiciary changed its mind in the mid-fourteenth century concerning the admission of trespass actions without a royal interest'.[111] This Revolutionary School is supported by Palmer. He has argued that the arguments of Plucknett and Dix 'remain determinative' but that there was 'a social rather than legal origin' to the remedy. For Palmer, the discussion of the Statute of Westminster II 1285 should 'play no further role in the historical discussion of Case'. His work sought to prove that the role of the statute, 'long the dominant consideration, is no longer relevant'.[112] Palmer's thesis regarded the changes in the third quarter of the fourteenth century as being brought about as a deliberate response to the economic and social upheaval caused by the Black Death. He argued that it provided a further example of 'overtly using the law as a means of social control'.[113] Palmer's contention was that while legal professionals did change the law, 'the justices acted as part of the government in implementing general policy in response to the Black Death'.[114] The relaxation arose as a result of 'decisions by officials made in accordance with governmental policy in direct response to social factors'.[115] For Palmer, the 'policy base' behind the writs differed depending on their purpose: those actions on the case that dealt with wrongs committed by horse doctors, innkeepers and the like were a means by which the post-Black Death labour legislation could be enforced.[116] By contrast, other actions on the case writs brought outside the context of occupational performance represented 'the more general governmental policy of making people stand to their ethical obligations by legal coercion'.[117]

The Traditionalist School provided a compromise between the two extremes of the Modernist and Revolutionary schools.[118] Led by Langdon himself,[119] this perspective maintained that actions on the case predated the Statute of Westminster II, but that its

---

[105] Fifoot, *History and Sources of the Common Law* 68.
[106] 'Trespass writs in which plaintiffs gave background information to their claims (usually in a subordinate clause beginning "whereas", *cum*) are found from the first half of the thirteenth century' (David J Ibbetson, *A Historical Introduction to the Law of Obligations* (Oxford University Press, 1999) 51).
[107] The criticism was formerly made that chapter 24 could not be an influence on the development of the action on the case since the action on the case was not very similar to the action of trespass. As Thomas Watkin noted, '[F]ar from being similar to general trespass writs, actions on the case were markedly dissimilar.' However, as Watkin has noted, this criticism has been overtaken by Milsom's research, which has shown that the allegations of direct force made in trespass writs were often fictional and so the two were indeed very similar; Thomas G Watkin, 'The Significance of "In Consimili Casu"' (1979) 23 *American Journal of Legal History* 283, 284.
[108] Fifoot, *History and Sources of the Common Law* 66.
[109] Theodore FT Plucknett, 'Case and Statute of Westminster II' (1931) 31(5) *Columbia Law Review* 778.
[110] Elizabeth Jean Dix, 'The Origins of the Action of Treaspass on the Case' (1937) 46 *Yale Law Journal* 1142.
[111] Watkin, 'The Significance of "In Consimili Casu"' 286.
[112] Palmer, *English Law in the Age of the Black Death 1348–1381* 147.   [113] Ibid. 141.   [114] Ibid. 61.   [115] Ibid. 141–2.
[116] Ibid. 143–4.   [117] Ibid. 144.   [118] Fifoot, *History and Sources of the Common Law* 66.
[119] Landon, 'Action on the Case and the Statute of Westminster II' 68.

172   *The Black Death (c.1307–1485)*

development could not have taken place without it. Their argument is that 'Chapter 24 ... gave the clerks enlarged powers which, with persistent enthusiasm, they used to invent the new writs upon which so much of the modern law is based.'[120] Fifoot, however, commented that this did not explain the eighty-year gap between the statute and the popularity of the writ.[121] However, Watkin has subsequently explained the gap on the basis that the 1285 statute provided the possibility for a new way of thinking.[122] It provided the potential for lawyers and clerks to develop the law by precedent: 'The decided case expands gradually by analogy by testing to see whether the novel fact-situation is sufficiently similar to the established legal rule to merit a remedy.'[123] However, so innovative was this change that it took time for the legal profession to appreciate its significance and to realise that they no longer needed the fictitious allegation.[124] Watkin reasoned that this new wave of thinking would only fully develop once there was a generation of law personnel in positions of authority who had been educated after the 1285 statute and so had not been brought up under the previous system. For Watkin, this explained the eighty-year gap between the statute and the popularity of the action on the case.

For Watkin, this was underlined in the case of *Waldon* v. *Marshall*.[125] It concerned a horse doctor (Marshall) who 'so negligently applied his cure' to Waldon's horse that it died. Waldon brought an action on the case against Marshall. Counsel for Marshall argued that this should have been an action for covenant, and so the wrong writ had been used. However, Counsel for Waldon maintained that an action for covenant could not be brought without a deed, and that 'this action is brought because you performed the treatment so negligently that the horse died, and therefore, it is right to maintain this special writ according to the case'. When Counsel for Marshall argued that the writ of trespass could have been used, Counsel for Waldon replied that this could not have been used 'because the horse was not slain by force but died for want of being cured'. The writ for the action on the case was judged to be good by the court. *Waldon* v. *Marshall* therefore provides an example of the action on the case being used instead of the writ of trespass where what happened was not the result of force.[126] It also, for Watkin, provided an example of the reasoning permitted by the Statute of Westminster II being applied. As he noted, '[T]he court accepted the similarity and sustained the writ once it was clear that no remedy existed, i.e. that the requirements of chapter 24 were made out.'[127]

Waldon v. *Marshall* also provides evidence of the start of a further development in the law of obligations. The court in upholding the writ of the action on the case not only dismissed the argument that the writ should have been in trespass but also rejected the

---

[120] Fifoot, *History and Sources of the Common Law* 68.   [121] Ibid. 74.
[122] Watkin, 'The Significance of "In Consimili Casu"'.   [123] Ibid. 311.
[124] As Watkin noted: '[W]hat occurred was a steady development within the jurisdiction granted by the "in consimili casu" provision, first by using fictions and then by recognizing new family groupings' (ibid. 300).
[125] (1370) YB Mich. 43 Ed III f 33 pl 38. Also known as *Dalton* v. *Mareschall*. It is extracted in Fifoot, *History and Sources of the Common Law* 80 and John Baker, *Baker and Milsom: Sources of English Legal History* (2nd ed., Oxford University Press, 2010) 400–2.
[126] This was affirmed in subsequent cases. Fifoot wrote that in 1373 in *The Farrier's Case* (1373) YB Trin. 46 Ed III f 19 pl 19, the 'writ of trespass *en sur case* was sustained against a farrier for laiming a horse', and in *The Surgeon's Case* (1375) YB Hil. 48 Ed III f 6 pl, 'an action of trespass *sur son case* failed against a surgeon who had negligently pursued his undertaking to heal' but only on factual grounds; Fifoot, *History and Sources of the Common Law* 75.
[127] Watkin, 'The Significance of "In Consimili Casu"' 301.

Effect upon Substantive Law   173

argument that the writ of covenant should have been used. In part, this was rejected because the writ of covenant could not have been used because there was no deed. However, the other argument put forward by Counsel for Waldron introduced another distinction that was seemingly accepted by the court. *Waldon* v. *Marshall* provides an example of the courts approving the action on the case instead of covenant where something has been done but it has been done badly.[128] A distinction was drawn between covenant that was concerned with the breaking of an agreement because the defendant had not done something (nonfeasance) and trespass or case that was concerned with the defendant having done something that had caused an injury (misfeasance/malfeasance). As David Ibbetson has noted, '[T]he principal thrust of the action on trespass on the case in its earliest manifestations in the middle of the fourteenth century was the provision of a remedy for cases of mis-performance of informal contracts.'[129] In this way, the action on the case (a tortuous remedy) filled a gap in the late medieval law of contracts. The law of covenant and debt had been 'stunted by technical rules': in covenant the insistence of a written contract under deed and in debt by the doctrine of quid pro quo.[130]

In time, however, the action on the case went further still and provided a contractual remedy for instances of nonfeasance too, where an agreement had been broken by the defendant's failure to complete it. This would become the action on the case for assumpsit.

2   *Assumpsit*

Waldon v. *Marshall* suggested that the dividing line between covenant and case was that covenant provided a remedy for a promise that had not been done while case provided a remedy where something had been done but done badly. However, as Ibbetson noted, there 'was from the start a degree of pressure for the expansion of the remedy [of case] to cover cases of contractual non-performance'.[131] Indeed, attempts had been made to bring such claims under the writ of trespass as early as 1303.[132] However, there was a serious concern that such a development would mean that the action on the case could be used to enforce all agreements. As Martin J noted in *Watkin's Case*,[133] 'a man would have an action of trespass for every broken covenant in the world'.[134] Yet, this is what eventually happened. At first, the rule was circumvented: an action on the case was allowed in an action against a defendant who had promised to act for the claimant in the buying of a manor but who instead acted for a third party, obtaining them the land.[135] The court's sleight of hand here was that, although the defendant had done nothing for the claimant (a nonfeasance), he had

---

[128] This principle was also recognised in the Humber Ferry case of 1348, *Bukton* v. *Townsend* (1348) YB 22 Lib Ass pl 1.41, in which a bill 'seemingly drafted in an essentially trespassory form' was upheld against a ferryman who had received the claimant's horse to carry across the river but the horse had died. The argument of the defendant's counsel that the claim should have been in covenant was rejected. For Ibbeston, 'that they allowed the claim to succeed strongly suggests that they saw no impropriety in the use of a trespassory action to recover damages for contractual misperformance' (Ibbetson, *A Historical Introduction to the Law of Obligations* 47). See also Palmer, *English Law in the Age of the Black Death 1348–1381* 173–6.
[129] Ibid. 126. This distinction was articulated in *Watton* v. *Brinth* (1400) YB Mich. 2 Hen IV f 3 pl 9.
[130] Fifoot, *History and Sources of the Common Law.*   [131] Ibbetson, *A Historical Introduction to the Law of Obligations* 126.
[132] Palmer, *English Law in the Age of the Black Death 1348–1381* 181, n1.   [133] (1425) YB Hill. 3 Hen VI f 36 pl 33.
[134] Ibbetson, *A Historical Introduction to the Law of Obligations* 127.
[135] *Somerton* v. *Colles* (also known as *Somerton's Case*) (1433) YB t11 Hen VI f 55 pl.26, discussed by ibid.

174   *The Black Death (c.1307–1485)*

done something positively inconsistent with the agreement, making fulfilling the agreement impossible.[136] From then on, claims for the failure to convey land 'became a routine if not frequent part of the business of the royal courts'.[137] Similar arguments became used in other situations: litigants could 'point to some positive act on the part of the defendant or they might simply reformulate the defendant's behaviour in terms of the language of wrongdoing rather than the language of rights' in order to make the claim an action on the case.[138]

This came to be known as the action of assumpsit (or the action on the case of assumpsit) and this 'took over the grounds of informal contracts'.[139] The word 'assumpsit' meant 'he undertook', which indicated 'that the word was based on undertakings'.[140] Much of what was to become known as the law of contract worked out from the action of assumpsit. Indeed, by 1600, 'it had largely eclipsed the traditional action of debt'. As Brian Simpson noted, '[M]odern English contract law grew up around the action of assumpsit, a special sub-species of the action on the case.'[141] This meant that the development of what was to become the modern law of contract was shaped by what was to become the modern law of tort. The lines that existed in the medieval law were not so much blurred but used to create new rules. As Milsom put it, 'The old law governing transactions was not changed but abandoned; and what we should call tortuous remedies came to create different contractual rules.'[142] As he noted, 'hindsight would find the challenges ... beyond belief if they had not happened' because 'hindsight has the eye of a law professor who assumes that life must always conform at least to his syllabus'.

Assumpsit was not the only 'spin-off' from the action on the case. Ibbetson noted that by the early sixteenth century, 'three principle satellite torts of the common law had emerged': the action on the case for nuisance had developed alongside the assize of nuisance; the action on the case for conversion had grown up alongside the action on detinue; and the action on the case for defamation developed alongside the ecclesiastical courts' jurisdiction on malicious allegations.[143] In all three situations, the original actions 'were not abandoned by their ingestion into trespass on the case, but all underwent mutations so as to fit with their new found trespassory home'. In each situation the result was the same: 'by 1600 all were firmly consolidated.' The development of the action of assumpsit had taken the same general trajectory as these other spin-offs:

first of all the argument that the trespassory remedy was simply supplementing the remedies that were otherwise available followed by a wholesale expansion into the ground covered by the other remedies. In addition – as had happened with nuisance, conversion and defamation – the structure of liability that remained after this shift into the trespassory matrix remained much of the framework of the earlier structure of liability but gave a tortuous twist to it. In the case of contractual liability, though, this tortuous dimension came to lie primarily on the surface of the action, whose substance

---

[136] This was followed in *Shipton v Dogge* (also known as *Doige's Case* (1442) YB T 20 Hen VI f 34 pl 4, discussed by ibid. 128
[137] Ibid. 129.   [138] Ibid.   [139] Ibid. 95.   [140] Palmer, *English Law in the Age of the Black Death 1348–1381* 169.
[141] He noted that 'we can now trace the history of assumpsit back into the fourteenth century, since in retrospect we can detect the significance of changes in pleading forms where contemporaries could not' (AW Brian Simpson, *History of the Common Law of Contract* (Clarendon Press, 1987) 199).
[142] Milsom, *Historical Foundations of the Common Law* 314.
[143] Ibbetson, *A Historical Introduction to the Law of Obligations* 95.

Effect upon Substantive Law 175

remained firmly defined by pre-existent contractual ideas. Modern law recognizes a tort of nuisance, a tort of conversion and a tort of defamation. It does not know a tort of breach of contract.[144]

This account has, however, been questioned by Palmer. Like the development of the action on the case, Palmer regarded the development of assumpsit as being 'the product of policy implementation, not the product of litigation strategy or of doctrinal evolution'.[145] He noted that the important decisions were made in Chancery and council. For Palmer, the role played by the Chancery in issuing the writ was vital:[146] he reasoned that 'the fact that these developments took years' reflected 'Chancery hesitation about a particular remedy or its formulation and prove Chancery control over the remedies'. Palmer's thesis regarded assumpsit as being developed to 'cure deficiencies' in labour law legislation by regulating the performance of employees.[147] He dated the development of assumpsit writs to an earlier date than other legal historians, back to the 1350s, when a more active Chancery provided assumpsit writs to reinforce the Statute of Labourers.[148] He contended that these early assumpsit writs were more closely related to detinue rather than covenant and a further shift occurred gradually in the 1360s towards a more covenant-like writ.[149]

Palmer also rebutted the conventional theory that the action of assumpsit developed from the action on the case. He maintained that if anything, it was the other way around since in 'some case writs first appeared in an assumpsit form'.[150] His view was that both writs 'derived from a more active Chancery responding to individual situations'.[151] Indeed, he stressed how 'each form of assumpsit was its own class, resting on an individual Chancery decision and with a somewhat independent history'.[152] For Palmer, the fact that assumpsit 'was not a coherent, recognized class subject to deductive thought or general descriptions affecting its forms' further indicated 'that the development could not represent lawyers thinking abstractly about the law: the Chancery decisions rather were responses to litigants'.[153] This was the crux of his argument: 'Assumpsit was Chancery reinforcement of governmental objectives, not the creation of lawyers concentrating either on the remedy structures or the litigation strategy.'[154] The Palmer thesis as it applies to the development of the law of obligations in the fourteenth century differs considerably therefore from the conventional accounts of legal historians. For Palmer:

The hypothesis that these innovations were related to the problems created by the Black Death is more plausible than the hypothesis that different legal innovations, occurring at the same time and embodying similar effects, developed without any relationship to each other and from isolated doctrinal concerns.[155]

---

[144] Ibid. 126.   [145] Palmer, *English Law in the Age of the Black Death 1348–1381* 141.

[146] He noted that this went against the view of Plucknett (Plucknett, 'Case and Statute of Westminster II' 786) that by the fourteenth century, Chancery 'had abandoned control over the issuance of new writs', a view that Milsom 'either got from or shared with Plucknett'. He noted that this view had been challenged by Holdsworth (William S Holdsworth, 'The Nature and Origins of Trespass on the Case' 47 (1931) *Law Quarterly Review* 355) 'but to no effect'; Palmer, *English Law in the Age of the Black Death 1348–1381* 296, 297.

[147] Ibid. 141, 143. It 'remedied problems with negligent carriers, builders, doctors, shepherd and cloth-workers as well as with miscellaneous artisans and labourers' (ibid. 169–70).

[148] Ibid. 169

[149] Ibid. 169–70. For Palmer, the development of assumpsit 'was unrelated to the deficiencies in the action of covenant' (ibid. 212).

[150] Ibid. 217.   [151] Ibid. 169–70.   [152] Ibid. 211.   [153] Ibid. 212   [154] Ibid. 143.   [155] Ibid. 61.

176   *The Black Death (c.1307–1485)*

Yet, it may be countered that in other periods of legal history, similar if not greater legal innovations occurred without the kind of stimulus provided by the Black Death. The Palmer thesis raises similar issues as the Maitland-Milsom debate as to the origins of land law. Palmer is adopting a centralist or royalist interpretation, regarding the changes as an intended and deliberate act on the part of the king's government, here enforced by clerks and justices. This runs contrary to the conventional understanding of the period and indeed Milsom's revisionist work on the origins of trespass, which presented the legal developments as happening through 'client-pleasing lawyers circumventing legal forms'.[156] This may run the risk of rationalising with the benefit of hindsight developments that were not a linear course of progression. The pragmatism implicit in Milsom's account seems preferable to the sense of design found in the Palmer thesis.

It is unobjectionable, however, that the developments of the action on the case and assumpsit were of significant importance. Although they were not the most common actions in the late fourteenth and early fifteenth centuries, these were the actions that were to dominate the common law for centuries (alongside the writ of trespass).[157] The common law of contract grew out of assumpsit and, as Milsom noted, by the eighteenth century, 'almost all litigation at common law were conducted in ... actions of trespass and case'.[158] This, together with how they closely correspond with the modern law of contract and tort, is why we have focused on these actions. Assumpsit grew out of the action on the case to become the major action in the law of contracts. This was underlined in a report in 1851 that stated that:

The forms of action most frequently in use are assumpsit, debt, covenant, detinue, trespass and debt. The first three are applicable to claims founded on contracts: thus assumpsit lies to recover damages, whether liquidated or unliquidated,[159] for the breach of a contract not under seal. Debt lies to recover a sum certain, or capable of being reduced to certainty by calculation, payable in respect of a direct and immediate liability by a debtor to a creditor. Covenant to recover damages for the breach of a covenant under seal. Detinue lies when good s or specific monies are lawfully detained. Trespass lies for direct injuries to person or property. Case is far more extensive than any other form of action and is applicable as a remedy for what are called consequential, that is, injuries supposed to arise indirectly and consequentially from the act complained of.[160]

This, however, is to get ahead of ourselves.[161] The developments of the action on the case and of assumpsit were symptomatic of a wider trend. Ibbetson noted that 'by the middle of the fifteenth century the common law was undergoing a crisis. Its rules were bafflingly

---

[156] Ibid. 296.

[157] Ibid. 141. For discussion of the development of writ of trespass, see Ibbetson, *A Historical Introduction to the Law of Obligations* chapter 4.

[158] Milsom, *Historical Foundations of the Common Law* 283.

[159] Liquidated damages are damages where the amount has been designated during the formation of the contract.

[160] *First Report of Her Majesty's Commissioners for Inquiring into the Process, Practice and System of Pleading in the Superior Courts of the Common Law* (PP, 1851, xxii 567) 31, quoted in Geoffrey Samuel, *Rethinking Legal Reasoning* (Edward Elgar, 2018) 78–9.

[161] Not least because the distinction between trespass and case was articulated in a number of cases in the eighteenth and nineteenth centuries: see Ibbetson, *A Historical Introduction to the Law of Obligations* chapter 8.

Effect upon Substantive Law 177

complex and its procedures so byzantine that even getting one's opponents into court was no simple matter.'[162] This was remedied in the century that followed, the century when the Tudors were firmly on the throne.

3   *Treason*

In some respects, the effect of the Black Death upon criminal law seems predictable. As Bennett has noted, there was clearly 'an upsurge in certain sorts of property crime'.[163] Yet, the plague did not lead to anarchy and lawlessness. Indeed, an increase in disorder can be dated before the Black Death. The 'trailbaston' sessions were a response to the violent affrays that were common place at the very start of the fourteenth century.[164] Palmer's thesis is that the Black Death had a considerable but unique effect upon criminal law, in that, while other areas of law became more punitive, 'criminal law became more considerate'.[165] He based this argument on developments of the law of treason, which became 'one of the very few crimes that were defined by statute in this period'.[166] Indeed, as Lyon pointed out, the law of treason provided 'a very early example of the translation of a vague concept of the common law into a more precise statutory form'.[167]

The courts had developed and expanded the scope of the law of treason so that it had become a means of subduing opposition.[168] This particularly affected the magnates and the knightly classes who were the most likely defendants. The Statute of Treasons 1352 curbed this trend by defining treason more narrowly. Recognising that 'divers opinions have been held before this time', the Act clarified that treason was limited to five situations: first, 'when a man doth compass or imagine the death of our lord King', his consort or heir; second, where 'a man do violate' the consort, the king's eldest daughter or the wife of the heir; third, where 'a man do levy war against our lord the King in his realm, giving to them aid and comfort'; fourth, where 'a man counterfeit the King's great or privy seal or his money'; and fifth, the slaying of 'the chancellor, treasurer, or the King's Justices'. Such treason was to be punished by forfeiture of land and goods to the crown.[169] The Act also recognised 'another manner of treason', known as petite or petty treason, which occurred 'when a servant slayeth his master, or a wife her husband, or where a man secular or religious slayeth his prelate to whom he oweth faith and obedience'. Such cases were to involve escheat but not forfeiture of lands. This was 'most beneficial to those with the most to lose: lords who would otherwise lose rights of escheat or whose land would be lost for their families'.[170] By contrast, the king, who previously would have benefitted from

---

[162] Ibid. 95.
[163] Bennett, 'The Impact of the Black Death on English Legal History' 192. There was also an increase in legal corruption: Jonathan Rose, *Maintenance in Medieval England* (Cambridge University Press, 2017) 111.
[164] John Hostettler, *A History of Criminal Justice in England and Wales* (Waterside Press, 2009) 60.
[165] Palmer, *English Law in the Age of the Black Death 1348–1381* 24.
[166] Plucknett, *A Concise History of the Common Law* 443.   [167] Lyon, *Constitutional History of the United Kingdom* 116.
[168] Palmer, *English Law in the Age of the Black Death 1348–1381* 24–5. For discussion of the early development of treason, see JG Bellamy, *The Law of Treason in England in the Later Middle Ages* (Cambridge University Press, 1970) chapters 1, 2 and 4.
[169] Plucknett, *A Concise History of the Common Law* 443.
[170] Palmer, *English Law in the Age of the Black Death 1348–1381* 26.

178   *The Black Death (c.1307–1485)*

gaining such land, missed out as a result of the narrowing of the offence. Provision was, however, made in the Act for Parliament to declare treason in future cases not covered by the Act.[171]

The legislation also included other changes to the administration of justice that benefitted the upper classes and represented kingly concessions. Those accused of felonies usually 'passed through two juries: a presentment jury that returned whether they were suspected of the crime and the trial jury that returned whether they were innocent or guilty'.[172] The Act gave the defendant the right to exclude a trial juror for being also on the presentment jury. As Palmer noted, this 'helped establish the necessary bifurcation between accusers and triers'. Moreover, the Act contained an 'updated restatement of the Magna Carta provision committing the king not to proceed against individuals by petition or suggestion but only by indictments and presentments or by ordinary writs at common law' and not to confiscate property outside the ordinary course of law. For Palmer, these provisions indicated 'a royal attitude toward his subjects decidedly more conciliatory than the approach of the royal courts in the 1340s'.[173] He regarded the statute 'as one part of a comprehensive alteration in governance to counteract the effect of the Black Death'.[174] It was part of the new consensus that the king and governing classes agreed to in order to cope with the economic and social effects of the pestilence. However, there are other interpretations of the Act. Bellamy noted that: 'Perhaps no English statute of the latter Middle Ages has yielded its secrets more reluctantly to the historian than the Treason Act of 1352. There have been at least as many opinions as commentators.'[175] As Bellamy pointed out, historians are divided as to whether 'Edward's design was either legal or political'. While some commentators agree with Palmer that the intention was political in that the Statute of Treasons sought 'to prevent reckless royal charges and arbitrary punishments', others regard the motive as being legal, settling the law on forfeiture, providing clarity and certainty about the king's coffers.[176] Even those who see political motives underlying the Act do not necessarily see it as a consequence only of the Black Death. Omrod regarded the statute as being the resolution of financial, political and judicial matters dating back to the 1330s.[177] Similarly, Lyon argued that the Statute of Treasons and other legislative changes of the times were enacted to persuade Parliament to agree to provide further revenue for the king and his wars, and to secure the long-term support of his subjects.[178] This is partly compatible with the Palmer thesis that 'these statutory provisions constitute an important element in the recognition of the standing of the knightly classes as full participants in governance, an attitude quite different from the confrontational and oppressive policies of the 1340s'.[179] However, it is impossible to say whether the changes effected by the Black Death were the cause or one of a number of causes of the statute. It is clear, however, that the Statute of Treasons represented a clear

---

[171] For discussion of how treason was interpreted during the rest of the Plantagenet period, see Bellamy, *The Law of Treason in England in the Later Middle Ages* chapters 5 and 6.

[172] Palmer, *English Law in the Age of the Black Death 1348–1381* 26.   [173] Ibid.   [174] Ibid. 25.

[175] Bellamy, *The Law of Treason in England in the Later Middle Ages* 59.

[176] Hostettler, *A History of Criminal Justice in England and Wales* 64.   [177] Ormrod, *The Reign of Edward III* 30.

[178] Lyon, *Constitutional History of the United Kingdom* 116.

[179] Palmer, *English Law in the Age of the Black Death 1348–1381* 27.

Effect upon Substantive Law 179

change. As Plucknett noted, the Act may have 'hampered the orderly growth of the law relating to offences against public security by including so few of them in the definition of treason, making no provision for the lesser (but still serious) crimes'.[180]

4   Murder

The Statute of Treasons was not the only significant change in criminal law during this period, though it is again difficult to determine whether these changes were directly or indirectly caused by the Black Death. The fourteenth century also witnessed significant developments in the law of homicide.[181] From the Norman Conquest onwards, a distinction had been drawn between the deaths of Normans and deaths of English men. The murdrum fine was only due in relation to deaths of Normans and until chapter 25 of the Statute of Marlborough of 1267, this included accidental deaths. Although it was increasingly difficult to distinguish Norman and English men, the practice continued since the murdrum fine was lucrative. Baker suggested that the distinction was used to differentiate killings by stealth (where the killer took the victim by surprise and without provocation), with these stealthy killings being regarded as murder.[182] While the term 'murder' was originally used to describe secretive and particularly heinous killings, it came to describe the situations where the murdrum fine was imposed on the local community for an explained homicide.[183] Maitland contended that this change had occurred by the 1220s. He noted that in Glanvill, it was whether 'the deed is done in secret' that distinguished murdrum from other forms of homicide.[184] He noted that by contrast, 'Bracton repeats Glanvill's distinction, but immediately blurs and probably perverts it by mentioning the murder fine'. As Maitland put it, 'from this we may conjecture that the word had already lost the sense attributed to it by Glanvill, namely that of manslaughter done in secret'.[185]

The Engleschrie Act of 1340 finally abolished the distinction between the death of Norman and English men and the murdrum fine.[186] As Maitland noted, from then on, the word murder 'was set free from the very technical and peculiar sense given to it' since the Norman Conquest.[187] However, murder 'did not apparently ever regain its oldest meaning'. Instead, murder came to signify a manslaughter with what became known as 'malice prepense' or 'malice aforethought'. It came to denote killings purposively done. The term murder came to denote the most serious forms of killing and, as Plucknett noted, the word murder 'slowly tends to get linked up' the phrase 'malice aforethought' and 'so we get the classical formulae describing the crime of murder'.[188]

---

[180] Plucknett, *A Concise History of the Common Law* 444.

[181] There were also developments in relation to other crimes such as larceny/theft, on which see, e.g., Ian Williams, '*The Carrier's Case* (1473)' in Philip Handler, Henry Mares and Ian Williams (eds.), *Landmark Cases in Criminal Law* (Hart 2017) 9.

[182] Baker, *An Introduction to English Legal History* 570, n63.

[183] Thomas A Green, 'The Jury and the English Law of Homicide, 1200–1600' (1976) 74 *Michigan Law Review* 414, 419 n19.

[184] The distinction mattered, according to Glanvill, in that 'in the case of murder, only the nearest kinsman of the slain can bring an appeal, while in the case of simple homicide, he appeal may be brought by anyone who is related to the slain by blood or tenure, and who has been the eye witness of the deed' (Frederic W Maitland, 'The Early History of Malice Aforethought' (1883), reprinted in Maitland, *The Collected Papers of Frederic William Maitland*, vol. 1, 304, 307).

[185] Ibid.   [186] This was chapter 4 of the first statute passed in 1340.   [187] Ibid. 304, 307–8.

[188] Plucknett, *A Concise History of the Common Law* 445.

180 *The Black Death (c.1307–1485)*

Ascertaining how this came to be is a complicated task. There was no clear legislative act. Rather, the change came about as a result of the changing law on pardons. In the thirteenth century, there existed two forms of homicide: felonious homicide, which was a capital offence, and non-felonious homicides, where the killing was justifiable because it was pursuant to a royal order or where it was excusable and led to a pardon.[189] The vast majority of homicides, including those that would later be classified as manslaughters, were felonious homicides.[190] This meant that 'for the stealthy slayer and for the one who acted on sudden impulse, the official sanction was the same'.[191] However, a significant number of pardons were issued, typically in cases of accidental homicides or those caused by self-defence.[192] As Plucknett noted, this meant that death by misadventure or by self-defence were recognised 'not so much as defences to a charge of homicide as circumstances entitling one to a pardon'.[193] Indeed, 'pardons were issued with liberality for all sorts of felonies throughout the middle ages and long afterwards'.[194] The granting of a pardon did not result in an acquittal: the slayer was absolved from liability under royal justice but the victim's kin could still bring about an appeal.[195] Nevertheless, the widespread granting of pardons proved controversy and led to legislation.[196] And it was this legislation that was indirectly to transform the law on homicide.

Whereas previously pardons had been a matter of royal discretion, the granting of pardons in cases of homicide had become in practice a matter for the common law courts by the end of the thirteenth century.[197] Various attempts were made throughout the next century to curb the number of such pardons.[198] It is possible that the social and political transformations caused by the Black Death may have accelerated this. In the late fourteenth century, the matter was considered by commissions of justices of the peace, who in official documentation began to use the word 'murder' to describe the most serious killings where there had been ambushing or planning.[199] However, the most significant development came via a pardons statute in 1390 that prohibited pardons in cases of killings by lying in wait, assault or *malice prepense*.[200] Plucknett explained that the effect that for 'cases of what we may call wilful murder' was that 'pardons were subjected to almost impossible conditions'.[201]

---

[189] Green, 'The Jury and the English Law of Homicide, 1200–1600' 419. The category of justifiable homicide 'was extended in the fourteenth century to include the slayers of felons caught in the act of burglary, arson, or robbery' (ibid. 436).

[190] Ibid. 414.   [191] Ibid. 421.

[192] Ibid. 420; See generally Naomi D Hurnard, *The King's Pardon for Homicide Before AD 1307* (Oxford University Press, 1969).

[193] Plucknett, *A Concise History of the Common Law* 445.   [194] Ibid.

[195] Green, 'The Jury and the English Law of Homicide, 1200–1600' 419.

[196] Green's work also highlights the role played by jury behaviour, noting that because the jury was relied upon to have 'first-hand knowledge of the events and persons in question', the judge was 'almost entirely dependent upon the jury for his knowledge of the case'. This meant that 'by stating the evidence in a way that made the result it wanted a necessary conclusion, the medieval jury was able to alter the impact of formal rules of law to conform with prevailing social attitudes' (ibid. 414).

[197] Ibid. 426.

[198] The Statute of Northampton 1328 called for restraint in issuing pardons; ibid. 457. See JM Kaye, 'The Early History of Murder and Manslaughter – Part One' (1967) 83 *Law Quarterly Review* 365, 377 *et seq.*

[199] Green, 'The Jury and the English Law of Homicide, 1200–1600' 461.

[200] This was the second statute passes in the thirteenth year of the reign of Richard and is sometimes dated to 1389.

[201] Plucknett, *A Concise History of the Common Law* 446.

Effect upon Substantive Law　　181

However, controversy has surrounded what the reference to *malice prepense* meant in the 1390 statute. One view, favoured by JM Kaye, was that the term referred to all culpable homicides.[202] A contrary view, adopted by Thomas Green, was that it was a new term of art, translatable as 'malice aforethought', which only covered 'homicides committed through true planning or premeditation'.[203] Under this interpretation, 'the statutory restraint on the royal pardoning power would have applied only to the most serious forms of felonious homicide'. This second interpretation is implicitly followed by Baker, who noted that the categories of killing in wait, killing by assault and killing by malice aforethought 'became confused over the next century into a single concept of murder'.[204] The effect of the 1390 statute was to create a distinction between murder committed with malice aforethought (which were not pardonable) and all other forms of felonious homicide (which were pardonable), and this second category became known by 1480 as 'manslaughter'.[205] The way in which this distinction crystallised over time makes it difficult to attribute to the Black Death.

Indeed, Green argued that the 1390 Act had a limited effect. He argued that the 1390 Act did not have any permanent effect upon the law in practice, in that throughout the period, all homicides 'that were deliberate but neither justifiable nor excusable' remained capital offences.[206] Moreover, he argued that the distinction attributed to the Act simply reflected the pre-existing social meaning. He contended that from the late Anglo-Saxon age to the end of the Middle Ages, a 'widespread societal distinction between "murder," i.e., homicide perpetrated through stealth, and simple homicide, roughly what a later legal age termed manslaughter' that was 'imposed upon the courts through the instrument of the trial jury', even when that was 'fundamentally at odds with the letter of the law'.[207]

Elizabeth Papp Kamali has suggested that the societal distinctions referred to by Green may refer to religious understandings.[208] Her work, alongside work by Penny Crofts, has suggested that many commentators have mistakenly read modern ideas about fault in criminal law and *mens rea* back into periods to which they do not belong. Papp Kamali has argued that ideas of *mens rea* operated implicitly in the late medieval period. She maintained that '*mens rea* was at work in medieval English felony adjudication' but not in the 'sense that there was no explicit doctrine of *mens rea* being discussed by lawyers and justices'.[209] She contended that the notion 'was implicit in the meaning of the word "felony" itself'. Central to her argument is that *mens rea* was a more expansive concept in this period, 'broader indeed than our current understanding of the phrase'.[210] Crofts has argued that the concept of *malitiam* was central to the characterisation of wrongdoing in

---

[202] Kaye, 'The Early History of Murder and Manslaughter – Part One' 391–5.　　[203] Ibid. 462.

[204] Baker, *An Introduction to English Legal History* 571. Green noted that 'by the middle of the fifteenth century, "murder" was employed in indictments as a catch-all term for felonious homicide' (Green, 'The Jury and the English Law of Homicide, 1200–1600' 469).

[205] Baker, *An Introduction to English Legal History* 571.

[206] Green, 'The Jury and the English Law of Homicide, 1200–1600' 457.

[207] Thomas A Green, 'Societal Concepts of Criminal Liability for Homicide in Mediaeval England' (1972) 47(2) *Speculum* 669.

[208] She wrote that 'there was a rift between the formal English common law of crime, which relied heavily on capital punishment, and popular and ecclesiastical understandings of culpability, which countenanced greater room for human growth and renewal' (Elizabeth Papp Kamali, *Felony and the Guilty Mind in Medieval England* (Cambridge University Press, 2019) 50).

[209] Ibid. 305.　　[210] Ibid. 4.

182   *The Black Death (c.1307–1485)*

medieval homicide law' and 'was a complex, malleable concept' which was structured by 'religious and secular order and informed by localised knowledge'.[211] For Crofts: 'The jury did not embrace the modern distinction between internal and external elements of crime. It was assumed that sin would be manifest. *Malitiam* was about essence, self and God – not about intention, harm or even about acts. *Malitiam* was a question of soul.'[212]

As Papp Kamali pointed out, '[J]urors drew upon ideas learned through sermons, literature and the practice of confession to determine whether the defendants hauled before them were guilty of innocent.'[213] Crofts criticised legal historians for their 'tendency to understand *malitiam* in terms framed by modern criminal legal doctrine', noting that: 'Far from being a primitive precursor of the contemporary emphasis upon wrongful intention, medieval *malitiam* was a highly ambitious, expansive, transcendental concept.'[214] Legal historians were to blame for the 'tendency to reduce *malitiam* to intention, and *malitia precogitata* to premeditation'.[215]

While conventional commentators can be criticised for misconstruing the medieval criminal law by understanding it through the lens of their experiences of the modern criminal law, over-reliance and simplication of Palmer's thesis runs the same risk by focusing on the Black Death as a mono-causal explanation. Both approaches fail to fully grasp the nuanced, complicated and messier realities of the past, imposing a modern mindset that assumes law is an autonomous and distinct system.

V   Conclusions

Determining the extent to which the Black Death caused or even accelerated legal and political changes is a difficult task. It is tricky to determine whether particular developments would have occurred anyway. Changes rarely operate in a linear, uniform and predictable way, and are seldom the product of a singular cause. The Palmer thesis, though valuable in correcting the neglect of the effect in Black Death in orthodox accounts, runs the risk of over-emphasising not just the importance of the pestilence but also the nature of the change that resulted. However, the Palmer thesis is also an important corrective in terms of stressing how law can be used as a manifestation of power. Central to Palmer's argument is that the crises caused by the Black Death united the ruling classes, who then used law as a means to curb class war and to further their own interests.[216] The use of law in such a way was not novel. For centuries previously, law had been used as a means of maintaining order and therefore sustaining the power of monarchs. Law had also become the battleground for power disputes between the monarch and the ruling classes, as shown by the number of kingly concessions over the ages. What was novel about the fourteenth

---

[211] Penny Crofts, *Wickedness and Crime: Laws of Homicide and Malice* (Routledge, 2013) 25, 26, 58. The word had 'a broad repertoire that could attach to different subjects and objects, across a broad timeframe, inviting and requiring individual, social and transcendental questions of good and evil' (ibid.).

[212] Ibid. 59.   [213] Papp Kamali, *Felony and the Guilty Mind in Medieval England* 304.

[214] Crofts, *Wickedness and Crime* 25, 27.   [215] Ibid. 33.

[216] However, see the critique of Bailey, *After the Black Death* 219, who maintained that the 'social conflict cannot, however, be categorized simplistically or crudely along class lines' because 'the experience of royal justice affected elements of the lower orders in different ways' and the interests of the land lord class were not closely aligned.

century, according to Palmer, was that the crises that ensued from the Black Death prompted a ceasefire amongst those at the top of society as they united to subordinate those at the bottom of society: law was being used to keep the villeins and the working classes in their place.

Such efforts were ultimately unsuccessful. Despite its name, the Peasants' Revolt was an uprising not just by the peasant classes but by those whom the Black Death was originally lucrative and liberating but who then lamented curbs that had then been imposed by taxation and legislation.[217] The Peasants' Revolt proved to be the most violent upheaval in medieval England. Attacks on sheriffs and tax collectors soon escalated into full riots that targeted anything with the seal of the exchequer. Simon Sudbury, the Archbishop of Canterbury and lord chancellor, was decapitated by the rebels. When King Richard II met with the leaders, including Wat Tyler, they demanded a new Magna Carta, with the assets of the Church being liquidated, serfdom being abolished and outlaws being pardoned. While the king agreed, the fighting continued. This led to the death of Tyler and the king charging at the army proclaiming 'I am your captain', reasserting his authority. Yet, this early success in reasserting royal authority was to be short-lived.

The post-Black Death consensus between the king and the ruling classes collapsed. Conflict with the barons followed with Parliament becoming once again the battleground, as it had so often been in Plantagenet England. Richard tried to bypass Parliament, while parliamentarians sought to charge those who they considered to have been treasonous and demanded a say over the choice of appointments. In August 1387, Richard summoned the chief justice of the King's Bench and his fellow judges, putting to them ten questions concerning his powers and prerogative, including whether he could control the business of Parliament and whether Parliament could impeach or remove the king's ministers.[218] On every issue, the judges found in favour of the king.[219] However, this simply fanned the flames of conflict with a group of aristocrats known as the 'Lords Appellant'. New forms of treason were created, including impeding the king in the exercise of his prerogative.[220] During the so-called Merciless Parliament from February to June 1388, many members of the King's Court were convicted for treason. This was achieved not under the Statute of Treasons but by particular Bills of Attainder that were passed by Parliament at the king's behest. An Act of Attainder 'not only deprived the offender of his titles and property, but "corrupted" his blood, preventing his issue from inheriting from or through him'.[221] This meant that entire families became deprived of their property.

Richard's 'brisk, not to say a ruthless, efficiency' was to prove his downfall.[222] His decision to go for broke, to attempt to make himself an absolute ruler, ruling without Parliament, led to him losing everything. Richard was deposed, losing the crown via a 'newly minted legal process', with the official report being read to Parliament.[223] This

---

[217] See ibid. chapter 5.   [218] SB Chrimes 'Richard III's Questions to the Judges, 1387' (1956) 72 *Law Quarterly Review* 365.
[219] Lyon, *Constitutional History of the United Kingdom* 128.   [220] Ibid. 129.   [221] Ibid. 131.
[222] Nigel Saul, *Richard II* (Yale University Press, 1997) 440–1.
[223] Laura Ashe, *Richard II* (Allen Lane, 2016) 4. On which, see David J Seipp, 'How to Get Rid of a King: Lawyering the Revolution of 1399' in Catharine MacMillan and Charlotte Smith (eds.), *Challenges to Authority and the Recognition of Rights: From Magna Carta to Modernity* (Cambridge University Press, 2018) 55.

184   *The Black Death (c.1307–1485)*

underscored the shift in the balance of power between king and Parliament. Moreover, as Lyon noted, the deposition showed that 'the king ceased to be truly set apart from other men: the crown and the power it bought were a prize fought over'.[224] This set the scene for the fifteenth century; a century that saw six Plantagenet kings on the throne before the dynasty ended on the battlefield with the birth of Tudor England. However, the fifteenth century has proved tricky to understand. While it has been the subject of powerful if exaggerated literary presentations through a series of Shakespearian plays, the century remains a comparatively neglected period in English history in general and in legal history in particular.[225] As Christine Carpenter has noted, the influence of Maitland has been more upon early medievalists than later medievalists.[226] She noted that much of the literature saw the fifteenth century as being one of transition and erroneously read back later assumptions and expectations of a limited parliamentary monarchy, which 'made it impossible to say anything worthwhile about the tangled and sometimes violent politics of fifteenth century England'.[227] For Carpenter, it was only the work of KB McFarlane in the mid to late twentieth century that provided 'a new paradigm' on the fifteenth century by being 'almost the first to study it for its sake, neither as the degrading of something good nor as the prelude for something better'.[228] McFarlane's work questioned that there was 'a fundamental weakness in fifteenth century government' and instead highlighted 'inadequate kingships', de-emphasising the importance of long-term causes of the War of the Roses.[229] McFarlane stressed that 'the history of this period should not be primarily the history of institutions but of people; that "the real politics" of the period constituted of the King's daily personal relations with his magnates'.[230]

The century of the last six Plantagenet monarchs provided plenty of evidence of 'inadequate kingships'. As Lyon noted, the reign of Henry IV (1399–1413) 'began in a blaze of popular enthusiasm, but soon degenerated into a holding pattern'.[231] In particular, the reign was plagued by rebellions in Wales led by Owain Glyn Dwr, who had studied law at the Inns of Court and summoned a Parliament at Machnylleth in 1403, seeking an independent Wales. The later years of the reign were marred by the king suffering from a serious and still mysterious illness. The king through Parliament had fixed the issue of succession so that the crown passed to his eldest son, Henry V (1413–22). Also called Henry of Monmouth (denoting his birthplace), Henry V played a significant role in the

---

[224] Lyon, *Constitutional History of the United Kingdom* 124.

[225] SB Chrimes, *Lancastrians, Yorkists and Henry VII* (Macmillan, 1964) xi.

[226] Christine Carpenter, *The War of the Roses: Politics and the Constitution in England c.1437–1509* (Cambridge University Press, 1997) 26.

[227] Ibid. 7, 8.

[228] Ibid. 16. Carpenter also considered the work of Chrimes, but concluded that, although he 'wrote in 1936 what should have been a seminal work on the fifteenth-century constitution from the perspective of legal records' (namely SB Chrimes, *English Constitutional Ideas in the Fifteenth Century* (Cambridge University Press, 2013 [1936])), the fact that it was published 'so close to the war years' meant that 'there was no time for its influence to spread' before it had been supplemented by the work of McFarlane. She also notes that Chrimes still worked within the parameters set by the previous historians (Carpenter, *The War of the Roses* 14, 15). See, however, the important collection of essays in SB Chrimes, CD Ross and RA Griffiths (eds.), *Fifteenth Century England 1399–1509* (2nd ed., Sutton publishing 1997) and the work this led to as described in Griffiths' foreword to the second edition.

[229] Carpenter, *The War of the Roses* 18. McFarlane's main works can be found in KB McFarlane, *England in the Fifteenth Century Collected Essays* (Hambledon, 1981) and KB McFarlane, *The Nobility of Later Mediaeval England* (Oxford University Press, 1980 [1953]).

[230] Carpenter, *The War of the Roses* 18.   [231] Lyon, *Constitutional History of the United Kingdom* 146.

Conclusions 185

conflict in Wales and had effectively run the kingdom during his father's illness. When he became king, he turned his attention to foreign affairs (most notably his victory at Agincourt) but there were some notable developments in relation to governance. The Riot Act of 1411, which was passed during the illness of Henry IV, gave justices of the peace and sheriffs powers to arrest in the case of 'any riot assembly, or rout of people against the law', and this was furthered by the Riot Act of 1414 that reiterated and reinforced the earlier statute, imposing imprisonment for a year for those engaged in significant riots and giving powers to the chancellor and court of the King's Bench to supervise the actions of justices of the peace and sheriffs through commissions of enquiry.[232] The Statute of Lollards of 1401 required justices of the peace to give the Church active support against the Lollard movement that sought reform of Catholic Church.[233] As Christopher Allmand noted, 'heresy was beginning to be viewed as a form of treason'.[234] Henry V's reign also saw legislation against piracy in the Statute of Truces and moves to develop the use of the English language in government.[235]

During the reign of Henry VI (1422–61), initially another infant monarch, power struggles broke out, leading to civil war. As Lyon noted, the situation came to a head from 1450, and the 'main motivation for activity at the highest political level was self-interest'.[236] The activity in question was invariably violence of some description. This is epitomised by the reign of Edward IV (1461–83), which began with the seizing of the crown by force at the Battle of Mortimer's Cross; this was followed by his deposition and exile a decade later, and then later again by his subsequent recovery of the throne.[237] This underscored how the throne was perpetually perilous in this period. As Lyon noted, even a strong king would be dependant 'on the continuing support of his greatest subjects, themselves virtual "mini-kings"'.[238] Edward IV's son Edward V (1483) was heir but was never crowned. Edward V and his younger brother were the 'princes in the tower' who disappeared in mysterious circumstances. The throne went instead to Edward's uncle, the duke of Gloucester, who had served as lord protector during his short reign and who is often seen as being responsible for the death of the two princes. The duke of Gloucester became Richard III (1483–5) by dint of the statute Titulus Regius in 1484, which declared that Edward IV's marriage was invalid and so Edward V and his other children had no claim to the throne. His reign was to be short and dominated by rebellions, leading to his death at the Battle of Bosworth Field in 1485.

Reform of government and the administration of justice took a back seat in the fifteenth century. Indeed, as Chris Given-Wilson noted, 'Westminster-based offices such as the Chancery and exchequer had by now developed a civil service ethos allowing them to bridge royal minorities and political crises with a minimum of disruption, and part from some changes at the higher levels, government could be expected to continue much as

---

[232] Anne Curry, *Henry V* (Allen Lane, 2015) 45.
[233] Ibid. 47; Christopher Allmand, *Henry V* (new ed., Yale University Press, 1997) 302.   [234] Ibid. 304.
[235] John H Fisher, *The Emergence of Standard English* (University Press of Kentucky, 1995) 22.   [236] Ibid. 151, 153.
[237] Charles Ross, *Edward IV* (new ed., Yale University Press, 1997) xxv.
[238] Lyon, *Constitutional History of the United Kingdom* 158.

186 *The Black Death (c.1307–1485)*

before.'[239] As conventional accounts have stressed, this resulted in consistency and continuity. As Lyon noted, the century 'did not see innovation in constitutional matters, but consolidation of previous practice', especially in terms of emphasising the importance of Parliament and 'the idea that the king was subject to the law'.[240] This consistency was perpetuated by the publication of works on law by holders of high judicial office during this period that were to become seminal in the years to come. Sir John Fortescue, chief justice of the King's Bench from 1422 to 1461, became renowned for his *In Praise of the Laws of England and the Governance of England*, which drew upon the intellectual and philosophical writings of the period to present the common law as being superior and continuous.[241] Sir Thomas Littleton, justice of the Common Pleas from 1466 to 1481, wrote his *Treatise on Tenures*, a book of English property law, which was outsold only by the Bible and which was notable for not only stating the law but also commentating on it, highlighting the features of the law 'which he believed most amenable to development to jurisprudential ends'.[242] All works on law inevitably take the form of a synthesis, but this was explicit for the first time with Littleton who 'carefully but vigorously undertook the enterprise of rationalizing and even refashioning English property law'.[243] The *Treatise on Tenures* itself became an authority, blurring the lines between stating, interpreting and re-constructing the law. Its longevity was remarkable and helped cement further a romanticised and unhistorical interpretation of the common law. This, coupled with the fact that reforms and tweaks to the administration of justice were not prioritised, meant that the common law became increasingly complex and ineffective.

The final years of Plantagenet England were dominated, therefore, by conflict, violence and uncertainty. Although Parliament and the common law had become used to operating regardless of personnel changes in the highest offices of the land, the War of the Roses did have an effect upon law and order. As Charles Ross noted: 'Most of the flagrant examples of open defiance of the law, ranging from bribery and intimidation, through murder and riot, to private war and general terrorism, were the work of gangs of men ... acting on behalf of powerful people, or at least afterwards being able to claim their protection'.[244]

In the end, it was not the Black Death that killed Plantagenet England. Although it left its mark on the legal system, the more deadly disease was that of civil war. Perhaps suitably for Plantagenet England, it was the resurgence of conflict with the barons that proved its undoing.

---

[239] Chris Given-Wilson, *Henry IV* (Yale University Press, 2016) 157.

[240] Lyon, *Constitutional History of the United Kingdom* 146. As McFarlane's work stresses, the key developments occurred at the personal rather than the institutional level.

[241] Thomas Garden Barnes, *Shaping the Common Law: From Glanvill to Hale, 1188–1688* (Stanford University Press, 2008) 47; Lyon, *Constitutional History of the United Kingdom* 166.

[242] Garden Barnes, *Shaping the Common Law* 33, 39–40.   [243] Ibid. 40.   [244] James Ross, *Henry VI* (Allen Lane, 2016) 393.

'The Tudor period is a distinct, well-marked period, and anyone who was writing the history of England would have to mark it as such ... The Tudor monarchy is indeed something very different from the Lancastrian – the latter was a very limited monarchy, the former if we regard its practical operation, seems almost unlimited'.

Frederic W Maitland, *The Constitutional History of England* (Cambridge University Press, 1941 [1908]) 237.

9

The Tudor Transformation (c.1485–1603)

I   Introduction

The year 1485 is usually considered to be the end of the medieval period.[1] That year saw the end of the Plantagenet dynasty and the beginning of the Tudor period.[2] As with the rise of the Normans and Plantagenets, the rise of the Tudors was the consequence of bloodshed: the Battle of Bosworth saw Henry Tudor accede to the English throne. Henry had no clear hereditary right to the crown but was appointed as such by the justices of the exchequer chamber.[3] When Parliament was called, his kingship was presented as a *fait accompli* rather than seeking the approval of the assembly.[4] A clear message had been sent: the kingdom was under new management.[5]

The reign of Henry Tudor ushered in a new dynasty. Henry Tudor became Henry VII (1485–1509), but his reign is often regarded as simply the prologue to what was become. The Tudors are perhaps the rock stars of English history and it is the reigns of Henry VIII (1509–47) and his children that are well taught in schools and are constantly the subject of television documentaries, dramas and even musicals.[6] However, as ever, such periodisation runs the risk of overstating the extent of change and understating the extent of continuity. This is particularly true in relation to law where talk of a Tudor transformation is difficult to reconcile with the evidence of legal continuity. John Baker, whose research has done much to shed light upon law in the Tudor period,[7] noted that:

---

[1] However, this is not always treated as a cut-off point. It has also been argued that the War of the Roses actually ended in 1471 and was 'restarted almost by accident in 1483' (Christine Carpenter, *The War of the Roses: Politics and the Constitution in England c.1437–1509* (Cambridge University Press, 1997) 19). John Baker's volume in the *Oxford History of the Laws of England* begins in 1483 in order to include the property legislation of 1483–4; John H Baker, *The Oxford Laws of England Volume VI 1483–1558* (Oxford University Press, 2003) v.

[2] Henry VII (1485–1509), Henry VIII (1509–47), Edward IV (1547–53), Lady Jane Grey (1553), Mary I (1553–8) and Elizabeth I (1558–1603).

[3] Indeed, Henry was himself an attained person disabled in law under an Act of Attainder. The justices of the exchequer chamber discussed this and concluded that Henry was discharged of his attainder as a matter of fact of becoming king; SB Chrimes, *Henry VII* (Yale University Press, 1999 [1972]) 61.

[4] Ann Lyon, *Constitutional History of the United Kingdom* (2nd ed., Routledge, 2016) 158.

[5] The Acts of Attainder and Titulus Regius were repealed but a new Act of Attainder was passed, naming twenty-eight supporters of Richard; ibid. 160.

[6] The musical *Six*, which focuses on the stories of the six wives of Henry VIII, is itself a work that could be regarded as a piece of feminist or subversive history.

[7] See, in particular, John H Baker (ed.), *The Reports of Sir John Spelman* (Selden Society, 1976); Baker, *The Oxford Laws of England Volume VI 1483–1558*; and John H Baker, *English Law under Two Elizabeths* (Cambridge University Press, 2021).

190   *The Tudor Transformation (c.1485–1603)*

Anyone who approaches the history of the common law during this age of intellectual revolution has to confront the rather surprising fact that the law of England seems on the surface hardly to have changed at all. The essential features of the law, and of the constitution, were settled long before the battle of Bosworth and were recognizably the same when Elizabeth I was crowned three-quarters of a century later.[8]

This echoed Frederic W Maitland's point that 'the history of our public law regarded as a whole is very continuous: the greatest events that occur in it do not constitute what can fairly be termed revolutions'.[9] Maitland noted that comparing the legal system under the Tudors to that of the Plantagenets, the monarchy under the Tudors seemed 'very different', in that by contrast the Tudors seemed 'almost unlimited'. However: 'Still the difference, when we look into it, is found not so much in the nature of the institutions which exist as in the spirit in which they work: the same machinery of king, lords, commons, council, law courts, seems to bring out very different results.' By 1485, most of the key legal institutions were in place but were in a state of early adolescence. Many of the features recognisable to modern eyes were there but they had not fully developed. Many developments occurred during the Tudor period as the rock star monarchs flexed their powers. Maitland noted that there was 'no one minute at which the change takes place'; it was only gradually overtime through development, experiment and regression that the common law reached maturity. The Tudor period was crucial to this but did not see such completion and, as ever, we need to be wary of linear accounts of progression. As we will see in the next chapter, much of the Tudor transformations came undone under the Stuarts.[10] Many of the Tudor legal innovations proved to be short-lived. This is particularly true of those developments that were added onto rather than integrated within the common law. Yet, some of the changes that crystallised during this period remain with us today. This is true of one word that would echo down the ages and continue to confound law students centuries later: equity. As we will see, this referred to a jurisdiction that developed separately from the common law.

This chapter, then, explores the growth pains experienced during the early adolescence of the common law: the Tudor transformation. This chapter examines how English law developed in this period of significant religious, political and social change. It asks whether there actually was a legal renaissance – a term coined by Baker.[11] The chapter falls into three sections. Section II explores the legal renaissance by examining the common law courts as they stood by the start of the Tudor period and before introducing the Tudor innovations that supplemented (and sought to supersede) the common law courts. These include the notorious and controversial Court of Star Chamber and also the less infamous but significantly more influential Court of Chancery from where the law of equity grew. Section III then examines in more detail the event for which Henry VIII is perhaps best known: the Reformation. It examines the breach with the Church in Rome and how a new Church of England was set up, headed now by the king rather than the Pope. However, the

---

[8] John H Baker, *The Oxford History of the Laws of England Volume VI 1483–1558* (Oxford University Press, 2003) 4.

[9] Frederic W Maitland, *The Constitutional History of England* (Cambridge University Press, 1941 [1908]) 236.

[10] For a detailed analysis of the period from 1485 to 1642, see also Christopher W Brooks, *Law, Politics and Society in Modern England* (Cambridge University Press, 2008).

[11] John H Baker, 'New Light on Slade's Case: Part II' (1971) 29(2) *Cambridge Law Journal* 213, 216.

focus here will be on the legal rather than the political or religious dimensions of the Reformation. The emphasis will be on how the Reformation legislation showed the growing power and importance of statute law. This was evident not only under Henry VIII but during the reigns of his children, when the religious identity of the realm was in flux but where it became clear that religious uniformity was shaped and enforced by means of Parliamentary statute. This cemented the power of what became known as the 'King in Parliament' whereby legislation is made by the crown acting together with the two Houses of Parliament. Section IV then examines some of the developments at common law during the Tudor period. This will focus on some of the key changes in what modern eyes call contract law (the development of the doctrine of consideration), property law (the writ of ejectment and the origins of trusts) and criminal law (the distinction between murder and manslaughter), continuing accounts from previous chapters.

Throughout this chapter, our focus will differ from the stories taught in schools and repackaged in various media that fixate on the lives of the rock star monarchs of this period. Instead, our attention will be on how English law developed during the Tudors; a story of the growing pains experienced during the adolescence of the common law as rivals began to grab the attention. This is an account not so much of the renaissance of English law but of its puberty.

II   The Legal Renaissance

Unlike the change in dynasty that occurred as a result of the Battle of Hastings, there was no invasion from overseas during the Battle of Bosworth. However, nevertheless, the question of the impact of foreign thinking upon English law still needs to be asked of Tudor England in the same way that it was asked of Norman England. The Tudor era in England needs to be placed in the context of wider political, social and theological trends that were affecting Europe as a whole at this time. As David Ibbetson put it:

The years around 1500 could be seen as a pivotal point in the Renaissance as Europe came out of the Middle Ages (though we would today not be so chronologically prescriptive). From a continental European point of view, law was a part of this Renaissance. From the last years of the fifteenth century there was a step-change in the use of the Roman law of the universities in legal practice ... and from the first years of the sixteenth century we can date the rise of 'legal humanism'.[12]

This was the era of what Maitland referred to as the 'triad of the three R's: Renaissance, Reformation and Reception':[13] the Renaissance was the cultural movement in Europe from around 1300 that placed an emphasis upon humanism and science; the Reformation was the religious movement against the Catholic Church by Protestant reformers such as Martin Luther and John Calvin from 1517 that began in Germany but spread throughout continental Europe; and the Reception was the rediscovery and adaption of Roman law by

---

[12] David J Ibbetson, 'The Renaissance of English Legal History' (2021) 80(S1) *Cambridge Law Review* s91, s92. On humanism, see Baker, *The Oxford History of the Laws of England Volume VI 1483–1558* 15–18.
[13] Frederic W Maitland, *English Law and the Renaissance* (Cambridge University Press, 1901) 9.

192 *The Tudor Transformation (c.1485–1603)*

continental legal systems (and Scotland) from around the middle of the sixteenth century. However, as Ibbetson has noted, 'whether English law was part of this legal Renaissance is problematic'.[14]

Although the three R's were felt in England, their effect was rather different here than on the continent. The Renaissance was felt in England much later and was only truly experienced during the reign of Elizabeth I (1558–1603).[15] As the leading Tudor historian Geoffrey Elton has commented, England 'wore her Reformation with a difference': the divorce from Rome in the 1530s under Henry VIII was not a religious upheaval that required political and constitutional reconstruction, it was a political and constitutional act that led in time to religious upheaval.[16] Moreover, although the Reformation statutes of the 1530s prohibited the academic study of Catholic canon law at the time of the Reformation and led the universities to focus on the teaching of civil law,[17] the English common law remained steadfast and there was no wholesale adaptation of Roman law or its jurisprudence.

This mismatch between the wider continental shifts and the English experience animated Maitland when he delivered the Rede lecture in 1901. He pondered: 'How was it and why was it that in an age when old creeds of many kinds were crumbling and all knowledge was being transfigured, in an age which had revolted against its predecessor and was fully conscious of the revolt, [that] one body of doctrine ... remained so intact'?[18] Maitland was referring to the common law; he was asking why the medieval common law survived the Renaissance. Looking at the Year Books of Henry VII and Henry VIII, he remarked that these 'ancient law reports are not a place in which we look for humanism or the spirit of the Renaissance: rather we look there for an amazingly continuous persistence and development of medieval doctrine'.[19] Indeed, renaissance-era writers were not only continuing to use but were actually praising medieval texts.

Maitland's Rede lecture continues to be controversial. Just over eighty years later in a Special Ford lecture in Oxford, Baker gave a lecture with an identical title.[20] In that lecture and in his subsequent publications, Baker pointed out that most of Maitland's 'major assumptions' have turned out to be mistaken.[21] Maitland's assumption was that a reception had been possible because the common law courts had been in decline. Subsequent commentators have agreed that Maitland 'over-emphasised the real danger of a reception of Roman law in England' and overplayed the decline of the common law courts.[22] Baker noted that 'there was no such dramatic decline as might be supposed from Maitland's literary references. Indeed, after a serious decline in King's Bench business down to the time of Wolsey's ascendancy, there was a steady increase in business after about 1530.'[23] Maitland emphasised the ending of the Year Books but did not mention, because he did not

---

[14] Ibbetson, 'The Renaissance of English Legal History' s92.
[15] Baker has suggested that 'many of the remarkable developments began in the half century between the 1490s and the 1540s, even if they did not all bear full fruit until the Elizabethan period' (John H Baker, 'English Law and the Renaissance' (1985) 44 (1) *Cambridge Law Journal* 46).
[16] Geoffrey R Elton, 'The Reformation in England' in Geoffrey R Elton (ed.), *The New Cambridge Modern History Volume 2: The Reformation, 1520–1559* (2nd ed., Cambridge University Press, 1990) 262.
[17] Maitland, *English Law and the Renaissance* 9.   [18] Ibid. 4.   [19] Ibid. 3.   [20] Baker, 'English Law and the Renaissance'.
[21] Baker, *The Oxford History of the Laws of England Volume VI 1483–1558* 4.
[22] Most notably, William S Holdsworth, *A History of English Law Volume IV* (Methuen & Co, 1924) 252 *et seq.*
[23] Baker, *The Reports of Sir John Spelman Volume II* vol 94, 25, 26.

The Legal Renaissance   193

know, that in their place existed manuscript reports and reporting traditions.[24] However, even accepting these criticisms, it is worth noting that Maitland appreciated that the decline of the common law courts as he saw it had been a temporary matter. Although Maitland stated that during 'the Tudor age the life of our ancient law was by no means lusty',[25] he added that English law soon displayed 'a new lease of life'.[26] Moreover, although at times Maitland suggested that the conditions had been ripe for a reception, his lecture was clear that such a reception had not taken place. Although Maitland said that the 'medieval law was open to humanistic attacks',[27] he added that no reception of Roman law took place or was desired by the king. So, although Maitland overplayed the likelihood of a reception occurring, he did not argue that such a reception had taken place and he accepted that the common law enjoyed a revival, albeit later in the period.

Baker has suggested that the criticisms made of Maitland's Rede lecture are 'directed at Maitland's arguments rather than his principal question and its answer.'[28] Although Maitland's apparent assumptions about the practicality of a reception are now questionable, the same is not true of the answer Maitland gave to his question of why the English experience remained so different from that of continental countries.[29] For Maitland, the difference was the fact that medieval England had places where the common law was taught.[30] In England, the Inns of Court developed, providing legal education for practitioners and the gentry. As Thomas Garden Barnes noted:

It became the vogue for young gentlemen of the landed aristocracy (or those who aspired to join the landed aristocracy) to be sent in their early teens to one of the universities for a few years and afterwards for a year or two to study at one of the four Inns of Court. It was not intended that these young men would take a degree at Oxford or Cambridge; that was for those bent on taking religious orders, or who sought to be civil lawyers or physicians. Rather, they were to be exposed to the higher element of basic Classical learning and introduced to polite manners. Likewise, sojourn at the Inns was not meant to produce barristers; it was to expose them to the city life of London and Westminster and to introduce them to the rudiments of law, so much law, particularly property law, as they would need to manage their estates.[31]

Maitland's argument was therefore that the common law survived because it was taught, studied and perpetuated by the Inns of Court and those they trained.[32] As Maitland commented, it is 'difficult to conceive of any system better suited to harden and toughen a traditional body of law than one which, while books were still uncommon, compelled every lawyer to take part in legal education and every distinguished lawyer to read public

---

[24] Indeed, Baker commented that the 'mass of parchment in the Public Record Office relating to Henry VIII's reign alone is so vast that, ironically, historians have been deterred from making any use of it at all' (ibid.); Ibbetson, 'The Renaissance of English Legal History' s95–6.

[25] Maitland, *English Law and the Renaissance* 22.   [26] Ibid. 29.   [27] Ibid. 17.

[28] Baker, *The Reports of Sir John Spelman Volume II* vol. 94, 26. Dafydd Jenkins has pointed out that some commentators such as Samuel Thorne (Samuel E Thorne, 'English Law and the Renaissance' in Samuel E Thorne (ed.), *Essays in English Legal History* (Hambledon Press, 1985) 187) have confused these arguments as being Maitland's thesis whereas in reality 'his discussion of the possible threat to continuity was only incidental to his main purpose' (Dafydd Jenkins, 'English Law and the Renaissance Eighty Years On: In Defence of Maitland' (1981) 2(2) *Journal of Legal History* 107, 108).

[29] Baker, *The Oxford History of the Laws of England Volume VI 1483–1558* 7, 12.

[30] Maitland, *English Law and the Renaissance* 23.

[31] Thomas Garden Barnes, *Shaping the Common Law: From Glanvill to Hale, 1188–1688* (Stanford University Press, 2008) 33.

[32] Maitland, *English Law and the Renaissance* 26.

194   *The Tudor Transformation (c.1485–1603)*

lectures'.[33] As he put it, 'Law schools make tough law.'[34] This conclusion has been supported by Dafydd Jenkins, who concluded that: 'Every piece of evidence which strengthens the argument that a Reception was unlikely also strengthens Maitland's argument that it was because English law was taught that a Reception did not occur.'[35] Baker agreed that the main causes of jurisdictional and procedural changes during the Tudor period were intellectual and owed to the growing influence of the Inns of Court.[36] As Ibbetson has noted, the Inns of Court were as central for Baker as for Maitland.[37] However, while Maitland saw the Inns 'as a gatekeeper against the supposed risk of a reception of Roman Law', Baker underlined how 'English law was already professional-ised, staffed and operated by learned lawyers, lawyers who had learned their law not in universities but in the Inns of Court and later through legal practice.' The revisionist account holds that there was no need for a further reception since English legal practice had already been transformed thanks to the Inns of Court.[38]

Although Baker agreed with Maitland's answer that the Inns of Court were the explanation, he also found that more recent evidence undermined Maitland's question of why England was unique in not succumbing to a reception. Maitland's understanding of the reception on the continent as the establishment of Roman law through the sweeping away national laws has now been questioned.[39] It is now thought that the general trend in Europe was 'the reverse of what Maitland had supposed: there was a nationalist tendency'.[40] For Baker, this has meant that 'at the same time as Maitland's solution is completely vindicated, his question dissolves away' since there 'was nothing remarkable in the survival of English law'.[41] On the one hand, this finding is unimportant: even if the English experience was unexceptional, the issue remains of why the common law survived.

Baker argued that 'Maitland, Holdsworth, and Plucknett, by stressing the continuity of English law, unconsciously perpetuated a misleading approach which long obscured the true story.' By highlighting the basic level of legal continuity, attention was not paid to the changes that did occur. Baker's work points to a legal renaissance. He referred to the Tudor period as experiencing a 'regeneration or renaissance of English law', writing that the 'medieval law lived on in an organic sense, but the rate of development, distortion and innovation was ... accelerated'.[42] For Baker, English law underwent 'something of a transformation',[43] raising the question of 'to what extent was there a sixteenth-century Reformation of English law?'[44] As he noted: 'By the seventeenth century the year books and old abridgments were regarded by the lawyer in the same way as bows and arrows were regarded by the soldier since the invention of gunpowder.'[45] Yet, these developments have traditionally been underplayed by legal historians. Baker has referred to the period 1500–1700 as the 'dark age of English legal history', noting that developments after Edward III have 'been seriously neglected by historians of law', and that, although legal

---

[33] Ibid. 27–8.   [34] Ibid. 25.   [35] Jenkins, 'English Law and the Renaissance Eighty Years On' 133.

[36] Baker, 'English Law and the Renaissance' 50. For a contrary view, see Thorne, 'English Law and the Renaissance' 187.

[37] Ibbetson, 'The Renaissance of English Legal History' s94.

[38] As we saw in the last chapter, this could be interpreted as an effect of the Black Death.

[39] Baker, *The Reports of Sir John Spelman Volume II* vol. 94, 27.   [40] Ibid. 28.   [41] Ibid. 27.   [42] Ibid. 23.

[43] Baker, *The Oxford History of the Laws of England Volume VI 1483–1558* 13.

[44] Baker, *The Reports of Sir John Spelman Volume II* vol. 94, 27.   [45] Ibid. 23.

The Legal Renaissance 195

history work begun to be written in the Elizabethan age, such writers 'were pre-occupied with dark and distant problems about the origins of the common law' and the 'sense of continuity which they conveyed was of rhetorical and emotional and political, rather than historical, value'.[46] Baker lamented this omission and highlighted the importance of what he has referred to as the 'legal renaissance of the sixteenth century'.[47] He insisted that this period is 'one of the most interesting and vital periods in the history of the common law. If the twelfth and thirteenth century saw the birth of the common law, the sixteenth century witnessed its renaissance – or at least its reformation.'[48]

However, the 'underlying causes' of this legal renaissance have been difficult to identify. Samuel Thorne has pointed out that there is a need to place the legal changes in the context of 'the progressive reorganization of 16th century society along new lines'.[49] He criticised Maitland for not taking into account the effect 'of the dissolution of the monasteries, of the commercialisation of land, enclosures, the agrarian revolution, of expanding trade, both domestic and overseas, of the new mobility of the population, or of the rise of an indeterminate middle class'.[50] Baker noted that it was unlikely that it was a 'mere coincidence' that these legal changes occurred during 'the age of many other changes – the age of Reformation, of Renaissance (in England), and of revolution in natural science and the arts'.[51] He argued that, although in 'detail the English story could not be more different from Continental legal history', nevertheless in 'the shift of emphasis from *doctrine* (or common learning) to *jurisprudence* (or judge-made law) the similarity is striking'.[52] The changes in England echoed what really occurred on the continent, which was less of a reception and more of an 'increasing sophistication':

What changes most was not the law as a body of principles, but the learned treatment of legal disputes by the doctors of law who advised and adjudicated in real cases. Courts which had been governed by laymen were replaced by courts composed of professional lawyers, who naturally used the material available to them in their tests and glosses when arguing and deciding cases.[53]

As Ibbetson has put it:

It may be that around 1500 there was a changed perception of law, shared between England and continental Europe, according to which disputes should be resolved according to determinate rules, a rise of legal positivism. No longer would it be seen as ideal to leave to the jury a very general issue . . . If dispute resolution was to be properly rule-based, then it be for the trained judges, judges who knew or who could discover the law, to say what those rules were and to apply them.[54]

He noted that although there 'is no doubt that medieval judges had acted more or less consistently', nevertheless 'the greater emphasis on judicial decision-making in the

---

[46] John H Baker, 'The Dark Age in Legal History, 1500–1700' in Dafydd Jenkins (ed.), *Legal History Studies* (University of Wales Press, 1975), reprinted in John H Baker, *The Legal Profession and the Common Law* (Hambledon Press, 1986) 435.
[47] Baker, 'New Light on Slade's Case: Part II' 216.   [48] Baker, 'The Dark Age in Legal History, 1500–1700' 435, 437.
[49] Thorne, 'English Law and the Renaissance' 195.   [50] Ibid.
[51] Baker, 'English Law and the Renaissance' 50. Though the precise question of the effect of the renaissance is kept open: 'The only safe generalisation to be made about the effect of the Renaissance on English law is that the humanist intellectual climate made it easier for the legal profession to react promptly and creatively to the new range of potentially lucrative problems thrust upon it by social, economic, and jurisdictional forces' (Baker, *The Reports of Sir John Spelman Volume II* vol. 94, 50–1).
[52] Baker, 'English Law and the Renaissance' 59.   [53] Ibid. 51.
[54] Ibbetson, 'The Renaissance of English Legal History' s104

196   *The Tudor Transformation (c.1485–1603)*

sixteenth century imparted a new flavour to this'.[55] As Ibbetson pointed out, 'in the years after 1600 authoritative weight was attached in particular to judicial precedent. The balance was now shifted towards what was to become the characteristic English mode of case-law reasoning.'

For Baker, the legal renaissance was therefore shown not only in the volume and range of parliamentary legislation in this period, but also in the development of the courts in light of increasing litigiousness.[56] He lamented that 'later historians, bedazzled by the exciting achievements of the Reformation Parliament, and perhaps misled by the paucity of printed legal literature, left well alone the common law of the early Tudor period'.[57] Although, as discussed later, the increase in the number and status of statutes was an important development, as shown in the Reformation legislation, Baker pointed out that in reality 'the legislation of the 1530s had little direct effect on everyday law, and such jurisdictional adjustments that took place had been on the way since the previous century'.[58] For Baker, it is important, therefore, that attention is also paid to the legal renaissance in the court room. He noted that: 'New courts rose up, and a new profession', and this has meant that historians 'cannot fully understand the later common law unless we first understand this later Tudor legal revolution'.[59] Indeed, it is not only the development of institutions that proved vital but also the development of thinking. As Thorne noted, 'the real story of English law in the Renaissance' is the tale of how 'English law found solutions within itself for the very serious and threatening problems' raised by the social and political changes of this period.[60] The way in which the law developed and its growing pains is the theme of this chapter. This section will begin by examining the structural changes in the legal system before Section III explores the development of statute law, as shown by the Reformation legislation, and Section IV follows Baker's advice in exploring common law developments.

1   The Common Law Courts

Much work has been completed on the development of legal institutions under the Tudors since Maitland gave his lecture.[61] Although the relationship between courts was often unsettled and at times controversial,[62] a number of general trends can be identified. The first is the decline of the local courts: justice was increasingly a matter for the royal courts, as by the sixteenth-century, matters of what we would call contract and tort were now routinely determined at Westminster rather than locally. As Baker noted, this may have been in part because such claims regularly 'exceeded the forty-shilling limit which common and statute law imposed on inferior jurisdictions',[63] and that that limit had not been increased as the value of money fell. However, a further cause may have been the influence of the Inns of Court and the development of a common view that regarded 'quaint

---

[55] Ibid. s104.   [56] Baker, *The Oxford History of the Laws of England Volume VI 1483–1558* 34, 39.
[57] Baker, *The Reports of Sir John Spelman Volume II* vol. 94 23.   [58] Baker, 'English Law and the Renaissance' 47.
[59] Baker, 'The Dark Age in Legal History, 1500–1700' 435, 437.   [60] Thorne, 'English Law and the Renaissance' 195.
[61] Baker, 'The Dark Age in Legal History, 1500–1700' 435, 436.
[62] Baker, *The Reports of Sir John Spelman Volume II* vol. 94 51.   [63] Ibid.

The Legal Renaissance 197

provincial jurisdictions as anomalous and outdated'.[64] The same trend can be seen in relation to the ecclesiastical courts, with litigants seemingly preferring royal justice. As Baker noted, '[T]he appearance of actions for defamation and breach of faith, and an action against executors for a legacy, all hint at a redirection of litigants from ecclesiastical courts.'[65] It is important, however, not to overplay the extent to which the Tudor common law courts resembled their present-day successors. The work of Baker, especially his Clarendon lectures on 'The Law's Two Bodies',[66] emphasised how the 'common learning' of the Inns of Court was as influential, if not more so, than the decisions of the common law courts. Lawyers 'put as much weight on opinions expressed in the Inns of Court as on what had been decided in Westminster Hall'.[67] As Ibbetson put it: 'Law was as much, perhaps more, the professional consensus of lawyers as it was something sent down from on high in judicial decisions. Moots and readings in the Inns of Courts, especially the latter, are quite as relevant as sources of the legal history of the period as reports of cases.' That said, the common law courts had become firmly established by the Tudor period. It had long become impractical for all significant disputes to be heard personally by the king and his council, and so three courts had been derived from the King's Court: the King's Bench, the Court of Common Pleas and the Court of the Exchequer. These royal courts grew and often overlapped with the effect that litigants often had 'the choice between these three courts and each of them will deal with his case in the same way and by the same rules'.[68]

The King's Bench was the court that was most closely connected with the King's Council, as shown by the king's actual presence until 1465.[69] The court originally dealt with pleas 'against the peace of our lord the king', including all writs of trespass and case and criminal matters in any county that it sat. However, it became settled at Westminster Hall from 1420 and came to hear all pleas touching the king. This included treason, murder, felony, trespass, indictments for misdemeanour, writs of right brought by the king himself and other private law actions in particular circumstances.[70] It also took on what we would now call a supervisory jurisdiction through a number of writs such as *habeas corpus* (which questioned the cause of detention), *quo warranto* (which enquired into the authority by which something was done) and the writ of error (which ordered the judges to send a record of their proceedings in a particular case to be inspected).[71] Over time, three 'prerogative writs' became used. The first was the writ of prohibition, which restrained a body from doing something outside their jurisdiction. This was first used against ecclesiastical courts before being applied to all courts.[72] The second was the writ of *mandamus* (Latin for 'we command'), which covered the reverse scenario and compelled a body to do something. This became a common order against local authorities, but precedents for the writ date back to the fourteenth century and was originally referred to as the writ of

---

[64] Ibid. 52.   [65] Ibid. 53.

[66] John H Baker, *The Law's Two Bodies: Some Evidential Problems in English Legal History* (Oxford University Press, 2001).

[67] Ibbetson, 'The Renaissance of English Legal History' s96. A pivotal publication was John H Baker, *Readers and Readings in the Inns of Court and Chancery* (Selden Society Supplementary Series, 2000) vol. 13.

[68] Frederic W Maitland, *Equity: A Course of Lectures* (Cambridge University Press, 1969 [1909]) 2.

[69] See generally Baker, *The Oxford Laws of England Volume VI 1483–1558* chapter 7.   [70] Ibid. 151.

[71] See, generally, John H Baker, *An Introduction to English Legal History* (5th ed., Oxford University Press, 2019) chapter 9.

[72] Ibid. 155.

198   *The Tudor Transformation (c.1485–1603)*

restitution.[73] The third was the writ of *certiorari* (Latin for 'to be informed'), which quashed a decision previously made. This included quashing indictments that were incorrectly worded.[74] The writs of *mandamus* and *certiorari* came to be used chiefly to control local government.[75]

According to the number of recorded cases, the business of the King's Bench underwent a temporary decline in the 1500s, which was halted and turned into an expansion from the 1530s.[76] This change in fortune was caused by the King's Bench developing the bill of Middlesex procedure described in the last chapter. Baker has argued that it was this bill procedure that allowed it to compete with the other courts in terms of possible remedies and the scale of costs.[77] This bill procedure allowed cases to be brought without writ; rather, a petition was made and it did not have to take any form or use any particular formula.[78] This new procedure allowed all forms of action other than those concerning land to be heard at the King's Bench. It was used in relation to the action on the case to such an extent that Baker wrote that 'one is hard put, in the rolls of the early sixteenth century, to find two actions on the case in exactly the same form'. For Baker, the result was a 'period of maximum fluidity' where 'the courts regained as much creative power as their predecessors had enjoyed in the twelfth and thirteenth centuries'.[79]

There were two other common law courts that had derived from the King's Council and were now firmly established. The Court of Common Pleas dated to the reign of Henry II (1154–89) and dealt with all pleas brought to the King's Court that did not concern royal rights.[80] The court 'continued to enjoy by far the greatest share of common-law business', but was unpopular given that only the expensive serjeants at law had the right to represent cases there.[81] Many of the actions were shared with the King's Bench (not least due to its bill procedure), but there were some actions on which it had a monopoly, such as reviewing the proceedings of local courts that were not of record. The vast majority of actions in this period were writs of debt. The third common law court was the Court of the Exchequer, which had developed from the exchequer of account and recipient (which was to become the modern-day treasury) and largely dealt with fiscal matters, including cases concerning the king's revenues.[82] In the Tudor period, this was 'a relatively small jurisdiction', but the court also performed numerous non-judicial functions, as shown by the fact that its judicial and clerical staff number was comparable in number to that of the King's Bench.[83]

Baker noted that the Court of the Exchequer had three 'sides'.[84] The first was the revenue or crown side, which mainly dealt with the recovery of sums of money due to the crown, including land and feudal dues. The second, the plea side – sometimes called the exchequer of the pleas – dealt with various forms of private litigation, including the writ of *Quominus*, which enabled a personal action to be brought by someone who owed money to

---

[73] John H Baker, *The Reinvention of Magna Carta 1216–1616* (Cambridge University Press, 2017) 203.
[74] Baker, *An Introduction to English Legal History* 159.   [75] Baker, *English Law under Two Elizabeths* 177.
[76] Baker, *The Reports of Sir John Spelman Volume II* vol. 94, 53–4.
[77] Ibid. 54. For discussion of the disgruntlement from other courts, see Baker, *The Oxford Laws of England Volume VI 1483–1558* 154 ff.
[78] Baker, *The Reports of Sir John Spelman Volume II* vol. 94, 86.   [79] Ibid. 87.
[80] See generally, Baker, *The Oxford Laws of England Volume VI 1483–1558* chapter 6.
[81] Baker, *The Reports of Sir John Spelman Volume II* vol. 94, 62.
[82] See generally, Baker, *The Oxford Laws of England Volume VI 1483–1558* chapter 8.   [83] Ibid. 159.   [84] Ibid. 161.

The Legal Renaissance 199

the king against those who owed him money.[85] This jurisdiction grew through the use of fictions by litigants whereby people would state that their claim concerned the king's revenues so that the writ of *Quominus* would give them entry to this court. The third and final side was the equity side, which has been referred to as 'by far the most obscure of all the English jurisdictions'.[86] Baker suggests that this jurisdiction grew from the *Quominus* jurisdiction 'so that the king's debtors could make equitable claims to money which would help them discharge their duties to the king'.[87] As we will see, the practice of giving remedies in situations where a common law remedy did not exist but it was considered equitable to do so, was to be developed further through the law of equity. This was to develop outside the courts of the common law, mainly in the Court of Chancery, one of the conciliar courts that had developed by this period.

2 *The New Conciliar Courts*

The main legal institutional development in this period was outside the common law courts entirely. The Tudor reigns saw the rise of a number of new courts that supplemented, circumvented and rivalled the common law courts, most notably the Court of Requests, the Court of Star Chamber and the Court of Chancery.[88] As Maitland noted, these new courts not only aroused 'professional jealousies' but were also controversial in that they 'did not proceed according to the course of the common law'.[89] This is surprising given that these new courts derived from the King's Council in the same way that the common law courts had.[90] Although the three common law courts became separate from the King's Court, the monarch continued to exercise residual powers, and those disputes that were not heard by the common law courts continued to be heard through the King's Council. This meant that the King's Council became increasingly attractive to litigants because it provided remedies not available under the common law courts. However, the council's power became controversial and 'complaints were soon heard of its arbitrariness'.[91] It therefore developed institutions of its own separate to and outside of the common law courts: the Privy Council (a body of the king's closest advisers that exists to this day), the Court of Chancery and the so-called conciliar courts, which included local courts (e.g., the Council of the North, the Council of the Marches and the Council of the West) as well as the Court of Requests and, most notoriously, Star Chamber.[92] The Court of Requests was set up to relieve the Star Chamber by dealing with small suits.[93] It came to exercise the civil jurisdiction of the king

---

[85] Ibid. 167.
[86] Theodore FT Plucknett, *Concise History of the Common Law* (5th ed., Little Brown and Co., 1956) 185. See further WH Bryson, *The Equity Side of the Exchequer* (Cambridge University Press, 1975).
[87] Baker, *The Oxford Laws of England Volume VI 1483–1558* 169.
[88] Holdsworth, *A History of English Law Volume IV* 252–3.
[89] Frederic W Maitland and Francis C Montague, *A Sketch of English Legal History* (GP Putman's Sons, 1915) 114.
[90] For discussion of the King's Council at the start of the Tudor period, see Chrimes, *Henry VII* chapter 4.
[91] Baker, *The Reports of Sir John Spelman Volume II* vol. 94, 70–2.
[92] There also existed ecclesiastical, admiralty and revenue courts as well as commissions, metropolis and local courts, on which, see Baker, *The Oxford Laws of England Volume VI 1483–1558* chapters 11–16.
[93] Ibid. 204.

200   *The Tudor Transformation (c.1485–1603)*

in council and dealt with petitions from the poor, affairs of the king's household and matters not important enough for other courts. In the end, it was effectively replaced by local litigation since it proved costly for small claims to be adjudicated at Westminster.[94]

The term 'star chamber' began as the name of a room rather than an institution, denoting a room in the Palace of Westminster where the King's Councillors met to deal with both judicial and administrative matters.[95] It pre-dated the Tudor period with the Star Chamber Act of 1487 that recognised a sub-group of the council that dealt with serious disorder.[96] It had both a civil and criminal jurisdiction but is mostly known for exercising the criminal jurisdiction of the king in council and seeking to keep order in the realm. The Court of Star Chamber developed a vast jurisdiction that dealt with a number of matters that were not crimes at common law such as attempts, as well as hearing civil cases to save time and expense and dealing with what it perceived to be the failure of common law courts to do justice. Baker noted that the court 'existed primarily for the benefit of private litigants seeking some form of relief, though plaintiffs frequently alleged misdemeanours which could be punished as criminal offences at the same time'.[97] Most of its subject matter comprised of property cases alleging some form of disorder, though it also dealt with the alleged perversion of justice.[98] As with the other conciliar courts, Star Chamber was a court to which people 'turned to circumvent the limitations of common law' and it 'was less formulaic and more flexible than common law courts'.[99] As KJ Kesselring and Natalie Mears have commented: 'Star Chamber offered some people relatively fast, flexible solutions to problems that other courts could not address, even while it provided others with evidence of the dangers of royal power when unchecked by law'.[100] The court used the procedure of the canon law: summoning parties and deciding cases without any jury, and as Maitland noted, the 'extraction of confessions by torture is no unheard-of thing'.[101] It also used a range of punishments aside from fines and imprisonment, including public humiliation such as wearing papers, standing in the pillory or losing an ear.[102] Many bills before the Court of Star Chamber concerned cases that were pending before other courts and so its records provide examples of legal pluralism in that they show litigants navigating multiple jurisdictions.[103]

Star Chamber was to achieve infamy as an illustration of royal excess under the Tudors and early Stuarts, but while it was important in terms of constitutional development, it made little mark upon English law, as Maitland commented: 'It had not added much to our national jurisprudence. It had held itself aloof from jurisprudence; it had been a law unto

---

[94] Baker, *An Introduction to English Legal History* 130.   [95] Baker, *The Oxford Laws of England Volume VI 1483–1558* 195.

[96] Ibid. 196. See JA Guy, *The Cardinal's Court: The Impact of Thomas Wolsey's Star Chamber* (Hassocks, 1977) and Geoffrey R Elton, *Star Chamber Stories* (Metheuen, 1958).

[97] Baker, *The Oxford Laws of England Volume VI 1483–1558* 197.   [98] Ibid. 198.

[99] Deborah Youngs, '"A Besy Woman ... and Full of Lawe": Female Litigants in Early Tudor Star Chamber' (2019) 58 *Journal of British Studies* 735, 736.

[100] KJ Kesselring with Natalie Mears, 'Introduction: Star Chamber Matters' in KJ Kesselring and Natalie Mears (eds.), *Star Chamber Matters: An Early Modern Court and Its Records* (University of London Press, 2021) 1.

[101] Maitland and Montague, *A Sketch of English Legal History* 118.

[102] Baker, *The Oxford Laws of England Volume VI 1483–1558* 197–8.

[103] Youngs, 'A Besy Woman ... and Full of Lawe' 737.

The Legal Renaissance

itself, with hands free to invent new remedies for every new disease of the body politic. It had little regard for precedents, and, therefore, men were not at pains to collect its decisions.'[104]

The same was not true of what Maitland has referred to as the Star Chamber's 'twin sister', the Court of Chancery.[105] This left an important and enduring mark upon English law.

3 *The Court of Chancery*

The Court of Chancery developed from the role of the chancellor: the figure who was effectively the king's secretary of state for all departments, keeping the king's seal and supervising all of the writing done under the king's name.[106] The chancellor was a member of the King's Council and usually a bishop. Over time, those who sought royal justice went straight to the Chancery to obtain a writ rather than going to the King's Council.[107] The Chancery became important in the development of English law not only in terms of providing, producing and developing the common law writs, but also because the chancellor considered all other petitions to the king and his council seeking remedies that could not be dealt with by the common law writs.[108] As Maitland observed, 'it is in dealing with these petitions that the Chancellor begins to develop his judicial powers'.[109] The chancellor and thereupon the Chancery began to give justice to those whose claims did not fit within a common law writ. The Court of Chancery developed its own separate and considerable jurisdiction, again outside the common law courts.[110] As Baker noted, the Court of Chancery provided 'a different juridical world, and it is a world which we see less sharply for want of complete records'.[111]

Maitland noted that the Court of Chancery had two sides: 'a common law side and an equity side'.[112] The common law side consisted of petitions against the king. Since no writ could be brought against the king, the petition had to be made to the chancellor, who would then send the question for trial to the King's Bench.[113] The equity side of the Court of Chancery concerned requests for relief where a person could not get a remedy in the ordinary course of justice through the writ system, but there it was held that they were nevertheless entitled to a remedy. Such petitions were often couched in pious terms, asking the king to find a remedy for the love of God and in the way of charity.[114] These requests became dealt with by the chancellor and where a writ could not be issued to bring the matter before the common law courts, the chancellor began to summon the person involved

---

[104] Maitland and Montague, *A Sketch of English Legal History* 119–20.   [105] Ibid. 120.   [106] Maitland, *Equity* 2.
[107] Ibid. 3.
[108] Robert Palmer noted that this innovation 'began in the decades after the Black Death' (Robert C Palmer, *English Law in the Age of the Black Death 1348–1381: A Transformation of Governance and Law* (University of North Carolina Press, 1993) 107). Gary Watt traces this to a proclamation on 23 January 1349; Gary Watt, *Equity Stirring: The Story of Justice Beyond Law* (Hart, 2009) 51.
[109] Maitland, *Equity* 3.
[110] See Timothy Haskett, 'The Medieval Court of Chancery' (1996) 14(2) *Law and History Review* 245.
[111] Baker, *The Oxford Laws of England Volume VI 1483–1558* 191.
[112] Maitland and Montague, *A Sketch of English Legal History* 121; Maitland, *Equity* 3. Baker refers to the Latin and English side of the Chancery's jurisdiction; Baker, *The Oxford Laws of England Volume VI 1483–1558* 173; Baker, *An Introduction to English Legal History* 108–9.
[113] Maitland, *Equity* 4.   [114] Ibid. 4–5.

202   *The Tudor Transformation (c.1485–1603)*

to order them to appear before him or forfeit a sum of money. The court became therefore a 'court of conscience': as Baker put it, '[T]he theoretical basis of its jurisdiction was that a party required a remedy in conscience where none was available at common law.'[115] This reflected the chancellor's role as the keeper of the king's conscience. As Chancellor Wolsey (1515–29) wrote to a judge giving advice: '[E]very counsellor to a King ought to have a respect to conscience before the rigour of the law.'[116]

The Chancery's jurisdiction operated outside and separate to the common law. Like the Star Chamber, the Court of Chancery followed canon law procedures. In particular, it borrowed the procedure used by the ecclesiastical courts for the suppression of heresy: the accused was examined upon oath and the chancellor decided questions of fact as well as questions of law.[117] However, unlike the Star Chamber, the Court of Chancery developed a particular jurisdiction that was to prove long-lasting. It became agreed that some matters fairly fell within the chancellor's jurisdiction, and these were summed up by an old rhyme:

These three give place in a court of conscience
Fraud, accident, and breach of confidence.[118]

Dubious rhyming aside, this underscored that the chancellor enjoyed a piecemeal jurisdiction over the frauds that the formal common law rules would not remedy, the accidental loss of documents and the like, and agreements that could not be enforced at common law. As we will see, this included the use (the forerunner for the modern trust), which meant that, in the words of Maitland, 'one great field of substantive law fell into his hand – a fruitful field, for in the course of the fifteenth century uses became extremely popular'. However, although Timothy Haskett calculated that over 40 per cent of cases in the later fifteenth century concerned uses,[119] Baker argued that recent studies have questioned this.[120] Research by Nicholas Pronay showed that only 12 per cent of cases concerned uses in a single perhaps unrepresentative bundle of 200 bills from 1480 to 1483.[121] However, as Baker has noted, 'the core of a Chancery disputes' is often hidden 'by jurisdictional fictions, or side issues', meaning that 'difficulty besets all attempts to analyse Chancery business by using the file of bills, and explains the radically different calculations which different observers have made'.[122] Cordelia Beattie, however, has argued that '[I]f we focus less on Chancery as a jurisdiction and more on how it fitted into the broader legal framework in late medieval England, the bills can be revealing.'[123] She presented a picture whereby claimants negotiated solutions to social and legal disputes, not just in the Chancery but through a variety of legal jurisdictions. Indeed, talk of the popularity of the Chancery needs to be tempered. As Baker noted, even 'by the 1550s, when Maitland

---

[115] Baker, *The Oxford Laws of England Volume VI 1483–1558* 174.   [116] Quoted in Watt, *Equity Stirring* 49.
[117] Maitland, *Equity* 5.   [118] Ibid. 7.   [119] Haskett, 'The Medieval Court of Chancery' 298.
[120] Baker, *The Oxford Laws of England Volume VI 1483–1558* 188.
[121] Nicholas Pronay, 'The Chancellor, the Chancery and the Council at the End of the Fifteenth Century' in Harry Hearer and HR Loyn (eds.), *British Government and Administration: Studies Presented to S B Chrimes* (University of Wales Press, 1974) 87, 92–4.
[122] Baker, *The Oxford Laws of England Volume VI 1483–1558* 188.
[123] Cordelia Beattie, 'A Piece of the Puzzle: Women and the Law as Viewed from the Late Medieval Court of Chancery' (2019) 58 *Journal of British Studies* 751, 753.

The Legal Renaissance 203

thought the common law was in deep trouble, the case-load of the Chancery was still only a tenth of that of Common Pleas'.[124]

Nevertheless, by the late sixteenth century, the rules that the chancellor were administering became known as 'the rules of equity and good conscience'.[125] However, limits to the powers of the Chancery were not set out and, even by the seventeenth century, it was said that the protection of equity varied with 'the length of the chancellor's foot'.[126] As Baker noted, the Chancery's 'informality was part of its strength, but it has made its history the more elusive'.[127] The scale of the jurisdiction proved controversial: although the House of Commons voiced such criticism of the Chancery and the role of the King's Council generally 'there was a certain half-heartedness in the opposition'.[128] It became accepted, however, that the chancellor was not to hear cases where the common law provided an adequate remedy.[129] However, the jurisdiction's elasticity posed further problems. The sheer number of claims led to delay and decisions when they were reached were not reported.[130] Cases were decided not on the basis of decided cases but rather by drawing analogies, not only with the common law but with maxims borrowed from canon or civil law.[131] As Maitland put it, 'English equity seems to live from hand to mouth.'[132] However, the scale of the enterprise meant that chancellors were no longer able to serve as the king's first minister, apart from in a symbolic sense. Wolsey was the last chancellor who ruled England; his successors were each 'more of a judge, less of a statesman'.[133]

As Baker noted, by Tudor times, the modern conception of law as a body of rules that are applied to given set of facts had been fostered while the term equity had been adopted for the form of justice provided by the chancellor.[134] The term 'equity' was by no means new and had been known to medieval lawyers, being mentioned in Glanvill. The work of Norman Doe has highlighted the extent to which ideas of conscience were known to medieval common lawyers.[135] In the Tudor period, however, there had been a shift from the rather more fluid and theological notion of conscience to the more legalistic concept of equity. This corresponded with the shift from chancellors being ecclesiastics to being lawyers. While chancellors had been typically trained in theology and canon law, with Wolsey having no legal training, his successor Thomas More had been educated in the common law as a bencher of Lincoln's Inn.[136] However, Dennis R Klinck has argued that 'for Wolsey and for More, conscience remained front-and-centre as far as Chancery was concerned', and so 'a transformation of occurred around or just after their times'.[137]

Commentators such as Timothy Endicott and JL Barton have argued instead that this transformation of equity was due to or at least reflected in the influential work of Christopher St Germain, and in particular his legal treatise *Doctor and Student*, which

---

[124] Baker, *The Oxford Laws of England Volume VI 1483–1558* 190.   [125] Maitland, *Equity* 7–8.
[126] Maitland and Montague, *A Sketch of English Legal History* 126.
[127] Baker, *The Oxford Laws of England Volume VI 1483–1558* 171.
[128] Maitland and Montague, *A Sketch of English Legal History* 122.   [129] Maitland, *Equity* 6, 7.
[130] Maitland and Montague, *A Sketch of English Legal History* 126.   [131] Maitland, *Equity* 8–9.
[132] Maitland and Montague, *A Sketch of English Legal History* 126.   [133] Ibid.
[134] Baker, *An Introduction to English Legal History* 114.
[135] Norman Doe, *Fundamental Authority in Late Medieval Law* (Cambridge University Press, 1990).
[136] Baker, *An Introduction to English Legal History* 115.
[137] Dennis R Klinck, *Conscience, Equity and Court of Chancery in Early Modern England* (Ashgate, 2010) 43.

204 *The Tudor Transformation (c.1485–1603)*

imagined a dialogue between a doctor of divinity and a student of the common law.[138] Klinck, however, pointed out that, although equity is a central concept in *Doctor and Student*, the book uses it in the same way as theologians and canonists did, and so 'one would expect at least the ecclesiastical chancellors to have been familiar with it'.[139] Moreover, *Doctor and Student* was mostly concerned with conscience.[140] It referred to equity sometimes as being outside the law and sometimes being intrinsic to the law. Although 'St. Germain does seem to assume – and indeed to assert – that there is a kind of equity, or perhaps conscience, that is peculiar to the Court of Chancery', this 'actually contributed to the continuing identity of Chancery as a court of conscience'.[141] In short, as Doe put it, St Germain 'follows the traditional medieval outlook'.[142] A further explanation is offered by Mike Macnair who argued that conscience did not have the meaning it has today nor that found in the work of St Germain.[143] Rather, it originally referred to the judge's and defendant's private knowledge of facts that they knew could not be proved in common law courts because of the technicalities of the common law. His argument is that the term equity did not so much replace the term conscience; it was just that conscience lost its specific meaning as the jurisdiction became applied outside the original limited subject area.

It is clear, however, that equity became used as a convenient label for the Chancery's extraordinary form of justice that could be contrasted with the common law. By the Tudor period, references to the 'common law' were widespread. As Maitland noted, the term common law had come to be used to describe 'that part of the law that is enacted, non-statutory that is common to the whole land and to all Englishmen' and could be contrasted with statute law, local custom, royal prerogative and, now, equity.[144]

The new conciliar courts and the Court of Chancery rivalled the common law courts, and this was to prove politically controversial, allowing for the growth of royal power under the Stuarts. However, it can be argued that during the Tudor period it was their development that allowed the common law to continue. Maitland argued that there is some truth in the statement that 'equity saved the common law, and that the Court of Star Chamber saved the constitution'.[145] This is because the conciliar courts provided 'a scheme for the reconciliation of permanence with progress': 'The old mediaeval criminal law could be preserved because a Court of Star Chamber would supply its deficiencies; the old private law could be preserved because the Court of Chancery was composing an appendix to it'.[146] These adjuncts to the common law allowed a renaissance to occur by stealth. Baker argued that the most significant change was 'not in the details of doctrine but in the procedures which enabled the law to become more detailed'.[147] The competition provided by the new courts motivated the common law to expand. Baker commented that courts showed a 'greater willingness . . . to decide points of law which had not been settled

---

[138] Timothy AO Endicott, 'The Conscience of the King: Christopher St. Germain and Thomas More and the Development of English Equity' (1989) 47(2) *University of Toronto Faculty Law Review* 549; JL Barton, 'Equity in the Medieval Common Law' in Ralph A Newman (ed.), *Equity in the World's Legal Systems* (Bruylant, 1973) 139.

[139] Klinck, *Conscience, Equity and Court of Chancery in Early Modern England* 43.   [140] Ibid. 44.   [141] Ibid. 49.

[142] Doe, *Fundamental Authority in Late Medieval Law* 51.

[143] Mike Macnair, 'Equity and Conscience' (2007) 27(4) *Oxford Journal of Legal Studies* 659.   [144] Maitland, *Equity* 3.

[145] Maitland and Montague, *A Sketch of English Legal History* 127–8.   [146] Ibid.

[147] Baker, 'English Law and the Renaissance' 58.

or raised before, and a corresponding tendency to employ procedures which encouraged them to do so'.[148] The same was true, he noted, of Parliament. This period saw the increasing use of statute law to deal with a wider range of matters and, like the conciliar courts, Parliament provided an adjunct to the common law, enabling English law to develop, while preserving the common law tradition. The next section will explore the Tudor transformation of statute law by reference to the Reformation legislation of the 1530s, where Acts of Parliament were used to remove the jurisdiction of the Pope, replacing it with royal authority over religious matters.[149]

III   The Reformation of Statute Law

For Baker, the Tudor era was the 'Age of Common Law': 'The common law was then revered as a body of accumulated wisdom, brought ever close to perfection by centuries of argument and refinement. Its basic principles were attributed to timeless natural reason, perceived though study, practical experience and precedent.'[150] By contrast, legislation was simply 'a necessary gloss upon this unwritten common law, sometimes intended to restore and rescue it from recent perversions, sometimes to supplement it, but rarely to replace it'.[151] Acts of Parliament were regarded as being 'essentially less perfect in nature' than the case law developed by judges.[152] This, for Baker, is in 'bald contrast' to the modern era, which is 'well into the Age of Statute'.

As Maitland noted, the 'desire for continuous legislation is modern': in the medieval period Parliament did not 'pour out statutes', it only passed legislation when absolutely necessary, and such enactments were seen as making small modifications.[153] It was thought that there existed ideally 'a perfect body of law, immutable, eternal, the work of God, not of man'.[154] How ironic, then, that it was religious matters that provided the catalyst for growth in the use of legislation. It was the role of Parliament in redefining the relationship between Church and State that made it clear that parliamentary statute could be used to enact widespread legal and social change. However, Parliament did not stand alone in this initiative. In addition to the requirement that the king approve his Parliament's legislative actions,[155] it was also true that many of these legislative actions had royal fingerprints all over them. The growth of statute law was a key element in the developing relationship between the monarch and Parliament. It was the product of what became known as the King in Parliament. However, the increasing role of statute law encouraged both parties in their conviction of their own constitutional importance, sowing the seeds of the Civil War that was to come in Stuart times.

---

[148] Ibid.

[149] This is not the only example of this trend. It should also be noted that there were other constitutional innovations under the Tudors, particularly in relation to the form of government. On this, see Geoffrey R Elton, *The Tudor Revolution in Government* (Cambridge University Press, 1962).

[150] Baker, *English Law Under Two Elizabeths* 87.   [151] Ibid. 87–8.   [152] Ibid. 88.

[153] Maitland and Montague, *A Sketch of English Legal History* 103. There were exceptions, but even under the reign of Edward I, the English Justinian (discussed in Chapter 7), statute law was still used sparingly compared to the Tudor period, though the use of legislation was to grow even more in the nineteenth, twentieth and twenty-first centuries.

[154] Ibid.   [155] Geoffrey R Elton, *The Tudor Constitution* (2nd ed., Cambridge University Press, 1982) 21.

206   *The Tudor Transformation (c.1485–1603)*

Prior to the Tudor period, when Parliament sat, it largely concerned itself with minor issues: although it would on occasion devise a new remedy or fill a gap in the register of writs, it generally played little role in controlling the development of the common law.[156] Maitland commented that the statute roll of the fifteenth century seems to provide evidence of 'the decline and fall of a mighty institution': while the War of the Roses blossomed, 'Parliament seems to have nothing better to do than to regulate the manufacture of cloth.'[157]

For Maitland, the Tudor period saw the transformation from what Bentham had referred to as the 'omnicompetence' of Parliament to the omnipotence of Parliament.[158] Previously, Parliament had been competent to do whatever it pleased but largely occupied itself with operating within existing systems: it could, for instance, 'determine the rate of wages, the price of goods, the value of money [and] decide that no man shall dress himself above his station'.[159] Under Henry VIII (1509–47), however, Parliament became all powerful. The change was in both form and substance: Tudor statutes became lengthier documents and much more detailed, teeming with exceptions and saving clauses as 'considerable legal exploits' were undertaken.[160] Now, statute law was used much more to make changes to the common law, with striking innovations being made to the laws of property and of crime. This had a considerable effect upon the centrality and operation of the common law: judges were now 'expected to attend very closely to the words that Parliament utters, to weigh and obey every letter of the written law'.[161]

In addition to the Reformation statutes, a number of important pieces of legislation were also passed during the Tudor period.[162] The Laws in Wales Act of 1536 is often referred to as an act of union that brought together England and Wales as one jurisdiction. As we saw in Chapter 7, under the Statute of Wales of 1284, Wales became annexed to the English crown under Edward I but the country still had its separate jurisdiction. This continued until Tudor time, although there was 'a noticeable tendency towards Anglicization' and the extension of English law to parts of Wales by the royal prerogative'.[163] The different Welsh laws and language proved controversial, however, particularly the finding that treason committed in Wales could not be tried in England. The Laws in Wales Act of 1536, together with later legislation and royal ordinances, afforded the Welsh the same 'freedoms, liberties, rights, privileges and laws' as those applied in England, including representation in Parliament, removed Welsh customs of inheritance, stated that all court proceedings were to take place in English, stated that no Welsh speaker was to hold public office unless they used the English language, and reformed the court structure in Wales.[164] A Lord President and Council of the Dominion and Principality of Wales took a role equivalent to Court of Chancery and the Great Sessions were set up as the equivalent to the King's Bench and Common Pleas.[165] Each of the four Welsh circuits was to be presided over by a 'person learned in the laws of England', and the judges of the Great Sessions were appointed from benchers of the Inns of Court. This

---

[156] Maitland and Montague, *A Sketch of English Legal History* 106.   [157] Ibid.   [158] Ibid. 105.   [159] Ibid.
[160] Ibid. 107–8.   [161] Ibid.   [162] For the primary materials, see Elton, *The Tudor Constitution*.
[163] Baker, *The Oxford Laws of England Volume VI 1483–1558* 103.
[164] Ibid. 107. For details, see Thomas G Watkin, *The Legal History of Wales* (2nd ed., University of Wales Press, 2012) chapter 7.
[165] Baker, *The Oxford Laws of England Volume VI 1483–1558* 107.

The Reformation of Statute Law 207

system remained in place, supplemented by the later equity jurisdiction, until 1830, when Wales was brought fully under the English court system.[166]

Other seminal pieces of legislation included the Statute of Uses of 1536, the Statute of Enrolments of 1536 and the Statute of Wills of 1540, which will be discussed in Section IV. The fact that such important developments were enacted by parliamentary statute did not, however, mean that ultimate authority rested in Parliament. The monarch played a central role: more often than not Parliament was just doing his bidding. This is particularly clear when looking at the Reformation legislation.[167] Maitland commented that Parliament itself played 'a subservient and ignoble part' in the Reformation statutes, but pointed out that paradoxically this role was to increase the power of Parliament in the longer term. The fact that the changes were made by legislation and 'by the authority of Parliament' created the expectation that Parliament would play a similar role in the future. As Maitland put it: 'In the end it was better that Parliament should for a while register the acts of a despot than that it should sink into the contempt that seemed to be prepared for it.'[168] The Reformation legislation underscored that now there was 'nothing that could not be done by the authority of Parliament', and this extended not only to constitutional and ecclesiastical changes but also any matter dealt with by the common law. This did not, of course, mean that English law became codified, only a small part of English law was to be found in the statute book, but the boldness of the Reformation statutes would have a long-term effect upon English law.[169] Two new supreme beings rose in the 1530s: the divine right of the king and the omnipotent power of his Parliament. And the tension between these two supreme beings would dominate for centuries to come.

However, the English Reformation revisited a different tension that had been present for some time, the uneasy co-existence of two legal systems in England: the king's common law on the one hand and the canon law of Rome being applied by the ecclesiastical courts on the other hand. The English Church operated as 'a state within the realm', with the ecclesiastical courts enjoying vast jurisdiction and a number of cases being appealed to Rome.[170] This tension was occasionally sparked by critical readings at the Inns of Court or by decisions by the common law courts who developed an increasingly 'vigilant control over the worldly consequences of spiritual power'.[171] A writ of prohibition or an action founded on the Statute of Winchester could be brought by those who were aggrieved to be brought before the ecclesiastical courts. However, for most of the time, the tension between religious and secular law was simply accepted. That said, it had been long acknowledged that there were areas where the king's law meant that the canon law could not apply and English kings had long interfered in ecclesiastical matters by taxing the clergy, for example.[172] The question of the status of Catholic canon law prior to the Reformation has been the subject of much scholarly discussion. It is often referred to as the so-called

---

[166] Ibid. 108. For details, see Watkin, *The Legal History of Wales* chapter 8.
[167] For a more general appraisal, see RK Gilkes, *The Tudor Parliament* (University of London Press, 1969) and Michael AR Graves, *The Tudor Parliaments: Crown, Lords and Commons, 1485–1603* (Longman, 1985).
[168] Maitland and Montague, *A Sketch of English Legal History* 107.   [169] Ibid. 109.
[170] Elton, 'The Reformation in England' 263.   [171] Baker, *The Reports of Sir John Spelman Volume II* vol. 94, 65, 66.
[172] Elton, 'The Reformation in England' 264. See Frederic W Maitland, *Roman Canon Law in the Church of England* (Methuen & Co., 1898) chapter 2.

208 *The Tudor Transformation (c.1485–1603)*

Stubbs-Maitland debate. The argument attributed to William Stubbs, the nineteenth-century bishop of Oxford and historian, was that the papal law of Rome, though of great authority in the medieval period, was not binding upon the English Church, and that the Courts Christian applied the native law developed by the Church in its assemblies of bishops and clergy, even where it was in conflict with the papal law.[173] The argument attributed to Maitland was that the ecclesiastical courts accepted and applied Roman canon law as 'binding statute law', only refusing to follow it in situations where royal law forced ecclesiastical practice to depart from canon law.[174]

Although modern scholarship has broadly supported the view of Maitland, scholars such as Richard Helmholz and Charles Donahue who have examined primary materials have concluded that Maitland's work needs to be qualified in certain respects.[175] Helmholz stressed how both Stubbs and Maitland thought in positivist terms that were not shared by medieval litigants and court personnel. The Stubbs-Maitland choice, either that Western canon law was binding statute law or that the English Church enjoyed an unfettered discretion, does not need to be made since in most cases there was no conflict between the canon and common law in relation to principle; the difference was to be found in the detail. Donahue in his study of study of the records of the Consistory Court of York of 1300–99 concluded that there were three important variables (the institution, the time and the type of case) that needed to be taken into account, but that overall the relationship between the English courts and Rome could be characterised as one of great deference but not of blind adherence.

The Stubbs-Maitland debate, however, concerned the relationship between Church and State prior to the Reformation. The Reformation radically recast the relationship. The English Reformation saw the Catholic Church under the authority of the pope replaced by a Protestant Church under the ultimate authority of the king. This shift was earth-shattering. As Geoffrey Elton has commented, while in 1529 'no cleric in England (except a few heretics) doubted the papal claim to be, under Christ, supreme head of the church', by 1534, no one could assert such a claim without jeopardy of his life.[176] The divorce from Rome would have also seemed unlikely at the time. Henry VIII was a monarch, after all, who had maintained extremely friendly relations with Rome: Henry VIII's critique of the Protestant reforms of Luther had led Pope Leo X to bestow on Henry the title of 'Defender of the Faith' in 1521. And, although there was an element of anticlericalism present in England due to the wealth of the Church and the supposed corruption of its courts, heresy was not prevalent and such popular dislike of ecclesiastical institutions was not advanced enough to provide the catalyst for reform.[177]

The Reformation in England was unexpected because it differed in cause from the Reformation on the Continent. As we have seen, the Reformation on the continent was a

---

[173] William Stubbs, 'Historical Appendix' in *Report of the Commissioners into the Constitution and Workings of the Ecclesiastical Courts* (1883).
[174] Maitland, *Roman Canon Law in the Church of England*.
[175] Richard H Helmholz, *Roman Canon Law in Reformation England* (Cambridge University Press, 1990) chapter 1; Charles Donahue Jr, 'Roman Canon Law in the Medieval English Church: Stubbs vs. Maitland Re-Examined After 75 Years in the Light of Some Records from the Church Courts' (1974) 72 *Michigan Law Review* 647.
[176] Elton, 'The Reformation in England' 266. [177] Ibid. 262–3.

religious movement where Catholicism was replaced by the Protestantism of Luther.[178] Although Protestantism also replaced Catholicism in England, the difference was that 'England's march away from Rome was led by the government for reasons which had little to do with religion or faith.'[179] Henry's transformation from Defender of the Faith to attacker of the Catholic Church was motivated not so much by a religious or intellectual development but a transformation in the status of his personal relationship with the pope: Henry's change from being the pope's protector to the being the pope's enemy.[180]

As countless school textbooks, documentaries and dramas have depicted, the cause of the breakdown of the relationship between Henry and the pope was Henry's intention in 1527 to end his marriage to Catherine of Aragon. As Elton has noted, 'Without the divorce there would therefore have been no Reformation, which is not at all the same thing as to say that there was nothing to the Reformation but the divorce.'[181] The termination of the marriage proved controversial because, although the pope was able to declare the marriage null on one of the grounds provided under canon law, he was reluctant to do so for two reasons: first, Catherine's earlier marriage to Henry's brother had been dissolved by papal dispensation and so the pope was being asked to declare null his previous decision; and second, Pope Clement VII was now under the military influence of Charles V of Spain who was also Catherine's nephew.[182] As Elton has commented: 'Spanish influence and Clement's timidity were too much for Wolsey',[183] the chancellor of the time. Wolsey was subsequently replaced by Sir Thomas More, but the fact that More only accepted the chancellorship 'in return for a promise that he would not have to involve himself in the business of the divorce' meant that Henry VIII had to pursue a different approach.[184] It is this approach that was to lead to the Tudor transformation of statute law when diplomacy with the pope was disregarded in favour of the use of Parliament.[185] However, this did not happen straightaway. It is possible to identify three phases in the Reformation legislation under Henry VIII:

1   *Regulating the Relationship with Rome*

The first phase was that of continuity with renewed policing. At first, Parliament was used in its usual way to solve particular problems. The summoning of Parliament in this way was by no means surprising. As Elton has noted, it would have been more surprising if Parliament had not been summoned.[186] Yet, as he conceded, Henry VIII displayed 'considerable skill in using Parliament', sowing the seeds for even more skilful manoeuvres in the near future. In the years 1529–30, a flurry of bills were drafted and enacted that attacked various aspects of the Church and its courts by limiting fees and pardoning the clergy but fining the Church for sending cases to the Rome that ought to have been

---

[178] For further discussion, see, e.g., Diarmald MacCulloch, *Reformation: Europe's House Divided 1490–1700* (Allen Lane, 2003).
[179] Elton, 'The Reformation in England'.   [180] Ibid. 265.   [181] Ibid.   [182] Ibid. 267.   [183] Ibid.   [184] Ibid. 268.
[185] For a fuller examination of the effect upon religion, see Eamon Duffy, *The Stripping of the Altars* (2nd ed., Yale University Press, 2005), especially chapters 11–13.
[186] Elton, 'The Reformation in England' 268.

210 *The Tudor Transformation (c.1485–1603)*

resolved under the common law. This included the Probate Fees etc. Act of 1529, Mortuaries Act of 1529, Clergy Act of 1529 and the Pardon of Clergy Act of 1530–1. Although Elton may have over-played their significance in saying that the 'whole system of church courts came under attack',[187] this legislation provided the first indications of what is to come.

Such measures did not, however, solve the issue of the royal divorce. At this time, that issue was still the subject of negotiations with Rome. Although Henry talked of using Parliament to settle matters, in December 1530, 'his legal advisers declared such spiritual matters outside its competence'.[188] Similarly, at this time, there was no thought that Henry should become spiritual head of the Church. Although he managed to get the Church Assembly to acknowledged him as 'their only and supreme lord and, as far as the law of Christ allows, even supreme head', the reference to 'Law of Christ' was interpreted as referring to the canon law, and at this time even Henry's own interpretation of the acknowledgment 'gave him only temporal and no spiritual rights of headship'.[189] The germs of a revolution could be found here, however. The English Reformation would be truly underway once it was accepted that spiritual matters were within Parliament's competence and that Henry could become spiritual head of the English Church. As Elton noted: 'Once Henry was persuaded that the lawyers (and he himself) had been wrong – that the divorce did not need papal sanction and that Parliament could act in the matter – the way was clear.'[190]

2   *Cromwell's Constitutional Clash*

The man responsible for clearing the way was the king's new advisor, Thomas Cromwell. For Baker, 'Henry VIII's government under Cromwell was essentially autocratic, in the sense that, although the outward forms of law were strictly observed, both the judges and the legislature were in practice amenable to the king's will.'[191] Cromwell built on the grievances expressed in the 1529–30 legislation to produce much further reaching reform. This represented the second phase in the reformation legislation: the constitutional attack.

A flurry of pieces of legislation were enacted that took back control from the papacy. The Restraint of Payment of Annates Act of 1532 stated that revenues from the first year of profits should no longer go to Rome. The Ecclesiastical Appeals Act of 1533 declared 'that this realm of England is an empire', that is 'governed by one supreme head' and forbad 'the intermeddling of any exterior person or persons', including 'the annoyance as well of the see of Rome', forbidding all appeals to Rome. The Submission of the Clergy Act of 1534 stated that the Church assemblies could now only make law under 'the King's most royal assent and licence', and that the existing canon law was only to apply provided it was not 'contrariant or repugnant to the King's prerogative royal, or the customs, laws and statutes of this realm'.[192]

The Act of Supremacy 1534 stated that 'by the authority of this present Parliament, ... the King our sovereign lord, his heirs and successors kings of this realm, shall be taken,

---

[187] Ibid. 269.   [188] Ibid.   [189] Ibid.   [190] Ibid. 270.

[191] Baker, *The Oxford History of the Laws of England Volume VI 1483–1558* 66.

[192] Similarities can be drawn between the treatment of canon law at this time and the treatment of European Union law following the 2016 referendum decision to leave the European Union.

The Reformation of Statute Law 211

accepted and reputed the only supreme head in earth of the Church of England' and shall have 'all honours, dignities, preeminences, jurisdictions, privileges, authorities, immunities, profits and commodities, to the said dignity of the supreme head of the same Church', including 'the full power and authority from time to time to visit, repress, redress, reform, order, correct, restrain, amend all such errors, heresies, abuses, offences, contempts and enormities whatsoever they be'. The Treasons Act of 1534 added criminal sanctions to this claim, while a host of statutes bestowed rights of appointment previously invested in the pope to the king: most notably, the provisions of the Appointment of Bishops Act of 1533 and the Suffragan Bishops Act of 1534 gave the king the power to appoint bishops following their election within the Church.

For Elton, the 1533–4 legislation showed that 'the real attack on the papacy had begun, with the undermining of its legislative and financial powers over the church in England'.[193] These statutes crucially enabled the dissolution of the king's marriage, with the Ecclesiastical Appeals Act of 1533 being used to declare Henry's marriage to Catherine of Aragon void. The legislation clearly provided not only a schism from Rome but also a statement of the supremacy of the king. However, as Elton has argued, this supremacy was not parliamentary; Henry understood that he derived his supremacy from God: '[B]y virtue of his kingship he was also God's vicar on earth as far as his temporal dominions extended.'[194] This supremacy was recognised not created by Parliament. As Elton put it, the king's supremacy was not 'exercised in or through Parliament: it was personal, monarchical, even despotic, as had been the pope's from which it derived'.[195] Yet, Parliament had played an essential role in the Reformation: only Parliament could create new treasons by criminal legislation that could allow the common law courts to enforce the supremacy.[196] This first batch of statutes, however, had a minimal effect upon the doctrine and teaching of the Church. This was underscored by the provisions of the Submission of the Clergy Act of 1534 that allowed the old canon law to be continued to be applied, provisions that were intended as a transitory provision pending the writing of a new code of canon law but its rule was 'lengthened by inertia into permanence'.[197] The main effect of this stage of the Reformation on the courts and the laws spiritual was the admittance of laymen to judicial office.

3   A Religious Revolution

The third phase under Henry VIII was the religious and practical change. This was, in the words of Elton, 'the working out of the problems raised by that revolutionary change', including the economic crisis that the assertion of national sovereignty had caused.[198] This phase began with the dissolution of the monasteries, an event that 'has at times been allowed to usurp the first place in the story ... though in fact it is of less importance than the establishment of the supremacy'.[199] All monastic orders vanished from England over

---

[193] Elton, 'The Reformation in England' 271.   [194] Ibid.   [195] Ibid.   [196] Ibid. 271–2.
[197] Baker, *The Reports of Sir John Spelman Volume II* vol. 94, 70.   [198] Elton, 'The Reformation in England' 274–5.
[199] Ibid. 272.

212   *The Tudor Transformation (c.1485–1603)*

the course of four years, beginning with the smallest. This orderly process was permitted by statute law under the Dissolution of the Monasteries Act of 1534.[200] However, the main reason behind the dissolution of the monasteries was temporal rather than spiritual: although there may have been fears that the religious orders were dangerously papalist, there is no evidence to support this, and the fact was that 'the Crown needed money and the gentry needed lands'.[201]

At this point, the English Reformation was beginning to have religious effects. Although Henry VIII seemed 'to have thought that the break with Rome could be carried through without altering the doctrine and worship of the English church', nevertheless 'the political Reformation was beginning to stir up religious turmoil' with a certain cautious drifting away from beliefs and practices that were particularly Catholic such as the doctrine of purgatory.[202] Further, statutes were now passed by Parliament working out the detail of the Reformation and in the same way as it had been accepted that Parliament had the competence to determine constitutional matters, it was now accepted that it had competence to determine matters of religious doctrine. So, for example, the See of Rome Act of 1536 denounced the authority of the 'pretend power and usurped authority of the bishop of Rome, by some called the Pope', which had 'deceived the King's loving and obedient subjects, persuading them, by his laws, bulls and other his deceivable means such dreams, vanities and fantasies as by the same many of them were decided and conveyed unto superstitious and erroneous opinions'. It made submission to Rome an act of treason. It was notable that parliamentary statute was now used to determine and enforce religious doctrine. The Act of the Six Articles of 1539 made it an offence to say or print any opinions contrary to the Articles and also made refusing to confess or receive the sacrament an offence. This third phase of the Reformation under Henry VIII was largely prompted by the need to maintain order. As Elton noted, by 1539, the existence of very different religious ideas caused concern to the king and his advisers: '[T]he country was being torn in two by the upstart arrogance of the new religion and the boorish stubbornness of the old.'[203]

However, it was the death of Henry VIII that allowed the religious Reformation to fully occur in England. The short reign of Edward VI (1547–53) 'witnessed a revolution in religion as great as the jurisdictional revolution of the 1530s'.[204] Again, Parliament was used to pass a series of statutes to provide for religious conformity that was now more recognisably Protestant.[205] Moreover, Parliament not only created criminal offences but also stipulated in detail forms of worship and doctrinal teachings. Most notably, the Sacrament Act of 1547 provided that Parliament had the power to excommunicate and stated that the sacrament of the Eucharist was to include both bread and wine; while Acts of Uniformity in 1549 and 1552 mandated the use of the Book of Common Prayer during worship and made the use of any other ceremony or the speaking of anything derogating from the book an offence. The effect of such provisions was that 'England was now a

---

[200] The process was furthered under the (Second) Dissolution Act of 1539.   [201] Elton, 'The Reformation in England' 272.
[202] Ibid. 275.   [203] Ibid. 276–7.   [204] Ibid. 279.
[205] This included the further acquisition of religious property under the Abolition of Chantries Acts of 1545 and 1547; Baker, *The Oxford Laws of England Volume VI 1483–1558* 715–17.

The Reformation of Statute Law 213

Protestant country, at least so far as legislation and decree could make her one'.[206] Yet, such changes were only 'skin-deep' and Edward's death meant that there was not the necessary time to the changes to bed in and be enforced.[207]

The acceptance of the constitutional role and importance of Parliament was underscored under Mary I (1553–8) who sought to bring about a counter-Reformation aimed to restore the Catholic faith. Although she considered the Reformation legislation to be invalid, she accepted the advice of her advisers that only Parliament could undo what Parliament had done.[208] Selected statutes of Edward VI and all the Reformation statutes of Henry VIII were therefore repealed *en masse* by new Acts of Parliament.[209] However, other than this, Parliament's role in Mary's counter-Reformation was reduced to creating offences of treason and heresy rather than reforming religious doctrine.[210] This was typical of a counter-Reformation that, for Elton, 'contented itself with persecution and attempted nothing like a true spiritual revival'.[211] Mary's persecution of Protestants was therefore, in the words of Elton, 'a political error of the first magnitude'. It was now 'Protestantism, however thinly spread so far, [that] represented a genuine spirit of religion'.[212]

This was reflected under Elizabeth I (1558–1603), when there was a reversion back to Protestantism. Although a question mark still hovers over the private religion of the Virgin Queen, she became the nominee of the Protestant faction who returned after Mary's death and which made up an 'enthusiastic core' of the new Parliament.[213] Statute law was used once again to bring about the *volte-face*. Indeed, by this period, the 'ever-increasing torrent of legislation' generally was perturbing lawyers, as Baker noted:

Although most if it was accepted as necessary, the volume alone was coming to be seen as a problem. The proliferation of new statutes, often overlapping each other, their piecemeal and often short-term character, their convoluted draftsmanship, the clash of statutes apparently dealing differently with the same subject matter, the lapse of temporary statutes, the revival of repealed statutes, and the ambiguity of some apparent repeals, all led to considerable dissatisfaction with the corpus of legislation in this period. Statutes were also becoming longer and longer.[214]

The religious legislation fitted this overall picture. The Act of Supremacy 1559 restored to the crown the powers under Henry VIII, and revived legislation under Henry VIII and Edward VI while repealing Mary's legislation. It clearly stated, however, that 'all usurped and foreign power and authority, spiritual and temporal, may for ever be clearly extinguished and never used nor obeyed within this realm'. The Act of Uniformity of 1559 resurrected Edward VI''s legislation that mandated the use of the Book of Common Prayer as the uniform liturgy. And further statutes were passed to make it treasonable to seek or bring in documents from Rome or to withdraw allegiance to either the queen or Church of England,[215] with the Popish Recusants Act of 1593 requiring that Catholics remain within five miles of their usual abode and register themselves so that they could be fined or exiled.

---

[206] Elton, 'The Reformation in England' 282. [207] Ibid. 282–3. [208] Ibid. 285.
[209] See Elton, *The Tudor Constitution* 408–9, 368–72. [210] Treasons Act 1553; Heresy Act 1554; Treasons Act 1554.
[211] Elton, 'The Reformation in England' 286. [212] Ibid. [213] Ibid. 287.
[214] Baker, *English Law under Two Elizabeths* 291–2.
[215] Act Against Bulls from Rome of 1571; Act Against Obedience to Rome of 1581.

214 *The Tudor Transformation (c.1485–1603)*

In 1583, the High Commission Court was set up to supervise matters concerning religion and Church government.

These Elizabethan statutes restoring the work of the queen's father would have a long-lasting effect upon English law in two respects. The first concerned their content. Membership of the Church of England was seen as being synonymous with being a subject of the crown and the line between heresy and treason was blurred. It would take centuries for other religions to be tolerated, and even today the Church of England as a Church established by law remains in a different legal position than all other faiths.[216] The second legacy of these statutes concerned their form. Not only did the continued use of statute law show the omnipotence of Parliament in terms of declaring constitutional and doctrinal matters and controlling uniformity through the creation of offences, it also created an expectation that Parliament was the place to create and instigate such laws. As Elton has noted, although Elizabeth 'fought tenaciously to keep her Parliaments from interfering in matters ecclesiastical, she could never deny their right to participate'.[217] The way in which the English Reformation was achieved by the assumption of power and authority by the King in Parliament would create increased expectations on the part of both the monarch and Parliament in terms of the role that they would play in the running of the country. This represented a ticking time bomb that would explode under the Stuarts.

Under the Tudors, it had become accepted that the crown could not abrogate, repeal or suspend any Act of Parliament and the requirement for royal assent to legislation was understood from around 1510 to consist of a right to veto not to amend.[218] However, there remained uncertainty as to the residual powers of the monarch: those powers, rights and privileges collectively called the royal prerogative. This was shown not only by the growth of the new conciliar courts of the Chancery and Star Chamber but also by the uncertainty concerning the status of proclamations by monarchs. Although Maitland referred to the Act of Proclamations of 1539 as giving 'the force of statute to the king's proclamations',[219] Elton has commented that few would regard the statute in that light today and that it is now thought that proclamations were 'regarded as inferior to statute and common law' and were not enforced by the common law courts but were enforced by the Star Chamber.[220] Moreover, although the Act of Proclamations of 1539 was repealed in 1547, this 'made no different to the range of proclamations issued'.[221] The practice became that proclamations were 'used to support statutes rather than to replace them'.[222]

Parliament, therefore, remained in a state of adolescence. In regulating constitutional and religious matters, it was now being trusted to deal with matters of the utmost importance. However, it was not independent from the monarch. Indeed, the legislation of the Reformation and counter-Reformation underscore that Parliament was doing the monarch's bidding, a matter that would lead to growing tension.

---

[216] See Russell Sandberg, *Law and Religion* (Cambridge University Press, 2011) particularly chapters 2 and 4.
[217] Elton, 'The Reformation in England' 283.   [218] Elton, *The Tudor Constitution* 20, 21.
[219] Maitland, *English Law and the Renaissance* 19.   [220] Elton, *The Tudor Constitution* 22.
[221] Baker, *The Oxford Laws of England Volume VI 1483–1558* 64.   [222] Ibid.

IV   The Tudor Common Law

In some respects, the teenager-like experience of Parliament was also reflected in the common law. As Ibbetson has put it: 'The sixteenth century marks a transitional stage between the medieval law, which was heavily dominated by the forms of action, and the modern law, with its focus on substantive rules and principles.'[223] This adolescent phase can be seen in several areas of the law. The following will briefly and selectively examine four developments in what we would call the law of obligations, land and crime. The four developments are: the concept of consideration in contract law; the development of the action of ejectment to recover freehold land; the creation of the trust; and the demarcation of murder and manslaughter.[224]

1   *Consideration*

The Tudor law of obligations was clearly in an adolescent state. As we saw in the last chapter, the action on the case had been used to overcome the limitations of the medieval law of contracts. As Baker noted, the action of debt remained 'bedevilled by a survival from Anglo-Saxon times called wager of war, which meant that an unprincipled debtor could swear way out of debt without a trial of the facts'.[225] This had meant that creditors seeking a better remedy had found one in assumpsit, and so for over a century had been 'treating a breach of promise as an honorary tort'.[226] This continued under the Tudors but 'governing principles' became established so that not all promises could be enforced by the action of assumpsit. By *Golding's case*,[227] it was held that there were three ingredients required for an action on the case for assumpsit: a promise, the breach of that promise and consideration. The concept of consideration, according to Baker, 'brought together the notion of a quid pro quo (a benefit to the promissor), which was the hallmark of a bargain, and the detriment to the plaintiff which was the requisite for an action in tort'.[228] With actions for assumpsit for debt being permitted by *Slade's case*,[229] the requirement of consideration became central to English contract law – a position that has remained ever since (at least in terms of contractual theory). Yet, the question of the origins of consideration remains unclear. Baker has argued that 'no other doctrine in English law can compete with "consideration" for the greatest diversity and complexity of historical explanations' and that 'anyone who attempts to augment, even by a few pages, all that has already been written on this vexed subject must at the outset acknowledge his own foolhardiness'.[230]

---

[223] David J Ibbetson, *A Historical Introduction to the Law of Obligations* (Oxford University Press, 1999) 95.

[224] These examples are illustrative. For a fuller discussion of the substantive law of the period, see Baker, *The Oxford Laws of England Volume VI 1483–1558* parts ix, x, viii and vi and Baker, *English Law under Two Elizabeths* chapter 2.

[225] Ibid. 64.   [226] Ibid.   [227] (1586) 2 Leon. 73.   [228] Baker, *English Law under Two Elizabeths* 64.

[229] (1598) 4 Co Rep 92b. The case was hailed by Milsom as 'the climax of the process by which a new law of contract was derived from trespassory remedies', though he noted that Edward Coke's report of the case showed that older ideas remained intact; SFC Milsom, *Historical Foundations of the Common Law* (2nd ed., Butterworths, 1981) 353. Recent scholarship has questioned whether developments occurred earlier; John H Baker, 'Indebitatus Assumpsit in 1447' (2021) *Cambridge Law Journal* 39.

[230] John H Baker, 'Origin of the Doctrine of "Consideration"' in Morris S Arnold, Thomas A. Green, Sally A. Scully and Stephen D. White (eds.), *On the Laws and Customs of England: Essays in Honor of S E Thorne* (University of North Carolina Press, 1981) 336, 336–7.

216   *The Tudor Transformation (c.1485–1603)*

As with the debate as to the origins of trespass, the debate as to the origins of consideration has been transformed by the realisation and appreciation that there is not one single answer or cause to the question, and that the question we are asking is a modern and anachronistic question. As Baker noted, '[T]here is no reason to suppose that sixteenth-century lawyers were unanimous as to the nature, let alone the intellectual sources, of the doctrine of consideration.' He noted that had 'the matter had been plain then, it would be more readily clarifiable now'.[231]

It is possible to identify two main groups of theories. The first group may be styled the 'internal development' arguments. These theories suggest that the doctrine of consideration was, in the words of CHS Fifoot, 'a domestic invention of the common law'.[232] One such theory, purported by Oliver Wendell Holmes Jr, is that the origin is to be found in the requirement of *quid pro quo* in the action of debt.[233] Another theory, put forward by JB Ames, is that the doctrine of consideration evolved from the law of assumpsit, and in particular the requirement that there was detriment to the claimant.[234] As we have noted, Baker suggested that consideration brought these two ideas together;[235] but this is not the same as saying that it was the result of one or the other (or indeed both). Fifoot saw the concept of consideration as the common law's response to the increase in commercial activity; the requirement for consideration stressed the commercial significance of the agreement and thus merited the court's involvement.[236] These 'internal development' theories all see consideration as a practical adaptation made within the legal system itself. As Fifoot put it, '[T]he "mystery of consideration" which the Victorian lawyers found so fascinating becomes no more than a practical answer to an urgent problem.' However, these explanations fail to convince. The work of Holmes and Ames do not explain why the existing common law concepts were adapted and fall down on the basis that the concept of consideration went further than these existing concepts. As for Fifoot, Brian Simpson showed that whilst merchants might have sought to enforce their contracts in court, they used the writ of debt not the action of assumpsit.[237]

The second group of theories may be styled 'external influence' arguments. These all see the doctrine of consideration as being 'an exotic imported from a more luxurious jurisprudence'.[238] These explanations rest on the assumption that the concept of consideration could not have been a logical development from within the action of assumpsit.[239] John Salmond suggested that the principle was derived from Roman law and had been imported through the Court of Chancery.[240] Yet, Theodore Plucknett countered that 'this possibility must not be over-estimated' on the basis that philosophical idea of conscience,

---

[231] Ibid.   [232] CHS Fifoot, *History and Sources of the Common Law* (Stevens & Sons, 1949) 399.
[233] Oliver W Holmes Jr, *The Common Law* (Dover Publications, 1991 [1881]) 253 *et seq*. See also William S Holdsworth, *A History of English Law Volume VII* (Methuen & Co, 1925) 3.
[234] JB Ames, *Lectures on Legal History and Miscellaneous Legal Essays* (Harvard University Press, 1913) 129 *et seq*.
[235] Baker, *English Law under Two Elizabeths* 64.   [236] Fifoot, *History and Sources of the Common Law* 399.
[237] AW Brian Simpson, *History of the Common Law of Contract* (Clarendon Press, 1987).
[238] Fifoot, *History and Sources of the Common Law* 399.
[239] John W Salmond, *Essays in Jurisprudence and Legal History* (Franklin, 1891) 187–94, 207–24; John W Salmond, 'The History of Contract' (1887) 3 *Law Quarterly Review* 171. See also WT Barbour, *History of Contract in Early English Equity* (Oxford University Press, 1914).
[240] Salmond, 'The History of Contract' 171, 176–7.

The Tudor Common Law

and the political idea of prerogative upon which Chancery took its stand, were alike 'anathema to the common lawyers'.[241] He reasoned that 'common lawyers were eager to afford rival remedies to those of Chancery, but equally stubborn in evolving these remedies from their own common law heritage, without borrowing Chancery's theories'.[242] Simpson argued that the concept of consideration began as a moral rather than legal term and can be understood as part of the theological influence upon law documented in St Germain's *Doctor and Student*.[243] Yet, assuming that judicial decisions existed within a theoretical framework not only assumes a wide knowledge on the part of legal actors but also seems unlikely given the pragmatic nature of legal decisions. KO Shatwell argued against this 'tendency to push analysis of the doctrine itself on to a plane of abstraction' on the basis that it 'complicates with unnecessary theoretical difficulties the practical approach of the common law to the practical requirements of daily life'.[244]

More recent historians have favoured a middle-way approach that stresses pragmatism and practicality. Milsom has argued that, yet again, historians 'have tried to be too precise, to trace the later meaning of a legal word back to some single source; and we have complicated the task by supposing that even in the later law the word had a meaning in the sense of representing an idea'.[245] Yet, he further argued that this does not mean that the potential causes highlighted by others are irrelevant. They do not provide a single origin of consideration in the same way as it is not possible to identify a single origin of trespass. Nevertheless, each possible origin is 'clearly ... part of a story which cannot be understood without it'.[246] When looking at cases before them, legal actors would have sought to develop ideas that were already developing in the common law, and they were also likely to have had ideas from Roman law and the Court of Chancery in mind. As Ibbetson has stressed, the development of the concept of consideration was a practical and pragmatic matter. Consideration was simply the term used to describe the 'necessary feature' that promises needed to have in order to be enforceable.[247] It served to identify the victim and whether they had standing to bring an action following the breach of a promise.

Regardless of its origin, the concept of consideration was to prove to be the bridge between the historic law and the modern law of contract. Of course, there were later developments in the law of contract that proved to be important. However, these built upon the law of assumpsit and the doctrine of consideration. As Ibbetson put it:

The seventeenth and eighteenth centuries marked a period of consolidation of the law of contract, the fleshing-out of the skeletal structure that had been locked into place by the end of the sixteenth century ... The eighteenth-century lawyers' model of contract owed a great deal to their predecessors. At its heart was the qualified idea of reciprocal agreement, in its essence indistinguishable from the conception formulated before the beginning of the seventeenth century.[248]

---

[241] Theodore FT Plucknett, *A Concise History of the Common Law* (5th ed., Liberty Fund, 2010 [1956]) 652.   [242] Ibid.
[243] Simpson, *History of the Common Law of Contract* 376.
[244] KO Shatwell, 'The Origin of Consideration in the Modern Law' (1954) 1 *Sydney Law Review* 289, 319.
     Ibid. 317.   [245] Milsom, *Historical Foundations of the Common Law*, 2nd ed. 358.   [246] Ibid.
[247] Ibbetson, *A Historical Introduction to the Law of Obligations* 142.   [248] Ibid. 202–3.

218   *The Tudor Transformation (c.1485–1603)*

2   *Ejectment*

Similar trends can be discerned in relation to the Tudor land law, which was also in a noticeable state of adolescence. On one hand, there were certain continuities back to the reign of Henry II (discussed in Chapter 5): land remained the principle form of investment and so land law, the law of real property, continued to dominate private law.[249] As Baker put it, '[L]and law was therefore by far the most important subject the law student had to tackle, beginning with his pocket copy of Littleton's *Tenures*.' Yet, the complex framework concerning the protection of land, discussed in Chapter 5, had become simplified: 'The perplexing array of medieval procedures, with the arcane learning built around them, had largely given way ... to the more straightforward action of ejectment.'[250]

This action of ejectment provides a further example of the blurring of categories and areas of law. Ejectment had begun as a remedy for those who were outside the feudal ladder. It gave a remedy to those who did not have seisin, those who were not the freeholders of land. It began as a remedy for those who leased the land – known as the termors – who paid for land for a set term of years and so who were what we would call leaseholders. The real actions described in Chapter 5 could not be a remedy for termors. As Milsom put it, they were 'simply not within the contemplation of those feudal customs for which novel disessin was meant to provide a further sanction'.[251]

Two writs of ejectment were originally drafted between 1235 and 1237. The first was limited to situations where there was a connection between the lord and ejector, and the second was limited to providing damages rather than giving the property back. However, the limitation on this second writ was gradually relaxed and ejectment became used to recover the land and not simply to receive damages.[252] This made the action an attractive one for freeholders as well as leaseholders. As Milsom noted, although the 'writs of entry did not fall out of use', *Novel Disseisin* had become the 'principal vehicle for litigation about the title to land'.[253] However, this began to fall out of use itself. Milsom speculated that a reason for this might have been the desire to 'keep the claimant out of a range of criminal sanctions', given that the justices of the assize were also a part of the criminal administration.[254] Regardless of the reason, freeholders began to look for a new action to cover disputes as to the title of their land, and they found it by appropriating the action that had developed for leaseholders: the writ of ejectment.

By the sixteenth and seventeenth centuries, this writ of ejectment was used by freeholders and became, in the words of Maitland, 'the common means of recovering possession of land, no matter the kind of title that the claimant asserts'.[255] He noted that the explanation of how this was so constitutes a complex story where 'it is hard to fix any dates', and which

---

[249] Baker, *English Law Under Two Elizabeths* 54.   [250] Ibid.

[251] Milsom, *Historical Foundations of the Common Law*, 2nd ed. 153.

[252] AW Brian Simpson, *A History of the Land Law* (2nd ed., Oxford University Press, 1986) 144.

[253] It became accepted that a claimant did not need to actually disseise the tenant of his land. Rather, if the claimant had what was called 'a right of entry', then he became seised when he entered the land, meaning that when the tenant removed him from the land, the claimant could then recover the land in *Novel Disseisin*. As Milsom pointed out, 'great artificiality resulted' (Milsom, *Historical Foundations of the Common Law*, 2nd ed. 157).

[254] Ibid. 161.   [255] Frederic W Maitland, *The Forms of Action at Common Law* (Cambridge University Press, 1965 [1909]) 57.

The Tudor period was characterised by adolescence, with medieval law only

included the 'cover of an elaborate fiction'.[256] It began by freeholders circumventing the law: freeholders would nominally grant leases to friends solely so they could use the writ of ejectment if their land was taken.[257] As Simpson noted, such leases 'would not be a serious lease' but would only be granted so that if there was a dispute over land, the nominal leaseholder could use the action of ejectment rather than the real freeholder using *Novel Disseisin*. Simpson stated that in the 1560s and 1570s this practice 'seems to have become fairly common', despite the 'inconvenience involved which required that the nominal plaintiff be ejected from the land'.[258]

Again, the Tudor period was characterised by adolescence, with medieval law only being superseded after the Tudor reign. From the early years of the seventeenth century, the fiction went further and the nominal termor became fictitious. Over time, the courts began to relax technical requirements and eventually 'the need for an actual entry and ouster came to be removed'.[259] As Milsom remarked 'an element of pantomime was involved', given that an imaginary leasehold tenant usually called John Doe was said to be dispossessed by an equally fictional servant of the third party often called Richard Roe.[260] Yet, as Simpson noted, the 'whole ingenious rigmarole did away with the need for any actual lease ... and was obviously more convenient.'[261] By the seventeenth century, the action of ejectment 'had become the usual mechanism for claiming land'.[262] The writ of ejectment was an action in trespass, and so, like the law of contract, the law of property was revolutionised and transformed by trespass, befitting Maitland's description of trespass as 'that fertile mother of actions'.[263]

3   *Trusts*

The way in which the Tudor law of property was an uneasy mixture of the medieval and the modern can also be seen in developments that were to lead to the trust, which Maitland famously hailed as 'the greatest and most distinctive achievement performed by Englishmen in the field of jurisprudence'.[264] In a modern trust, the settlor (the legal owner) transfers property to trustees who then hold the legal title but who are compelled to allow another (the beneficiaries) to use and enjoy the property. The interest of the beneficiaries is not a matter of common law but of equity. The use was the forerunner of the modern trust and similarly split the enjoyment of the property from the ownership of the property. In the medieval context, the terminology was different: the tenant of land created a use by feoffing (giving the fee) to feoffees, who were the legal owners and had seisin of the land; the feoffees would hold the land for the *cestui que use*, that is, those to whose use the feoffment was made. The tenant therefore was the equivalent of the modern settlor; the feoffees the equivalent to the trustees

---

[256] Ibid. 59, 57.   [257] Simpson, *A History of the Land Law* 145.   [258] Ibid.   [259] Ibid. 146.

[260] Ibid. 147–8. They were sometimes alternatively spelled 'Doo' and 'Roo'; Milsom, *Historical Foundations of the Common Law*, 2nd ed. 161–2.

[261] Simpson, *A History of the Land Law* 148.

[262] The Doe-Roe fictions only finally disappeared in the Common Law Procedure Act 1852; Milsom, *Historical Foundations of the Common Law*, 2nd ed. 162, 163.

[263] Maitland, *The Forms of Action at Common Law*, 2nd ed. 48.

[264] Frederic W Maitland, *State, Trust and Corporation* (Cambridge University Press, 2003 [1911]) 52.

220   *The Tudor Transformation (c.1485–1603)*

and the *cestui que use* were the equivalent to beneficiaries. As JMW Bean put it, 'What happened was that a distinction was drawn between the actual ownership of the land and the view which the common law took of its ownership.'[265]

The interests of the *cestui que use*, like that of the beneficiaries of the modern trust, were not recognised by the common law. The arrangement was therefore risky in that if anything went wrong, the *cestui que use* could not use the law to invoke their rights. As Plucknett noted, the use began as a 'situation rather than an institution'.[266] However, there has been controversy over what was the situation. Both 'Pollock and Maitland'[267] and William Holdsworth[268] stated that there were records of uses having been created before the Norman Conquest. Indeed, implicit reference is made to it in the Doomsday Book. There is much debate as to the origin of the use: the situation or situations in which it arose, and whether it was derived from an older idea.[269] It is often asserted that the use became popular during the Crusades but Bean contended that 'their growth of popularity within the ranks of the nobility and gentry coincided with the opening stages of the Hundred Years' War with France'.[270] In both possible situations, the use was the means by which property was disposed of and kept safe before the tenants went abroad. It was a means by which tenants could secure their land against political instability or bankruptcy, could avoid feudal dues or commit simple fraud.[271] The use provided a means of making an unofficial will of land. As Simpson pointed out, it was a 'definite and extremely important settled rule' that 'uses could be disposed of by will' whilst 'common law estates, of course, could not'.[272] The landholder could transfer his land to the feoffees, who would hold it for him for the rest of his life and then the land could be passed for the enjoyment of persons who he named after his death in a document that he has executed.

These uses would neither be interpreted nor enforced by the common law courts because the common law recognised only the legal title of the feoffees.[273] Helmholz's research has supported Maitland's suggestion that the early uses may have been enforced by the Church courts.[274] However, by the end of the fifteenth century, they had become enforced by the Court of Chancery as part of what would be known as its equity jurisdiction. Holdsworth said that the use was the product of the equitable jurisdiction of the chancellor.[275] However, Bean rejected this view on the basis that it 'puts the cart before the horse', in that the use was commonly used before the Court of Chancery sought to regulate it.[276] As Milsom argued, '[I]t is likely that uses were as much a cause as a product of regular Chancery intervention.'[277] Moreover, as Helmholz has pointed out, his research shows that 'the rise of the Chancellor's jurisdiction over feoffees to uses is not, therefore,

---

[265] JWM Bean, *The Decline of English Feudalism* (Manchester University Press, 1968) 104.

[266] Plucknett, *Concise History of the Common Law* 579.

[267] Frederick Pollock and Frederic W Maitland, *The History of English Law* (2nd ed., Cambridge University Press, 1968 [1898]) vol. 2, 229, 234

[268] Holdsworth, *A History of English Law Volume IV* 412.

[269] Milsom, *Historical Foundations of the Common Law*, 2nd ed. 200. See Avisheh Avini, 'The Origins of the Modern English Trust Revisited' (1996) 70 *Tulane Law Review* 1139 and Bean, *The Decline of English Feudalism* 126 *et seq.*

[270] Ibid. 144.

[271] AW Brian Simpson, *An Introduction to the History of Land Law* (2nd ed., Oxford University Press, 1986) 174–5.

[272] Ibid. 182.   [273] Richard H Helmholz, 'The Early Enforcement of Uses' (1979) 79 *Columbia Law Review* 1503.

[274] Cf. Pollock and Maitland, *The History of English Law* 232.   [275] Holdsworth, *A History of English Law Volume IV* 417–18.

[276] Bean, *The Decline of English Feudalism* 129.   [277] Milsom, *Historical Foundations of the Common Law*, 2nd ed. 210.

The Tudor Common Law   221

the story of the creation of a legal remedy where previously there had been none. Rather it is the story of continuing enforcement in a new setting.'[278]

The Tudor period saw the decline of the use and the rise of the trust because legislative actions were taken against the use. Uses were seen negatively because they undermined the position and finances of lords (including the king) by providing a means to make an unofficial will and to avoid feudal incidents. Henry VII legislated so that feudal incidents were levelled on interests under uses.[279] However, Henry VII was 'not powerful enough' to force through major reform.[280] Such reform was needed under Henry VIII, however, as the Reformation disputes with Rome and other foreign ambitions meant that funds were desperately needed.[281] Following a Draft Bill in 1529, which was defeated in the House of Commons,[282] Henry turned to the courts instead. His challenge to how Lord Dacre of the South had left much of his land tied up in uses that was presented as an act of 'fraud and collusion between Lord Dacre and his counsel to defraud the king' showed that Henry was serious about reform and would make uses unlawful if Parliament did not compromise.[283] As Bean pointed out, '[T]he king got his way by means of extra-parliamentary manoeuvres that ultimately gave him a victory over uses in courts of law.'[284]

The Statute of Uses of 1536 was a piece of 'radical legislation', which constituted five years' work.[285] Its preamble has been described by Simpson as 'a diatribe against the supposed evil' of uses and as 'mere propaganda'.[286] The statute decreed that where feoffees held land to the use of the beneficiary and had seisin vested in them, then the use is to be executed so that the seisin passes to the beneficiary.[287] This would mean that legal ownership passes to the beneficiary. This would apply 'where one stands seised to the use of another'. The reference to 'standing' was interpreted to only refer to uses where the feoffees had nothing to do; that is, they have no active duties to perform. If the feoffees had active duties to perform because, for example, the beneficiary was an infant (an heir under twenty-one), then the feoffee is not seen to 'stand', and thus the use is not executed. The reference to seisin means that only uses of freehold land were to be executed. Some uses continued to exist, therefore. This also applied to the use upon a use: the situation where land was conveyed to A to the use of B to the use of C.[288] The first use would be executed but the second would not, and this became known as a trust.[289] Simpson noted that, while the terms 'use' and 'trust' had become interchangeable, now the 'use' referred solely in relation to purposes for which they were executed under the statue and so the unexecuted use became known as a trust.[290]

---

[278] Helmholz, 'Early Enforcement of Uses' 1513.
[279] This was by no means the first attempt. A statute was passed under Edward IV but this was repealed under Richard II; Bean, *The Decline of English Feudalism* 238–9.
[280] Ibid. 256.   [281] Ibid. 257.   [282] Ibid. 259, the bill is printed in Holdsworth, *A History of English Law Volume IV* 572–4.
[283] See Bean, *The Decline of English Feudalism* 275–84 and JH Baker and SFC Milsom, *Sources of English Legal History* (2nd ed., Oxford University Press, 2010) 127–32.
[284] Bean, *The Decline of English Feudalism* 272.
[285] Simpson, *An Introduction to the History of Land Law* 184; Bean, *The Decline of English Feudalism* 258.
[286] Simpson, *An Introduction to the History of Land Law* 186.   [287] See Watkin, *The Legal History of Wales* 125, 136–7.
[288] Ibid 201.
[289] *Ash* v. *Gallen* (1668) 1Ch. cases. Barton has argued that the use upon the use was enforced in Chancery before *Ash* v. *Gallen*; JL Barton, 'The Statute of Uses and Trusts of Freeholds' (1966) 82 *Law Quarterly Review* 562. See also NG Jones, 'Tyrrel's Case (1557) and the Use upon a Use (1993) 14(2) *Journal of Legal History* 75.
[290] Simpson, *An Introduction to the History of Land Law* 204.

222   *The Tudor Transformation (c.1485–1603)*

Such trust came to be enforced through the Court of Chancery, and became a main feature of what was to become known as the equity jurisdiction.

Two other pieces of legislation were also important: the Statute of Enrolments of 1536 and the Statute of Wills of 1540. Together, they show the adolescence that character-ised property law at the time.[291] The Statute of Enrolments of 1536 overcame an issue created by the Statute of Uses, while the Statute of Wills of 1540 reduced the potency of the Statute of Uses. It used to be said that the Statute of Enrolments of 1536 followed the Statute of Uses in quick succession in order to remedy a lacuna. However, according to JM Kaye,[292] the two statutes were produced together. Simpson wrote that the second statute is 'best considered as a sub-provision of the first'.[293] The Statute of Enrolments of 1536 pro-vided that records needed to be kept of the exchange of freehold land; this was necessary since the Statute of Uses of 1536 executed uses, and therefore transferred ownership. The Statute of Wills of 1540, by contrast, was a reaction to the popular reaction against the 'nightmare results' of the 1536 Statutes, which had removed the ability to make an unofficial will of land.[294] The Statute of Wills of 1540 remedied this by providing for the first time the chance for landholders to make an official will of freehold land. Socage tenants could dispose of all of their land by will, whilst those of military tenure could dispose of two-thirds of their land by will. The preamble to the 'long and complicated' statute emphasised the king's benevolence.[295] Commentators, however, have seen it as a right royal defeat:

The details of the Act of Wills show clearly that in consenting to its promulgation Henry VIII was surrendering a large part of the gains he had secured through the Statute of Uses ... There can be no doubt that the Statute of Wills constituted a *volte face* on the part of the Crown that can only be explained in terms of hostility which the Statute of Uses have evoked among the country's landowners.[296]

For Bean, the Statute of Wills was a compromise.[297] It was not a complete failure for Henry in that it still gave him 'a measure of control over the loss of feudal incidents through uses which had been denied to his predecessors for almost two centuries'.[298] It also, in the words of Simpson, reflected the 'chaotic state of the land law', which 'was all the more lamentable during a period of social upheaval marked by an increase in the property and social status of the lesser landowners'.[299] The Tudor legislation showed how property law was caught in a state of transition between the medieval and the modern: land could now be inherited and was fast becoming like any other good. The reforms them-selves were also unprecedented. As Milsom noted, no radical reform as serious as the Henrician legislation was considered in any branch of law until the eighteenth century.[300]

---

[291] See, generally, AR Ruck, 'The Politics of Land Law in Tudor England, 1529–1540' (1990) 11(2) *Journal of Legal History* 200.

[292] JM Kaye, 'A Note on the Statute of Enrolments, 1536' (1988) 104 *Law Quarterly Review* 617.

[293] Simpson, *An Introduction to the History of Land Law* 184.

[294] Milsom, *Historical Foundations of the Common Law*, 2nd ed. 218.

[295] Ibid. See Baker and Milsom, *Sources of English Legal History* 215–18.   [296] Bean, *The Decline of English Feudalism* 294.

[297] Ibid. 301.   [298] Ibid. 258   [299] Simpson, *An Introduction to the History of Land Law* 198.

[300] Milsom, *Historical Foundations of the Common Law*, 2nd ed. 220.

The Tudor Common Law 223

4   *Murder and Manslaughter*

The adolescence of what we would call criminal law was a different experience than that found in other areas of law. This is perhaps most emphasised – and perhaps overstated – by Milsom. The sole chapter on crime in his *Historical Foundations of the Common Law* described its history as 'miserable', lamented that 'nothing worth-while was created' and argued that 'the main interest of the subject is as a control against which to assess the development of other branches of the law'.[301] Milsom's argument was that, while by the sixteenth century the common law had created 'one intellectual system' based upon the forms of action, by contrast, 'in criminal matters, there had been almost no substantive developments'.[302] The criminal process 'was still seen more as an administrative exercise' reliant on the local community and justices of the peace rather than 'a forensic exercise in the investigation of evidence'.[303] A substantive criminal law did not have the chance to develop in the King's Court because, when the defendant was accused of a felony, the jury would simply 'render its yes-or-no verdict, and the defendant would stand convicted or acquitted'.[304] Although there would likely be professional conversations in the Inns of Court, 'until the twentieth century, a point arising in an actual trial would be formally discussed only if the judge decided to reserve the case'.[305] A criminal trial, therefore, did not allow for the 'kind of discussion by which law develops as an intellectual system'.[306]

Milsom was not alone in making such comments. James Fitzjames Stephen wrote that the criminal law could 'scarcely be said to have a history', in that there was 'no such series of continuously connected changes in the whole system as the use of the word "history" implies'.[307] Lindsay Farmer has argued that criminal law does have a history but:

there is an important sense in which the history of the criminal law begins only in the modern period. Before that time there were individual crimes or wrongs, and rules for their punishment, which have a rich and distinctive history of their own, but, as Stephen suggests, there was no separate understanding of the idea of criminal law as a unified and purposive body of rules – of criminal law as an institution – that could have its own history.[308]

James Gordley has made a similar point more generally about the common law, contending that it was not until the nineteenth century and the abolition of the writ system that there developed a substantive law detached from the law of procedure.[309] For Gordley, the dominance of the writ system and of the jury meant that decisions were being made

---

[301] Ibid. 403.   [302] Ibid. 413.
[303] Baker, *English Law Under Two Elizabeths* 68. For discussion of 'the ways in which questions of criminal law could be asked, discussed and resolved', see John H Baker, 'The Refinement of English Criminal Jurisprudence 1500–1848' in Louis A Knafla (eds.), *Crime and Criminal Justice in Europe and Canada*, (Wilfrid Laurier University Press, 1981) 17, reprinted John H Baker, *Collected Papers on English Legal History* (Cambridge University Press, 2013) 989.
[304] Thomas P Gallanis, 'The Evolution of the Common Law' in Troy L Harris (ed.), *Studies in Canon Law and Common Law in Honor of R H Helmholz* (The Robbins Collection, 2015) 61, 70.
[305] Milsom, *Historical Foundations of the Common Law*, 2nd ed. 424. See further Baker, *The Oxford Laws of England Volume VI 1483–1558* 526–8.
[306] Milsom, *Historical Foundations of the Common Law*, 2nd ed. 403.
[307] James Fitzjames Stephen, *History of the Criminal Law of England* (Macmillan, 1883) vol. 1, 6
[308] Lindsay Farmer, *Making the Modern Criminal Law: Criminalisation and Civil Order* (Oxford University Press, 2016) 63–4.
[309] James Gordley, *The Jurists: A Critical History* (Oxford University Press, 2013) 21.

224 *The Tudor Transformation (c.1485–1603)*

without reasons, resulting in a 'patchwork of unrationalized decisions laid down as the judges dealt with particular cases'.[310]

However, it depends upon what you are looking for. To return to Patrick Wormald's suggestion, discussed in Chapter 3, it depends whether you are looking at the history of law or the history of lawyers – that is, the history of the legal system or the history of law as experienced.[311] If the focus is on the history of law understood as the history of the legal system, then the Milsom-Gordley thesis stands; it could possibly be said that the history does not begin until the modern era. If, however, the focus is on the history of lawyers, the history of law as experienced, then the history begins before this. This second approach is to be preferred. The early history of crimes before the development of the legal system should not be omitted from our study, and the reason for this can be found in the work of Milsom itself.

There is a notable difference between the texts of the opening page of Milsom's chapter of crime in his first and second editions. His first edition stated: 'There is no achievement to trace. Except in so far as the maintenance or order is itself admirable, nobody is to be admired before age of reform. Centuries of civilisation have passed the subject by, so that the law itself still largely reads like an Anglo-Saxon tariff.'[312] By contrast, his second edition stated that: 'There are only administrative achievements to trace. So far as justice was done throughout the centuries, it was done by jurors and despite of savage laws. The lawyers contributed humane but shabby expedients, which did not develop into new approaches.'[313]

The language of his first edition of his book was considerably stronger. In his second edition, by contrast, he conceded that there were 'administrative achievements to trace'. It may be recalled,[314] that his book began by stating that: 'The common law is the by product of an administrative triumph, the way in which the government of England came to be centralised and specialised during the centuries after the Conquest.'[315] This recognises that the early criminal law was in the same state as the early common law: the focus was more on order than law. Law (or at least the creation, application and enforcement of rules that we could now identify as law) was an administrative means of maintaining order that was employed in a pragmatic manner without any thought of developing an overall system, an overall intellectual framework. It follows that the study of the early criminal law is as important as the early common law. The study of the history of law is limited if it extends only so far back as the development of the legal system, to the development of law as an intellectual system.

The history of criminal law, like the history of the common law generally, needs to go back beyond the development of a system. It needs to extend to how law was used as an administrative means to maintain order. Law still performs this function, even when an intellectual system has come into existence. The creation of the legal system, of the criminal justice system, is historically significant but it is not the starting point. The

---

[310] Ibid. 26.   [311] Patrick Wormald, *Lawyers and the State: The Varieties of Legal History* (Selden Society, 2006) 19.
[312] SFC Milsom, *Historical Foundations of the Common Law* (1st ed., Butterworths, 1969) 353.
[313] Milsom, Historical Foundations of the Common Law, 2nd ed. 403.   [314] See Chapter 3.
[315] Milsom, *Historical Foundations of the Common Law*, 2nd ed. 11.

The Tudor Common Law 225

development of such systems promotes the idea that law is autonomous, self-perpetuating, universal and natural. This hides how the system is both constructed by people and how it can be changed by people. 'The law' operates as a form of artificial intelligence. It is illusionary. The development of law as an intellectual system limits not only the scope of change and legal reform but also of the legal imagination. The development of such systems is not natural and is far from universal; it is a late development.

Milsom, Farmer and Gordley, therefore, are talking about the origins of criminal law as an intellectual system. Even then, there is a debate to be had about when that system arose and whether it came into existence later than the development of the modern legal system generally. As we have seen, Baker's account dated the development of modern legal thought and reasoning to the sixteenth century.[316] However, this should not distract us from going further back in time. Regardless of how developed it was as a system compared to other parts of the common law, it is clear that important developments in criminal law and order occurred during this period.[317]

The criminal law, in the words of Baker, 'was kept simple and undeveloped because it was designed to be understood by common jurors'.[318] This meant that hard rules were often made fairer by creative means.[319] Milsom gave the example that a jury 'could save a thief from the gallows by adjusting the value of property he had stolen'.[320] Although murder and all felonies[321] had a fixed sentence of death, most of those sentenced to death were not actually executed.[322] Many prayed 'benefit of clergy', which by 1490 was routinely used by laymen as well as clerics.[323] The test had become whether the accused could read or recite a particular passage from the Bible while on his knees. By the sixteenth century, around half of all men charged with felony escaped death by this means.

There were, however, some developments in the substantive criminal law in the Tudor period.[324] This was particularly true of murder and theft, which Milsom described in the first edition of his book as 'legal monoliths, because they are unalterable parts of the social landscape'.[325] Some uniformity was beginning to be achieved, 'though the discussion of reserving cases from the assizes for discussion back in town'.[326] Judicial decisions clarified matters such as the definition of breaking and entering, while statute law created new treasons in part to suppress opposition to the Reformation reforms.[327] One lasting distinction that became established occurred in the law of homicide, where in addition to the basic distinction between felonious and excusable homicides, a distinction became drawn within

---

[316] See Geoffrey Samuel, *Rethinking Legal Reasoning* (Edward Elgar, 2018) 74–9.

[317] See generally Gregory J Durston, *Jacks, Knaves and Vagabonds: Crime, Law and Order in Tudor England* (Waterside Press, 2020). For criticism of Milsom and an elucidation of the criminal law in this period, see Cynthia B Herrup, *The Common Peace: Participation and the Criminal Law in Seventeenth Century England* (Cambridge University Press, 1987). It is also possible to talk of an intellectual history of criminal law before the development of an intellectual system.

[318] Baker, *English Law Under Two Elizabeths* 71.

[319] For a detailed account, see KJ Kesselring, *Mercy and Authority in the Tudor State* (Cambridge University Press, 2003).

[320] Milsom, *Historical Foundations of the Common Law*, 2nd ed. 425. [321] Other than petty larceny.

[322] Baker, *English Law under Two Elizabeths* 70.

[323] Baker, *An Introduction to English Legal History* 555. See further Baker, *The Oxford Laws of England Volume VI 1483–1558* chapter 30.

[324] See ibid. chapter 31. [325] Milsom, *Historical Foundations of the Common Law*, 1st ed. 353.

[326] Baker, *English Law under Two Elizabeths* 69.

[327] Ibid. 69–70; Baker, *An Introduction to English Legal History* 569. See further Baker, *The Oxford Laws of England Volume VI 1483–1558* chapter 32.

the category of felonious homicides between murder and manslaughter. However, as Kesselring has observed, although the distinction persists today and has 'come to seem natural', it 'had a messy, protracted birth and called forth new legal fictions about "constructive malice" or "malice implied" as judges sought to reserve certain cases as acts of murder even though they seemed to fall on the other side of the newly drawn line'.[328] Further, the line drawn 'reflected gendered assumptions about human nature' and 'historically specific notions of legitimate force'.[329]

Milsom stressed how the development of the murder-manslaughter distinction did not occur 'in the common law itself' but was achieved through 'external matters'.[330] It came about through developments in the law on pardons.[331] As discussed in the previous chapter, a pardons statute in 1390 had prohibited pardons in cases of killings by lying in wait, assault or *malice prepense*, and this led to malice – often referred to as malice aforethought – being central to the definition of murder. The consensus of writers such as Maitland and Stephen was that the 1390 statute had defined 'one particularly heinous form of homicide, killing by *malice prepense*, and attempted to make it impossible, or at least very difficult, for the Crown to pardon it', and this had meant that the meaning of murder had changed once again since the word 'had somehow become attached to this species of homicide and had thus embarked on a fresh career with malice aforethought'.[332] However, this was not a straightforward process. The 1390 statute was 'only a limited and temporary success' and doubt has been expressed as to whether it was observed at all after 1430.[333] It became the norm for all homicide indictments to read as if they were the particularly heinous type named in the 1390 Statute. Murder was no longer a term of art.[334] Moreover, the decrease in the use of pardons was mitigated by the increase in the use of pleading benefit of clergy.

The 1390 Statute was, therefore, not the source of what was to become the definition of murder, let alone the architect of the distinction between murder and manslaughter. It was a series of statutes under the Tudors that 'turned what had hitherto been an administrative difference into one of substance'.[335] A statute of 1488 sought to limit benefit of clergy by stating that those who committed particular crimes including murder could not rely on it twice.[336] Although this did not define murder or distinguish between types of homicide, it marked 'an important first step in the gradation of punishment for felony'.[337] A further statute in 1512 excluded laymen who were convicted of certain felonies from being able to rely on benefit of clergy at all. The statute covered murders or felonies committed 'in any church, chapel or hallowed place, or of and upon malice prepensed' as well as robbings and murders on the king's highway or in a person's house.[338] As Thomas A Green has noted, the 1512 'legislation appears to have been aimed primarily at predatory and truly

---

[328] KJ Kesselring, *Making Murder Public: Homicide in Early Modern England, 1480–1680* (Oxford University Press, 2019) 20. Constructive malice was not abolished until the Homicide Act 1957.

[329] Ibid.   [330] Milsom, *Historical Foundations of the Common Law*, 2nd ed. 424.

[331] On which see generally Kesselring, *Mercy and Authority in the Tudor State*.

[332] The idea that there was one understanding of murder was questioned by Kaye; JM Kaye, 'The Early History of Murder and Manslaughter – Part One' (1967) 83 *Law Quarterly Review* 365, 368, 369.

[333] Thomas A Green, 'The Jury and the English Law of Homicide, 1200–1600' (1976) 74 *Michigan Law Review* 413, 473.

[334] Ibid. 474.   [335] Kaye, 'The Early History of Murder and Manslaughter – Part One' 368.

[336] Green, 'The Jury and the English Law of Homicide, 1200–1600' 475.   [337] Ibid.   [338] Ibid. 475–6.

The Tudor Common Law 227

premeditated attacks upon the person or property of others'.[339] It led to a distinction being made by judges and writers[340] between 'non-clergiable murder', characterised by *malice prepense*, and a residual category of 'clergiable homicides', which became known as 'manslaughter', involving killing by 'chance-medley',[341] where there was no malice aforethought.[342] The meanings of all of these terms, however, remained unclear. Green pointed out that '[T]he records do not allow us to determine exactly what test of murder was applied.'[343] He noted that '[I]t is possible that any degree of true premeditation, rather than sudden deliberation, turned a manslaughter into a murder.'[344]

Further legislation in the middle of the century provided a cementing of the distinction between murder and manslaughter. A 1530 statute stipulated that one of the requirements for those entitled to sanctuary was where the act was 'petit treason, felony or manslaughter by chance medley, and not murder of *malice prepensed*'. A statute of 1532 dealing with the situation where someone was killed because that person had attempted to rob or murder the defendant on a highway or in his dwelling similarly did not apply to those who 'by chance medley' killed others in self-defence.[345] A statute in 1547 states that 'wilful murder' and 'murder of malice prepensed' would be excluded from clerical privilege.[346] These and other statutes now recognised a 'dual classification' between murder and manslaughter.[347] As Kesselring noted, '[T]wo distinct labels attached to two categories of criminal homicide, and benefit of clergy served as the primary mechanism for making that distinction matter.'[348] The effect was to 'redefine' both murder and manslaughter, 'making the distinction between them depend on the presence or absence of premeditation'.[349] Murder required malice, and this required more than a chance killing. Those who committed manslaughter rather than murder were less culpable and this distinction had some legal effects. However, as Green pointed out, '[M]anslaughter had not yet become a lesser gradation of homicide, automatically meriting a lesser punishment.'[350] Both murder and manslaughter were felonies punishable by death, but 'those people who made and enforced the law adapted and secularised the medieval practice of providing clerics with immunity from the King's Courts to allow a lesser punishment for men convicted of manslaughter', provided that it was their first such offence and that they had met the literacy test.[351]

Contrary to Milsom's argument that the murder-manslaughter distinction came from outside the common law, Kaye argued that the creation of the crime of manslaughter occurred in the early sixteenth century and 'was the work not of Parliament but of the courts and ... certain writers'.[352] Kaye contended that the distinction drawn between murder and manslaughter by the courts was 'based not on whether it was premeditated

---

[339] Ibid. 476.   [340] See ibid. 476–8.

[341] Meaning a sudden fighting; Baker, *The Oxford Laws of England Volume VI 1483–1558* 558. This was the main type of manslaughter.

[342] Guyora Binder, 'The Origins of American Felony Murder Rules' (2004) 57 *Stanford Law Review* 59, 77.

[343] Green, 'The Jury and the English Law of Homicide, 1200–1600' 479.   [344] Ibid.   [345] Ibid. 482.

[346] Kesselring, *Making Murder Public* 23.   [347] Green, 'The Jury and the English Law of Homicide, 1200–1600' 483.

[348] Kesselring, *Making Murder Public* 23.

[349] Some exceptions to this rule were permitted, in which case it was said that the 'malice was implied by law'; Kaye, 'The Early History of Murder and Manslaughter – Part One' 370.

[350] Green, 'The Jury and the English Law of Homicide, 1200–1600' 483.   [351] Kesselring, *Making Murder Public* 23.

[352] Kaye, 'The Early History of Murder and Manslaughter – Part One' 369.

228   *The Tudor Transformation (c.1485–1603)*

or not, but on whether it was accidental or deliberate'.[353] Yet, by contrast, as Guyora Binder noted, some cases closely identified *malice prepense* with premeditation.[354] What is clear is that malice had become a requirement for murder. *Lord Dacres's case*[355] established that all participants who had agreed to kill anyone who resisted them were liable for murder since they had *malice prepense* in terms of their intent to kill.[356] *Mansell and Herbert's case*[357] relied on this to hold that 'an unsuccessful attempt to kill one person that resulted in the unintended death of another should be viewed as murder.'[358] These decisions were mostly important in establishing this idea of transferred malice, which was further articulated in *R* v. *Saunders and Archer*.[359] They did not develop a clear distinction between murder and manslaughter. Moreover, caution is required as to what words such as 'malice' meant at the time. As Penny Crofts argued, providing malice with a legal meaning was the product of the work of treatise writers; she contended that 'the central function of malice was to persuade that the State had the authority to speak in and of the law'.[360] It was not a legal term of art but simply denoted wickedness.

R v. *Salisbury and others*[361] has been called 'the earliest reported verdict of manslaughter'.[362] This concerned an ambush by Salisbury and two conspirators but also crucially involved Salisbury's servant, who was not one of the conspirators but came to Salisbury's aid, wounding the man who died.[363] The jury were instructed that the servant should be found liable for manslaughter and not murder if he did not act with *malice prepense* but suddenly acted with those who had *malice prepense*. While they found the other defendants liable for murder, they found the servant liable for manslaughter only on this basis. For Green, the 'distinction between murder and manslaughter drawn in *Salisbury's case*' was to form the heart of the law on homicide for centuries.[364] However, he contended that this actually represented the way that 'by 1550 the formal rules of the law of felonious homicide were being reconciled with the persistent popular feeling' about the definition of homicide. For Green, 'it represented the final stage of a long process by which the common law adapted to social views on capital felony' that 'are ultimately traceable to the ancient Anglo-Saxon tradition making homicide through stealth unemendable and homicide committed in the open a matter for monetary compensation'.[365]

The *Salisbury case* did not resolve all matters concerning the distinction between murder and manslaughter. It was noticeable that the servant was still sentenced to death.[366] However, it became the orthodox position that a defendant who killed with malice would

---

[353] Ibid.   [354] Binder, 'The Origins of American Felony Murder Rules' 78–9.   [355] (1535) 72 ER 458.
[356] Binder, 'The Origins of American Felony Murder Rules' 77. See also Kesselring, *Making Murder Public* 26–7.
[357] (1558) 3 ER 279.
[358] Binder, 'The Origins of American Felony Murder Rules' 78. See also Baker, *The Oxford Laws of England Volume VI 1483–1558* 556–7 for discussion of how the case divided judicial opinion.
[359] (1573)75 ER 706. On which, see John H Baker, 'R v Saunders and Archer (1573)' in Philip Handler, Henry Mares and Ian Williams (eds.), *Landmark Cases in Criminal Law* (Hart, 2017) 28 and Kesselring, *Making Murder Public* 27–8.
[360] Penny Crofts, *Wickedness and Crime: Laws of Homicide and Malice* (Routledge, 2013) 64, 65.   [361] (1553) Plowd 100.
[362] Green, 'The Jury and the English Law of Homicide, 1200–1600' 484.
[363] Binder, 'The Origins of American Felony Murder Rules' 78.
[364] Green, 'The Jury and the English Law of Homicide, 1200–1600' 485.   [365] Ibid. 498.
[366] As Baker put it, a tripartite distinction therefore existed: first, a killing done out of malice was punishable by death and forfeiture; second, a killing without prior malice was clergiable provided it was a first offence and therefore punishable only by forfeiture; and third, an accidental or excusable killing was pardonable; Baker, *An Introduction to English Legal History* 572.

Conclusions 229

be liable for murder; a defendant who did an unlawful act and by chance killed another would be liable for manslaughter, while someone who killed through misadventure or misfortune while carrying out a lawful act would not be liable, provided that they had no malice.[367] The basic distinction between malice and chance medley was that between cold and hot blood. However, over time, complications eroded this. The definition and ambit of murder and manslaughter would exercise judges and writers for centuries to come. Malice proved difficult to define: it did not require an intention to kill and so a general evil intent would suffice. As Kaye noted, '[T]he history of culpable homicide in the seventeenth and eighteenth centuries was largely dominated by attempted to extend the scope of Murder at the expense of Manslaughter, attempts that culminated in the modern rule that any deliberate killing, whether done "upon a sudden occasion" or not, is murder.'[368] Over time, one test for manslaughter became not the hot bloodedness of the killing but the degree of provocation.[369] As with other areas of the law, the law on homicide was clearly in an adolescent stage during the Tudor period: it had moved beyond its medieval childhood but was yet to reach its modern state.[370]

V   Conclusions

Although the experience was different from that on the Continent and that there were also clear signs of continuity, it is clear that there were a number of transformations under the Tudors. Maitland observed that '[W]e were having a little Renaissance of our own: or a gothic revival if you please.'[371] He pointed to how English law was experiencing a 'new lease of life': 'The medieval books poured from the press, new books were written, the decisions of the courts were more diligently reported, the lawyers were boasting of the independence and extreme antiquity of their system.'[372] This chapter has shown that this was the period that saw the developments of courts outside the common law that were to cast long shadows, of Reformation statutes that showed the unlimited powers of the King in Parliament, and a number of significant developments inside and outside the common law courts. In the law of obligations, the various forms of the action on the case continued to grow with the doctrine of consideration being developed in order to regulate the action on the case for assumpsit, which had become a law of contract. In the land law, the writ of ejectment that had previously been a remedy only for leaseholders was adopted by freeholders by means of a legal fiction. This meant that in land law as in the law of obligations, the writ of trespass and its spin-offs dominated litigation. In Chancery, outside the common law, the use was on its way to becoming the trust via the Statute of Uses. And in criminal law, where procedural matters often precluded discussion of principles and distinctions, nevertheless, a distinction developed between murder and manslaughter as

---

[367] Baker, *The Oxford Laws of England Volume VI 1483–1558* 561.
[368] Kaye, 'The Early History of Murder and Manslaughter – Part One' 365–6.
[369] *R* v. *Mawgridge* (1707) Kel 119; Baker, *An Introduction to English Legal History* 572. See Jeremy Horder, *Provocation and Responsibility* (Oxford University Press, 1992). Today, a number of different forms of manslaughter exist for culpable killings that fall short of murder.
[370] See further Thomas G Watkin, 'Hamlet and the Law of Homicide' (1984) 100 *Law Quarterly Review* 282.
[371] Maitland, *English Law and the Renaissance* 29.   [372] Ibid. 29.

230 *The Tudor Transformation (c.1485–1603)*

two forms of felonious homicide. In all of these areas of law, there are glimpses of the modern law and the modern legal system beginning to emerge.

It is important, however, not to overplay how advanced such changes were and also not to confuse change with progress. The Reformation statutes underscored the extent to which this was an era of discrimination and intolerance. Indeed, it is during the Tudor period that 'an intermittent programme of minority persecution' began as 'the Tudor state bowed to political concerns over the presence of observable ethnic and racial minorities'.[373] A firm message was being sent that 'minorities were not just unwelcome but also effectively outlawed'.[374] An increasingly confident and assured State was also an arrogant, self-centred and prejudiced one, and this arrogance was to come to the fore in the centuries of empire and colonisation that were to come – the shame of the common law.

English law was also increasingly complex, as shown by the growth of literature, including the rise of what Ibbetson has referred to as a new 'form of treatise literature, beginning with Littleton's Tenures'.[375] In addition to the ongoing influence and popularity of the work of Littleton (with his *New Tenures* being published shortly after the author's death in 1481) and the publication of St Germain's *Doctor and Student*, this was the era in which John Perkins' *Profitable Book* on conveyancing was published and in which William Staunford published his Exposition of the King's Prerogative and *Les Plees del Coron* (the first textbook of English criminal law).[376] It was also the epoch in which Francis Bacon and Edward Coke began their careers and works on English law. As Ibbetson noted, this literature was 'placed alongside the reported cases, but by the early seventeenth century the dominant authorities in legal reasoning were judicial precedents; case law prevailed over doctrine'.[377] Once again, the Tudor experience represented a midway position between the medieval and the modern: a state of adolescence, following which some innovations would continue to develop while others would be stopped in their tracks.

There was, however, no straightforward bridge from the medieval law to the modern law. Things fell apart in the Stuart period. While English history had until now been littered with civil wars, with whole periods dominated by such conflict as epitomised by the Anarchy and the War of the Roses, the Civil War that broke up the Stuart period was something different. It deserves the definite article and capitalisation because the Civil War saw the unthinkable happen: it saw the killing of the king and his replacement with a different constitutional head of State. The Civil War was the culmination of tensions that had been felt for centuries and the growth of the powers of the monarch that had grown under the Tudors but had been hidden. As Elton has commented, '[O]ne of the major differences between the Tudors and the Stuarts lay in their treatment of the royal

---

[373] W Mark Ormrod, Bart Lambert and Jonathan Mackman, *Immigrant England 1300–1550* (Manchester University Press, 2019) 3.

[374] Ibid.; Baker, *English Law under Two Elizabeths*. [375] Ibbetson, 'The Renaissance of English Legal History' s92.

[376] Baker, *The Oxford Laws of England Volume VI 1483–1558* 501–5.

[377] Ibbetson, 'The Renaissance of English Legal History' s97.

Conclusions   231

prerogative: where the Stuarts spoilt acceptance by defining, the Tudors by not analysing reserved to themselves a large undefined power.'[378] These unresolved tensions between the crown and Parliament led to a marked change in fortunes for the monarchy from being the supreme head of the Church under the Tudors to the head on the chopping board under the Stuarts, as the next chapter will discuss.

---

[378] Elton, *The Tudor Constitution* 17.

'Everywhere we see difficulties before King Charles I. The system by which England has of late been governed is a questionable system, it is being questioned in Parliament, it is being questioned in the law courts ... Whether a wiser man than Charles could have averted or guided the coming storm, is a question over which we may well think; but everywhere we see that the storm is coming'.

Frederic W Maitland, *The Constitutional History of England* (Cambridge University Press, 1941 [1908]) 275.

10

The Stuart Suicide (c.1603–1649)

I   Introduction

Maitland's observation that 'such is the unity of all history that anyone who endeavours to tell a piece of it must feel that his first sentence tears a seamless web' applies as much to the question of where to end historical accounts as it does to the question of where to begin them.[1] The last sentence in any historical account also 'tears a seamless web'. There are several points where an account of the origins of the common law could end. We have passed some of them. It would be possible to end with the death of the father of the common law, with the English Justinian or just before the Tudor transformation. Yet, as we saw in the last chapter, the Tudor period can be understood as part of the growing pains of the common law, as part of the story of its growth and early development. Indeed, it is also possible to close an account of the growth of the common law nearer to the present day, to continue the analysis up to the abolition of the writ system, the death of Maitland or perhaps even the late twentieth century with developments in international law and the United Kingdom's short-lived membership of the European Union. However, to continue the account for centuries to come would be questionable because there the common law is no longer in a stage of youth; indeed, one may say that it is in a state of decay. Moreover, the closer the account comes to the present, the more troubling is the problem of where legal history ends and the current law should begin. Indeed, more recent centuries require a somewhat different approach to exploring their legal histories.[2] As Steve Hedley has pointed out, those who seek 'weighty tomes on "the law of contract in the 1890s"' can actually 'consult the weighty tomes written at the time'.[3]

---

[1] Frederick Pollock and Frederic W Maitland, *The History of English Law* (2nd ed., Cambridge University Press, 1968 [1898]) vol. 1, 1.

[2] As shown by specialist works on modern legal history: see e.g., AH Manchester, *Modern Legal History* (Butterworths, 1980); William R Cornish et al., *Law and Society in England 1750–1950* (2nd ed., Hart, 2019); Ian Ward, *English Legal Histories* (Hart, 2020) and the work cited by David Sugarman and GR Rubin, 'Towards a New History of Law and Material Society in England 1750–1914' in GR Rubin and David Sugarman (eds.), *Law, Economy & Society: Essays in the History of English Law 1750–1914* (Professional Books, 1984) 1.

[3] Steve Hedley, '"Superior Knowledge or Revelation": An Approach to Modern Legal History' (1987) 18 *Anglo-American Law Review* 177, 177.

233

234 *The Stuart Suicide (c.1603–1649)*

Establishing when the common law had reached a state of adulthood is difficult. The common law, of course, has never been fully formed. The language of adulthood is helpful only in so far as we do not confuse experience and longevity with progress. Achievements and setbacks during your life do not run in a linear line, and the same is true of the history of the common law. Experiments and concessions can sometimes result in significant but unforeseen change. There is very rarely a plan even though the benefit of hindsight often makes us retrospectively construct one. The comparison of the common law's move to adulthood to that of humans is also useful in that it underlines that there is not one set answer. Different people would say that they reached a state of adulthood or became truly themselves at different points. It often corresponds with a time not only of change but of challenge, typically but not always leaving the security of home and having to fend more than ever before for oneself. Applying these ideas to the history of the common law, it could be said that one candidate for a date of when the common law reached adulthood could be when it faced its greatest challenge. The Civil War of the seventeenth century would be a prime candidate for this. Previous chapters have told stories concerning the growth of kingly powers and the development of a common law that arose from the administrative consolidation of those powers. We have seen how rights came from kingly concessions and compromises and how, despite tensions between the two, the role of the King in Parliament has become ever powerful. The connection between English law and the monarchy has been central through-out the previous chapters: the common law is the product of the decisions in the king's courts; statutes are the product of the King in Parliament; and other forms of justice such as the courts of Chancery and Star Chamber also have their origins in the business of the King's Council. It follows that the common law's greatest challenge, the day it truly reached maturity, could be plausibly said to have occurred following the Civil War in the seventeenth century where the common law had to operate without the king and with a different head of State.

There is another reason for ending our account at the outbreak of the Civil War. We have noted numerous other civil wars and conflicts that have taken place, including the change of royal houses, but the seventeenth-century civil war deserves its designation as 'the Civil War' given that it was the culmination of pressures that had built up over centuries. The growth of the power of the King in Parliament and the escalation of tensions that we have seen throughout previous chapters, between kings and their advisers, between kings and parliaments, between feudal lords and tenants all ultimately led to the Civil War. In many respects, the rise and demise of the feudal system has been the backbone of the stories that we have been telling. And it was the decline of feudal revenues that reduced royal outcome and led to a greater dependence by monarchs upon parliaments that stoked the tensions between them. The transformations of the Tudor period worsened matters further in that the rock star monarchs got away with abuses for which their Stuart successors would be criticised.

This chapter, therefore, provides the end of our account of the origins of the common law by exploring the early Stuart period, the reigns of James I (1603–25) and Charles I (1625–49), the years that led up to the Civil War.[4] The period was a tumultuous one for

---

[4] The Interregnum occurred from 1649 to 1660. The later Stuart monarchs were Charles II (1660–85); James II (1685–8), Mary II and William III (1688–94); William III (1694–1702) and Anne (1702–14).

Introduction   235

England and for the common law.[5] However, as we have already noted, the story of the origins of the Civil War cannot be told by simply starting with the Stuarts. Maitland in his lectures on constitutional history remarked that there were three claimants for sovereignty: '(1) the king, (2) the king in parliament, (3) the law'.[6] He noted that under the Tudors, the powers of Parliament had grown and that it had been asserted that the 'king in parliament was absolutely supreme, above the king and above the law':

> The practical despotism of the Tudors had laid a terrible emphasis upon the enormous power of parliament – there was nothing that parliament could not do – it could dissolve the ancient dual constitution of church and state, it could place the church under the king, it could alter the religion of the land, it could settle the royal succession, it could delegate legislative powers to the king, it could take them away again.[7]

Yet, noted Maitland, much power remained in royal hands. This was shown in practical terms by the growth of the conciliar courts and in theoretical terms by the belief in the divine rights of king. Indeed, the seemingly all-powerful Parliament was actually simply doing the king's bidding. As Maitland remarked, it depended for its very existence on the will of the monarch: 'It comes when he calls it, it disappears when he bids it go; he makes temporal lords as he pleases, he makes what bishops he pleases, he charters new boroughs to send representatives.' For Maitland, this raised the question of whether Parliament was 'an emanation of the kingly power'.[8] This led to repeated tensions between the king and Parliamentarians.

The Stuart period saw this tension between king and Parliament come to the boil but it also saw the rise of a third contender, that of the common law. During this time the confidence and autonomy of the common law solidified, articulating the idea that no one or no group was above the law. For Maitland, this position was the legacy of Sir Edward Coke (1552–1634), pronounced 'Cook'.[9] Maitland attributes Coke as distinctly claiming 'that the common law is above statute, and above prerogative – it assigns a place to both king and parliament, and keeps them in it'.[10] The common law, according to Coke, was therefore above both king and Parliament.

The story of the tensions that led to the Civil War and particularly the role of the common law in that story is therefore the tale of Sir Edward Coke. In a letter to William S. Holdsworth, Maitland said that Coke's books 'are the dividing line' between the medieval and the modern law.[11] Both the man and his works have been seen as being of great significance. Holdsworth called Coke 'the greatest master of the common law' and

---

[5] See further Alison Wall, *Power and Protest in England 1525–1640* (Hodder Arnold, 2000) and Christopher W Brooks, *Law, Politics and Society in Modern England* (Cambridge University Press, 2008).
[6] Frederic W Maitland, *The Constitutional History of England* (Cambridge University Press, 1941 [1908]) 298.   [7] Ibid.
[8] Ibid.
[9] A number of recent book-length biographies and accounts of Coke's legal achievements exist, including: Catherine Drinker Bowen, *The Lion and the Throne: The Life and Times of Sir Edward Coke 1552–1634* (Hamish Hamilton, 1957); Stephen D White, *Sir Edward Coke and 'The Grievances of the Commonwealth' 1621–1628* (University of North Carolina Press, 1979); John Hostettler, *Sir Edward Coke: A Force for Freedom* (Barry Rose, 1997); Allen D Boyer, *Sir Edward Coke and the Elizabeth Age* (Stanford University Press, 2011); and David Chan Smith, *Sir Edward Coke and the Reformation of the Laws: Religion, Politics and Jurisprudence 1578–1616* (Cambridge University Press, 2014).
[10] Maitland, *The Constitutional History of England* 300–1.
[11] William S Holdsworth, 'Sir Edward Coke' (1935) 5(3) *Cambridge Law Journal* 332, 344.

236   *The Stuart Suicide (c.1603–1649)*

went as far as to claim that Coke was to English law 'what Shakespeare has been to literature'.[12] Indeed, like Shakespeare, there is much debate as to what Coke actually said. There is scant evidence that he 'had a coherently thought-out constitutional position' other than being shaped by the traditional medieval understanding of 'mixed-monarchy', the governance of kings and his advisers.[13] Moreover, there are contradictions in his judgments and works: sometimes he suggested that the common law was supreme and that courts can sit in judgment of parliamentary statutes, while other times he was insistent that Parliament was supreme.[14] This may result from the fact that Coke held both high judicial office and was a parliamentarian. However, occasional inconsistencies should not distract from what was ever present in his life and works: what Holdsworth referred to as Coke's 'fanatical reverence for the common law'.[15]

This chapter therefore explores the early Stuart period by focusing upon the life and achievements of Sir Edward Coke, exploring how the common law's claim for sovereignty was made in the run-up to the Civil War. Our analysis will extend from the late Tudor era into the reigns of the first two Stuart kings, reflecting not only the longer-term causes of the Civil War but also the fact that Coke's judicial and parliamentary career did not coincide exactly with the early Stuart period. He was born in 1552 and died in 1634, and so he was active towards the end of the Tudor period as well as into the early Stuart period. As Maitland rather colourfully put it, '[E]ven in the days of Elizabeth and James I, Sir Edward Coke, the incarnate common law, shovels out his enormous learning in vast disorderly heaps.'[16] His influence would prove longer lasting with the authority of his works being felt for generations.

This chapter will fall into three parts. Section II will explore the period running up to and including the Civil War by particular reference to Coke's career as a lawyer. Section III, however, will look at a more negative side to Sir Edward. As Thomas Garden Barnes has noted, 'Coke was a complex man.'[17] Authors extolling his impact upon the common law have not shied away from noting that in some respects Coke 'was not a wholly attractive character'.[18] This was particularly true of Coke's domestic affairs, which often got very public indeed. Section III focuses upon the negative side of Coke's character to explore the relationship between women and the law in this period. The third part will explore Coke's other significant contribution to the common law: his writings and the influence his work had after his death in the years following the Civil War, examining how his work was used to justify slavery. Section IV completes our examination of the genesis of the common law by exploring how English law was now crystallised in the works of Coke.

II   Coke the Lawyer

Edward Coke was born on 1 February 1552 and played a seminal role in the development of the common law during the late Tudor and Stuart periods. As Samuel E Thorne put it,

---

[12] Ibid.   [13] Thomas Garden Barnes, *Shaping the Common Law* (Stanford University Press, 2008) 131.
[14] Christopher Hill, *Intellectual Origins of the English Revolution* (Clarendon Press, 1965) 253.
[15] Holdsworth, 'Sir Edward Coke' 334.
[16] Frederic W Maitland and Francis C Montague, *A Sketch of English Law* (GP Putnam's Sons, 1915 [1899]) 113.
[17] Garden Barnes, *Shaping the Common Law* 121.   [18] Hill, *Intellectual Origins of the English Revolution* 225.

Coke the Lawyer 237

Coke had 'a hand in every important law-suit for more than forty years when far-reaching questions of private and public law were before the courts'.[19] During the late Tudor period, Coke rapidly rose as a barrister.[20] By 1588, Coke was speaking in about a hundred cases a year and was referred to by a law reporter as 'the most famous barrister of Inner Temple'.[21] He was involved with a number of cases that transformed central aspects of the common law, from *Slade's Case*,[22] which established that the action on the case for assumpsit could be used in place of debt to *Shelley's Case*,[23] and *Chudleigh's Case*[24] that transformed on the law of property and the interpretation of the Statute of Uses, respectively.[25] Coke also began his judicial career in 1585 sitting as a Recorder, and from 1589 he also became a Member of Parliament. He was then appointed to legal offices within Parliament, becoming Solicitor General in 1592 and then Attorney-General in 1594, as well as serving as Speaker of the House of Commons. Certain character traits that were to come to the fore in his later career were already present at this time. He was 'a fighter: toughly adversarial, aggressive, never wont to lose a case by faint prosecution'.[26] Yet, the later Coke would come to disagree with the younger Coke on a number of fronts. Although Coke's focus was on protecting the integrity of the law, noting that justice was the 'most beutyfull thing in the world', the offices he held required Coke to protect royal interests.[27] As Attorney-General, Coke formally approved 'acts and doctrines which he later denounced as unconstitutional – such acts as the infliction of torture'.[28]

The legend of Coke became fully formed, however, during the reign of the Stuarts. On the death of the childless Elizabeth I in 1603, James VI of Scotland became James I of England (1603–25) and the first monarch to unite the kingdoms. Many English lawyers saw the accession of King James as being 'potentially catastrophic from the constitutional point of view'.[29] In his *Trew Law of Free Monarchies* in 1598, James had written that kings were answerable to God alone, and were the makers of law who could suspend the law at will. As John Baker noted, this was 'completely contrary to constitutional monarchy as understood in England since the fourteenth century, to everything that Coke believed in'.[30]

At the very start of James's reign, Coke continued as Attorney-General and was responsible for prosecuting Guy Fawkes and his co-conspirators in the Gunpowder Plot

---

[19] Samuel E Thorne, *Essays in Legal History* (Hambledon Press, 1985) 224 (originally published as 'Sir Edward Coke, 1552–1952' (Selden Society lecture, 1952)).

[20] For discussion of his early career, see Allen D Boyer, *Sir Edward Coke and the Elizabethan Age* (Stanford University Press, 2003) chapters 1–4 and Chan Smith, *Sir Edward Coke and the Reformation of the Laws* chapter 1.

[21] John Baker, *The Reinvention of Magna Carta 1216–1616* (Cambridge University Press, 2017) 335.

[22] (1598) 4 Co Rep 92b, discussed in the previous chapter. See AW Brian Simpson, 'The Place of *Slade's Case* in the History of Contract' (1958) 74 *Law Quarterly Review* 381, reprinted in Allen D Boyer (ed.), *Law Liberty and Parliament: Selected Essays on the Writings of Sir Edward Coke* (Liberty Fund, 2004) 70 and David Ibbetson, 'Sixteenth Century Contract Law: *Slades's Case* in Context' (1984) 4 *Oxford Journal of Legal Studies* 295.

[23] (1581) 1 Co.Rep 93b. The rule provided that a conveyance of freehold to A for life, then to the heirs of A would be interpreted as giving full ownership to A. See DA Smith, 'Was there a Rule in *Shelley's Case*?' (2009) 30(1) *Journal of Legal History* 53.

[24] (1594) 1 Co Rep 1136. The case established that common law principles on property transfers also applied to transfers made by use.

[25] For analysis of all three cases, see Boyer, *Sir Edward Coke and the Elizabethan Age* chapter 8.

[26] Garden Barnes, *Shaping the Common Law* 112.

[27] Quoted in Chan Smith, *Sir Edward Coke and the Reformation of the Laws* 59, 60. John Baker has argued that 'Coke as Attorney-General consistently showed a judicious concern for the central importance of the common law in a constitutional monarchy' (Baker, *The Reinvention of Magna Carta 1216–1616* 337).

[28] Holdsworth, 'Sir Edward Coke' 333.   [29] Baker, *The Reinvention of Magna Carta 1216–1616* 339.   [30] Ibid. 340.

238 *The Stuart Suicide (c.1603–1649)*

of 1605.[31] Garden Barnes noted that 'Coke's vigorousness and harshness in prosecution were remarked upon by his contemporaries only as manifestations of remarkable patriotism and loyalty to his sovereign'.[32] Yet, outside the courtroom, tensions were beginning to show. In 1604, Coke published the fourth volume of his law reports and in his title page he dated his work to 'the first year (the spring time of all happiness) of the most happy rule of the most high and most illustrious King James', before putting the boot in by stating that 'the king is under no man, but under God and the law, for the law makes the king'.[33] As Baker noted, '[F]or an Attorney-General thus to school his royal master in print was both unprecedented and audacious.'[34] It reflected how Coke saw his position as the king's chief law officer was not only to serve the king and to defend the royal prerogative but also and more importantly to share with the judges 'the duty of ensuring the survival of English law'.[35]

Further high office soon followed for Coke. In 1606 he was appointed Chief Justice of the Court of Common Pleas, the first judge of Common Pleas in almost a century who had never practiced in that court as an advocate.[36] And in 1613 he was appointed Chief Justice of the King's Bench before being dismissed in 1616. However, these promotions were 'of honour rather than of fees' and so it has been suggested that 'Coke would have preferred to remain where his work was more lucrative'.[37] Francis Bacon, who was Coke's long-term nemesis, was said to have influenced the king's decision to move Coke. When Coke accused him of this, Bacon's reply was that 'your lordship all this while hath grown in breadth; you must now grow in highth, else you would be a monster'. Ironically, however, it was Coke's tenure on these courts that was to prove monstrous. It was a 'turbulent' period that was marked by friction with the king.[38] Coke, like James, came to his new post 'fully formed' and with set ideas that were untouched by the situation that he now found himself in.[39] In particular, there was an important difference between Coke and the king. James saw judges as officers of the crown; while Coke saw judges as the sole and unfettered exponents of the common law, which was supreme.[40] It was unsurprising, therefore, that 'Coke's tenure of the judicial office should be marked by a series of conflicts with the king',[41] which were leveraged open by Francis Bacon, Coke's rival.[42]

1 *Disputes with the Ecclesiastical Courts*

The first dispute was with the ecclesiastical courts and the Archbishop of Canterbury, Richard Bancroft, who complained that the common law judges were issuing writs of

---

[31] See further, Drinker Bowen, *The Lion and the Throne* chapter 19 and Hostettler, *Sir Edward Coke* 47–57.

[32] Garden Barnes, *Shaping the Common Law* 120.   [33] Quoted in Baker, *The Reinvention of Magna Carta 1216–1616* 343–4.

[34] Ibid. 345.   [35] Ibid. 346.   [36] Garden Barnes, *Shaping the Common Law* 121.

[37] Laura Norsworthy, *The Lady of Bleeding Heart Yard: Lady Elizabeth Hatton 1578–1646* (John Murray, 1935) 25.

[38] Allen D Boyer, 'Introduction' in Boyer, *Law Liberty and Parliament* vii, viii.

[39] Garden Barnes, *Shaping the Common Law* 121.   [40] Holdsworth, 'Sir Edward Coke' 334.

[41] However, the nature of the confrontation should not be distorted: WL Jones, 'The Crown and the Courts in England, 1603–1625' in AGR Smith (ed.), *The Reign of James VI and I* (Macmillan, 1973). It has been stressed that James 'was careful always to operate within the framework of the common law; he never imprisoned anyone without trail, he never levied money from his subjects without authorization from parliament or the courts of the common law': JP Kenyon, *The Stuart Constitution* (Cambridge University Press, 1966) 8.

[42] Baker, *The Reinvention of Magna Carta 1216–1616* 422.

Coke the Lawyer

239

prohibition to stop the ecclesiastical courts hearing claims.[43] The king supported the archbishop, though he stressed that it was for judges to decide to which court cases should go, they were his delegates and the law was founded upon reason that he and others had as well as the judges.[44] Francis Bacon supported this view, describing judges as lions, but 'lions under the throne, being circumspect that they do not check or oppose any points of sovereignty'.[45] Coke disagreed, saying that the king was under God and the law:[46] judges decided cases not by natural reason but 'by the artificial reason and judgment of law, which law is an act which requires long study and experience before that a man can attain to the cognizance of it'.[47]

A number of conflicts subsequently occurred. Coke repeatedly advised against the ecclesiastical courts, and in particular the Court of High Commission, which was an ecclesiastical court established by the monarch. Coke held that the High Commission had no power to fine or imprison except for heresy and schism and policed this by using writs of prohibition to stop both the High Commission and Star Chamber from hearing cases that would result in imprisonment.[48] In *Fuller's Case*,[49] Coke wrote that '[W]hen there is any question concerning what power or jurisdiction belongs to ecclesiastical judges ... the determination of this belongs to judges of the common law.'[50] Fuller was a barrister who had been held in custody for contempt of court for calling the High Commission 'popish, under the jurisdiction not of Christ but of anti-Christ', after a number of his clients had been fined by the court for non-conformity.[51] The question arose of whether he ought to be tried by the King's Bench or the High Commission with Coke mediating between the two. In the end, he was convicted by the High Commission. Catherine Drinker Bowen described the debacle as 'a notable defeat' for the common law.[52]

2   Tensions between the King and the Common Law

The dispute grew from its original ecclesiastical context to concern the prerogative powers of the king more generally. At first, there was another clear defeat. In *Bate's Case*[53] a merchant refused to pay a customs duty imposed by the king on the basis that such taxation required the consent of Parliament. The Court of Exchequer gave judgment unanimously for the king. Chief Baron Fleming, though holding that the common law 'cannot be changed without Parliament', held that the decision under discussion fell under matters of 'policy of government' and therefore was within the king's 'extraordinary power'. Coke approved of the decision, only later denouncing it in writings as a judgment that 'was against the law, and diverse Acts of Parliament'.[54] However, in the case of *Proclamations*[55] Coke decreed that the king's power to make proclamations could not be used to change the

---

[43] See ibid. 353 *et seq.*   [44] Maitland, *The Constitutional History of England* 268.
[45] Drinker Bowen, *The Lion and the Throne* 253–4.   [46] Ibid. 254.
[47] Quoted in Maitland, *The Constitutional History of England* 268–9.   [48] Hostettler, *Sir Edward Coke* 67.
[49] (1607) 12 Co Rep 41.   [50] Quoted in Boyer, 'Introduction' vii, viii.
[51] See Baker, *The Reinvention of Magna Carta 1216–1616* 356 *et seq.*
[52] Drinker Bowen, *The Lion and the Throne* 258. But compare Baker who argues that 'it was not wholly unreasonable' (Baker, *The Reinvention of Magna Carta 1216–1616* 362).
[53] (1606) 2 St Tr 371, also known as the case of *Impositions*. See Kenyon, *The Stuart Constitution* 54–6.
[54] Quoted in Hostettler, *Sir Edward Coke* 65–6.   [55] (1611) 12 Co Rep 74.

240   *The Stuart Suicide (c.1603–1649)*

common law or create new offences: offences could only be made by common law or legislation. Moreover, offences could not be made punishable by Star Chamber by proclamation.[56] However, the king and the conciliar courts resisted, with the result being that 'of the government constantly doing what the judges consider unlawful.'[57]

Coke reached his peak perhaps in *Bonham's Case*,[58] concerning a fine imposed by the Royal College of Physicians under Acts of Parliament. Coke's judgment in the case dealt with 'wider issues' that the claim provoked and declared that the 'common law will control Acts of Parliament, and sometimes judge them to be utterly void: for when an Act Parliament is against common right and reason, or repugnant, or impossible to be performed, the common law will control it, and adjudge such Acts to be void'.[59] As Drinker Bowen noted, this was the 'most controversial judicial dictum of the Coke's life, due to be celebrated out of all proportion to its real significance – once of those public statements which, as history progresses, men seize upon and interpret according to their needs'.[60] The judgment has been variously interpreted.[61] On the one hand, it can be seen as the foundation of the judicial review of legislation.[62] Yet, on the other, it can be seen as a statement of the supremacy of the common law over Parliament that was simply not followed. Coke's suggestion that judges could strike down statutes was not followed and instead the sovereignty of Parliament became established over time. The legal authorities put forward by Coke to support his assertion have been criticised. Maitland argued that the precedents Coke cited did not show that 'the judges of the Middle Ages had considered themselves free to question the validity of a statute on the ground of its being against natural law'.[63] And Coke himself later, most notably in his writings, seemingly changed his mind and accepted the supremacy of Parliament. Christopher Hill has suggested that lawyers and political theorists have made too much of this case.[64] Yet, it shows the opening of a road that was not taken – at least not in England. As John Hostettler pointed out, Coke's idea had an immense influence in the United States, leading to the role of the Supreme Court to review and disallow statutes that they hold to conflict with the Constitution.[65]

The tensions between the king and the common law continued to simmer after *Bonham's Case*. In March 1610, James I made a speech in Parliament, saying that 'for a king to despise the Common Law, is to neglect his own crown', but noting that no law but the law of God was 'perfect and free from corruption' and that there was a need for the law to be clearer.[66] Referring to the relationship between the common law and the conciliar courts, the king 'gave admonitions to both sides' to ensure that 'every court contain himself within their own limit'. This instruction resulted in an apparent appetite for reform. In

---

[56] Maitland, *The Constitutional History of England* 257.   [57] Ibid. 257–8.   [58] (1610) 8 Co Rep 107
[59] Quoted in Boyer, 'Introduction' vii, xi.   [60] Drinker Bowen, *The Lion and the Throne* 272.
[61] For further discussion see, e.g., Theodore FT Plucknett, '*Bonham's Case* and Judicial Review' (1926) 40 *Harvard Law Review* 30; Samuel E Thorne, '*Dr Bonham's Case*' (1938) *Law Quarterly Review* 543; R Berger, '*Doctor Bonham's Case*: Statutory Construction or Constitutional Theory' (1969) 117(4) *University of Pennsylvania Law Review* 521; and HJ Cook, 'Against Common Right and Reason: *The College of Physicians v Dr Thomas Bonham*' (1985) 29 *American Journal of Legal History* 301.
[62] Boyer, 'Introduction' vii, xi.   [63] Maitland, *The Constitutional History of England* 301.
[64] Hill, *Intellectual Origins of the English Revolution* 236.   [65] Hostettler, *Sir Edward Coke* 75.
[66] Kenyon, *The Stuart Constitution* 81–3.

Coke the Lawyer 241

1611, the king made a further address to the members of the three common law courts and announced a reform of the High Commission that would 'reduce it to certain spiritual charges'.[67] The king's real motive was perhaps revealed by the inclusion of Coke and six other judges on this new High Commission: no doubt the intention was to silence them.[68] The plan backfired, however, when Coke literally refused to sit during the first meeting at Lambeth Palace. The other justices followed Coke's example, and by refusing to take the oaths required of a commissioner declined to accept the legality of the commission. It became clear that the 'matter lay too deep for compromise'.[69] Both the High Commission and Coke continued to be active rivals to one other. By 1613, the common law judges were not only issuing writs of prohibition against ecclesiastical courts but were also declaring that the king had no right to stop them from hearing cases that had already commenced.[70] At this point, the impasse had become too much. The king summoned the judges to appear before him and all bar Coke hastily reversed his position.

Coke was transferred from Common Pleas to the King's Bench, the king's motive being that Coke's capacity for harm would be lessened in a court concerned with the rights of the king rather than the rights of the people.[71] Again, the king's hope was misguided and further quarrels dogged Coke's three-year tenure of this office. Coke objected to the practice whereby the king would seek the opinions of judges one by one on a matter that was yet to come to them judicially.[72] As Maitland noted, this 'was an old well-established practice, and it was even possible to contend that the judges were bound by their oaths to give the king legal advice whenever he asked for it'.[73] The conflict between Coke and the king was to escalate further in relation to the Court of Chancery.

3   *The Conflict with Chancery*

The clash concerned the Court of Chancery and its practice of providing relief after the matter had been resolved at the common law courts.[74] This was very different from Chancery providing a remedy where the common law did not;[75] here the court was effectively providing 'another bite of the cherry'.[76] Coke opposed this practice in a number of cases,[77] declaring that there was no appeal from the King's Bench 'to any court except the High Court of Parliament'.[78] However, in the end, the matter was referred to a group of the King's Council,[79] who sided with the Chancery against Coke. As Maitland noted, 'The victory of the Chancery was final and complete-and if we were to have a court of equity at

---

[67] Drinker Bowen, *The Lion and the Throne* 280.
[68] Hostettler, *Sir Edward Coke* 75. As Drinker Bowen noted, 'Name a man to a place of honour, give him a share and a title and his opposition fades: it is the ancient strategy of power' (Drinker Bowen, *The Lion and the Throne* 280).
[69] Ibid. 283.   [70] Hostettler, *Sir Edward Coke* 77.   [71] Holdsworth, 'Sir Edward Coke' 335.
[72] Maitland, *The Constitutional History of England* 270; Hostettler, *Sir Edward Coke* 83.
[73] Maitland, *The Constitutional History of England* 270.
[74] See further John H Baker, 'The Common Lawyers and Chancery: 1616' (1969) 9 *Irish Jurist* 368, reprinted in Boyer, *Law Liberty and Parliament* 254.
[75] The dispute was not about the need for the equitable jurisdiction of Chancery; Baker, *The Reinvention of Magna Carta 1216–1616* 410.
[76] Hostettler, *Sir Edward Coke* 85.   [77] See Baker, *The Reinvention of Magna Carta 1216–1616* 410–22.
[78] Drinker Bowen, *The Lion and the Throne* 310.
[79] Comprising of Attorney-General Bacon, the Secretary General, two King's Serjants and Prince Charles' attorney: Ibid. 313.

242   *The Stuart Suicide (c.1603–1649)*

all, it was a necessary victory.'[80] 'From this time forward the Chancery had the upper hand. It did not claim to be superior to the courts of law, but it could prevent men from going to those courts, whereas those courts could not prevent men from going to it.'[81] This facilitated legal pluralism: litigants could now pick and choose between the common law Courts and Chancery, which became a separate legal system with its own courts and lawyers. Chancery became a busy but over-stretched institution.[82] This was to cause problems for the future in terms of delays and a sense that justice was not really being done

4   *The End of Coke's Judicial Career*

However, Coke's judicial quarrelling was not quite over. The case of *Commendams*[83] concerned the legality of the king's decision to issue a commendam writ that transferred Church property and the resulting revenues but without the bishop actually carrying out the duties.[84] A letter was written on the king's behalf instructing common law judges not to hear the case since it involved the royal prerogative.[85] Francis Bacon had persuaded the king that to question the writ in court was to question the king's supremacy as head of the Church.[86] Led by Coke, the common law judges wrote back a letter of response that stated that 'knowing your majesty's zeal to justice, we have, according to our oaths and duties . . . proceeded' to hear the claim.[87] James was said to have torn up the letter and eventually responded to them that he knew 'the true and ancient common law to be the most favourable to kings of any law world', and so 'to which law I do advise you my judges to apply to your studies'.[88] The king noted that while his private interests could be subject to litigation, 'his supreme and imperial power and sovereignty' was not to be disputed 'in vulgar argument'.[89] Coke stood his ground, however, and Bacon as Attorney-General was invited to argue against him. Coke lost and the judges knelt before the king as he asked them one by one whether they would obey his instruction to pause the lawsuit until they had consulted him. All of the judges except Coke submitted and so the case was halted. Coke said that he would 'do that which shall be fit for a judge to do'. This was the final straw and Coke was dismissed for his 'perpetual turbulent carriage' towards the Church and the prerogative.[90]

As Garden Barnes has noted, Coke was 'merely the first judicial martyr of Stuart England'.[91] In a speech to the judges in Star Chamber in June 1616, the king was adamant that: 'As kings borrow their power from God, so judges from kings; and as kings are to account to God, so judges unto God and Kings.'[92] He added that judges were 'no makers

---

[80] Maitland, *The Constitutional History of England* 270.
[81] Frederic W Maitland, *Equity: A Course of Lectures* (Cambridge University Press, 1969 [1909]) 10.
[82] 'Bacon said that he made 2000 orders in a year, and we are told that as many as 16,000 causes were pending before it at one time: indeed it was hopelessly in arrear of its work' (ibid. 10).
[83] Also known as *Colt and Glover v. the bishop of Coventry* (1615–17) 1 Rolle Rep 451.
[84] Baker, *The Reinvention of Magna Carta 1216–1616* 424.   [85] Hostettler, *Sir Edward Coke* 90.
[86] Baker, *The Reinvention of Magna Carta 1216–1616* 424.   [87] Drinker Bowen, *The Lion and the Throne* 320.
[88] Hostettler, *Sir Edward Coke* 91.   [89] Quoted in Baker, *The Reinvention of Magna Carta 1216–1616* 425.
[90] Hostettler, *Sir Edward Coke* 92. For discussion of Coke's dismissal and its aftermath, see Baker, *The Reinvention of Magna Carta 1216–1616* 435 et seq.
[91] Garden Barnes, *Shaping the Common Law* 126.   [92] Kenyon, *The Stuart Constitution* 84.

Coke the Lawyer 243

of law, but interpreters of law', and that he would 'never trust any interpretation that agrees not with my common sense or reason'.[93] James was adamant that the common law had to be 'kept within her own limits', it should not encroach upon the prerogative of the crown, and if a question concerned the 'prerogative or mystery of state', judges should consult the king or his council before hearing them because 'that which concerns the mystery of the king's power is not lawful to be disputed; for that is to wade into the weakness of princes, and to take way the mystical reverence that belongs unto them that sit on the throne of God'.

5   *Coke the Parliamentarian*

Coke's judicial career under the Stuarts illustrated the growing confidence and demands of the king. These were also clear in the king's dealings with other constitutional bodies including Parliament. Indeed, Coke's dismissal from judicial office simply meant that the location of the dispute moved from the law courts to Parliament.[94] James ruled without Parliaments from 1611 to 1414 and 1621 to 1624, assisted instead by the Star Chamber and the High Commission courts. However, in 1621, he was forced to summon Parliament to provide funds for his costly foreign policy, and Sir Edward Coke became one of the prominent leaders of the Commons.[95] In Parliament, 'Coke found again a forum worthy of his talents, his learning, and his activism.' Coke 'ended up as somewhat of a statesman, moving into opposition to the crown'.[96] Coke allied himself with the parliamentary opposition. He played a leading role in the impeaching of state officers by Parliament by supplying precedents and conducting hearings. As Holdsworth has noted, this was 'a momentous step, which had large consequences both for Parliament and for the common law' in that it 'cemented the old standing alliance between Parliament and the common law' by enlisting 'in favour of the Parliament that superstitious reverence which men felt for the common law'.[97] This was manifested in the Protestation of 18 December 1621 produced under Coke's guidance, where the Commons declared that the privileges of Parliament were 'the ancient and undoubted birthright of subjects of England – that the Commons may handle any subject and enjoy a complete freedom of speech'.[98] The king is said to have responded by calling for the journals of the Commons, ripping out the sections featuring the protest and dissolving Parliament. Coke was imprisoned in the Tower of London for nine months.[99]

In 1625, James died and Charles I (1625–49) acceded to the throne. The new king furthered the approach of James. Martial law was introduced.[100] The Star Chamber 'became more and more tyrannical' and had become 'a court of politicians enforcing a policy, not a court of judges administering the law. It was cruel in its punishments, and often has recourse to torture'.[101] The king raised loans without parliamentary consent and

---

[93] Ibid. 85.   [94] For a detailed account, see White, *Sir Edward Coke and 'The Grievances of the Commonwealth' 1621–1628.*
[95] Garden Barnes, *Shaping the Common Law* 127.   [96] Boyer, 'Introduction' vii, xi.
[97] Holdsworth, 'Sir Edward Coke' 335.   [98] Maitland, *The Constitutional History of England* 243.
[99] Hostettler, *Sir Edward Coke* 114.   [100] Ibid. 127.   [101] Maitland, *The Constitutional History of England* 263.

244   *The Stuart Suicide (c.1603–1649)*

imprisoned those who did not pay them. In *Darnel's Case*,[102] the imprisonment of knights who refused to pay a forced loan 'by his majesty's special commandment' was upheld on the basis that freeing such a prisoner 'was probably too dangerous for public discussion'.[103] While lawyers such as Coke accepted that the crown had a prerogative right to imprison suspected traitors and terrorists, here they considered that it had 'been abused as a means of enforcing an unconstitutional form of taxation'.[104] The court's decision gave the crown 'the apparent right to detain the four prisoners until such time as Charles decided to let them go free'.[105] Parliamentarians saw this as yet another sign of Stuart absolutism: the growing powers of the king.

Coke's role in Parliament changed from being the tireless litigator to being one of the main opposition figures who 'pressed a series of initiatives uncongenial to the new king – criticizing his foreign policy, challenging his decisions on religion, and hesitating to grant financial support'.[106] Coke led the argument in Parliament that these actions were thought contrary to Magna Carta, which he considered to be a fundamental law that could not be annulled by statute.[107] He accepted that the royal prerogative was part of the law but said that 'sovereign power has now parliamentary word: in my opinion, it weakens Magna Carta'.[108] In 1628, these concerns resulted in the first major constitutional document since Magna Carta, the Petition of Right. Framed largely by Coke himself and defended by him in a number of parliamentary sessions, the Petition of Right was eventually agreed to by the king when his need to raise funds became desperate. The Petition of Right declared that no person should be compelled to pay a loan, benevolence or tax without the consent of Parliament and that no subject should be imprisoned or detained without due cause shown or be tried by martial law.[109] The document was greeted by the ringing of church bells and bonfires, but it also set alight a much larger fire. The fuse for Civil War had been lit.

In 1629, King Charles I was so angered by the refusal by Parliament to impose the taxation that he required to support his foreign wars that he decided to rule without them. Parliament was shut for eleven years. In the era of the king's 'personal rule', Coke retired to his estate in Buckinghamshire where he worked to complete his books. Coke's lifelong addiction to the common law proved controversial to the end. As he laid dying in 1634, the king's men raised and ransacked his home study and his files at the Inns of Court.[110] His papers vanished for seven years.

The king meanwhile assumed that his prerogative powers could raise the revenue that he needed. This came to the fore in the case of *R* v. *Hampden*,[111] where John Hampden refused to pay the king's tax on ships. The majority of the judiciary decided for the king, and the language used showed how far the pendulum had swung. Berkley J held that the law knew no 'king-yoking policy': 'The law itself is an old and trusty servant of the king's; it is his instrument or means which he useth to govern his people by'. He held that there

---

[102] Also known as the *Five Knights' Case: R* v. *Warden of the Fleet ex parte Darnel* (1327) 3 State Tr 1.
[103] Hostettler, *Sir Edward Coke* 126.
[104] John H Baker, *An Introduction to English Legal History* (5th ed., Oxford University Press, 2019) 508.
[105] JA Guy, 'The Origins of the Petition of Right Reconsidered' (1982) 25(2) *The Historical Journal* 289, 293.
[106] Boyer, 'Introduction' vii, xii.   [107] Hostettler, *Sir Edward Coke* 128.   [108] Quoted in Boyer, 'Introduction' vii, xii.
[109] Hostettler, *Sir Edward Coke* 138.   [110] Boyer, 'Introduction' vii, xiii.
[111] (1638) 3 State Tr 825. Also known as the 'ship money' case. See Kenyon, *The Stuart Constitution* 98–103.

were two maxims of the laws of England: 'the king is a person trusted with the state of the commonwealth' and 'the king cannot do wrong'. Finch CJ added that 'no Act of Parliament can bar a king of his regality'. As he colourfully put it, 'Acts of parliament may take away flowers and ornaments of the crown, but not the crown itself.' As Maitland pointed out, these words lacked precision: who was to decide what an ornament was and what was a substantial part of the crown?[112] The limitations of both the king and parliament were unclear, and this 'would satisfy neither king nor nation'. For Maitland, *R v. Hampden* 'hurried on the Civil War' by setting a contest 'between the sovereignty of a king, and the sovereignty of a king in parliament'. Finch CJ's words were to prove prophetic. In just over a decade, Parliament would indeed take away the crown, but this was only to be achieved by war.[113]

The catalyst came when Charles eventually summoned a new parliament in April 1640 to provide royal funds. When they refused to do so, this 'Short Parliament' was dissolved within a month. This was followed by the summoning of the 'Long Parliament' in November 1640, where Parliamentarians not only refused to do the royal will but also composed the 'Grand Remonstrance', listing the unconstitutional Acts of the king, demanding the appointment of ministers by Parliament and attacking the 'malignant and pernicious design of subverting the fundamental laws and principles of government' by 'papists who hate the laws' and bishops who sought 'ecclesiastical tyranny'.[114] Parliament reversed the judgment in *R v. Hampden* and overturned the effect of *Darnel's Case*.[115]

The attempted arrest of leading members of Parliament followed, culminating in the king setting up the royal standard on the Castle Hill at Nottingham, summoning his loyal subjects to join him against his enemies in Parliament. The country was at war with itself. From 1642 onwards, the Civil War blazed through the kingdom, eventually culminating in the abolition of the office of king and the House of Lords and the introduction of a Council of State and a new religion: Presbyterianism.[116] In 1649, an Act abolishing kingship declared 'by authority derived from Parliament' that Charles was 'to be justly condemned, adjudged to die, and put to death, for many treasons, murders and other heinous offences'.[117] The Act stated that it had 'been found by experience that the office of a king in this nation and Ireland, and to have the power thereof in a single person, is unnecessary, burdensome and dangerous to the liberty, safety and public interest of the people'.

It did not take long, however, for this assessment to be revisited. The squabbling of parliamentary factions persuaded Oliver Cromwell in 1653 of the need for power to be invested in one person, a 'Lord Protector', and the need for Cromwell himself to fill this position and to take on powers akin to that previously enjoyed by monarchs. The Instrument of Government of 1653, the country's only written complete constitution, stated that 'the supreme legislative authority of the Commonwealth of England ... shall

---

[112] Maitland, *The Constitutional History of England* 300.
[113] For further discussion on the numerous causes of the Civil War, see, e.g., the essays in Conrad Russell (ed.), *The Origins of the Civil War* (Macmillan, 1973).
[114] See Kenyon, *The Stuart Constitution* 207–17.   [115] Baker, *An Introduction to English Legal History* 509.
[116] See, further, e.g., the essays in Gerald E Aylmer (ed.), *The Interregnum* (Macmillan, 1972).
[117] Kenyon, *The Stuart Constitution* 307.

246 *The Stuart Suicide (c.1603–1649)*

be and reside in one person, and the people assembled in parliament'.[118] During the Commonwealth, a number of legal changes were made: the official language of the law was now English, reform of Chancery and the Exchequer took place, and there was a ban on performing plays, and eventually upon Christmas itself. A number of puritan provisions were enacted such as fines for swearing, punishments for adultery, incest, prostitution, duelling and cockfighting. Even more reforms were discussed but not implemented, including evidence under oath, civil marriage, new laws of inheritance and the wearing of 'immodest dress'. Indeed, a 'comprehensive reform of the law, especially the rules of procedure, was frequently demanded in the time of the Commonwealth'.[119] However, the Commonwealth experiment and its reforms were to prove short-lived. On Cromwell's death, he was succeeded by his son Richard but financial and military chaos ensued, Parliament was dissolved and Richard overthrown. It was eventually resolved that only the restoration of the king could end the chaos, and so the son of the decapitated king was invited to return from exile. In 1660, Charles II was restored to the English throne, having been already been acknowledged as king in Scotland in 1651. The restoration led to the rejection of almost all of the reforms made under the Commonwealth. As a matter of law, the Acts of Parliament that had not received royal assent were simply void. As Maitland noted, at the time, 'no lawyer would have appealed to them as law, and no lawyer would do so at the present day: they have no place in our statute book'.[120] It was as if it had all been a dream.

However, it was not only the Commonwealth that had been rejected but also the absolute monarchy of the Stuart kings. From now on, supremacy was to rest in the King in Parliament but this did not simply mean that Parliament was there to do the king's bidding. The powers of Parliament and the common law had been strengthened. Judges were increasingly free of interference by the crown and the prerogative courts were in decline.[121] The Court of Chancery ceased to be an instrument of the royal prerogative and its jurisdiction grew to meet 'the needs of the subject, not to the ambition of the monarch'.[122] The rules of equity began 'to take a very definite shape, comparable in rigour to the rules of the common law'.[123] In contrast, as Maitland put it, the Star Chamber was abolished 'in the name of the common law', with its role taken over by the common law courts.[124] Despite existing throughout the Tudor and early Stuart periods, the Star Chamber added little to the national jurisprudence because it had 'held itself aloof from jurisprudence [and] been a law unto itself'. The same was true of the era of absolute monarchy and the Commonwealth as a whole. The fires of the Civil War had left scars, not least in highlighting the dangers of personal rule. However, although it singed the common law, these were temporary scars, showing the perseverance and maturity of the common law. Stuart absolutism in the end had little long-term effect upon the letter of English law . The same could not be said of the contribution of Sir Edward Coke.

---

[118] See Kenyon, *The Stuart Constitution* 308–13. [119] Maitland and Montague, *A Sketch of English Legal History* 131.
[120] Maitland, *The Constitutional History of England* 282.
[121] The Church of England was restored by the Act of Uniformity of 1662, which mandated a single liturgy for whole realm.
[122] Maitland and Montague, *A Sketch of English Legal History* 131. [123] Ibid. 127. [124] Ibid. 119.

III Coke the Husband

As Holdsworth has observed, although it was Coke the man that had a 'vast influence upon the law and politics of the seventeenth century', it was the work of Coke that secured 'the permanence of his influence upon the future development of English law'.[125] However, it is true that both his publications and work as a lawyer has taken attention away from more negative aspects of his character. Coke's treatment of his wives and children shed a different light upon the man. It shows that, however addicted to the common law Coke was, he was more addicted to ensuring that he had his own way and that justice was achieved for him. As Laura Norsworthy noted in her biography of Coke's second wife, Lady Elizabeth Hatton, Coke expected both his wife and children 'to remember that his word was law' and he 'had visions of holding the same despotic sway at home as he had in the King's Bench'.[126] Coke's domestic but very public controversies underscore that he was autocratic and shamelessly used the law in order to protect his own interests. In addition to revealing much about his character, exploring Coke the husband also shines a light upon the social and legal position of women in this era.

There are four particular incidents that explain why when Coke died in 1634 his widow, Lady Elizabeth Hatton, reflecting upon thirty-six years of married life, is said to have remarked, 'we shall never see his like again – praises to be God'.[127] The first surrounded the fact that their marriage had breached ecclesiastical law. Following the death of Elizabeth's first husband, Sir William Hatton, Coke was one of the suitors for her hand alongside his long-time rival Francis Bacon.[128] At this point, Coke was aged forty-seven, had been widowed, had ten children and was Attorney-General. Lady Elizabeth was twenty.[129] Coke was 'courting advancement as well as a wife' and, although Coke was preferable to Bacon, he was still reluctantly accepted by Lady Hatton as a suitor.[130] Indeed, '[S]he showed no enthusiasm in the proceedings and refused to allow her engagement to be made public.' It is possible that this coloured what happened next. Lady Hatton agreed to marry Coke but only if it took place at Hatton House at night without banns being read. This would be illegal. Her biographer, Laura Nosworthy, suggested that Lady Hatton was aware of this because she had been married before and interpreted it as either being mischief, given that both Coke and the Archbishop of Canterbury were known for their egos, or as wanting to prove Coke's love to her, given his devotion to the law.[131] In any case, the two were married secretly on the night of 6 November 1598.[132] And this set in course 'a whole train of legal proceedings', which would usually 'only end in imprisonment and excommunication'.[133] Coke's response to this predicament was to go to the Archbishop of Canterbury and plead ignorance of ecclesiastical law. As Hill noted, 'the greatest legal expert in the country pleaded ignorance of the law, made humble submission – and got off'.[134] The archbishop provided a dispensation, but Lady Hatton had made a fool of Coke and this was to sour relations between the two.[135] Moreover, the

---

[125] Holdsworth, 'Sir Edward Coke' 337.   [126] Norsworthy, *The Lady of Bleeding Heart Yard* 34.
[127] Thorne, *Essays in Legal History* 224.   [128] Norsworthy, *The Lady of Bleeding Heart Yard* 8.   [129] Ibid. 12.
[130] Ibid. 10.   [131] Ibid. 11.   [132] Ibid. 12.   [133] Ibid. 14.   [134] Hill, *Intellectual Origins of the English Revolution* 226.
[135] Norsworthy, *The Lady of Bleeding Heart Yard* 15.

248 *The Stuart Suicide (c.1603–1649)*

incident showed Coke's hypocrisy and the way in which, despite his grand-standing rhetoric of the importance of the law, he was not above undermining the law to further his own interests.

This was also evident in the second incident: the way in which Coke dealt with his wife's property. Norsworthy noted that Coke 'began at once to meddle with her wealth and with the affairs of her late husband'.[136] The doctrine of coverture meant that married women were effectively seen as the property of their husband's given that the marriage had created 'one flesh' or, in Maitland's language, a guardianship over the wife by the husband.[137] A woman's income and property now generally belonged to their husband's. For Lady Hatton, this means that 'what was hers was also the Attorney-General's. He could do with it what he liked.'[138] Coke took possession of her entire estate, meaning that Lady Hatton would live in her own houses 'as though they were his, under his rules and regulations, dependent on him for everything, and without a penny to spend'.[139] This provoked conflict between the two already unhappy newlyweds. This worsened after the death of the queen, who had personally provided a check on the behaviour of Coke, and following the birth of two daughters, Elizabeth and Frances, when Coke broke his promise to his wife to settle her estate and lands he had purchased after their marriage on these children.[140] Coke and Lady Hatton 'found themselves fighting out their grievances before the Council Table'.[141] The conflict not only concerned financial matters but Coke's behaviour. Norsworthy noted that Coke had 'a caustic tongue, disagreeable manners and an abominable temper. He could be cruel.'[142] At the King's Council, Lady Hatton alleged that Coke and his son had broken into Hatton House, taken all her goods and had threatened all her servants, sending them away without any wages.[143] She claimed that she had 'suffered beyond measure of any wife, mother, nay of any ordinary woman in the kingdom'.[144] This was not the only example of Coke's violence: on another occasion, Lady Hatton had noted that 'his rage was such as he came violently in to my chamber, rent my ruff from my neck offering unworthy blows'.[145] Even later in their marriage, when the two were leading separate lives, Coke continued to cling to his marital rights.[146] Not only did Lady Hatton have to sell her jewellery, other belongings and land in order to survive, she also had to ask for Coke's consent to do so.[147] For Norsworthy, this humiliation was 'made a thousand times worse by having to pay the author of her wrongs for consent to sell what belonged to her that she might have the bare means to live'.[148] Throughout the marriage, Coke was 'as obstinate as he was dictatorial, and persisted in clinging to the letter of the law'.[149]

Coke's dictatorial streak was even clearer in the third incident, in which he kidnapped and beat his daughter Frances in order to make her marry his choice of husband.[150] Coke

---

[136] Ibid. 12. [137] Pollock and Maitland, *The History of English Law* 485. See also the previous discussion in Chapter 6.
[138] Norsworthy, *The Lady of Bleeding Heart Yard:* 13. [139] See further ibid. 22–4, 27. [140] Ibid. 25, 15. [141] Ibid. 30.
[142] Ibid. 10. [143] Ibid. 31. [144] Ibid. 32. [145] Lady Hatton, quoted in ibid. 24. [146] Ibid. 82.
[147] This was because a married woman had 'right in law to dispose of her estate without permission and concurrence of her husband: ibid.
[148] Ibid. 82–3.
[149] Indeed, his actions later in their marriage led to the pair once again going before the King's Council. Even when Lady Hatton had successfully argued her case to the council, refuting Coke's argument that she was 'unfit to have maintenance according to her birth and fortune', this 'made no difference to Sir Edward Coke' who continued to insist upon his legal rights: ibid. 83.
[150] Tim Stretton, *Women Waging War in Elizabethan England* (Cambridge University Press, 1998) 219–20.

was keen that Frances marry Sir John Villiers, who was a favourite of King James.[151] Lady Hatton and Frances were bitterly opposed to this, and one night after Coke had gone to bed, they both crept out of the house and left to stay in a nearby mansion where they tried to arrange an alternative marriage suitor.[152] Coke sought a warrant from the Privy Council to search the mansion but this was blocked by Bacon.[153] He therefore sought an order from elsewhere and, although 'there was some question as to whether this was in order, Sir Edward Coke did not let any little irregularity of that sort trouble him'. He armed himself, his attendants and his sons and 'forced his way into the grounds by taking done the doors of the gatehouse' before searching the place. Coke shouted, '[I]f we should kill any of your people it would be justifiable homicide but if you should kill any of us it would be murder.'[154] When Coke found them, he 'dragged Frances out of the closet' and 'began a tussle of force' with his wife, carrying off Frances and leaving on horseback.

Lady Hatton then successfully sought a warrant from Bacon.[155] Bacon then summoned Coke to the Star Chamber on a charge of housebreaking, Coke then summoned Lady Hatton for taking away their daughter and arranging a marriage for her without his consent.[156] Lady Hatton chose to plead her own case in which she railed against Coke's 'threats and ill usage' of her daughter, and maintained that 'the end justifies – excuses the act'.[157] She argued that if she had taken away Frances, so had Coke, and he had done so with the 'most notorious riot' and threats of 'justifiable homicide'.[158] The king, however, supported Coke, leading the rather sneaky Bacon to suddenly disclaim any disapproval of Frances's marriage.[159] The incident once again showed that Coke's obedience of the law was selective and he did not slavishly follow the law when it was not in his interests to do so.

Coke's creative use of the law underpinned the fourth incident. In order for Frances's marriage to take place, Coke worked with Bacon for once and dealt with Lady Hatton by putting her in prison.[160] Coke applied for the warrant and Bacon issued it, with Lady Hatton then being arrested and lodged in a house and kept in close confinement. As Norsworthy noted, this was not atypical in this period since being whisked off to jail 'was one of those things that might have happened to almost anyone in the century that she lived'. It was not only Lady Hatton who was mistreated. Frances was repeatedly 'tied to the bedposts and whipped 'till she consented to the Match'.[161] Such punishment was within Coke's rights. Indeed, as Norsworthy noted: 'He had sent many a recalcitrant resister to the stocks, the pillory, the tumbrel, and the cage. He had stood over prisoners in the torture chamber – had watched them dragged through the street at the cart's tail. What was a whipping at the bedpost compared with these?'[162] Coke dictated a letter for Frances to write to her mother, saying that she would now obey him, and declaring that she has suffered no violent means by words or deeds.[163] The wedding was fixed and took place in Hampton Court Palace in the presence of the whole court, with the king giving orders that

---

[151] Norsworthy, *The Lady of Bleeding Heart Yard* 37.   [152] Ibid. 41.   [153] Ibid. 44.   [154] Ibid 45.
[155] However, while the clerk of the council went off with the warrant, she prepared to attend as well, accompanied by sixty men with pistols: ibid. 46, 47.
[156] Ibid. 48.   [157] Ibid. 49.   [158] Ibid. 50.   [159] Ibid. 53.   [160] Ibid. 61.   [161] Ibid. 62.   [162] Ibid. 63.
[163] Ibid. 63, 64.

250   *The Stuart Suicide (c.1603–1649)*

festivities were to be carried out on a very grand scale.[164] At the ceremony, Coke gave his daughter to the king who then gave her to Sir John Villers.[165] Lady Hatton was not present: as a prisoner on parole, she could have attended as the king's guest but she pleaded illness.[166] The events leading up to the marriage underlined not only the subordinated position of married women and daughters in this period but also how commonplace violence remained not only in the justice system but also within the domestic arena.

The four incidents also underscore how common recourse to the law was during this period. As Tim Stretton has noted, '[D]uring the reigns of Elizabeth I and James I, levels of civil litigation rose to unprecedented levels, directly or indirectly touching the lives of the majority of the population.'[167] Moreover, despite the letter of the doctrine of coverture, this included cases brought by women.[168] As Stretton noted, '[D]espite the paucity of rights they enjoyed compared to men, many Tudor and Stuart women went to the law seeking redress for wrongs.'[169] This nuances if not questions the classic statements about coverture as articulated by Maitland.[170] Indeed, Stretton has noted that the historical literature written in the nineteenth and twentieth centuries has 'witnessed a see-sawing of historians' perceptions of the legal status of women in early modern England'.[171] While late nineteenth- and early twentieth-century feminist historians such as Charlotte Stopes,[172] Alice Clark[173] and Doris Stenton[174] 'agreed that women enjoyed a degree of legal independence in England prior to the seventeenth century under customary law', they also then claimed that this was then eroded by capitalism, industrialisation and the rise of the common law.[175] By contrast, later writers have questioned these two statements. As Stretton noted, '[M]odern feminist historians are sceptical about the existence of in the past of a "Golden Age" of equality between men and women.'[176] It is now accepted that women 'enjoyed fewer rights, fewer privileges, less wealth, less influence in spheres of power and less control over domestic affairs, than English men' and that this was perpetuated by legal institutions. The history shows that 'bias against women in English law can be found at every turn'.[177] For Stretton, the acceptance of this has led historians to shift focus and 'to investigate the practical effect of that bias'.[178] There has been a move in recent historical work towards exploring litigation through the study of court records and what they reveal about the lived experiences of litigants. This includes work by Maria Cioni,[179] Amy Erickson,[180] Laura Gowing[181] and Stretton himself.[182] This work has shown that, although

---

[164] Ibid. 64. This included some 'boisterous' behaviour on the part of the king himself, who was 'playing the buffoon about his palace' and who disturbed the newlyweds 'jumping up and down on the great four-post bed and making a most unkingly display of the royal prerogative' (ibid. 68).

[165] Ibid. 66.   [166] Ibid. 68.   [167] Stretton, *Women Waging War in Elizabethan England* xi.

[168] There is evidence of this before the early modern period, as shown by Gwen Seabourne's work on medieval law, discussed previously: Gwen Seabourne, *Women in the Medieval Common Law c.1200–1500* (Routledge, 2021).

[169] Stretton, *Women Waging War in Elizabethan England* 3.   [170] Pollock and Maitland, *The History of English Law* 482, 485.

[171] Stretton, *Women Waging War in Elizabethan England* 21.

[172] Charlotte Carmichael Stopes, *British Freewomen: Their Historical Privilege* (Cambridge University Press, 1907).

[173] Alice Clark, *Working Life of Women in Seventeenth Century* (Routledge, 1982 [1919]).

[174] Doris Stenton, *The English Woman in History* (Routledge, 1957).

[175] Stretton, *Women Waging War in Elizabethan England* 21.   [176] Ibid. 22.   [177] Ibid. 23.   [178] Ibid. 24.

[179] Maria L Cioni, *Women and Law in Elizabethan England with particular reference to the court of Chancery* (Garland, 1985).

[180] Amy Erickson, *Women and Property in Early Modern England* (Routledge, 1993).

[181] Laura Gowing, *Domestic Dangers: Women, Words and Sex in Early Modern London* (Oxford University Press, 1996).

[182] Stretton, *Women Waging War in Elizabethan England*; Tim Stretton, *Marital Litigation in the Court of Requests 1542–1642* (Cambridge University Press, 2008).

'a discriminatory ethos underpinned many areas of law', it was also true that 'discrimination against women was neither even nor universal and women could use the law as well as fall victim to it'.[183] The discussion of Lady Hatton's experiences provides evidence of this.

The public legal controversies of Sir Edward Coke and Lady Hatton also underscore a further factor that was ignored in the classic account of the legal rights of women. Statements of coverture only referred to the position at common law. Yet, this was a period of advanced legal pluralism. A number of other jurisdictions operated outside the common law and were open to litigants. These included the conciliar courts such as the Star Chamber, the courts of equity and the Church courts as well as the continued importance of local custom. As Stretton has put it, historians have downplayed 'the vast complexity of early modern English law' and a key aspect of this complexity, which is often overlooked but has a 'particular bearing on evaluating women's legal rights', is 'the simple fact that the common law enjoyed no monopoly in sixteenth century England, even if it at times is has monopolised the attention of historians of women's rights'.[184] The account of women's rights changes by including discussion of litigation in other courts outside of the common law. Stretton argued that the 'existence of these alternatives means that bleak prognoses about women's legal position' built up around coverture 'need to be modified using news from other legal quarters'.[185]

This point needs to be borne in mind not only in the discussion of the legal position of women but throughout this book. The focus, following Maitland, has been on the common law. In the periods that we have studied and beyond, the common law was not the only form of law and the common law courts were not the only place where litigants can seek recourse. We have been telling just one story about the historical development of law in England. A further point emphasised by Stretton in the context of adding nuance to the doctrine of coverture is also similarly of wider application. He noted 'the gulf between obvious statutory and judge-made rules, on the one hand, and practice on the other'.[186] This highlights the difference between the law as found on the page and law as interpreted and applied in practice. This difference can be particularly pronounced in writings about the law – treatises and textbooks – that seek to describe but actually interpret and crystallise the law. We have seen how such books have been crucial to the development of the common law dating back at least as far as Glanvill. However, perhaps the most important books written that synthesised the common law were those penned by Sir Edward Coke, which showed how the medieval law was mutating into its early modern form.

IV   Coke the Jurist

Coke's addiction to the common law led him to spend the little leisure time he had restating its principal doctrines in what was published as his *Institutes* and summarising the decisions of the judges in his *Reports*. Four parts of his *Institutes* were published: the first, a

---

[183] Stretton, *Women Waging War in Elizabethan England* 24.   [184] Ibid. 24–5.   [185] Ibid. 25.   [186] Ibid. 33.

252 *The Stuart Suicide (c.1603–1649)*

commentary on Littleton's *Tenures*; the second, a commentary on statutes of significance beginning with Magna Carta; the third, an account of the criminal law; and the fourth, a work on the courts and government bodies.[187] The first part of the *Institutes* was published in 1628, while the last three were all published in the 1640s after his death. Eleven volumes of *Reports* were published in his lifetime, with a further two being published posthumously. The publication of his works in the 1640s had an important short-term impact. As Holdsworth noted, they were published during 'the hour of the triumph of Parliament and the common law; and so the *Institutes* and *Reports* were accepted without question as an accurate statement of the law'.[188]

Moreover, Coke's work gave the parliamentary movement a cause worth fighting for. As Hill has pointed out, Coke's works provided 'a historical myth of the English constitution', casting the Norman Conquest as a popish perversion of the pure English laws, and presenting Magna Carta and subsequent statutes as monuments to the ancient liberties of all Englishmen.[189] Coke's work meant that 'the struggle of common lawyers and Parliamentarians was given historical significance and dignity, the prestige of a thousand-years old tradition'.[190] Such claims were clearly overstated. As we have seen, the common law developed in a pragmatic and piecemeal way, and these changes cannot be presented as being intended as part of a deliberate process over many centuries. The development of the common law was much more a means of securing control. The key term was not law but order. Focusing on law was exceptional; as shown by the way in which we have acknowledged Henry II as the father of the common law and Edward I as the English Justinian.

Like Magna Carta, Coke's work became a symbol that was often understood out of context. It became used for political purposes. As Hill put it, Coke's works stimulated a revolutionary movement that got out of control.[191] Coke's works were used by the parliamentary side to 'read into Coke's writings conclusions as remarkable as those which Coke himself had read into Magna Carta'.[192] This underscores how history can never be neutral, and that there is a thin line between history and nostalgia, and indeed between history and propaganda. Yet, this does not mean that Coke's work was not valuable. Like Magna Carta, it operated as a pragmatic text of its time and as a symbol for all ages. Leaving to one side, its later symbolic importance, Coke's writings were important because of the time in which they were produced.

Coke's work provided the first statement of English law following the legal renaissance. It reconciled the medieval and the early modern law. As Holdsworth noted, 'a great deal of restatement was needed' given that the 'sixteenth century – the century of transition from medieval to modern – had seen many changes in all branches of private law'.[193] Coke's

---

[187] Maitland, *The Constitutional History of England* 243. After Coke's death, some of his other writings were published: Boyer, 'Introduction' vii.

[188] Holdsworth, 'Sir Edward Coke' 340.

[189] Hill, *Intellectual Origins of the English Revolution* 257. For fuller discussion of the changing historical interpretations and uses of the Norman Conquest and Magna Carta over time, respectively, see George Garnett, *The Norman Conquest in English History* (Oxford University Press, 2021) vol. 1 and Baker, *The Reinvention of Magna Carta 1216–1616*.

[190] Hill, *Intellectual Origins of the English Revolution* 2258.   [191] Ibid. 253.   [192] Ibid. 260.

[193] Holdsworth, 'Sir Edward Coke' 343.

Coke the Jurist 253

work brought 'the medieval and the modern rules ... into harmony'. This was by no means an easy task given the scale and pace of the changes in this period. Thorne went so far as to argue that 'England under James and Charles had more in common than the nineteenth century than the fifteenth.'[194] It was during this period in which Coke lived that the medieval world was 'dissolving and reshaping into another'; although there was 'a background of continuity', 'the clash and fusion of the old and the new' was visible in the law in the same way that it was in 'religion or science, politics or economics, literature, music, medicine or architecture'. It was the work of Coke that 'systematized English law and in the process continued and extended the process of liberalizing it, of adapting it to the needs of a commercial society'.[195] His work was not only the bridge between the medieval and the modern but was also crucial in terms of repackaging the common law so that it survived the journey.

Given Coke's addiction to and protection of the common law, it was fitting that his works helped the common law to thrive as it adapted to the new commercial world. Coke's works educated common law lawyers of the new ideas and legal developments found in the conciliar courts.[196] The common law had been the product of an agrarian society, and it had seemed that 'Chancery and the prerogative courts would secure jurisdiction over commercial cases with which the procedures of the common law were ill-adapted to cope'.[197] However, in the sixteenth century, the common law 'made a remarkable comeback' and Coke's work played a significant part in this in terms of educating lawyers of the common law about other these legal systems. Coke's work also crystallised the common law in ways that would help make it endure. For Holdsworth, it was Coke's success in restating and adapting common law principles to meet modern needs that 'made the English legal system a much more uniform system than it might otherwise have been'.[198]

Coke's work had a longer-term impact upon the common law providing 'the nearest England had so far come to a codification of the law'.[199] His *Reports* filled a gap left by the discontinuation of the Year Books. They 'became the model for all subsequent reporting' and were 'the most frequently cited and most often argued-over reports the common law was known'.[200] Few doubted their authority until the nineteenth century: as Garden Barnes noted, the fact that the 'reports were often rambling and sometimes so opaque to be virtually incomprehensible mattered less than the fact that they bore the stamp of authenticity of Coke's reputation'.[201] This was also true of Coke's *Institutes*, which provided 'the first comprehensive statement of the common law since Bracton'.[202] The statements of the common law found in the *Institutes* became accepted 'as the law of the land'.[203] Passages and sentences from them continue to be quoted in court judgments today. Indeed, Coke is often cited as providing the common law definition of murder:

Murder is when a man of sound memory, and of the age of discretion, unlawfully killeth within any country of the realm reasonable creature *in rerum natura* under the king's peace, with malice

---

[194] Thorne, *Essays in Legal History* 226.   [195] Hill, *Intellectual Origins of the English Revolution* 256.
[196] Holdsworth, 'Sir Edward Coke' 343.   [197] Hill, *Intellectual Origins of the English Revolution* 227.
[198] Holdsworth, 'Sir Edward Coke' 344.   [199] Hill, *Intellectual Origins of the English Revolution* 231.
[200] Garden Barnes, *Shaping the Common Law* 133.   [201] Ibid. 134.   [202] Thorne, *Essays in Legal History* 225.
[203] Hill, *Intellectual Origins of the English Revolution* 245.

254 *The Stuart Suicide (c.1603–1649)*

fore-thought, either expressed by the party, or implied by law, so as the party wounded, or hurt etc die or the wound or hurt etc within a year and a day of the same.[204]

This underlined the key requirements for the *actus reus* (causing an unlawful killing) and *mens rea* of murder (malice aforethought), which have since remained largely settled.[205] The definition of murder is today the best known but is just one example of the enduring legacy of Coke's synthesis of the common law.[206] A further and more troubling example can be found in the use of Coke's works to justify slavery.

The seventeenth century saw a significant traffic in slaves from Africa to primarily provide labour in the West Indies and North America.[207] Although Charles I had promoted bound labour in his empire, the practice was to grow dramatically when Charles II was restored to the throne, in part as a means to cover lost sources of royal revenue.[208] The use of Coke's work to regulate and justify slavery was, on the face of it, unlikely. Despite the fact that his work would later become celebrated in America as the champion of the common law, Coke's judicial career and legal writings were very much concerned with the law of English subjects in England.[209] A partial exception can be found in *Calvin's Case*[210] in which Coke sat on a panel that had decided that a child born in Scotland after the union of the crowns was not an alien and therefore had the right to hold land. This not only extended common law rights in England to Scots but also provided an opportunity for Coke to outline some not particularly relevant general principles that might reflect that his eye was more upon the colonies than on Scotland. Coke used the opportunity to note that infidels were 'perpetual enemies' and that when a Christian king conquered the kingdom of infidels then the laws of the infidel would be abrogated. For Robert A Williams Jr, this effectively provided permission for the London Virginia Company to ignore the rights of Native Americans as they settled there.[211]

However, although Coke's writings very much focused on the common law in England, in so doing, they also packaged and transformed the common law 'from a limited royal legal system into a national constitutional resource' that could be transplanted and made 'available to all royal subjects throughout the expanding empire'.[212] The first volume of his *Institutes*, which updated Littleton, became 'the most important legal text of the seventeenth century across the empire, and the core of the printed common law'.[213]

---

[204] Edwardo Coke, *The Third Part of the Institutes of the Laws of England* (Brooke, 1797 [1640]) 48.

[205] The requirement that the death needed to happen within a 'year and a day' of the defendant's actions has been superseded by medical advances and so was abolished by the Law Reform (Year and a Day Rule) Act 1996. There have also been clarifications of the *mens rea* of murder. Constructive malice was abolished by the Homicide Act 1957. Malice aforethought is now taken to require intention to kill or cause grievous bodily harm: *R v. Vickers* [1957] 2 QB 664. The meaning of the word 'intention' has been the subject of a significant case law and body of academic writing.

[206] For further discussion, see Louis Blom-Cooper and Terence Morris, *With Malice Aforethought: A Study of the Crime and Punishment for Homicide* (Hart, 2004) chapter 2.

[207] Baker, *An Introduction to English Legal History* 513.

[208] Holly Brewer, 'Creating a Common Law of Slavery for England and Its New World Empire' (2021) 39(4) *Law and History Review* 765, 772, 778.

[209] Daniel J Hulsebosch, 'The Ancient Constitution and the Expanding Empire: Sir Edward Coke's British Jurisprudence' (2003) 21(3) *Law and History Review* 439, 440. Though it has been suggested that Coke played a role in settling the first Charter of Virginia: Frederic W Maitland, *English Law and the Renaissance* (Cambridge University Press, 1901) 12.

[210] (1608) 77 ER 277.

[211] Robert A Williams Jr, *The American Indian in Western Legal Thought* (Oxford University Press, 1990) 208.

[212] Hulsebosch, 'The Ancient Constitution and the Expanding Empire' 443.

[213] Brewer, 'Creating a Common Law of Slavery for England and Its New World Empire' 771.

Coke the Jurist 255

Coke's discussion of feudal rights and of the position of villeins were repurposed to apply to slaves. For instance, in Barbados in 1636, the governor declared that 'Africans and Indians who arrived "without contracts" would serve for life', a position that fitted with the 'feudal law then being republished and reprinted in texts such as Coke upon Littleton'. Between 1620 and 1660, English courts began to allow limited ownership claims that accorded with supposedly ancient laws of villenage.[214] Coke's work was also cited in *Butts v. Penny*[215] in which the English courts held that human beings could be considered to be property.[216] The judges reasoned that non-Christians were not subjects and so they could be 'litigated over as though they were a thing'.[217] Although this view would later be rejected as part of the constantly changing common law on slavery during the seventeenth and eighteenth centuries,[218] it nevertheless showed how Coke's reformulation of the common law could be used for nefarious purposes. As Holly Brewer has noted: 'In the seventeenth century the English common law became an instrument – the best the Stuart kings of England had – to create new laws, in the form of new precedents, and thus to both expand their own power and to legitimate slavery.'[219] And the common law that was exported and perverted was very much Coke's synthesis.

Indeed, while statutes and judgments only covered discrete legal issues, Coke's *Institutes* not only put the pieces of the jigsaw together but filled in the gaps. In this respect, the *Institutes* were like other treatises going back to Glanvill and similar to textbooks published today. However, the difference was the weight afforded to what was said in the *Institutes* because they were authored by Coke. The centuries that followed would see many other legal treatises produced that would not only be cited for legal propositions in courts and in Parliament but would also be used to teach generations of lawyers. What the writers said was the law became the law for such readers. No court and no Act of Parliament or code has ever sought to describe in detail the general principles of English criminal law, contract law, tort law and so on. It is the writers of the common law who have sought to synthesise and rationalise these and other bodies of law. Over time, they have come to remarkably similar conclusions so that it is possible to talk about general principles and these have become referred to in primary legal materials. However, this disguises how the elucidation of general principles and of bodies of law is an act of construction. It is a work of interpretation and therefore shaped by the assumptions, values and biases of the author. Yet, the role of writers is often overlooked and their statements are not understood as being authored. The work of Coke and those he followed and those who followed him – down to the dozen almost identical student textbooks now routinely published on each major area of law and the authoritative bulky practitioner tomes – are regularly cited but little attention is afford to the lives of the names given on the spine. It is often overlooked how the common law is supplemented and furthered by the 'common lore' developed in the textbook tradition.[220]

---

[214] Ibid. 774–5.   [215] (1677) 2 Lev 201.

[216] Butts' lawyer made reference to 'Coke's first volume of the Institutes, his section on the status of villeins (serfs), and to a discussion of whether feudal lords could own, buy, and sell them. That section articulated the obligations of villeins to their lords' (Brewer, 'Creating a Common Law of Slavery for England and Its New World Empire' 790, 792).

[217] Ibid. 795.   [218] Ibid 768.   [219] Ibid. 766.

[220] See further Russell Sandberg, *Subversive Legal History: A Manifesto for the Future of Legal Education* (Routledge, 2021) 202 *et seq.*

256 *The Stuart Suicide (c.1603–1649)*

Coke's writings, to which more attention has been afforded than most scholarly syntheses, underscores how the common lore can take on a life of its own. Coke was not simply describing the law or even interpreting it; in part he was making the law. Elucidation gave way to synthesis that developed into codification that resulted in the modernisation of the law. And Coke, it seems, was more creative than most legal authors. Garden Barnes noted that Coke was quite content 'not only to make up maxims, but also to shape the doctrine to fit them'.[221] Thorne has provided the useful advice that when reading Coke: 'As a rule of thumb it is well to remember that sentences beginning "For it is an ancient maxim of the common law", followed by one of Coke's spurious Latin maxims, which he could manufacture to fit any occasion and provide with an air of authentic antiquity, are apt to introduce a new departure.'[222] Such new departures were often small and technical but were not always so. Indeed, overtime even the smallest of tweaks would have significant impact. As Garden Barnes noted, Coke was not engaging in a deliberate act of creation. The exercise was 'a matter of discovery, or at least recovery, not of fabrication'.[223] In this respect, the thin line between interpretation and creation can be found in all legal works – both judgments and textbooks. It is on one level simply what lawyers do. As Thorne pointed out: 'Law must grow through the re-interpretation of the past, for only in such ways do judges and lawyers solve the paradox that law must be stable yet must never stand still.'[224]

Yet, Coke's actions stand out not only because his reputation meant that his interpretations of the law stuck but also because Coke drew upon 'his own uncritical acceptance of historical legends'.[225] In Coke's hands, Magna Carta became re-read as a declaration of the rights of all free Englishmen and feudalism gave rise to the principle that 'the house of an Englishman is to him as his castle'.[226] Coke created a historical context for the common law that fitted his values, assumptions and arguments about the place and significance of the common law.[227] Coke's fabricated historical context stuck. The lines between history and nostalgia, between history and propaganda, became blurred as the common law became appropriated as an emblem for Englishness. Rather than being seen as a pragmatic mechanism that enables and facilitates each generation (or more precisely, the ruling classes of each generation) to respond to the challenges that they face, the common law became linked to the idea of tradition. Legal change remained possible but the parameters narrowed and the pace declined.

V   Conclusions

The period leading up to the Civil War was tumultuous, not only politically but also legally. The steady concentration of royal power under the Tudors using Parliament developed into a long and bloody conflict between king and Parliament that resulted in a number of constitutional and legal innovations. Some experiments were short-lived but others –most

---

[221] Garden Barnes, *Shaping the Common Law* 133.   [222] Thorne, *Essays in Legal History* 227.
[223] Garden Barnes, *Shaping the Common Law* 133.   [224] Thorne, *Essays in Legal History* 233.
[225] Holdsworth, 'Sir Edward Coke' 338.   [226] Hill, *Intellectual Origins of the English Revolution* 236.
[227] Holdsworth, 'Sir Edward Coke' 340.

Conclusions

notably the understanding after the Restoration of the place of the monarch– were to provide the foundations of the modern State. Moreover, it is a simplification to present the period that led to the Civil War as simply a battle between king and Parliament. As Maitland pointed out in his lectures on constitutional history, there were three claimants for sovereignty: '(1) the king, (2) the king in parliament, (3) the law'.[228] This is why the role of Sir Edward Coke was so crucial. Not only was he the main advocate and author of the common law's claim for sovereignty but he was a parliamentarian and a holder of various high offices of State, which led him to often clash with the monarchy. While there are multiple stories that can be told about the legal history of this period, this justifies our focus on Coke.

Our focus of the life and works of Sir Edward Coke also underscores that it is misleading to make too watertight distinctions between the Tudor and early Stuart monarchies. Although the influence of Coke the man was mostly felt in the Stuart period and the influence of his works dominated English law from the Civil War onwards, Coke was formed in the Tudor period. As Holdsworth noted, he 'had the outlook of a Tudor lawyer and statesman, and a lawyer and statesman of the Elizabethan age'.[229] It was Coke who provided continuity across this period. He was also the bridge between the medieval and early modern period. It was Coke's achievements as a lawyer and as an author that melded the medieval and early modern laws. As Holdsworth put it, 'Coke succeeded in remoulding the medieval common law in such a way that it was made fit to bear rule in the modern English state'. It was ultimately Coke's writings that 'ensured the continuity of the development of the rules of English law'.[230]

Yet, both the man and his works were informed by the past. Coke's addiction to the common law, which resulted in radical action in his day, was based upon a fabricated nostalgic and patriotically idealised understanding of the past. This meant, as Maitland commented in his Rede lecture, that the 'medieval tradition was more than safe in his hands'.[231] However, it also meant that legal history was not safe in Coke's hands. Coke's work shows how history can be used to stabilise and can be perverted to suit particular causes. In Coke's hands, history became a form of fictional nostalgia and a means of propaganda whereby the common law was presented as a patriotic achievement. Yet, our account has questioned this. The stories we have told may on first glance point to the rise of law to promote order in place of violence. Yet, even in Coke's time, centuries after the heyday of the feud, violence remained ubiquitous, not just in relation to public punishments but also in domestic life. Talk of progression seems fanciful in an age of commonplace subordination of and violence towards women and where the evils of slavery were only just beginning. Indeed, such talk remains optimistic in our own age. Then and now, we often present law as the saviour but forget how English law was often complicit in perpetuating systems of discrimination.

This does not mean that you should be downhearted, however. The role of the law student and the informed citizen is to challenge, not accept, disadvantage and discrimination,

---

[228] Maitland, *The Constitutional History of England* 298. [229] Holdsworth, 'Sir Edward Coke' 336. [230] Ibid. 343–4.
[231] Maitland, *English Law and the Renaissance* 29.

258   *The Stuart Suicide (c.1603–1649)*

however systematised and ingrained that is. As this book has argued, history can play a part in this. History can be used to subvert rather than stabilise the present. History can be used as a means of showing how alternatives can be realised. It can subvert the most ingrained assumptions, values and ideas of the common law and indeed of the common lore. A historical analysis questions what we take for granted and the doctrines that overtime become indoctrinated. This includes being suspicious of progress narratives and also of what is omitted in legal sources and accounts. As Maitland once noted, 'Law schools make tough law.'[232] By this he meant that legal education can blind students and practitioners from the context in which rules exist and are applied.[233] A historical approach can recognise this and better equip you not only to be able to think like lawyers but also, and more importantly, to question like citizens.

By being able to place your study of the current law in its history, you are able to see the limits and possibilities of the law. The historical context teaches that law is a construct, a pragmatic product of its age. This raises the questions of who benefits from the law and who does not. It also underscores that legal change is possible and nothing is truly fixed. This is not how things will appear at first sight, of course. Looking at the syllabuses of your courses or the almost identical contents pages of corresponding textbooks presents a picture where the framework is by and large fixed and appears to be universal, where legal change is likely to be slow, piecemeal and in a foreseeable direction. History, however, shows that this is both a construction and a fabrication. As historically informed law students, you can challenge this and go beyond it. As Maitland commented at the end of his lectures on constitutional history:

> I have some little fear lest the study of what we call general jurisprudence may lead you to take a false view of law. Writers on general jurisprudence are largely concerned with the classification of legal rules. This is a very important task, and to their efforts we owe a great deal – it is most desirable that law should be clearly stated according to some rational and logical scheme. But do not get into the way of thinking of law as consisting of a number of independent compartments, one of which is labelled constitutional, another administrative, another criminal, another property, so that you can learn the contents of one compartment and know nothing as to what is in the others. No, law is a body, a living body, every member of which is connected with and depends upon every other member ... Life I know is short, and law is long, very long, and we cannot study everything at once; still no good comes of refusing to see the truth, and the truth is that all parts of our law are very closely related to each other, so closely that we can set no logical limit to our labours.[234]

Reference to the history of the common law shows not only that law is indivisible but also that it cannot be separated from it political, economic and social context. It also casts a light upon the nature of law that differs from the nostalgia of Coke or the rationalisation found in the textbook tradition. We have seen how law is the manifestation of order, nothing more than politics written up; how legal ideas ebb and flow, ridiculing talk of progress; and how

---

[232] Ibid. 25.

[233] This is reflected in Anthony Bradney's warning that in order to 'become a law student the student must forget who he or she is' (Anthony Bradney, 'Law as a Parasitic Discipline' (1998) 25(1) *Journal of Law and Society* 71, 77).

[234] Maitland, *The Constitutional History of England* 539.

Conclusions 259

legal changes come often as a result of creative responses on the ground that pay little attention to legal classifications. This is underscored by the pragmatic development of the first forms of action concerning land; the contract and property law developments reverberating from that 'fertile mother of actions',[235] the writ of trespass; and other examples discussed throughout this book, which are just the tip of the iceberg. It becomes clear from these studies that law is both important and ordinary; although laws seem to cover large topics and can have great effects, the creation, enforcement, adjudication and interpretation of law are often practical compromises designed to simply deal with the matters in front of the parties. They are more mundane and therefore more malleable than may first appear.

Focusing on Coke is therefore apt not only in terms of understanding the period up to the Civil War but also in providing an appropriate end point for our study of the genesis of the common law. Focusing on Coke to understand the early Stuart period, underscores how law is nothing more than the consequence of human interaction; how it is the product of personal politics and the clash of ideologies; and how it is decided upon and written about by human hands. It underscores many of the general points that we have come across in previous chapters. Moreover, our focus on Coke and our brief discussion of his life and behaviour brings to mind a criticism of legal history made by Ian Ward, who noted that nowhere was the risk of writing a history that forgets 'faces' greater than in legal history.[236] This justifies the ending of our account here. While the story of the genesis of the common law can just about be told by reference to the impact of successive monarchs upon law and governance,[237] the same is not true of stories of how the common law subsequently developed. Such stories deserve different perspectives and more faces.[238] Identifying an end point is invariably arbitrary and runs the risk of simplifying understandings of historical changes and continuities. However, the age of Coke seems an appropriate place to end, but with a semi-colon rather than a full stop. Coke's life and works as a bridge between the medieval and the early modern represents both change and continuity; it provides both a number of endings and several beginnings. It therefore seems a good enough place as any to tear the seamless web.[239]

---

[235] Frederic W Maitland, *The Forms of Action at Common Law* (Cambridge University Press, 1965 [1909]) 48.

[236] Ward, *English Legal Histories* 12.

[237] Cf. Chrimes's insistence that his biography of Henry VII was 'not to be regarded as primarily a biography' nor was 'intended to be a history of England during his reign' but could be 'perhaps best be described as a study of the impact of Henry Tudor upon the government of England' (SB Chrimes, *Henry VII* (Yale University Press, 1999 [1972]) xxi).

[238] The same can be said of the periods discussed in this book and the reader is encouraged to follow the leads discussed in Chapter 2 to explore additional perspectives on the stories that we have narrated. This book has been designed to fulfil the 'need for texts that introduce the conventional stories and authors of those stories, enabling students to understand these before they question them' (Sandberg, *Subversive Legal History* 223).

[239] Cf. Pollock and Maitland, *The History of English Law* 1.

'The forms of action we have buried, but they still rule us from their graves'.

Frederic W Maitland, *The Forms of Action at Common Law* (Cambridge University Press, 1965 [1909]) 2.

Epilogue

Destiny of the Common Law

'Is that it?'

The Man of Law stared back at the Commander following his interruption, pondering quite how he was to respond.

'Well, history – as Frederic W Maitland put it –is a seamless web and these stories that I have told you are just some of threads. Even in the periods that we have focused on, there is a multitude of other stories we could tell; other focuses we could adopt; other perspectives we could and should tell.'

The Commander nodded. He had already indulged quite the lecture. But he found himself asking for more. The words just fell out of his mouth: 'And what about later periods?'

'Oh, there's so many tales that can be told of the later developments in English law', replied the Man of Law. 'The stories I have told relate to the genesis of the common law where Maitland has been our main tour guide. But there are so many stories that can be told about the destiny of the common law: how it increasingly developed a life of its own and became overly complicated, restrictive and closed to change. As ever, the common law developed in a pragmatic, non-linear manner. The restoration of the monarchy in 1660 did not result in the development of the modern constitution and legal system overnight. The centuries that followed saw two revolutions that were to prove pivotal.'

The Commander's silence was taken as permission for the Man of Law to talk about these two revolutions.

'The first revolution was the so-called Glorious Revolution. Tensions had continued to exist between the king and Parliament in the reigns of Charles II (1660–85) and particularly under James II (1685–8). When James fled abroad, William of Orange (who had a legitimate claim to the throne through his grandfather Charles I) assembled Parliament and they decided that James had broken the contract between people and king and had therefore abdicated the government. William and his wife Mary (James II's daughter) were formally proclaimed king and queen. And a raft of important constitutional statutes followed: the Bill of Rights of 1688, the Act of Toleration of 1689, the Act of Settlement of 1701 and the Act of Union of 1707, which united England and Scotland.'

The Commander, fearful of a further lengthy lecture, interjected, 'That sounds like the beginnings of a written constitution to me.'

262   *Epilogue: Destiny of the Common Law*

'Not really', the Man of Law smiled. 'It's true that the supremacy of Parliament had been underlined both in terms of the king being below statute and also the common law being below statute. But in other respects, not much had changed. Monarchs still had significant powers known as the royal prerogative. Maitland in his lectures on constitutional history remarked that for centuries to come the extent of the royal prerogative was vague because kings and queens had rarely gone near to breaking the law.'

'And what was the second pivotal revoution?' enquired the Commander, who was clearly enjoying the account more than he had realised.

'That was the Industrial Revolution. The population dramatically increased and England went from being a country based on land and agriculture to an empire-builder focusing upon industry and commerce where smog-filled cities dominated the landscape and mass movement became facilitated for the first time by advances in road and railway transport. Like other major social and economic changes, this was reflected in English law. The country had now undeniably moved away from its feudal basis and so the common law with its feudal foundations looked increasingly outdated.'

The Commander nodded, giving permission for the Man of Law to continue.

'The role of Parliament increased yet again, particularly in terms of creating new criminal offences. Criminal law became larger and harsher. The Black Act of 1723 alone created over 350 new criminal offences. And the number of crimes punishable by death soared. This became known as the Bloody Code. And it was not just criminal law that grew. This period saw the seeds sown for seeds of commercial, company and employment law.'

'The common law was evolving then', remarked the Commander.

'No, it wasn't a deliberate, linear story of progress', the Man of Law replied, 'Far from it. People cheer at how the law stopped slavery, gave rights to women and gave everyone the rights to vote, but these changes were pragmatic and dragged out. And people overlook how it was the common law that facilitated slavery, patriarchy and the interests of the upper classes. The stories I have told have shown how law is used as a means of maintaining order. And this was to remain true not only in England and in other parts of what was to become the United Kingdom but also throughout the Empire. We often present the law within a story of freedom, when it was actually used as a means of subordination and control.'

The Commander was taken aback at how angry and frustrated the Man of Law was getting. This was atypical for such a meeting. The Commander's questions usually provoked sighs, eye-rolls and the occasional tut.

'But people could still use the law, presumably?' the Commander tentatively suggested.

'Not really,' came the retort, 'the common law was in a terrible mess. English law was becoming increasingly complex and unjust. The writ system was increasingly tangled. By the nineteenth century, it was laughable how the antiquated the law was. And, so, there were moves towards its rationalisation. There were lots more statutes on all sorts of new topics: giving some but limited rights to workers, providing some levels of education and what would become known later as consumer rights. And there were moves to rationalise the way in which the common law operated. The Uniformity of Process Act 1832 and

Epilogue: Destiny of the Common Law   263

Common Law Procedure Act 1852 abolished the writ system. Now, just one writ of summons was to be used and people did not need to specify the form of action.'

'That sounds like progress', reacted the Commander before correcting himself with a question, 'Was it?'

'Yes and no. Maitland in his lectures on "The Forms of Action" said that "the forms of action we have buried, but they still rule us from their graves". People –lawyers and textbook writers – continued to think in terms of the different actions corresponding to the now abolished writs. This was particularly true in tort law, which continued to distinguish between different torts, different actions. But, yes, overall, some of the curious technicalities and strange anomalies were removed and large parts of the law were now prescribed in statute law. Ideas of personal freedom and personal responsibility increasingly underscored the law, particularly in contract and criminal law where the number of capital offences was decreased. Although attempts to produce a criminal code proved unsuccessful, particular areas of law and particular offences did become codified to varying degrees.'

The Commander's interview continued, 'And people could go to court, I suppose?'

'Have you read *Bleak House* by Charles Dickens?' was the Man of Law's lightning response. The Commander paused, decided to be honest and shook his head. This candour momentarily baffled the Man of Law but he then continued: 'Well, I haven't either but that novel shows how the legal systems were also in need of rationalisation. There were extraordinary delays. In the preface to *Bleak House*, Dickens wrote that he was aware of a current case that had been ongoing for nearly twenty years; in which thirty to forty counsels had appeared and which was apparently no nearer to its termination now than when it was begun!'

'So you've read that bit?!'

The Man of Law ignored the Commander's taunt and continued. 'The problem was in part that the courts of equity had developed into a separate system of law, providing rights where the common law did not, with its own courts and separate lawyers. And so, litigants went from court to court and often had to go to both courts in order to secure their rights. In the middle of the nineteenth century, this led to a number of piecemeal changes that allowed common law courts to grant some equitable remedies and allowed the Court of Chancery to award common law remedies such as damages. However, real reform came shortly afterwards. The Supreme Court of Judicature Acts 1873 and 1875, generally known as the Judicature Acts, consolidated and unified the courts into two parts: the High Court (which by 1880 would have three divisions: the King's Bench, Chancery and Probate, Divorce and Admiralty) and the Court of Appeal. Appeals would go from the High Court to the Court of Appeal and then to the Judicial Committee of the House of Lords (which over a century later would become known as the Supreme Court). All of these courts now administered the rights, reliefs and defences found in both the common law and in equity. Common law and equity remained separate bodies of rules but were now enforced in the same courts.'

'That sounds complicated', remarked the Commander.

The Man of Law nodded. 'And it only got more complicated in the centuries that followed Maitland. Ideas and approaches ebbed and flowed. In the twentieth century, for instance, the horrors of global warfare inspired a new spirit of international collaboration and the growth of the welfare state, including the provision of legal aid to allow people

264 *Epilogue: Destiny of the Common Law*

access to the law. But this collapsed into renewed parochialism, and the rolling back of the State and savage cuts to legal aid put the courts out of the reach for many people. And then in the twenty-third century . . .'

The Man of Law stopped himself. He was aware that he had said enough.

'That's the problem with history', he smiled, 'there's just so much of it! But history is crucial to understanding English law. People don't realise that. They think that the past is an irrelevance or confuse history with nostalgia. History should not be used to stabilise the present but to challenge it, to subvert it. It shows us that other ways of thinking and doing law are possible because they have been considered or adopted in the past. Everything that we think is fixed about the law is not – every piece of law, each legal institution, every legal idea was created at a particular time usually by happenstance to respond to particular problems.'

The Commander nodded, thinking of what he had heard about how the common law had developed as a means of maintaining order, how this development had occurred pragmatically over centuries, how kingly concessions had come and gone, how criminal and civil law had once not been distinguished, how the dividing line between contract and tort had been malleable throughout the ages and how law was basically a political tool: Acts of Parliament, as their name suggests, were basically politics written up while lawyers were focusing on the difficulties of the clients in front of them and the line between judicial application, judicial interpretation and judicial law making was constantly blurred.

The Man of Law concluded, 'And this is why the most important thing we can do going forwards is to ensure that our students of law are taught legal history. An appreciation of law's history not only makes sense of the law today but also points to the need and often the direction of legal change. It underlines the limit of law too. Unfortunately, all too often law is studied without its history and a collective amnesia takes hold. Indeed, I have one more story to tell . . .'

***

On Monday 26 May 1817, Mary Ashford, who was about twenty years old, attended a dance at Tryburn House. Abraham Thornton, a local bricklayer, also attended the dance. Ashford and Thornton danced together frequently throughout the night and left after midnight. The next morning, Mary Ashford's drowned body was pulled from a nearby pit of water. Thornton acknowledged that he had had sexual relations with Mary but insisted that this had been consensual and he had not killed her. The case came to criminal trial. The prosecutor argued that he had assaulted her and thrown her unconscious body into the watery pit. The jury found Thornton not guilty on grounds of alibi evidence that he had been some distance away from the murder site shortly after the crime had said to have been committed. William Ashford, Mary's brother, then brought an action in the civil courts against Thornton, known as the appeal. In response, Thornton pleaded not guilty – and demanded trial by battle.[1]

---

[1] For detailed discussion of the case see John Hall (ed) *Trial of Abraham Thornton* (William Hodge, 1926); Naomi Clifford, *The Murder of Mary Ashford* (Pen and Sword, 2018).

Epilogue: Destiny of the Common Law 265

Although no one had claimed trial by battle since 1638,[2] the King's Bench came to the conclusion that there was 'a regular chain of authorities proving that the trial by battel [sic] is the defendant's right' and that it had not been proved that any of the recognised exceptions to this applied.[3] Lord Ellenborough concluded:

The general law of our land is in favour of the wager of battel, and it is our duty to pronounce the law as it is, and not what we may wish it to be. Whatever prejudices therefore may exist against this mode of trial, still as it is the law of the land, the Court must pronounce judgment for it.

William Ashford refused to fight Thornton and so Abraham Thornton was a free man. Legislation was quickly introduced into Parliament, however, to abolish both trial by battle and the appeal.

Ashford v. *Thornton* can therefore be seen as an illustration of how the ghosts of legal history can come back to haunt us. This was the view of some spectators and commentators at the time that saw the proceedings as 'unearthing vestigial brutality'.[4] Yet, the case also underlines that no neat line can be drawn between the past and the present in the common law. Even in the century of reform and rationalisation, the legacy of medieval values, feudal connections and blood ties was ever present. Even centuries after Coke, the supposed bridge between the medieval and the modern law, there remained a 'delicate balance between medievalist sensibilities and modernist reforms'.[5] Trial by battle was by no means the sole vestige of the medieval period, and abolition of similar relics was often not so straightforward. In 1815, a bill to abolish the pillory failed and it was retained for a time for crimes of fraud and perjury.[6] Furthermore, duels of honour existed entirely outside the law and remained both 'permissible and illegal'.[7]

Ashford v. *Thornton* also demonstrates how legal decisions often attract significant public interest. The case quickly became the focus of five pamphlets and three plays.[8] These representations invariably both stressed Mary Ashford's virginity before the dance while casting aspirations on her character in terms of how she dressed for and behaved at the dance.[9] This underscores how public attention in legal matters is often gendered and shows the gendered bias of the legal system. The possibility of trial by battle also invoked interest. It was not only sex and violence that attracted attention, however. The medieval dimension of the case also piqued interest. The age of reform was also a period of nostalgia. There was a revival in interest in the medieval period amongst architects, painters and authors.[10] Legal writers were not immune from this, with Maitland's work in the decades that followed shedding new light and prompting further interests in the

---

[2] *Claxton v Lilburn* (1638) Cro Car 522.   [3] *Ashford v Thornton* (1818) 1 B & Ald 405.
[4] Gary R Dyer, '"Ivanhoe", Chivalry and the Murder of Mary Ashford' (1998) 39(3) *Criticism* 383, 387.
[5] Mark Schoenfield, 'Waging Battle: Ashford v Thornton, Ivanhoe and Legal Violence' (2000) 23(2) *Prose Studies* 61, 67.
[6] The pillory was finally abolished in 1837. The stocks were never abolished but fell out of use.
[7] Clifford, *The Murder of Mary Ashford* 89; Schoenfield, 'Waging Battle' 68.
[8] Dyer, '"Ivanhoe", Chivalry and the Murder of Mary Ashford' 387.
[9] A pamphlet by the Reverend Luke Booker, 'Moral Review of the Conduct and Case of Mary Ashford', consisted of sixty-four pages of lessons to young women to deter them from attending 'scenes of amusement, unsanctioned and untended by proper protection' (Clifford, *The Murder of Mary Ashford* 102).
[10] Ibid., 384.

medieval law and its legacy. Yet, history should not be confused with nostalgia. The past should neither be glorified nor dismissed as a barbarous fantasy world far removed from our own.

Exploring the genesis of the common law is not to tell a story that has a definite ending. *Ashford* v. *Thornton* shows that seemingly archaic and forgotten legal ideas, institutions and practices can rise from the coffin marked legal history. The precedent system at the heart of the common law means that lawyers cannot help but look backwards. Yet, by understanding the past, they can also look forwards. Similar issues have arisen down the centuries; the facts of *Ashford* v. *Thornton* are far from period-specific. The law needs to be moulded in order to respond to the needs of each generation. Exploration of the law's past, therefore, is not just a pleasant and distracting time travel trip but is necessary for what it reveals about the possibilities for law's present and future. As Maitland noted, the lesson of legal history is that 'each generation has an enormous power of shaping its own law'.[11] Lawyers, of course, do not operate in a vacuum. There are all sorts of structural issues that provide obstacles. And laws and legal institutions will never be perfect; they exist in a constantly choppy sea of complexity and chaos. But Maitland was right. Each generation has the power, and therefore the responsibility, to shape their own law and are better equipped to do so if they know where that law has come from. It is over to you ...

---

[11] Frederic W Maitland, 'Letter from Maitland to AV Dicey, c. July 1896', quoted in CHS Fifoot, *Frederic William Maitland* (Harvard University Press, 1971) 143.

'Nowhere so busy a man as he there was
And yet he seemed busier than he was
In termes had he case and doomes all
That from the time of King William were fall'.

Geoffrey Chaucer, The Canterbury Tales (Duke
Classics, 2013) 39
(Introduction to the Man of Law (a Sergeant of
the Law) from the 'General Prologue')

'Though there was no one so busy as he,
He was less busy than he seemed to be,
He knew of every judgment, case and crime
Ever recorded since King William's time'.

Modern translation in Geoffrey Chaucer, The
Canterbury Tales (Penguin, 1975) 27–28;
translated by Nevill Coghill

Afterword

The prologue and epilogue to this book are both works of fiction. Whether the same is true of the chapters in between is for the reader to work out. Legal writing is always an exercise in interpretation. There is always an element of invention: even attempting to join the dots requires choices as to made, judgments to be formed, and values and biases to be inevitably displayed. This is all the more pronounced in relation to works of legal history: the larger canvas means that brush strokes are more visible and the omissions more obvious. Perhaps this means that the authored nature of legal history works is also more noticeable. This is shown in how the actual titles of a number of legal historical works – especially those that cover a large ground – have often become irrelevant and those books become known by the name of their author. Legal historians, for instance, refer to 'Pollock and Maitland', 'Baker' and 'Milsom', rather than the titles of those seminal works.

Yet, the subtitle of this book has been carefully chosen. The subtitle is not '*The* Genesis of the Common Law', as if it is a definitive account. It is rather a collection of stories that reflect upon the beginnings of the common law – its genesis. It does not pretend to cover anything other than the early stages of the common law; it is just the start of the story (or, to be more precise, a number of starts). The word 'genesis' has been chosen in preference to words such as 'foundations' or even 'origins' in order to reject a narrative of progress. It has also been chosen because it is less clear where the genesis of the common law can be said to have started and if it can ever be said to have ended. As you will have seen, the text repeatedly raises these questions to show the arbitrariness of the decisions made in the text, not only in terms of where the book as a whole begins and ends but what the chapters focus upon and what they do not.

This is intended to highlight that this book is my personal interpretation of the genesis of the common law. There is much more that could have been said and everything here could have been said differently. This is my attempt to bring it together but not to impose an order on it. That is why the book follows a chronological approach. My purpose is to underline the pragmatic and therefore the inevitably haphazard and disordered nature of English law – the chaos of the common law. This will hopefully show how the law is never perfect but is always capable of change. Structural forces will make this difficult and self-interests will often result in a conservative clinging to the status quo. Yet, change is not only possible but also can be achieved on a bigger scale than is often realised. History can help with this; as we have seen and as I have argued at length elsewhere,[1] history can be used to subvert what we think we know about the law. This means that the scope for reform now and in the future is greater than we often realise. The message of this book for law students is that this potential for change is in their hands. We are all capable of the most incredible change.

This book is written for students beginning law courses or specialist modules on legal history and hopefully it shows that a historical approach to law is necessary. The intention is to demonstrate how understanding the historical 'backstories' of the common law can make more sense of the rest of law courses that focuses on the current law of discrete legal areas. It also questions and exposes such classifications. In other words, it seeks to question what law schools and legal textbooks often tell you about the law! This book is intended to whet the reader's appetite for legal history. It is hoped that this will be the first book you read on the topic but not your last. That is why the pages have been packed with footnotes: you are encouraged to follow the footnote references, read more widely, question what I have written and develop your own interpretations.

This book has had an exceptionally long gestation period. It is fitting that this book will be first published in 2023 since that year marks twenty years since I first studied legal history at Cardiff. The weekly lectures by Professor Thomas Watkin, delivered without notes but with erudition, humour and passion, not only reawakened my interest in history generally but also made my whole law degree make sense. Suddenly, I could see how the common law fitted together, where it came from and why modules on contract, tort and land law were structured as they were. It was the most important module I studied during my degree.[2] And Professor Watkin's exemplary teaching shaped how I see the subject and the importance of legal history. With his departure to Bangor, I regretted that subsequent students would be deprived of such an opportunity. Ten years later, in 2013, returning from study leave, I became determined to remedy this, I seeded an argument for the need for legal history in the conclusion to the book that I had written while on sabbatical.[3] And I made plans to re-introduce an undergraduate module on the topic and to write the book that you currently have in your hands.

It took me considerably longer to achieve one of these objectives than the other! A module on legal history was re-introduced in 2014 and was at first co-taught with Professor Norman Doe and then with Dr Sharon Thompson. In addition to benefitting from their friendship and good humour, I have learnt a great deal from both Norman and Sharon who are both first rate legal historians.[4] I have also benefitted from the patience of successive cohorts of students on the course who have tolerated draft versions of much of this book. It has been gratifying to see the subject have the same effect on them as it had

---

[1] Russell Sandberg, *Subversive Legal History: A Manifesto for the Future of Legal Education* (Routledge, 2021).

[2] I would wholeheartedly recommend reading his articles on legal history subjects as well as his awesome book: Thomas G Watkin, *The Legal History of Wales* (2nd ed., University of Wales Press, 2012).

[3] Russell Sandberg, *Religion, Law and Society* (Cambridge University Press, 2014) 260–3.

[4] Norman Doe, *Fundamental Authority in Late Medieval Law* (Cambridge University Press, 1990) is a groundbreaking study of how legal ideas develop in ways different from what is often assumed, while Sharon Thompson, *Quiet Revolutionaries: The Married Women's Association and Family Law* (Hart, 2022) is a masterpiece in terms of a grounded feminist study that focuses on how it is important to pay attention to the role of activism, even where that leads only to piecemeal reform and even failures.

on me, and it is pleasing to continue the long association between Cardiff University and the study of legal history – a connection that goes beyond the law school.

I have racked up a number of other debts during the long period in which this book has been written. I am grateful to the staff at Cambridge University Press for their patience and for their support for the book. Earlier versions of some of the arguments made in this book have been made elsewhere. Very abridged versions of the main points of Chapters 1, 2 and 8 have been published in *Law and Justice*.[5] And aspects of the first two chapters were developed in my recent monograph *Subversive Legal History: A Manifesto for the Future of Legal Education*.[6] However, somewhat appropriately, lines of cause and effect between the two are far from straightforward. That whole book came into existence because of ideas in early drafts for this book. However, the fact that that book was published first now means that I am crediting that book for ideas that it developed from this book! I have also presented aspects at various conferences, workshops, seminars and public lectures over the years. I am grateful to all who have engaged with my work and its arguments, including in more informal settings and on social media. Almost every work conversation has fed into this book in some way. As ever, however, my largest debt is to my family and especially my wife Emma.

Russell Sandberg
Neath
July 2022

The Man of Law will return

https://twitter.com/themanoflaw_

---

[5] Russell Sandberg, 'The Time for Legal History: Some Reflections on Maitland and Milsom Fifty Years on' (2018) 180 *Law & Justice* 21–37; Russell Sandberg, 'The Unexpected Benefit of Hindsight: Reassessing the Legal Importance of the Black Death from the Vantage Point of the Covid Pandemic' (2022) 188 *Law & Justice* 38–50.

[6] Sandberg, *Subversive Legal History*.

Index

Act Abolishing Kingship 1649, 245
Act of Proclamations 1539, 214
Act of Supremacy 1534, 210
Act of Supremacy 1559, 213
Act of the Six Articles 1539, 212
Act of Uniformity 1559, 213
action on the case, 169–74, 176
Acts of Uniformity in 1549, 1552, 212
Acts of Union. *See* Laws in Wales Acts 1535 and 1542
Æthelbert, laws of, 52, 56
Æthelstan (king), 53
aids, 74
Allmand, Christopher, 185
Ames, J. B., 170, 216
Anarchy, the, 66, 82, 86–7, 96, 230
Anglo-Saxon law, 47
  absolute liability in, 54
  as archaic, 47
  cautionary perspective on, 48, 55
  codes of law in, 56–7
  ecclesiastical matters in, 58
  folk-moots in, 57
  folkright in, 56
  'franchisal courts' in, 59
  hundred courts in, 57
  King's Court in, 60–1
  liability in, 54
  'Lord's courts' in, 59
  maximalist perspective on, 48, 50–1, 55, 67
  minimalist perspective on, 47–8, 51, 54–5, 67
  notion of criminal law in, 53
  'private' courts in, 59
  royal initiative in, 56
  shift from feud to compensation in, 55
  shift from kin to lord's responsibility in, 60
  shire courts in, 58
  trial by compurgation in, 61
  trial by ordeal in, 61–2
Anglo-Saxon period
  definition of, 49
  feuds in, 50–1
  importance of kindred connections in, 60
  localisation of justice in, 61–2

  powers of kings in, 56
  rise in governance in, 55
  shift from feud to compensation in, 50
  slavery in, 58
anti-essentialism, 34
anti-Semitism, 121–2
appeal
  as Norman innovation, 69–70
Appointment of Bishops Act 1533, 211
assize courts
  formation of under Henry II, 90
Assize of Clarendon 1166, 88–90, 98
Assize of *Darrein Presentment*, 99
Assize of Mort D'Ancestor, 99–100, 104, 143
Assize of Northampton 1176, 88, 90, 99
Assize of Novel Disseisin, 98–100, 104, 106–7, 152
Assize of *Utrum*, 99
Assize of Windsor 1179, 97
assizes, petty, 98
assizes, possessory, 98
assumpsit, action of, 174–7
Auchmuty, Rosemary, 10–11, 30–1, 34, 39
Augustine, Saint, 57, 81

Bacon, Francis, 238–9, 242, 249
Bailey, Mark, 161, 165–6
Baker, John H., 12, 20–1, 225
  Clarendon lectures, 197
  on Court of Chancery, 201, 203
  on Court of Exchequer, 199
  on criminal law, 225
  on English vs. Continental legal development, 194
  Ford Lecture, 192–3
  on Inns of Court, 194
  on land law, 218
  on law of obligations, 215
  on Magna Carta, 132
  on murder and manslaughter, 179
  on Novel Disseisin, 98
  on Tudor period, 189, 194, 196, 198, 205, 216
  view of Black Death, 158
  on villeins, 77
Bancroft, Richard (Archbishop of Canterbury), 238

Index

Barnes, Thomas G., 193, 236, 238, 242, 256
Barton, J. L., 203
Bate's Case, 239
Batlan, Felice, 31
Battle of Bosworth Field, 185, 189, 191
Battle of Evesham, 129
Battle of Hastings, 45, 72, 191
Battle of Lewes, 128
Battle of Mortimer's Cross, 185
Bean, J. W. M., 146, 220, 222
Beattie, Cordelia, 202
Becket controversy, 86–7
Becket, Thomas, 86–7
Bell, Derrick, 35, 37
Bellamy, J. G., 178
benefit of clergy, 86, 225–7
Bennett, Michael
   on Black Death, 161, 168–9
   on labour legislation, 162–3, 165
Beowulf, 50
Biancalana, Joseph, 107
Binder, Guyora, 228
Black Death
   as catalyst for legal change, 161, 167, 169, 176, 180
   and consolidation of state power, 161–2, 165–7
   and criminal law, 177, 179–81
   as end of Planagenet England, 186
   and Justices of the Peace, 167
   King's Council under, 167
   King's Court under, 167
   and labour legislation, 162–3, 167, 171, 175
   and laws of obligaton, 169
   legal profession in, 168–9
   neglect of in legal history, 157–61
   and treason, 177–8
black-letter tradition, 2, 24
Bonham's Case, 240
bot. See compensation, system of
Bowen, Catherine Drinker, 240
Boydston, Jeanne, 67
Bracton, Henry, 134
Bracton's Note Book, 105
Bradney, Anthony, 16
Brand, Paul, 21, 107, 130, 142
Brookes, Christopher, 23
Burgage tenures, 74
Burt, Caroline, 139
Butterfield, Herbert, 27
Butts v. *Penny*, 255

Calvin's Case, 254
Cameron, James, 48
canon law, 81, 192, 200, 202–3, 207–11
Carpenter, Christine, 184
Carpenter, D. A., 119
Carta Mercatoria, 121
Case of Commendams, 242
Case of Proclamations, 239

Castle Guard, as feudal tenure, 73
Catherine of Aragon, 209, 211
certiorari, writ of, 198
cestui que use, 219
Chancellor, formation of role, 81
Charles I (king)
   martial law under, 243–4
   Parliament under, 244–5
   and royal prerogative, 244
Charles II (king)
   restoration of, 246, 254
Charter of Liberties, 86
Charter of the Forest 1217, 114, 125–6
Chudleigh's Case, 237
church courts, 5
   in Norman period, 68
   under Henry II, 86–7
   under Henry VIII, 210
Church of England, 6, 87, 190, 207, 211, 213, 246
Cioni, Maria, 250
Circumspecte Agatis 1286, 140
Civil War
   as challenge to common law, 234–5
   origin of, 245
Clanchy, M. T., 148
Clark, Alice, 250
Clement VII (pope), 209
Clergy Act 1529, 210
Cnut (king), 48, 57–9
Coke, Sir Edward
   on Acts of Parliament, 240
   as Attorney General, 237–8
   as Chief Justice, 238
   conflict over Court of Chancery, 236
   conflict with James I, 239–41
   disputes with ecclesiastical courts, 239
   as husband, 247–51
   as judicial martyr, 242
   on judicial review, 240
   as jurist, 251–6
   on King's Bench, 241
   as lawyer, 236–8
   legacy of for common law, 252–7
   as MP, 237, 243–4
   on murder, 253
   and royal sovereignty, 238–9, 242
   scholarly reception of, 256
   selective obedience to the law, 249
   on slavery, 254
   and sovereignty of common law, 235–6
   Tudor influence on, 257
common law
   Anglo-Saxon foundations of, 55
   biblical notions of kingship in, 57
   defined, 4–5
   and development of King's Court, 109
   development of, 252
   and Edward I, 138

274   *Index*

common law (cont.)
  entropic development of, 20
  evoutionary development of, 20
  and feudalism, 93
  first principle of, 95
  Henry II as father of, 88
  and history of legal system, 48–9
  King Edward I's importance to, 148
  lore of, 256
  and need for order, 109
  origins of, 45, 48, 92, 109
  and rejection of feudal system, 76
  second principle of, 98
  as unwritten law, 4
  women's rights in, 250–1
  and writ system, 92–5
common law effet of statute law on, 138–9
Common Law Procedure Act 1852, 93
Commonwealth period
  common law under, 246
  Court of Chancery under, 246
  legal reforms of, 246
compensation, system of, 52–3
Conaghan, Joanne, 30, 32, 34
consideration, theories of, 216–17
The Constitutional History of England (Maitland), 6
Constitutions of Clarendon 1164, 87, 90, 99
contract, modern law of
  and tort law, 174
Coronation Charter, 80
Coroner, Office of, 142
Council of the Marches, 199
Council of the North, 199
Council of the West, 199
counterfactual legal history, 41, 79–80
Court of Chancery, 190, 199, 201–4, 216, 220, 222, 241, 263
  canon law procedures in, 202
  in Commonwealth period, 246
  jurisdiction of, 202
Court of Common Pleas, 91, 168, 197–8
  formation of, 91
Court of Exchequer, the, 91, 122, 198, 239
Court of High Commission, 239
Court of Requests, 199
Court of the Exchequer, 198
Courts Christian, the, 68
covenant, actions for, 149
coverture, doctrine of, 79, 133, 248, 250–1
Crenshaw, Kimberlé Williams, 35
criminal justice
  history of, 24
criminal law, 48, *See also* manslaughter;
    murder
  development of, 224–5
  as intellectual system, 225
  in Tudor period, 223–4, 227
critical legal history, 26–30
critical legal studies, 26, 29, 38, 42

critical race theory, 26, 35–6
  and legal history, 38
  and storytelling, 37
critical turn, the, 19, 26, 29
Crofts, Penny, 181–2, 228
Cromwell, Oliver, 245
Cromwell, Thomas, 210
Crouch, David, 107
Curia Regis. See King's Court
customary law, 4

Darnel's Case, 244–5
Davis, Kathleen, 71
De Donis Conditionalibus, 139, 144
De Legibus et Consuetudinibus, 134
de Montfort, Simon, 114, 128–9
Delgado, Richard, 35, 37
Dictum of Kenilworth, 129–30
Dissolution of the Monasteries Act 1534, 212
divine justice, 61–2
divine right of the king, 207, 235
Dix, Elizabeth Jean, 171
Doctor and Student (St. Germain), 203, 217, 230
Doe, Norman, 203–4
Donahue, Charles Jr., 208
Doomsday Book, 76, 88, 220
Durkheim, Emile, 27

ealdorman, 58
Ecclesiastical Appeals Act 1533, 210–11
Edward I (king)
  and alien rights, 121
  as codifier of English law, 139, 145
  centralisation of power under, 140
  as codifier of English law, 139, 145
  as English Justinian, 137–41, 153
  as Hammer of the Scots, 139
  legacy of, 148, 153
  and Parliament origins, 124–30
  Parliamentary opposition to, 148
  as prolific legislator, 137
  reforms of, 140, 142
  royal justice under, 148
  and statute law, 135
  statute law under, 139–42, 154
  treatment of Jews under, 122
Edward II (king)
  legacy of, 159
Edward III (king)
  legacy of, 160–1, 194
  and writs of trespass, 169
Edward IV (king), 185
Edward the Confessor (king), 48, 65–6
Edwards, Laura F., 23
ejectment, writ of, 15, 191, 218–19, 229
Elizabeth I (queen), 192, 213, 237
  civil litigation under, 250
  legal legacy of, 214

Index 275

Elton, Geoffrey R., 192, 208–11, 213–14
Endicott, Timothy, 203
Engleschrie Act of 1340, 179
English law. *See* common law
entropic complexity, 39–41
equity, law of, 190
  and common law, 219
  and Court of Chancery, 203–4
Erickson, Amy, 250
Escheat and Forfeiture, as feudal incident, 75
Eves, William, 100
The Evolution of English Justice (Musson and
    Ormrod), 160
evolutionary functionalism, 27–8, 40
Exchequer, formation of role, 80

Farmer, Lindsay, 223
fault, 53–5
fealty, swearing of, 76–7, 103
feminism, approach to law of, 31–4
feminist legal history, 26, 31, 34
  and women's legal history, 30
feminist legal studies, 30
marriage, as feudal incident, 75
primer seisin, as feudal incident, 75
wardship, as feudal incident, 75
feudal courts, 75
feudal incidents, 74–5
feudal tenures, 72–4
feudalism
  bastard, 145, 147
  decline of, 102, 145–8
  as invention of historians, 70–2
  in Norman period, 70–3
'feudalist' account (Milsom), 102
feuds, 50–1
  importance of to legal history, 51–2
  maximalist view of, 52
Fifoot, C. H. S., 21, 151–3, 170, 172, 216
Flambard, Ranulf, 80
folk-moots, 57
folkright, 56
The Forms of Action (Maitland), 6, 86, 93–4, 103
  Milsom's critique of, 102–5, 108
Fourth Lateran Council, 118
frankalmoign, as feudal tenure, 73
frankmarriage, as feudal tenure, 74
frankpledge, 60, 69, 90
freehold estates, 72, 95, 101, 162, 215, 221–2
freeholder estates, 148–9
freeholders, 70, 218–19, 229
Freeman, Alan, 35
Fuller's Case, 239

Gallanis, Thomas P., 99, 107
Given-Wilson, Chris, 185
Glanvill. *See On the Laws and Customs of England*
    (Glanvill)

Goff, Lord, 2
Golding's Case, 215
Gordley, James, 223
Gordon, Robert W., 3, 21, 26–9, 38
Gowing, Laura, 250
Grand Assize, 97
grand jury
  origin of, 90
Grand Sergeanty, as feudal tenure, 73
Great Plague of 1665, 157
Green, Thomas A., 90, 181, 226, 228
Gunpowder Plot of 1605, 238

habeas corpus, writ of, 197
Hamill, Sarah E., 23
Hampden, John, 244
Harding, Alan, 59, 62
Harold I (king), 65
Harold II (king), 48
Hatton, Lady Elizabeth, 247–9, 251
Hedley, Steve, 24, 233
Helmholz, Richard, 208, 220
Henry I (king), 66, 80
Henry II (king), 45, 48, 82
  and assize courts, 90
  centralisation of justice under, 91, 107
  and church courts, 86–7
  and Church and State tensions, 87
  development of writ system under, 94–7, 101–2,
      104, 106–7
  emergence of professional judiciary under, 91
  experiments for maintaining order, 86, 91
  as father of common law, 46
  and formation of Court of Common Pleas, 91
  and juries of presentment, 89–90
  Maitland's view on, 85–6
  stabilsation of royal justice, 88
  transformation of common law under, 92
  and writ system, 92–3
Henry III (king)
  and common law, 134
  dispute with countess of Flanders, 121
  growth of common law under, 114–15
  and Parliament origins, 123–7, 130
  treatment of Jews under, 122
Henry IV (king), 184–5
Henry VI (king), 185
Henry VII (king), 189, 192
Henry VIII (king), 189
  challenge of trusts under, 221
  conflict with Rome, 209–10
  and divine supremacy of king,
      211
  Parliament under, 206
  and Protestant Reformation, 208
  religious revolution of, 214
Hicks, Michael, 146–7
High Commission, 214, 239, 241, 243

Index

Hill, Christopher, 247, 252
historical approach to law
benefits of, 3, 8, 12, 16, 42, 258
challenge of, 16
as comparative, 9
and contingency of law, 9
as critque, 11
importance of, 1–3, 258
as interdisciplinary, 9, 26
and legal change, 10
neglected by lawyers, 2–3
and relationship of law and society, 10–11
as subversive, 20, 39–41
Historical Foundations of the Common Law (Milsom), 223–4
The History of English Law (Pollock and Maitland), 5–6, 47–9, 53–4, 90, 103, 106, 157, 269
new introduction to, 7, 93, 103, 105
Holdsworth, William S., 21, 109, 247
on Coke, 235, 243, 252–3, 257
Holmes, Oliver Wendall Jr., 216
Holt, J. C., 21, 113
homicide, law of, 179–81
Horwitz, Morton, 11, 26
Hostettler, John, 240
Hudson, John, 21, 50, 59–60, 62, 108, 110, 116
hundred courts, 57, 60
Hundred Rolls, 140, 142
Hunt, Alan, 27
Hurnard, Naomi D., 89
Hyams, Paul R., 21, 48, 50–2, 56, 69, 90, 92, 111

Ibbetson, David J., 13, 21, 150, 230
on assumpsit, 174, 176
on consideration, 217
on trespass, 173
on Tudor period, 191, 194, 197
Inns of Court, 168, 184, 193–4, 196, 206–7, 223
inquests, 69, 88, 118
Institutes (Coke), 252–5
Instrument of Government 1653, 245
intellectual history tradition, 14, 19–22, 24, 28
complementarity with social history, 24–5
complentarity with social history, 25
defined, 20
and legal archaeology, 22
intersectionality, 34
and critical race theory, 36

James I (king), 237
on common law, 240–1
conflict over Court of Chancery, 241
conflict with Coke, 242
High Commission under, 241
on limits of common law, 242
Parliament under, 243
on royal prerogative, 243
Jenkins, D., 194

Jenks, Edward, 170
John (king)
excommunication of, 111
tryanny of, 117
and writ of *praecipe*, 96
John, Eric, 70
jury of presentment, 89–90
justices in eyre, 88, 90, 98, 130, 148
Justices of the Peace Act 1361–1362, 166

Kamali, Elizabeth Papp, 181–2
Karn, Nicholas, 111
Kaye, J. M., 181, 222, 227, 229
Kerr, Margaret, 89
Kesselring, K. J., 200
King in Parliament, 191, 205, 214, 229, 234, 246
King's Bench, 91, 167–8, 183, 185–6, 192, 197–8, 265
King's Court, 60, 75
centralisation of under Henry II, 88, 91
King's Peace, the, 55–6, 61, 69, 87–8, 90, 150, 169
Klinck, Dennis R., 203
knight service, as feudal tenure, 73

labour legislation, 162, 164–6, 171, 175
Landon, P. A., 170–1
Lawrence, Charles, 35
Laws in Wales Act 1536, 206
Laws in Wales Acts 1535 and 1542, 143
leasehold estates, 72
legal archaeology, 22
legal humanism, 191
legal memory, age of, 109, 141
Leges Henrici Primi, 81
Les Plees del Coron (Staunford), 230
Lewis, Matthew, 134
Lobban, Michael, 6, 20
London Charter, the, 65
Lord Dacres's Case, 228
Lovelace, H. Timothy Jr., 38
Loyn, H. R., 59, 140
Lyon, Ann, 13, 139, 143, 154, 177, 184, 186
Lyon, Bryce, 116–17, 123

MacCormack, G., 54
Macnair, Mike, 204
Maddicott, J. R.
on Magna Carta, 123
on Parliament origins, 124–30
Magna Carta, 256
alien rights in, 120–1
centralisation of royal justice in, 117
and Church freedom, 122
and due process, 118
and Edwardian statues, 140
as end to Angevin absolutism, 119
enforcement provisions of, 119
failures of, 113, 115
and feudal incidents, 74

Index

and feudalism, 116–17
free trade in, 120
governance in, 119
guarantee of trial in, 118
immigration in, 120
importance of to common law, 115
new perspective on law of justice in, 116
and Parliament origins, 123, 130
radicality of, 113
reforms of Henry II as basis of, 113–15, 117, 134
reissuing of, 125, 135, 148
role of women in, 131–3
safeguards of, 118
as symbol, 116
versions of, 114
and writ of *praecipe*, 96, 101
Maitland, Frederic W., 2, 4, 46
  on Anglo-Saxon law, 47
  on assizes, 98
  as authority, 4–5, 7, 13
  on Black Death, 157–8
  on canon law, 208
  and claimants on sovereignty, 257
  on claimants for sovereinty, 235
  on Coke, 235–6, 240–1
  on Commonwealth period, 246
  on Court of Chancery, 202–3
  downplay of feuds, 52
  on English vs. Continental legal development, 193–4
  on feudalism, 72, 80
  as founder of intellectual and social history, 25
  on importance of Edward I, 137–8, 140, 154
  on importance of historical approach to law, 258
  on importance of Edward I, 137–8, 140, 154
  influence of, 49
  on Inns of Court, 193–4
  and intellectual history tradition, 21
  on labour legislation, 162
  on Magna Carta, 113–15, 119–20
  method of, 6–7
  on murder, 179
  on murder and manslaughter, 226
  neglect of criminal law, 48
  on *R v.Hampden*, 245
  publications of, 5
  Rede Lecture 1901, 192–3, 257
  on the Sarum Oath, 77
  and the Selden Society, 6
  and 'triad of the three R's', 191
  on trusts, 219
  on Tudor period, 190–1, 193, 199, 206–7
  view of Henry II, 85–6, 91
  view of jury of presentment, 89
  view of Norman Conquest, 66
  on women and the law, 132–3
  on writ system, 93–7, 100–2

Maitland-Milsom debate, 102–8, 176
malice, 229
malice prepense, 179–80, 226–8
malitiam, 181
mandamus, writ of, 197
Mansell & Herbert's Case, 228
manslaughter, 226–9
Mary I (queen)
  counter-Reformation of, 213
Matsuda, Mari, 35
McFarlane, K. B., 184
McLaren, John, 10, 54
McSweeney, Thomas J., 118
Mears, Natalie, 200
mens rea, 181
Merciless Parliament, 183
Milsom, S. F. C., 7, 21, 46
  on Assize of Novel Disseisin, 98
  on assumpsit, 174
  on consideration, 217
  on criminal law in Tudor period, 223–4
  critique of, 106–7
  critique of Maitland on writs, 93, 96, 99–102, *See also* Maitland-Milson debate
  on ejectment, 218
  on feudalism, 71, 74, 218
  and history of criminal justice, 24
  and intellectual history tradition, 21–2
  on murder and manslaughter, 226–7
  on *Quia Emptores*, 146–7
  as refiner of Maitland, 107
  on Statute of Westminster II, 144
  on trespass, 151–3, 170, 176
Milsom-Gordley thesis, 224
Minikkinen, Panu, 38
The Mirror of Justice, 145
Mise of Lewes, 128
'Model Parliament' of 1295, 148
Modernist School
  view of action of the case, 170
Moore, Sally, 54
Mortuaries Act 1529, 210
Munro, Vanessa, 31–2
murder, 179, 197–226, 253
Musson, Anthony, 116, 141

Norman Conquest, 45, 55
  as replacement of ruling class, 66
  liguistic inheritance of, 67–8
  period before, 47, 49
Norman period
  decline in women's legal position in, 78–9
  focus on order over law in, 66
  formalisation of royal justice in, 81
  legal innovations of, 68–73, 80–1
  marriage in, 78
  order over law in, 80
  slavery in, 77–8

Index

Norman period (cont.)
  as time of centralisation, 80
  trial by battle in, 69
Norsworthy, Laura, 247–50

obligations, laws of, 148, 175
Odujirin, Adekemi, 47, 53–5
On the Laws and Customs of England (Glanvill), 109–10, 148, 179
Ordinance of King Edgar, 57–8
Ordinance of Labourers and Servants 1349, 162–4
Ordinance of London 1285, 140
Ormrod, Mark, 120
The Oxford History of the Laws of England (Baker), 13, 20
The Oxford History of the Laws of England (Hudson), 50

Palmer, Robert C.
  on action of assumpsit, 175
  Black Death thesis of, 159, 161–3, 165, 167, 169, 171, 175–8, 182–3
  on Statute of Labourers, 164
  on treason, 178
  on writ system, 105–6
Pardon of Clergy Act 1530–31, 210
pardons
  and law of homicide, 180–1
Pardons Statute 1390, 181
Parliament
  consolidation of, 160–1
  origins of, 123–30
Parliament, Long, 245
Parliament, Short, 245
Parsons, Talcott, 27
Peasants' Revolt, 183
Pelteret, David, 78
periodisation, of history, 66–7, 157, 189
Perkins, John, 230
Petition of Right, 244
Petty Sergeanty, as feudal tenure, 74
Phillips, Jim, 3
Plucknett, T. F. T., 21
  on action on the case, 171
  on Edward I, 139, 141
  on murder, 179
  on Statute of Westminster II, 144–5
  on pardons, 180
  on Statute of Treasons, 179
  on Statute of Wales, 142
  on Statute of Winchester, 145
  on trespass, 151
'Pollock and Maitland', *See The History of English Law* (Pollock and Maitland)
Pollock, Frederick, 5
Popish Recusants Act 1593, 213
Privy Council, 199
Probate Fees etc Act 1529, 210
Profitable Book (Perkins), 230

Pronay, Nicholas, 202
Provisions of Merton. *See* Statute of Merton 1235
Provisions of Oxford 1258, 114, 125, 127–9, 137, 143–4
Provisions of Westminster 1259, 125, 128–9
Purvis, June, 30
Putnam, Bertha Haven, 161

Quia Emptores 1290. *See* Statute of Westminster III 1290
Quo Warranto, writ of, 142, 197
Quominus, writ of, 198

R v. *Hampden*, 244–5
R v. *Salisbury and Others*, 228–9
R v. *Saunders and Archer*, 228
Rabin, Andrew, 56
Rackley, Erika, 30–1, 34, 39
Ragman Statute 1276, 139, 142
Rawlings, Philip, 145
Reformation legislation, 191, 196, 205, 207, 209, 213, *See also* Tudor period:statute law in
Reformation statutes, 15, 192, 206–7, 213, 229–30
Reformation, English, 207–14
Reports (Coke), 253
Restraint of Payment of Annates Act 1532, 210
Revolutionary School
  view of action on the case, 171
Reynolds, Susan, 71
Richard I (king)
  anti-Semitic massacres under, 121
Richard II
  legacy of, 160
Richard III (king), 185
  downfall of, 183–4
  and writ of *praecipe*, 96
Riot Act of 1411, 185
Roebuck, Derek, 50, 60
Roman law, 46
Rose, Jonathan, 25
Ross, Charles, 186
Royal Chancery, formation of, 81
royal writs, 104
'royalist' account (Maitland), 102

Sacrament Act 1547, 212
Salisbury Oath. *See* Sarum Oath
Salmond, John, 216
Sarum Oath, 76–7, 80, 110
Sayles, G. O., 21, 127
Seabourne, Gwen, 132–4, 212
See of Rome Act 1536, 212
Selden Society, 6
  foundation of, 21
Shelley's Case, 237
sheriffs, in Norman period, 69
shire courts, 58
Simpson, Brian, 13, 56, 76, 221
  on assumpsit, 174

Index

on consideration, 217
and fiscal feudalism, 145
on freeholders, 219
and legal archaeology, 22
on trusts, 220
on writ of *praecipe*, 96
Slade's Case, 215, 237
socage tenures, as feudal tenure, 74
social entropy theory, 40
social history tradition, 14, 19, 23
complementarity with intellectual history, 24–5
defined, 22
and history of criminal justice, 24
as interdisciplinary, 23
socio-legal studies, 23, 26
St. Germain, Christopher, 203–4, 230
Star Chamber, 190, 199–200, 204, 214, 243
canon law procedures in, 200
in Commonwealth period, 246
Star Chamber Act 1487, 200
Statute of Acton Brunell 1283. *See* Statute of Merchants 1283
Statute of Bigamy, 142
Statute of Enrolments 1536, 207, 222
Statute of Gloucester 1278, 139, 142
Statute of Jewry 1253, 122
Statute of Jewry 1275, 139
Statute of Labourers 1351, 162, 166
Statute of Lollards, 185
Statute of Marlborough 1267, 55, 101–2, 129–30, 141, 179
Statute of Merchants 1283, 139
Statute of Merchants 1285, 140
Statute of Merton 1235, 125–6, 130
Statute of Merton 1236, 132
Statute of Mortmain 1279, 139, 145–6
Statute of *Quo Warranto* 1290, 140
Statute of Rhuddlan 1284. *See* Statute of Wales 1284
Statute of the Jewry 1275, 122
Statute of Treasons 1342, 177–9
Statute of Treasons 1352, 159, 183
Statute of Truces, 185
Statute of Uses 1536, 207, 221–2, 229
Statute of Wales 1284, 139, 142–3, 206
Statute of Wesminster 1275, 141
Statute of Westminster 1275, 132, 139, 149
Statute of Westminster I 1285, 171
Statute of Westminster II 1285, 138–9, 141–5, 153, 171–2
Statute of Westminster III 1290, 138, 140, 146–8
Statute of Wills 1540, 207, 222
Statute of Winchester 1285, 139, 145, 207
Staunford, William, 230
Steedman, Carolyn, 24
Stefanic, Jean, 35–7
Stenton, Doris M., 21, 78, 86, 250
Stenton, Frank M., 21
Stephen (king), 66, 82

Stephen, J. F., 223
Stopes, Charlotte, 250
Stretton, Tim, 250–1
Stubbs, William, 208
Stubbs-Maitland debate, 207–8
subinfeudation, 72
Submission of the Clergy Act 1534, 210–11
subversive legal history, 38–41
Subversive Legal History (Sandberg), 13, 25, 40–1, 271
Suffragan Bishops Act 1534, 211
Sugarman, David, 11, 24, 26
Sutton, Ralph, 170

Tenures Abolition Act 1660, 74, 93
Thomas, Kendall, 37
Thompson, E. P., 23
Thompson, Sharon, 30–4
Thorne, Samuel, 195, 253, 256
Thorne, Samuel E., 106, 196, 236
Tomlins, Christopher, 29
Tout, Thomas F., 21
Traditionalist School
view of action on the case, 171–2
treason, law of, 178
Treasons Act 1534, 211
Treatise on Tenures (Littleton), 186, 218, 252
Treaty of Wallingford, 82
trespass, law of, 153
and Lord's Prayer, 152
origin of, 151–2
and tort law, 150
Trew Law of Free Monarchies (James I), 237
trial by battle, 69
trial by compurgation, 61
trial by ordeal, 61
trials by jury, emergence of, 118
trusts
in Tudor period, 219
Tudor period. *See also* Reformation, English; Reformation legislation; Reformation statutes
church courts, 220
common and canon law in, 207–8
common law courts in, 197–9
conciliar courts in, 199–200, 204, 214
criminal law in, 223–5, 227
decline of local courts, 196
increase of statute law in, 205
King's Bench in, 197–8, 201, 206
King's Council in, 199–201, 203
King's Court in, 223
land law in, 218–22
law of obligations in, 215
as legal renaissance, 194–6
legal innovations of, 189–90
murder and manslaughter in, 226–8
Parliament in, 205–7, 209, 211–14

280   *Index*

Tudor period. (cont.)
   religion as catalyst for legislation, 205
   and rise of legal humanism, 191
   statute law in, 205–7, 209–11, 222
   trusts in, 221
Turner, Ralph V., 106–7

Valverde, Mariana, 29
Van Caenegem, R. C., 88, 110
Vinogradoff, Paul, 21

Waldon v. *Marshall*, 172–3
War of the Roses, 15, 154, 159, 184, 186, 206, 230
Ward, Ian, 27, 259
Watkin, Thomas G.
  on Assize of Novel Disseisin, 98, 106
  on Assize of Mort D'Ancestor, 143
  on Revolutionary School
    revolutionary, 171
  on the Sarum Oath, 76
  on Traditionalist School, 172
  on trespass, 153, 172
  on trial by battle, 69
  on Welsh law, 12
Watson, Alan, 10
wergild, 52, 78
Westminster Council of 1102, 78

Whatmore, Richard, 24
William I (king), 66
William II (king), 66
William the Conqueror, 46, 65, 70
Williams, Patricia, 35, 37
Williams, Robert A. Jr., 254
Williams, Rowan, 11
Witenagemot. See King's Court
women
  under Medieval law, 131–4
  women's legal history, 30–1
Woodbine, G. E., 151
Wormald, Patrick, 21, 46–7, 53, 224
  critique of Maitland, 47, 60
  on frankpledge, 60
  maximalist perspective of, 52
writ *breve de recto. See* writ of right
writ of covenant, 173
writ of error, 197
writ of *praecipe*, 96–7, 101, 113, 117, 150
writ of restitution, 198
writ of right, 95–7, 197
writ of trespass, 150, 153, 169–70, 173, 176
writ system
  development of under Henry II, 92–4, 105
  and feudalism, 93
writs of entry, 100–2

For EU product safety concerns, contact us at Calle de José Abascal, 56–1°,
28003 Madrid, Spain or eugpsr@cambridge.org.

www.ingramcontent.com/pod-product-compliance
Ingram Content Group UK Ltd.
Pitfield, Milton Keynes, MK11 3LW, UK
UKHW052003090825
461507UK00011B/592